C000230980

Railways and culture
in Britain

MANCHESTER
UNIVERSITY PRESS

STUDIES IN
POPULAR
CULTURE

General editor: Professor Jeffrey Richards

Railways and culture in Britain

The epitome of modernity

IAN CARTER

Manchester University Press
Manchester and New York
distributed exclusively in the USA by Palgrave

Copyright © Ian Carter 2001

The right of Ian Carter to be identified as the author of this work
has been asserted by him/her in accordance with the Copyright, Designs
and Patents Act 1988.

Published by Manchester University Press
Oxford Road, Manchester M13 9NR, UK
and Room 400, 175 Fifth Avenue, New York, NY 10010, USA
http://www.manchesteruniversitypress.co.uk

Distributed exclusively in the USA by
Palgrave, 175 Fifth Avenue, New York,
NY 10010, USA

Distributed exclusively in Canada by
UBC Press, University of British Columbia, 2029 West Mall,
Vancouver, BC, Canada V6T 1Z2

British Library Cataloguing-in-Publication Data
A catalogue record for this book is available from the British Library

Library of Congress Cataloging-in-Publication Data applied for

ISBN   0 7190 5965 8   *hardback*
        0 7190 5966 6   *paperback*

First published 2001

10 09 08 07 06 05 04 03 02 01   10 9 8 7 6 5 4 3 2 1

Typeset by
D R Bungay Associates, Burghfield, Berks

Printed in Great Britain
by Biddles Ltd, Guildford and King's Lynn

STUDIES IN POPULAR CULTURE

There has in recent years been an explosion of interest in culture and cultural studies. The impetus has come from two directions and out of two different traditions. On the one hand, cultural history has grown out of social history to become a distinct and identifiable school of historical investigation. On the other hand, cultural studies has grown out of English literature and has concerned itself to a large extent with contemporary issues. Nevertheless, there is a shared project, its aim, to elucidate the meanings and values implicit and explicit in the art, literature, learning, institutions and everyday behaviour within a given society. Both the cultural historian and the cultural studies scholar seek to explore the ways in which a culture is imagined, represented and received, how it interacts with social processes, how it contributes to individual and collective identities and world views, to stability and change, to social, political and economic activities and programmes. This series aims to provide an arena for the cross-fertilisation of the discipline, so that the work of the cultural historian can take advantage of the most useful and illuminating of the theoretical developments and the cultural studies scholars can extend the purely historical underpinnings of their investigations. The ultimate objective of the series is to provide a range of books which will explain in a readable and accessible way where we are now socially and culturally and how we got to where we are. This should enable people to be better informed, promote an interdisciplinary approach to cultural issues and encourage deeper thought about the issues, attitudes and institutions of popular culture.

Jeffrey Richards

Sylvain rises, slips on his sandals, and goes to fetch his railway timetable. He adores trains. He once told Mathilde that if he weren't married, his dream would be to take a train to anywhere, to visit cities he didn't know and didn't even want to know, to stay alone overnight in the Hotel Terminus that's always across the street from the station, and to leave next morning for somewhere else. He claims that trains are magical, bewitching, and that only a very few superior souls understand this.

Sebastien Japrisot, *A Very Long Engagement* [1991], translated by Linda Coverdale, London, HarperCollins, 1995, 280–1.

For G, for ever

Contents

List of illustrations

General editor's foreword

'Romance' the season tickets mourn,
'*He* never ran to catch His train,
'But passed with coach and guard and horn–
'And left the local – late again'
'Confound Romance!' ... And all unseen
Romance brought up the nine-fifteen.

Thus wrote Rudyard Kipling in his poem *The King*, affirming that for him as for so many writers, whatever the day-to-day exasperations of commuters, the world of the railways, their workings, their essential mystery, was steeped in romance. The railways have inspired a wealth of literature. Books on railway engines, railway rolling stock, railway equipment, railway lines, railway stations, are legion. Books about the cultural importance of the railways are far fewer in number – and Ian Carter's is one of the very best. In this formidably detailed and subtly argued work, he takes us on an exhilarating ride from the recognised classics of railway art such as J. M. W. Turner's *Rain, Steam and Speed* and Émile Zola's *La Bête Humaine* to the teeming and largely unexplored hinterland of railway detective stories and thrillers, comic novels, cartoons and films. In Carter's intoxicating pages, the works of Tolstoy, Dickens and Turner rub shoulders with the works of P. G. Wodehouse, Agatha Christie, Arthur Quiller-Couch, Graham Greene, Eric Ravilious and Heath Robinson. He makes a persuasive case for the currently forgotten Arnold Bennett novel *Accident* as *the* great British railway novel. Throughout, he integrates and cross-references railway history, railway literature, railway mythology and critical theory to examine the role of the railways both in modernity and postmodernity. This is a book packed with insights, discoveries, reconsiderations and fresh assessments, all delivered with a wit and authority which will ensure that it will become a standard work on the subject.

Jeffrey Richards

Acknowledgements

I thank those copyright holders identified in the list of illustrations for permission to reproduce copyright images. Despite strenuous effort, my efforts to locate other images' copyright holders proved unavailing. If such people contact me then I shall ensure that this problem is rectified in any later edition of this book.

An earlier version of Chapter 2 appeared in *The Oxford Art Journal*, vol. 20, 1997, pp. 3–12.

I

History, modernity, fiction

For its proponents in the mid-1980s, Aramis signalled a revolution in guided transportation. Part train and part taxi, this cutting-edge hybrid would transform Paris' underground transport system. Sold overseas, it should more than recoup development costs. So enthusiasts urged as they persuaded French governments to pour fifty billion francs into state and private sector research and development. Then, quietly and mysteriously, Aramis expired. What happened? Did this death follow from accident, murder or natural causes? Sociology of science's *enfant terrible*, Bruno Latour, determined to find out. His book's form is calculatedly quirky. Part pathology report and part professional sociological monograph (an almost equally morbid genre), it blends in strong elements from another form: the literary novel. Different voices puncture this text's smooth façade. No disembodied puppeteer, the author speaks directly to his readers as he educates an open-minded but unlettered engineer. As with a thriller, we follow our author's gathering understanding. When we have followed his tangled tale's details for almost three hundred pages, Latour introduces yet another narrative form. 'In detective fiction there is always a moment when all the suspects and their buddies gather in a big circle', he reminds us, 'quaking, to hear Inspector Columbo or Hercule Poirot name the perpetrator.'[1] Any experienced reader knows what is coming now: the Big Surprise, the Final Twist.

Removed from the library's bloodstained Turkey carpet, Aramis lies in a morgue's drawer. Clearly enough, we have a corpse. Equally clearly, this corpse died neither from natural causes nor from accident. But in a thoroughly conventional way – Michael Innes' whodunnits often end like this – we now discover that there was no villain. No single person wielded that murderous knife. Latour turns his story into a casebook for actor network theory, examining how decisions to initiate and then to abort an ambitious high-technology programme emerged through a cloud of decisions and non-decisions, formal meetings and memoranda, nods and winks, in huge networks linking engineers, politicians and administrators. For anybody familiar with current sociology this conclusion looks mundane:[2] but Latour stalks different game. Telling a story about failed technological innovation, he establishes subversive claims about applied science. Natural scientists preen themselves about painstaking effort spent constructing walls of truth from tiny solid bricks of validated (or, at least, unfalsified) evidence; Latour uses Aramis to show how distant this story is from their mundane experience. No timeless glazed edifice like Stanley Kubrick's monoliths in *2001: a Space Odyssey*, science on the hoof is a social practice imbricated with all the messy personal, political, social and economic impedimenta which confuse and enrich other parts of our daily lives. Dethroned from Olympian intellectual privilege, science becomes available for social analysis and evaluation, like other social practices.

One-eyed kings in a scientifically blind public domain, claims like these often drive practising natural scientists close to apoplexy. No bad thing. Bruno Latour is a sociologist; and the notion of critique lies at the sociological enterprise's heart. If actor network theory stings unreflective practical scientists into contemplating deeper questions about what they do, then definite benefit follows – even if that means no more than forcing them to find better reasons for denying sceptical observers' arguments and conclusions. Latour opens his text with a question pointing directly towards this consummation. 'Can we unravel the tortuous history of a state-of-the-art technology from beginning to end', he asks, 'as a lesson to the engineers, decisionmakers, and users whose daily lives, for better or worse, depend on such technology?' So far, so familiar. Then Latour swerves his rail-guided vehicle in an interesting new direction:

> Can we make the human sciences capable of comprehending the machines they view as inhuman, and thus reconcile the educated public with bodies it deems foreign to the social realm? Finally, can we turn a technological object into the central character of a narrative, restoring to literature the vast territories it should never have given up – namely, science and technology?[3]

In a manner different from that which Bruno Latour chooses, these questions inform this book. Like their contemporaries elsewhere in the world, for nineteenth-century Britons modern railways's emergence exemplified economic (and other) change on a huge, a qualitatively novel, scale. 'It is impossible to regard the vast buildings and their dependencies, which constitute a chief terminal station of a great line of railways', Dionysius Lardner wrote in 1850, 'without feelings of inexpressible astonishment at the magnitude of the

capital and the boldness of the enterprise, which are manifested in the operations of which they are the stage. Nothing in the history of the past affords any
parallel to such a spectacle'.[4] By turns exhilarating and terrifying, in the mid-
nineteenth century one had to be confident that railways' onrushing modernity
would infuse and transform British cultural understandings: 'It would be
absurd to deny that the great and material changes which our progress in civilisation and the arts should not impress literature, as well as manners', C. J. Lever
wrote in 1845. But it did not. Astonishingly, denial survived Victoria's reign,
and her son's. Writing from a literary culture dismissively ignorant about science (and complacently naive about technological novelties which, in complicated combination with social and economic changes, had transformed Britain
through industrialisation), creative authors in the long nineteenth century
ignored science and technology. One major exception makes the point. H. G.
Wells enjoyed a solid scientific education. His 'scientific romances' gained rapid
popular and scholarly reputation principally because they differed so sharply
from run-of-the-mill late-Victorian fiction. Half a century before Wells wrote,
Lever sketched what British writers (and reading classes) would miss by taking
so little interest in pure and applied science.

> From the palace to the poor-house, from the forum to the factory, all has been
> searched and ransacked for a new view of life, or a new picture of manners. Some
> have even gone into the recesses of the earth, and investigated the drama of a coal
> mine. Yet, all this time, the great reformer has been left to accomplish his operations
> without note or comment, and while thundering along the earth, or ploughing the
> sea, with great speed and giant power, men have not endeavoured to track his influ-
> ence upon humanity, nor work out any evidences of those strange changes he is
> effecting over the whole surface of society. The steam-engine is not merely a power to
> turn the wheels of mechanism – it beats and throbs within the heart of a nation, and
> is felt in every fibre, and recognised in every sinew of civilised man.[5]

This book examines cultural representations of the modern steam railway in
the country where it was born: Great Britain. That action needs some modest
preliminary justification. George Ottley lists more than thirteen thousand
items pertaining to British railway history published up to 1987. And still the
presses roll, churning out yet more books, articles and magazines. Why add
another spoonful to this flood, this 'Railway Book Mania?'[6] Two reasons. First,
while leaning in a different direction, scholarly and popular accounts of British
railways's development and operation are no less lopsided than Victorian fiction. Focussed closely on mechanical engineering and economic history, they
pay little attention to social issues and less to culture. 'One of the writer's earnest

hopes', P. L. Scowcroft confided some years ago, 'is that someone will publish a comprehensive survey of railway fiction demonstrating not only its entertainment value but its usefulness in providing authentic, or reasonably authentic, railway backgrounds for the enthusiast and even for the railway historian.'[7] This book may not be quite what Scowcroft called for. Necessarily exploratory, it makes no claim to comprehensive coverage. It takes authenticity to be a less than simple notion, and it does not share Scowcroft's humility before empiricist British railway historians. Second, as Bruno Latour noticed, another group needs to be informed about the relationship(s) between railways and culture. As the central symbol for nineteenth-century modernity, British railways should intrigue humanists, freeing disciplined study of this fascinating topic from guilt by association with railwayacs, railfans and trainspotters (three terms used, in different places and at different times, to stigmatise a single pariah group). Transport by rail might have been largely superseded by cars, trucks and aircraft today, but the railway age laid tracks along which our world still runs. As William Everdell reminds us, we 'call "modern" everything that happened to any other culture after it had built its first railroad'.[8]

Writing history

'It is not a little remarkable', Henry Grote Lewin wrote in 1914, 'that although the English people may claim to be the pioneers of railways, no adequate history of the development of the British railway system has yet made its appearance.'[9] Time has rectified this anomaly. Today, railway history is a flourishing cottage industry. 'Perhaps the most encouraging thing about the practice of railway history in the past ten years or so', Michael Robbins wrote in 1957, 'has been a genuine attempt to seek out new evidence, to probe new sources, and to bring a more vigorously critical approach to bear on the traditional accounts.'[10] Reading forty years' issues of *The Journal of Transport History*, one wonders at that judgement. Still dominating other forms of transport history,[11] British railway history has explored some new sources in recent decades; but vigorous criticism remains trammelled in a narrow range. That journal's founding editors regretted failing to bridge divisions between historians in academic and other worlds,[12] but their sense of who constitutes a proper historian has been policed strictly. George Ottley thanks a 'fraternity' of railway historians and enthusiasts for contributing items to his bibliography,[13] but professional academics' habitually guarded and suspicious attitude to swarming railway amateurs contrasts sharply with the trajectory in certain other areas. Industrial archaeology was invented by amateurs, then enriched by professional expertise. Much the same tale can be told for people's history – centred on *History Workshop Journal*, that creatively strident organ. The membrane between academics laboriously conducting family reconstitution studies and enthusiastic amateur (but impressively expert) genealogists leaks ever more insistently. Nor is this argument limited to history. To take one spectacular example, for several centuries professional astronomy rested firmly on evidence provided by amateur observers. Meteorology showed a similar pattern until remote sensing replaced human recorders scattered across the globe. This broad lesson should be learnt. Maintaining a *cordon sanitaire* between professional academics writing for *The Journal of Transport History* and folk writing for publications catering to amateur interests (from *The Journal of the Railway and Canal Historical Society* down to the gricers' bible, *Rail*) might assuage academics' fears about pollution, but at excessive cost. Consider train-spotting's massive upsurge at the end of the Second World War. This alarmed older railway enthusiasts, with the young and the rootless polluting serious study. A medical doctor and railway fanatic, Philip Ransome-Wallis illustrates the point. Discussing railway enthusiasm, he constructs it as a human pyramid. The huge bottom layer corrals squirming juvenile number 'snatchers'. These are merely despicable. Above them stand somewhat older folk who know more about a locomotive than simply where to find its number. Third come railway photographers, both technical and pictorial. Only at the peak of this heap, firmly holding their noses, does one find men like Philip Ransome-Wallis himself: professional men with profound knowledge about railway operation, able to talk to senior railway officers on equal terms in London's Railway Club (admission by election only).[14] This pyramid now is nearly fifty years old, but attitudes have not softened. 'The severer students of transport history', we were told recently, 'rightly eschew sentimental nostalgia.' They despise 'a nostalgic "sights and sounds and smells" version of railway history'. They discount 'the enthusiast's intuitive and emotional "understanding" of the subject'.[15] Eschewing Max Weber's *Verstehensoziologie* this rigidly, scholars wall themselves in ever tighter and more restrictive keeps. Bringing to term 'a truly comprehensive science and art of the history of transport'[16] must see new lines built out from engineering and economic history's well-developed territory into less-charted spaces in social and cultural history.[17] Without abandoning proper canons of evidence, this wider work must worry much less about patrolling academic respectability's boundaries. It must also blend a concern for explanation with an interest in understanding social actors' life-worlds. Gently criticising historians writing about Victorian railways,

Bryan Morgan noted almost forty years ago that 'there is rarely reflected much sense of the gap of *feeling* which divides the ages of the past and present queens – of the technical, aesthetic and social revolutions which have rumbled behind Bourne and Frith and Pick, Stephenson and Stirling and English Electric, Midland and L.M.S. and B.R'.[18] His strictures about technology (and, to a lesser extent, about social history) might seem outdated today; those to do with feeling remain true. They point to aesthetic distinctions with which we will become familiar, as a realism derived directly from Enlightenment rationalism crashes against sundry anti-realisms: romanticism, Gothic, whimsy, post modernism.

However modestly, this book explores this contested territory, paying partic-ular attention to how railways are conjured in fiction – and, intermittently, in the visual arts and cinema. Chapters in Part I probe an absence just as curious as that which Henry Grote Lewin identified in 1914: the lack of a single major railway novel in the nation where modern railways were born. Given railway historians' deep concerns about patrolling respectability's boundaries, such a novel would have to be canonical: admired, discussed and taught by academic literary critics. In a curious way, their own practice has stopped railway histo-rians looking very insistently for this book. Consider Jack Simmons, the leading current figure. Written at the instigation of A. L. Rowse, his first single-authored book was a study of Robert Southey, the Lake poet.[19] An early anthology showed that Simmons had read a great deal of imaginative literature about railway (and other) travel, and was perfectly comfortable in handling it.[20] Then, for four decades, his railway monographs abjured fiction for engineering and economic history.[21] Not until 1991 did Simmons' literary sensibilities emerge again, in a second anthology.[22] But even in that year his magisterial survey of Victorian railways' social impact told readers that 'The success of the first steam railways evoked little interest from English imaginative writers.'[23] For some critics, this lack of interest long outlasted railways' early days. Reviewing Jeffrey Richards' and John M. Mackenzie's *The Railway Station: a Social History*, Richard Boston inquired what would be lost if, by some vanishing trick, all works of art and entertainment which involved trains and railway stations were to disappear.[24] Russell McDougall offered a costing for England.

> The list of dearly departed would include: *The Railway Children*, *Billy Liar* and *Paddington Bear*. In *The Wind in the Willows*, Toad would be unable to complete his escape from prison. Quite a bit of Dickens would be lost, a fair amount of Hardy, and almost all of Trollope – not to mention the many scenes from Wodehouse that are set in railway carriages. Holmes and Watson would be left

sitting at Baker Street. And we would lose Saki's story about the girl who won medals for good behaviour only to be eaten by a wolf, which tracked her down by the sound of their jangling, for it is told on a train (to keep some children quiet).[25]

A thin haul. Who, on this account, would mourn the railway's absence from English literature? That judgement is too hasty. Literary and social historians have trawled up a larger corpus of serious Victorian (and later) writing about railways than McDougall's list suggests.[26] And, as we shall see below, disdained literary genres offer largely unexploited oceans in which to fish. By triangulating (as we say in my part of the academic enterprise) railway historians' work with material from literary critics, art historians and social theorists, we can begin to lay out a less cramped agenda for railway studies: an agenda which takes culture more seriously than in most previous work.

Writing modernity

Springtime of freedom

Throughout this book, we will be interested in relationships between railways and modernity. Defining the modern railway is not a simple task,[27] but it pales before the challenge of defining modernity. One important difficulty is that so many other people have travelled this track in earlier years. As one proto-sociologist after another sought to understand what distinguished *this* world from what went before, so the notion of 'modernity' inflated to cover ever wider ranges of meaning. For some current critics, the term now signifies such broad territories that it excludes very little – by explaining everything, 'modernity' explains nothing. Perhaps we should simply dump the notion and set about forging sharper, more discriminating tools?[28] Since our interest lies in exploring what Victorian, Edwardian and Georgian writers and visual artists made of the railway we can evade this awkward conclusion, even if we thought it rooted in anything more admirable than rank cowardice. Like the fact or loathe it, none of sociology's eminent dead denied that something bearing world historical significance happened when modernity was born, nor that the modern era was different in kind from what preceded it. Nineteenth- and early twentieth-century intellectuals struggled to understand how, and why, their social world changed shape around them. Major figures produced different accounts of what mattered most: a shift from custom to contract as law's fundamental plank (William Lecky); from mechanical solidarity to organic solidarity (Émile Durkheim); from feudalism to capitalism (Karl Marx); from simple social forms to complex

(Herbert Spencer); from traditional domination to legal-rational domination (Max Weber); from community to association (Ferdinand Tönnies: the last great synthesiser). Conceptually, modernity's value lay in its ability to undergird attempts to understand bewildering different economic, social and political changes.[29] In one recent condensed formulation, these changes saw

> the emergence of an advanced industrial capitalism with powerful modernising forces that generated a fluid and pluralistic social structure, new social classes and fractions of classes, new professions, new industries and services, and populations increasingly concentrated in burgeoning urban centres.[30]

Unpacking this a little, we will take the notion of modernity to conflate seven elements: *capitalism* and *bureaucracy*, both organised on ever wider spatial scales; increasing *divisions of labour* and *technical specialisation in knowledge and skill* (inducing rapid changes in professional occupations, and rendering citizens increasingly dependent on specialists' technical expertise); novel forms of physical and social *engineering* (altered physical landscapes, with new arrangements for moving through them; human bodies disciplined and penetrated through increasingly adept medical interventions; modified human needs and consumption patterns); social meanings and value systems reconstructed through strong tendencies to *cosmopolitanism*, with family and community structures eroded to suit; and global physical *environments* ruthlessly plundered for resources to keep modernity's Juggernaut car moving forward.[31]

These lists help us understand why, one hundred years ago, H. G. Wells predicted that future historians would take 'a steam engine running upon a railway' to be the nineteenth century's central symbol.[32] Victorians took the train to be modernity's cutting edge. Karl Marx was clear that 'the eradication of space by time' – accelerating the circulation of commodities through new forms of exchange and communication (the railway, the electric telegraph and fast, efficient mail services) – marked an upward gear shift within capitalist industrialisation.[33] He was not alone in appreciating this point. 'Nothing', the modern American art historian Leo Marx insists, 'provided more tangible, vivid, compelling icons for representing the forward course of history than recent mechanical improvements like the steam engine'; or, in Jonathan Carrick's simpler terms, 'If people can make trains, people can do anything they want.'[34] Here, too, many elements lay bundled together. New railways represented 'the first of the large-scale, complex, full-fledged technological systems'[35] with which modernity's children would become ever more familiar. Many years after the event, Paul Jennings saw this pioneer modern *machine ensemble* (to adopt

Wolfgang Schivelbusch's useful term[36]) in a rusting cast iron warning notice: 'a masculine Victorian spring morning of mechanics; puffs of white steam in a blue sky, the ring of shovels, men in oilskins on windy nights, creaking signals, new cast-iron piers in high tides, tarred planking – the immense solid brand-new Railway itself'.[37] For L. T. C. Rolt and Patrick Whitehouse, social and physical order and discipline – exemplary modern virtues – lay at this machine ensemble's heart. 'A great railway system is perhaps the most elaborate and deli-cate, yet at the same time one of the most successful feats of organisation ever evolved by man', they insisted. 'The steel rail is a symbol of disciplined move-ment, but that movement is itself ordered and controlled by a complex human and mechanical hierarchy which extends from the central control room to the loneliest lineside signal box.'[38] In fiction no less than in fact, this standardised and disciplined order discountenanced many pioneer railway travellers. Sam Weller senior speaks for them, deprecating 'alvays comin' to a place, ven you come to one at all, the wery picter o' the last, with the same p'leesemen standin' about, the same blessed old bell a ringin', the same unfort'nate people standin' behind the bars, a waitin' to be let in; and everythin' the same except the name, vich is wrote up in the same sized letters as the last name, and vith the same colours'.'[39] Habit and convention soon laid a crust over complaints like these, as the railway's discipline came to seem mundane. In Victoria's last years, 'From the railway station in the distance came the sound of shunting trains, ringing and rumbling, softened almost into melody by the distance. My wife pointed out to me the brightness of the red, green and yellow signal lights hanging in a framework against the sky. It seemed so safe and tranquil.'[40]

Writing from London about the new Liverpool and Manchester line in 1830, a *Quarterly* writer anticipated that railways would produce 'a better phys-ical distribution of our population – a check to the alarming growth of cities, especially of manufacturing towns, and of this Babylon in which we write'.[41] Vain hopes! Modern British railways encouraged urbanisation.[42] While never particularly cheap in real terms, passenger travel provided many Britons with novel possibilities for personal mobility: as later commentators thought the Duke of Wellington muttered into his boot, railways encouraged lower orders to travel too far, and too often.[43] Social space and social understandings were transformed, as train travel radically widened many people's physical horizons. Local production and marketing structures withered in the face of specialised rail-borne regional production tailored to national markets. To be beached seven miles from a railway station in King's Gnaton, a remote Somerset village, was to be 'singularly untouched by civilisation'.[44] Not for nothing did Harold

Perkin dubbed railways 'the Great Connector'.[45] British society always had displayed social stratification markers, but the manner in which railways refined crude coaching distinctions between 'inside' and 'outside' travellers[46] into elaborate typologies (seven main classes, supplemented by Pullman and other 'super-first' forms, cross-cut by class-segregated smoking and ladies' compartments) sedimented *class* as the central notion through which modern British people thought about social hierarchy.[47] Measured against inhabitants' mundane understandings in the 1820s, railways annihilated space and time. By state fiat in Britain, through a conference of otherwise warring private companies in the United States of America, new railway networks stabilised time zones to facilitate rational train timetabling, cementing Edward Thompson's 'industrial time' on a world scale.[48] As new railways cut imperiously over and through physical landscapes, their hard, engineered tangents mocked softly rounded landforms. Building and operating new railways impelled reconstruction in older specialisms – notably stockbroking, surveying and civil engineering – and crystallised new professions like mechanical engineering and accountancy.[49] The need to control vast enterprises efficiently and profitably generated the novel organisational principle which Max Weber would dub bureaucratic rationality: 'line managers' were born on the railway line.[50] 'Without the Bourse, where would the railways be?' Condette demanded in 1884. 'Where would be those grand and magnificent works from which we have so greatly profited?'[51] His point is better reversed. Appalled by fall-out from the mid-1840s Railway Mania, that under-regulated speculative bubble, between 1855 and 1862 the British Parliament legislated to perfect the limited liability joint stock company, calming investors' qualms while satisfying railway companies' vast hunger for capital to fund construction and operation.[52] This sturdy envelope has stood time's test: bureaucratised capitalism in its (to date) fullest flowering, today's giant transnational corporation is little more than a pumped-up Victorian limited liability railway company.[53] Railway workers and passengers alike found themselves constrained by fierce discipline, blending features from older military organisation (uniformed staff, administrative procedures based on strict hierarchical delegation, senior staff as 'officers') with features drawn from newer capitalist industry (enforced rule-bound behaviour, intense divisions of labour, close surveillance, professionalised technical expertise, rigid time discipline).[54] Beset by competitive pressures, by newspapers attacking railway directors for elevating company profits over passengers' safety,[55] and by regulation from state authorities pressed by public demands that safety standards be improved, directors and technical staffs sought technological improvement, driving railways relentlessly towards the future.[56] Engineering historians shows us what happened in that future: efficiency gains in prime movers, as steam yielded to internal combustion engines and then to electric motors.[57] Not only efficiency was involved here. As Scott McQuire insists, 'If velocity has been at the heart of each of these revolutions [the train, the automobile, the aeroplane, the rocket], it is not only the increased speed each new wave of vehicles has achieved, but also the ascending rate at which they have transformed social and political relations.'[58] For almost two centuries humankind has experienced continuous acceleration in transporting not only people and things but also information, culminating (so far) in the Net;[59] but the qualitative break came on the modern railway when, for the first time in history, people travelled faster than any galloping horse could manage. Significantly titled *Faster! Faster!*, a forgotten novel anticipated much of this fashionable social theory half a century ago. Built around metaphors for acceleration, urbanisation and class stratification, this novel conjures British society as a long train divided into three class-specified sections. Organisers and administrators ride in first-class carriages. Minor executives, inspectors and supervisors ride second. Drivers, cooks and cleaners – 'those who labour perpetually that the pace of the train may be faster and ever faster' – are condemned to third-class carriages. Breaching discipline in a higher class brings downward mobility to the hoi polloi's third. Velocity precludes any thought of escape. Passengers are trapped as their train accelerates onward, fuelled by pressures to expanded reproduction.[60] As this case suggests, increasing velocity is more than a simple matter of technological determinism: social and economic innovation intimately interlards mechanical novelty. When many Victorian railway companies built their own factories to manufacture steam locomotives, rolling stock, signalling equipment, prefabricated buildings and a host of other items, they fought in a thoroughly modern fashion to limit artisans' control over work processes. 'The labour policies of railway companies', Eric Hobsbawm tells us, 'sometimes look as though they had been specifically designed to replace craft autonomy and exclusive control by managerial control of hiring, training, promotion to higher grades of skill and workshop operations'.[61] Believing that it was invented in early twentieth-century American auto plants, late twentieth-century scholars made this managerial onslaught on craft mysteries a Fordist thrust to install high capacity/low unit cost standardised production regimes. As Hobsbawm hints, these regimes might better be called Webbist, after the Victorian autocrat who commanded the world's largest railway workshops, built by the London and North Western Railway in Crewe – 'the archetypal Victorian company town', a settlement conjured from nothing by (and for) the railway company which Webb served so ruthlessly.[62]

Born in Britain, the modern railway's machine ensemble bundled together many different technical, economic and social novelties in that place. But the modern railway picked up subtly different inflections as export trades developed, coloured by local meanings in other national jurisdictions.[63] Lucius Beebe insinuates that robust sentiments about 'republican simplicity' prevented American railroads from developing offensively visible passenger classes after the European manner – but then he sets us down beside the New York Central's high iron near Garrison early one May morning in 1934. Round the bend from Albany ('or, if you prefer, Ultima Thule') comes The Parade: six passenger trains pounding towards Manhattan, all scheduled to pass Garrison within a single hour. First comes Train No. 36, *The Genessee*, 'an undistinguished bread-and-cheese sleeper', 'a train of no great pedigree'. Prestige rises steadily as the next four trains pass. *The Iroquois, The Fast Mail, The Montreal Limited* and *The New York Special* all thunder south dead on schedule, 'leaving the stage set for the big event of the day'.

> This is the passage in glory of Train No. 26, *The Twentieth Century Limited*, all-Pullman extra fare flyer from Chicago to New York on the tightest schedule known, with deluxe standard Pullmans with drawing rooms, staterooms and compartments, single and double bedrooms, valet, barber and maid service. There is Porterhouse steak on the menu, fresh flowers on every table, a steward on bowing terms with the great of the great world, a conductor with a pink in his button-hole and Pullman porters who are the *haute noblesse* of the social midst in which they move. The names on its sailing list are the names of headlines, and beside a passenger list of exalted dimensions, *The Century* carries an intangible but equally glittering freight, the pride of a great operation and a tradition of complete excellence unmatched by any railroad in the world.[64]

So much for rugged republican simplicity! Disdainful as European patricians riding *Le Train Bleu*, members in *The Century*'s pampered business elite hurled onward. Spleen's root differed from one side of the Atlantic to the other, but neither social nor monied pretension placated local groundlings' envy.[65] Elsewhere, a British art student in Munich early this century 'carried a cast-iron conviction that foreign [steam] locomotives were either funny or hideous'.[66] Walter Hillyard entertained less monolithic prejudices than this. Travelling from Paris to Milan, he refused to take the Simplon-Orient Express because it dived under the Alps through the culturally boring Simplon tunnel. He preferred to savour the St Gotthard's sharp social contrasts. 'Deadly depressing Swiss-German efficiency' ruled as his train eased into the tunnel at Göschenen, 'solemn and self-conscious and by numbers'. Thirteen minutes later it burst into Italian open air at Airolo. This was a 'delicious escape … into another world, a vivid, Latin world, another civilization'.[67] Nuanced differences from the British prototype flourished in complex mixtures, we see, in different places. National chauvinism compounded with thoughtful adaptations to local customs, traffics and topography – and with state policy. British state policy specified that, subject to sanction through a private act of parliament (and mediation from a strong 'Railway Interest', comprising directors and other railway company lackeys in the House of Commons) private promoters could build railway lines where they chose.[68] Things were different on the European peninsula. In France the state planned a comprehensive railway network, then contracted private companies to construct and operate particular segments.[69] The Belgian state both planned and operated its own centrally designed, and remarkably comprehensive, railway system. This example infused the only disinterested argument advanced against British railway nationalisation in Edwardian years: that a state-run British system would hand vast new patronage resources to shifty politicians.[70] Fearing that private railway companies' powerful economic heft might generate competing power bases, autocratic European regimes viewed railway development with fear and distaste. If railways had to come, then they must be kept firmly under central state control. In chapter 4 we shall see something of how this happened in Russia. The first line in Austro-Hungary, from Linz to Budweis (1827) was engineered by a Frenchman, Franz Zola. We will meet his son Émile in chapter 5. Bizarrely enough, authorities in this shambling empire named new trunk railways after members of the royal family. Struggling to buttress crumbling imperial political structures against modern nationalisms spawned in and against the 1789 French Revolution, Hapsburg emperors sought legitimacy from railways – master symbol for the onrushing modernity which would destroy imperial power within three generations.

Vienna and St Petersburg were not the only European capitals where furious debate raged over modern railways' social, political and economic effects. Early Victorian pamphleteers, poets and novelists wrangled over new British railways' social and cultural cost–benefit ratios.[71] Accustomed to cleaving blithely untrammelled paths through civil society, many patricians objected strongly to railway companies' stringent discipline at stations and on trains. But the train brought liberty, not constraint, for other social groups. 'Railways have introduced *freedom*', two late Victorian liberals enthused.

> When 'penny a mile' came in all feudal links with the past were snapped, including
> the traditional deference to surroundings from which one saw no means of escape;
> the abrupt freedom has produced an 'independence' of manners which is no doubt
> 'commoner', but perhaps not more unsatisfactory, than the laboured insincerity of
> former times. The railway has made the poor 'stand up to' the rich much as Luther
> stirred the nations to defy the Church.[72]

Their own workers found it more difficult to stand up to railway company
directors and senior officers. In early decades sharp divisions between and
within grades among railway workers, and officers' covert identification of particular workers as 'loyal' or as 'troublemakers', allowed companies to dominate
their workforces through particularistic paternalism.[73] Struggle continued in
the railway's labour process, as in every other economic sector; but paternalism's
broad effectiveness waned as organised trades unionism strengthened in the
later nineteenth century. Railway workers' industrial muscle hardened. The
Amalgamated Society of Railway Servants (merged with two other unions to
form the National Union of Railwaymen in 1913) was formed in 1872. Much
early twentieth-century labour law was born on the railway: the 1900–1 Taff
Vale Case, briefly establishing the principle that a trade union could be sued in a
representative action, is the most famous example. Union recognition issues
provoked the first national rail strike, in 1911.[74] By this time, loose collaboration among unions representing railwaymen, coal miners and engineers had
gelled in a fearsome 'triple alliance'. Capable of challenging industrial capital in
warfare whose scale and intransigence threatened to resemble First World War
battles, this triple alliance brought British capital (sustained by the British state
in unusually open collusion) to its knees in the 1926 General Strike; but after
nine days the railwaymen's leader, J. H. Thomas, buckled.[75] With no broader
social and economic programme to buttress a narrow economism born from
struggles against capitalist companies, railway industrial unionism hit history's
buffers. Because these buffers were pneumatic, the collision's significance was
veiled from contemporaries. In a longer perspective than we yet can bring to
bear,[76] future historians may date British organised labour's long decline from
railwaymen's and engineers' doomed sympathetic support for locked-out coal
miners in the 1926 General Strike.

Beyond Europe, railways' modern glamour shimmered no less brilliantly
than in Britain. 'Railroads are more than trucks and trains', Daniel Headrick
tells us; 'they are a whole new way of life, the forerunners of a new civilization.'[77]
Note the language here. As civilisation expunged barbarism, the Enlightenment
project rode serenely forward. 'There is no civiliser like the railway', H. H.

Johnston insisted for British West Africa, that white man's graveyard.[78] 'You cannot maintain a net of railways over an immense country', Karl Marx told the *New York Daily Tribune*'s readers,

> without introducing all those industrial processes necessary to meet the immediate and current wants of railway locomotion, and out of which there must grow the application of machinery to those branches of industry not immediately connected with railways. The railway system will therefore become, in India, truly the forerunner of modern industry.[79]

In later Victorian years railways spread throughout non-European territories wherever traffics in persons or goods could sustain heavy construction and operating costs.[80] Everywhere they went, these lines carried social meanings alongside copra or indentured labourers, tea or sahibs. As G. O. Trevelyan (an Indian Civil Service wallah whose mandarin brother deployed Manchester liberalism to justify state inaction in the face of widespread Irish distress in famine years) reported, in India all signs of civilisation disappeared beyond one hundred yards on either side of the railway track.[81] But 'civilisation' looked a different animal when viewed from each end. 'The railways of the nineteenth century, like the airlines of today, were extensions of distant financial centres, factories, and consumers', Headrick reminds us. 'Such enterprises can operate for decades as alien enclaves, linked to distant suppliers and customers, with little or not local articulation.'[82] Protected by guarantees, new Indian railways swallowed massive capital exports from Victorian Britain. Construction began from Calcutta towards Gangetic cotton districts in the late 1840s, spurred by the 1846 American cotton crop's failure. Writing in 1848, the promoter John Chapman considered that Lancashire merchants regarded this railway 'as nothing more than an extension of their own line from Manchester to Liverpool'.[83] No wonder, perhaps, that the man at Colombo's railway station (narrow gauge side) who discountenanced Ian Jack with such detailed knowledge about George Stephenson and the Liverpool and Manchester Railway turned out to be on day release from the local madhouse.[84]

Decline; and dark modernity

Modern railways annihilated distance and time through practical science disciplined to maximise profit. 'Type of the modern' in Walt Whitman's famous phrase, riding roughshod over and through the landscape, Victorian railways drove to the heart of the modern impulse as they demonstrated humankind's increased control over nature. In Marx's social philosophy (but not only there) increased control over nature opened vistas to illimitable human possibility.

Rejecting neo-classicism's penchant for mourning dead social worlds, romanticism trumpeted open-ended potential.[85] This mirrored modernity's future orientation. It infused socially patterned individual hopes. 'Psychically, modernity is about identity', Zygmunt Bauman tells us, 'about the truth of existence being not-yet-here, being a task, a mission, a responsibility.'[86] Like nothing else, for our great-grandparents railways exemplified the modern world crystallised in wood, iron and steel.[87] As apparently limitless futures unfolded, so railways would transport passengers to material cornucopias and political freedoms, to new heavens on a new earth. Grumpy early Victorians might grouch about particular companies' intrusions in loved landscapes[88] (and, often almost in the same breath, about inadequate local train services) but, Wolfgang Schivelbusch insists, 'To adherents of progressive thought in the first half of the nineteenth century, the railroad appears as the technical guarantor of democracy, harmony between nations, peace, and progress.'[89]

That confidence has disappeared like exhausted steam. International harmony and peace evaporated rapidly as, from the American Civil War onwards, warfare took to the rails with dreadful enthusiasm. The climax arrived with the First World War, as dense networks of lightly laid narrow-gauge lines on the Western Front allowed defensive positions to be reinforced quicker than attackers could be gathered, dooming millions of men to death and injury in set-piece battles along static trench lines.[90] If peace and harmony could not be assured by railway development, then progress was no more certain. Male, white and comfortably-circumstanced, few Enlightenment writers bothered to wonder whether some social groups benefitted less than others from secular applied science.[91] The Enlightenment project in a remarkably pure form, as modern railways spread their webs across Europe and beyond, distribution effects laid persistent discords under paeans of praise to railway-borne progress. Waiting for the Orient Express near the Black Sea's shores in the 1930s, Gregor von Rezzori's narrator's

> picture of himself [was] as a dandified, smarmy adolescent standing in his gold-buttoned navy-blue blazer on the scruffy railway platform in Braila among ragged porters and gray-faced railwaymen, loiterers and third-class passengers with their goats, hens, wives and children – for him this image summoned all the tumult of socialist polemics in this century. An epoch charged with class hatred pointed its accusing finger at the brass-and-blue railway cars.[92]

Recalling Indian stations seen on wartime service – 'the teeming families squatting round their brass drinking pots; the glistening brown bodies washing at the pumps' – Paul Jennings ruminated 'the curious translation of that British thing, the railway, from its proper Emett milieu of clanking Wolverhampton goods yards and Charles Keene cartoons, to the blinding, indifferent East'.[93] Imperialism rides the rails here, with other peoples' cultural arrangements viewed through a single constricting glass.[94]

Peering back across the First World War's caesura, 'the train ran as smoothly – Tietjens remembered thinking – as British gilt-edged securities'.[95] By the early 1920s Christopher Tietjens understood that this smooth security would not return, that the railway had ceased to be modernity's epitome. British railways' route mileage reached its greatest extent in 1927. National mineral traffic by rail (which means largely coal) peaked in 1913, total goods traffic in 1920, total passenger journeys in 1927.[96] For eighty years British railway history has been a story of decline, of contraction at a slower or faster rate. Interwar enthusiast literature disguised this unpalatable fact by celebrating bigger but scarcely more sophisticated steam locomotives, showpiece passenger train acceleration (the Great Western's *Cheltenham Flyer*, the LMS's *Coronation Scot*, the LNER's *Silver Link*), and modest track improvements; but difficulties gathered. 'Are not the trains already merely elongated buses without the racing instincts of the bus?' one grouch enquired as early as 1921.[97] Inheriting fixed capital assets degraded by wartime exigencies, caught between declining traffic receipts and increasing road competition, the Big Four railway companies earned low dividends after the 1923 Grouping. All contemplated upgrading through extensive electrification. None could afford it save the Southern Railway, and then only on intensively-worked London commuter lines. In their great days, sombre death prinked and highlighted railways' powerfully progressive life. As we shall see, both Carker the manager (in Charles Dickens' *Dombey and Son*) and Anna Karenina (in the novel which Leo Tolstoy graced with her name) died under trains' wheels: but their passing shocks through incongruity. When discussing railways in more recent years death, not life, rules the discourse. The dominant tone has become elegiac. Branch lines close; stations close; vast redundancies devastate railway workers' family dynasties. Sitting in the Orient Express in the late 1960s, Henry Pulling stared (in Yugoslavia) at 'the lines of stationary rolling-stock which looked abandoned as though nothing was left anywhere to put in the trucks, no one had the energy any more to roll them, and it was only our train which steamed on impelled by a foolish driver who hadn't realised that the world had stopped and there was nowhere for us to go'.[98] In 1986 Paul Theroux visited Beijing's 'Death Road', a nondescript chunk of railway track where, during the Cultural Revolution, extinction under a train's wheels became such a routine event that it turned into a social institution. 'One person a day, and sometimes more, jumped in front of the train', a young man told Theroux. 'In those days the buildings in Beijing weren't very tall – you couldn't kill yourself by jumping out of the window of a bungalow. So they chose the train because they were too poor to buy poison'.[99] Death Road's railway track was a cheap and reliable instrument for suicide. Back in Britain, George Sim's whodunnit sets us on a more complicated dark journey. Ned Balfour (significant name – remember the Balfour Declaration) investigates his friend's apparent suicide. Sam Weiss (significant name) was a Jewish art dealer who survived imprisonment in Dachau. Both men shared close friendships with another dealer, Max Weber (*highly* significant name). Weiss fell from a high window in Paddington (significant location). Dreaming one night, Balfour finds himself in a tall building.

> Then he heard a hurdy-gurdy grinding out a waltz and clambered up on a chair to one of the tiny awkward windows to look with difficulty down on a group of men, women and children being shepherded along a narrow street: as he stared down Max Weber and Sam Weiss looked up and waved gaily, shouting some words he could not hear. From his vantage point he alone could see that at the end of the street a train composed of closed goods wagons waited for them. He had rushed down the stairs as the music changed to that of a military band with loudly clashing cymbals playing at an increasing tempo. In a panic, unable to think, he had charged with his shoulder at the locked door to find that it opened into a small, crowded court-room with someone calling out in a dead-sounding voice *'Wiervel Stück?'* over and over again, despite the answering repetition '650 pieces in 12 goods wagons'.[100]

Rushing from his dream building, Balfour collides with a beautiful young girl, stripping her naked. The train chugs away. Any competent reader now knows that this 1960s London whodunnit will turn on Holocaust events: and that readers will be invited to distinguish different degrees of guilt, not to separate guilt from innocence. Max Weber's hired thugs killed Weiss to stop him taking evidence about Weber's Nazi-era activities to London police. Racked by conflicting loyalties to his two friends, Balfour makes his choice. He phones the police. Bearing witness against transcendental evil, he lifts one drachm from Europeans' collective guilt (whether of direct complicity or complacent passivity) in Nazi atrocities.

Sociology is the academic discipline charged with the specific duty to analyse modernity. All too often, this has meant no more than celebrating How We Live Now.[101] But twentieth century history insists that uncritical celebration will not do. Norbert Elias' multi-volume *The Civilizing Process* stands among this century's most imaginative and distinguished sociological attempts to understand how modernity budded and flowered. Elias' first volume was published in German in 1939. Turn the title page in this volume's English translation and read rendingly spare words: 'Dedicated to the memory of my Parents: Hermann Elias, d. Breslau 1940; Sophie Elias, d. Auschwitz 1941(?)'[102] The final solution. The civilising process twisted into its negation. The Enlightenment project spawning the twentieth century's worst monsters. Building on the other Max Weber's conceptual framework for understanding modernity (bureacratisation, rationalisation, the Iron Cage, disenchantment with the world), Zygmunt Bauman's *Modernity and the Holocaust* explains why this happened. Changes to German legal codes stripped civil rights from certain categories of people – Jews most prominently, but also disabled people, homosexuals, gypsies, socialists, trades unionists, certain nations' prisoners of war. With that task completed, these people stood exposed for treatment as sub-human things by Nazi state apparatuses. Slave labour underpinned the German war effort in a vastly ramified system of concentration camps. At this system's dark heart, in the death camps, fellow humans were exterminated wholesale in an obscene machine ensemble compounding well-tried technologies from different industrial sectors: chemical engineering, crematorium design, soap-boiling, metals recovery.[103]

And railway freight haulage. Watching (if we can) Claude Lanzemann's nine-hour documentary movie *Shoah* [1985], we might imagine that the phrase 'railway of death' was coined to describe this essential element in the final solution's perverted machine ensemble. Not so. It comes from humankind's first successful attempt to industrialise slaughter – hog-killing lines in meat packing plants surrounding late-nineteenth-century Chicago's stockyards.[104] In those years Chicago was the world's classic railroad city, growing at an optimally-sited node on America's spreading rail network. Western railroads brought hogs and cattle to the stockyards for slaughter; eastern railroads carried away canned and frozen dead meat to satisfy national and international market demand. This trade anticipated the Holocaust – except that in this case almost all loaded rail traffic travelled in one direction. As Muller reports while explaining how 400,000 Hungarian Jews could be murdered in the Auschwitz camp complex in a few weeks, 'In order to transport 10,000 people from Hungary to Birkenau about 100 railway carriages were needed. It needed only a few trucks to take their ashes to the Vistula.'[105] As in Ned Balfour's personal nightmare, the modern railway in Nazi-conquered lands stands complicit in the death camps, Europe's half-century deep collective nightmare.[106] Celebrating the railway age's progressive optimism, historians often provide their readers with maps showing how Victorian iron rails spread and connected, wrapping Britain in ever tighter modern webs. Martin Gilbert also prints a map; but this one identifies routes along which Auschwitz transports carried their imprisoned human cargoes from Europe's uttermost limits.

1.1   The British railway system in 1842

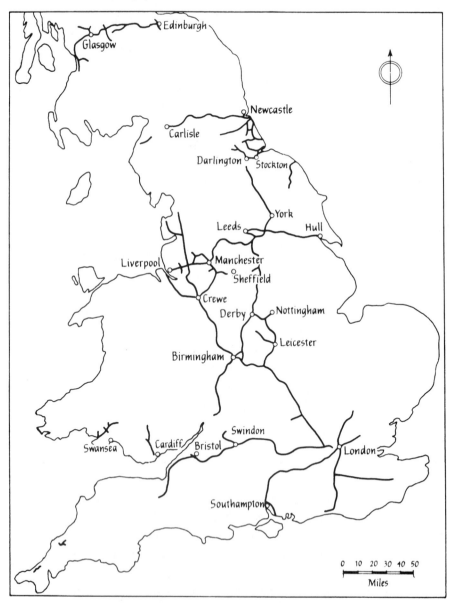

Deportation railway routes to Auschwitz, 1942–45   **1.2**

Many involuntary passengers died on journeys along the railway lines depicted in Martin Gilbert's map.[107] Lucky survivors – if that phrase can suggest other than a second kind of hell – found themselves selected to work as slave labourers, until they died or fell sick, in the huge Auschwitz complex's satellite camps. The halt and the lame, the too-young and the too-old, were herded directly from selection on the rail-side arrival platform (Birkenau-Auschwitz needed no departure platform) to the gas chambers.

The whistle of a train engine, the scream of wheels, the hiss of steam escaping from the valves, and the loud shriek of brakes, indicated that yet another transport had come up to the ramp. ... Almost daily several trains consisting, on average, of forty or fifty cattle trucks, arrived on the newly-built ramp at Birkenau. The trucks into which up to 100 people had been crammed were bolted; they were unlocked only when the train had reached its destination. ... Since the previous night 10,000 people had perished in the three gas chambers of crematorium 5 alone, while on the site of bunker six with its four gas chambers corpses were burnt in four pits. In addition, in crematoria 2, 3 and 4, with a total of five gas chambers and 38 ovens, work went on at full speed.[108]

Railways' deep complicity in the Nazi final solution, modernity's darkest single episode,[109] stains cultural understanding. No quantity of water rids us of this deed. 'Stockton to Darlington, 1825', Roy Fuller tells us in *The Nineteenth Century*:

> Stephenson on the sparkling iron road -
> Chimney-hatted and frock-coated – drives
> His locomotive, while the Lydian mode
> Of Opus 132 may actually be
> In the course of making. At twelve miles an hour
> The century rushes to futurity,
> Where art will be mankind-destroying power.[110]

Beethoven's noble faith in human progress crashes to cruel nullity. *Lyon*, or *Athens*, or *Oslo*, or (name your occupied town or city) *to Auschwitz, 1942*. Mankind-destroying power in fullest flower. Spanking Deutsches Reichesbahn steam locomotives, black above the running plate and scarlet below, dragging dreadful cargoes towards the distant ovens. [111] Like Roy Fuller, we ache to celebrate railways' unspotted childhood. That possibility always was remote for anybody who knew much about railways' social history. Today, it is erased. As Theodore Adorno insisted, no more railway poetry after Auschwitz.

Writing fiction

Exemplified by the modern railway, who could be surprised that the Enlightenment project's massive attempt to obliterate the past in the interest of creating a better future should impress itself deeply on British literary mentalities? 'Prominent if not paramount among world-changing inventions in the history of man', H. G. Wells reported in one of his less well-known scientific romances, 'is that series of contrivances in locomotion that began with the railway.'[112] Contrasts between *express train* and *slow coach* litter early- to mid-nineteenth-century fiction. 'The presence of either the railway or coach travel', Richard Altick notes, 'was, to the reader, an instantaneously recognisable clue to the time setting of a novel's plot'.

> Although the term 'modern novel' antedated the railway age, the very definition of modernity in early Victorian fiction may be said to have hinged on the railway. It served as a key signature, a mechanism that automatically fixed the reader's sights, encouraged him to translate into contemporary terms all the other, time-neutral, details the author may have supplied. Once a train was mentioned, everything fell into place. It was the prime way by which an action could be fixed in the present, as surely as spikes held down the rails.[113]

In his preface to the 1902 edition of *Far From the Madding Crowd* (1874) Thomas Hardy marked off Bathsheba Everdene's ineffably old, lost world from 'A modern Wessex of railways, the penny post, mowing and reaping machines, union workhouses, lucifer matches, labourers who could read and write, and National school children'. Hardy was born in 1840, the year when Rowland Hill's new adhesive penny black and twopenny blue postage stamps went on sale. Union workhouses dated from 1834; National Schools (and thus, for a few lucky labourers' children, literacy) from 1844; lucifer matches from 1831; reaping machines (in their earliest, primitive form) from 1811. The first modern railway, the Liverpool and Manchester, opened for traffic in 1830. Hardy's fiction lies rooted in the stories about her girlhood's local world which his mother told him in childhood. A child's natal world is flat and timeless, taken for granted. Appreciating that the place into which one is born has three dimensions, that a local universe enjoys its own historical depth, takes time and experience to achieve. In many novels and stories, Hardy's narratives reveal his striking ability to conjure his own childhood's mindset, measuring accelerating change against early Victorian Higher Bockhampton's deceptively timeless facticity. Very often he shows us characters minced between past and present. The modern present's potent symbol, steam railways, appear frequently in Hardy's fiction; but in the integrated manner that we might expect from an author who grew to manhood in years when railway travel had become routine. Thus steam power and steam railways intrude rarely (but always significantly) in his scandalous penultimate novel, *Tess of the d'Urbervilles* (1891). Chapter 30 shows us Tess and her worthy but vacillating admirer Angel Clare driving Dairyman Crick's churns to the local station, for consignment to London's town milk retailers.[114] This new railway has spawned a specialised dairying industry in Blackmoor Vale, permitting Tess her idyll milking cows on Talbothays farm. That idyll soon fades. By chapter 43 she labours on 'starve-acre' Flintcomb-Ash, hacking sheep-nibbled swedes from sodden winter fields. Five chapters later we find her driven to exhaustion on this farm, by a steam-driven threshing machine's relentless pace. Rascally Alec d'Urberville's price for rescuing Tess from degraded outdoor agricultural work is that she become his mistress. Travelling by train, in chapter 55 Angel Clare tracks them down in Sandbourne (Bournemouth). This location is not adventitious. Hitherto valued principally as a secluded watering-place, modern Bournemouth grew to be a middle-class coastal resort wholly through its railway connections.[115] Angel Clare's railway journey to this railway resort precipitates the novel's final crisis, with Tess murdering Alec in their boarding house, then hanged at Wintoncester (Winchester) prison. Hardy's bitter subtitle made Tess a 'pure woman'. As maid, wife and mistress, as murderer and victim, her tragedy lies in her failure to understand how pre-modern atavism leached through a modern present when change accelerated beyond human capacity to absorb its effects.

Writers were well aware that accelerating change could be found everywhere in early Victorian Britain. Disraeli's last novel identified four key innovations: 'railroads, telegraphs, penny posts and penny newspapers'.[116] Widening the frame, a modern historian tells us that in the 1840s transoceanic steam ships, cheap postal services, the electric telegraph, photography, and the modern railway 'contributed mightily to changing forever the quality of European – and ultimately the world's – life and the structure of society'.[117] Jerome Blum set the railway last in his list. Like Disraeli, most contemporaries gave it pride of place as modernity's prime symbol. 'We who have lived before railways were made, belong to another world', William Makepeace Thackeray told the *Cornhill Magazine*'s readers in October 1860.

> It was only yesterday; but what a gulf between now and then! …There it lies on the other side of yonder embankments. The young folk have never seen it; and Waterloo is to you no more than Agincourt, and George IV than Sardanapulus. We elderly people have lived in that prae-railroad world, which has passed into limbo and vanished from under us. I tell you it was firm under our feet once, and not long ago. They have raised those railroad embankments up, and shut off the old world that was behind them. Climb up that bank on which the irons are laid, and look to the other side – it is gone.

With remarkable perspicacity, Thackeray understood that steam-powered railways and transoceanic travel signalled a beginning, not an end:

> We are of the age of steam. We have stepped out of the old world on to 'Brunel's' vast deck, and across the waters *ingens patet tellus*. Towards what new continent are we wending? to what new laws, new manners, new politics, vast new expanses of

liberties unknown as yet, or only surmised? … I used to know a man who had
invented a flying machine. 'Sir', he would say, 'give me but five hundred pounds,
and I will make it. It is so simple of construction that I tremble daily lest some
other person should light upon and patent my discovery.' Perhaps faith was
wanting; perhaps the five hundred pounds. He is dead, and somebody else must
make the flying machine. But that will be only a step forward on the journey
already begun since we quitted the old world.[118]

Just so. Two generations later, in 1902, H. G. Wells speculated about which new
forms of locomotion this exciting new century would bring. A man born in
Thackeray's new world, he recognised that 'People of today take the railway for
granted as they take sea and sky; they were born in a railway world, and they
expect to die in one.'[119] Like Thackeray, Wells understood that the modern
railway merely initiated accelerating change in moving things and people from
one place to others. He scouted the possibility that air travel would ever come to
much ('Man is not … an albatross, but a land biped'), and his armchair-
equipped travelators speeding massed folk over and under every city street have
not been installed; but Wells' entertained a clear appreciation that the freedom
and personal autonomy provided by 'explosive engines' mounted in steerable
carriages running on soft tyres would challenge railways' inflexibility very
severely.[120] Jaded children of Wells' exciting new century, we know that the long
nineteenth century was the railway's golden age; that from 1914 gold yielded to
iron, just as Hesiod predicted all those centuries ago.

One hundred and seventy years after the Liverpool and Manchester Railway
opened for traffic, it is not easy for us to appreciate how radically railway travel
disturbed contemporaries' cultural understandings. Some people were
enchanted – like delicious Fanny Kemble, flirting with George Stephenson on
her footplate run along the soon-to-be-opened Liverpool and Manchester
Railway, intoxicated by her half-sexualised 'sensation of flying'.[121] The world's
first fictional female detective echoed Fanny's emotion thirty years later, then
drew larger conclusions. 'There is to me always something very exhilarating in
the quickly rushing motions of a railway carriage', she told her readers. 'It is typ-
ical of progress, and raises my spirits in proportion to the speed at which we
career along.'[122] Some people were less enchanted with progress than this –
notably John Ruskin, puce at railway companies' encouragement for
Derbyshire folk to gad about; and Wordsworth, railling at railway construction's heedless desecration of precious rural retreats.[123] The railway soon became
a metaphor for human experience. 'Our life is like one big train journey', Vitali
Vitaliev suggested remarkably recently. 'The express train runs forward along

the rails, rattling its wheels on the joints of days and weeks. It runs past the whistle stops of Childhood and Youth, slows down at the stations of Maturity and Old Age, and then, there on the hazy horizon, one can already discern the sad, blinking lights of the Terminal…'[124] Imaginative writers began playing with this conceit: 'For up to a certain time of life one is like a traveller who is seated facing the engine and ever looks ahead of what is immediately opposite him', E. F. Benson insisted. 'But that time past, for fear of draughts or what not, we gather up a railway rug, seat ourselves with our back to the direction of progress, and see only that which has passed us.'[125] Other writers joined Thomas Hardy in contrasting a stable and unchanging older world with the new railway's rush and hurry, offering 'a talisman for memory in an era in which the past was under threat and time itself seemed to be accelerating'.[126] Elizabeth Gaskell made mid-century Cranford (Knutsford) a town from which eighteenth-century manners, ideas and women's fashions had not completely disappeared. This backwardness threw into greater contrast modernity's restless intrusion, symbolised by the new railway connecting Cranford with Drumble (Manchester).[127] As he established groundworks for his running contrast between Michael Henchard's Wessex life world (based on handfast trust and personal reputation) and that Scottish interloper Donald Farfrae's new British world (operating strictly on double-entry book-keeping principles), Thomas Hardy's panoptic description of Casterbridge (Dorchester) in the late 1840s suppressed not only a union workhouse and a gasworks, but also the London and South Western's railway station – through whose portals Dorchester's citizens could escape Henchard's closed, regional world at the blast of a guard's whistle.[128] We understand what Bernard Miles' Buckinghamshire yokel managed to get right sixty years ago, among his jumbled errors. 'That was built by the Voikins in the 'leventh century', the Sage of Ivinghoe told credulous townies about his village church: 'afore the railway come'.'[129] Big historical markers. Before Christ and Anno Domini. Before the railway and after the railway. Before the modern world and in the modern world.

Bradshaw's Guide

The next five chapters bring recent criticism from specialists in many different disciplines to bear on canonical railway-related texts. We begin by pondering early railways' most significant image, J. M. W. Turner's oil painting *Rain, Steam and Speed: the Great Western Railway*. This discussion takes us to Charles Dickens' *Dombey and Son* – a book often linked to Turner's image, and always taken to be Britain's canonical railway novel. Since direct railway interest is so slight in *Dombey*, and for some other reasons, we choose not to endorse that judgement. To establish what Britain misses by having no canonical railway novel, chapters 4 and 5 examine two European novels which frequently are taken to be just that – Leo Tolstoy's *Anna Karenina*, and Émile Zola's *La Bête Humaine* – and conclude that the case is stronger for Zola than for Tolstoy. The book's first part closes by suggesting that if we really wanted to find a British railway novel capable of being installed in some literary pantheon, then Arnold Bennett's *Accident* provides the best candidate. It seems both odd and apt that it should be forgotten so completely today.

As railway historians so rarely do, in Part II we explore railways' representation in some nooks and crannies of British popular culture's rambling edifice, notably crime fiction and comic fiction. A chapter dissects Eric Ravilious' watercolour painting *Train Landscape*. This directs our attention to pictorial narrative conventions familiar to Turner and his contemporaries, but also connects to comic fiction by leading us to consider work from Britain's most celebrated twentieth-century railway cartoonists: William Heath Robinson and Rowland Emett. Exploring work in all these largely disparaged popular genres reveals an important register shift over time in the manner through which British railways were represented, a shift which influences (in ways which largely lie beyond our compass here) British railways' current public reputation.

Moving from canonical texts to popular culture is an academically risky enterprise. 'Popular narrative has not traditionally been well regarded in academic institutions', Jerry Palmer tells us. 'The clearest expression of this disregard is silence.'[130] Silence can signify not disparagement, but cowardice. 'Until very recently', Harriett Hawkins reports, 'it would most certainly have been, even as in some circles it may still be, academic suicide to admit to any interest in, much less an enjoyment of, certain works popular with "bourgeois" (middle-class, middle-brow) audiences'.[131] How could one compare a major novelist like Charles Dickens with Freeman Wills Croft, a mere crime writer? Several justifications spring to mind, beyond the primitive instinct that any academic worth her or his salt should face down paper tigers like these. First, as Gore Vidal notes, today's border between canonical and extra-canonical literature neatly divides involuntary from voluntary readers.[132] Dickens' novels sell more copies in university bookshops than supermarkets today, and students have to be threatened with examination questions before they will read *Dombey*, but Dickens' novels were immensely popular in his own time. Some jewels in today's literary crown once could be appreciated outside precious literary coteries, we see.[133] Second, genre, not quality, excludes some excellent writers from serious consideration. Highly praised by Belloc, Orwell, Waugh and Auden, perhaps twentieth-century English's finest prose stylist, only his stubborn insistence on writing (profitable) comedy kept P. G. Wodehouse outside the canon.[134] Paul Fussell sets Robert Byron's *The Road to Oxiana* (1937) alongside T. S. Eliot's *The Waste Land* and James Joyce's *Ulysses* as a modernist literary monument, directly comparable with them in technique and significance. Only because it is taken to be a 'travel book' rather than a novel or poem is it ignored.[135] Third, genre fiction can offer unexpected pleasure to those whose first reflex is not to despise it. D. A. Peart insists that the railway compartment short story was well developed by the 1860s. Wihin three decades it had declined, he claims; now 'several writers relied wholly on cheap melodrama and well-worn plots for their efforts'.[136] This judgement directs attention to crime writers, jewels in 1990s' popular culture. But we will see in chapter 7 that one chief delight in the railway crime literature which has flourished so richly over the last century in Britain is to watch authors play ingenious variations on well-worn plots and settings (including the compartment), tantalising expert readers with new twists and misdirection. As Umberto Eco tells us, in order to invent freely the writer must create constraints.[137] Fourth, smoke and gunfire from America's 'culture wars'[138] has diverted attention from the awkward truth that material in which involuntary readers must simulate an interest in university literature classes is no stable body of work. Particular authors move into favour over time, then find themselves cast to the outer darkness once more. Decisions about which authors may lounge in the canon and which must batter against its outside walls differ from one canon-builder's list to another. Anti-canonical critics howl against particular authors' exclusion, then construct parallel canons by drawing up their own reading lists for their own students.[139] Fifth, and most interestingly for our purpose, both armies in the culture wars legitimise their struggle by appealing to Enlightenment ancestors. Allan Bloom's trumpet-call for a revitalised 'Great Books' undergraduate programme swoons for the codified and warranted knowledge in Diderot and d'Alembert's *Encyclopédie* (1751–72). On the barricade's other side, as they seek to insert into university curricula some authors hitherto excluded by reason of gender, class or ethnicity, anti-canonical writers honour Voltaire's ringing injunction to critique existing social arrangements. 'The Enlightenment Project' is no single expressway. Understood in its full richness, that project insists that we ignore boundaries between literary and sub-literary work as completely as we ignore boundaries separating one academic discipline from others. Cultural studies, an empirically rooted interdisciplinary enterprise whose spongy marshes protected British academic life from American culture wars' marches and countermarches, provides a useful site for that enterprise. Cultural studies' onlie begetter was the critic, novelist and political activist Raymond Williams.[140] A railway signalman's son, Williams' cultural materialism will prove particularly fruitful for our purposes. More or less openly, it will guide our steps as we explore relationships between railways, modernity and culture in later chapters.

Notes

1   Bruno Latour, *Aramis, or the Love of Technology* [1993], translated by Catherine Porter, Cambridge, Mass., Harvard University Press, 1996, p. 289.

2   Contributors to a recent conspectus (John Law and John Hassard (eds), *Actor Network Theory and After*, Oxford, Blackwell, 1999) reveal the remarkably wide arenas in which actor network theory – simply one more way in which scholars have tried to articulate those old sociological enemies, structure and agency – has been employed. Use it to analyse anything else, and nobody much takes any notice. Use actor network theory to analyse science, and all hell breaks loose. Is this not instructive?

3   Latour, *Aramis*, p. vii.

4   Dionysius Lardner, *Railway Economy* [1850], quoted in Jack Simmons, *St Pancras Station*, London, Allen & Unwin, 1968, title page.

5   C. J. Lever, *Tales of the Trains*, London, Orr, p. v.

6   George Ottley, *A Bibliography of British Railway History, Supplement*, London, HMSO, 1988, p. 14. The base volume for this monumental work of amateur scholarship was published by HMSO in 1965. A further supplement appeared in 1998: Grahame Boyes, Matthew Searle and Donald Steggles (eds), *Ottley's Bibliography of British Railway History: Second Supplement*, York, National Railway Museum.

7   P. L. Scowcroft, 'Railways and detective fiction', *Journal of the Railway and Canal Historical Society*, 1981, pp. 16, 27.

8   William R. Everdell, *The First Moderns*, Berkeley, University of California Press, 1997, p. 4.

9   Henry Grote Lewin, *The British Railway System: Outlines of its Early Development to the Year 1844*, London, Bell, 1914, p. v. His easy conflation of England with Britain shows that Lewin was born south of the Tweed. His broad judgement could have been challenged in his own day, notably by those familiar with W. M. Acworth's *The Railways of England*, fifth edition, London, Murray, 1900. The first serious modern attempt at a synoptic survey was C. Hamilton Ellis' *British Railway History*, two volumes, London, Allen & Unwin, 1954–59. It now is buttressed, if not supplanted, by Jack Simmons' three-volume study: *The Railway in England and Wales, 1830–1914: the System and its Working*, Leicester, Leicester University Press, 1978; *The Railway in Town and Country, 1830–1914*, Newton Abbot, David & Charles, 1986; *The Victorian Railway*, London, Thames & Hudson, 1991.

10   Michael Robbins, 'What kind of railway history do we want?', *Journal of Transport History*, 1st series, 3, 1957, p. 66.

11   T. R. Gourvish, 'What kind of railway history did we get?', *Journal of Transport History*, 3rd series, 14, 1993, p. 112.

12   Jack Simmons and Michael Robbins, 'Forty years on: a message from the founding editors', *Journal of Transport History*, 3rd series, 14, 1993, p. v.

13   Ottley, *Bibliography* [1965], p. 21.

14   Philip Ransome-Wallis, *On Railways at Home and Abroad*, London, Spring, n. d., pp. 15–19.

15   These phrases are culled from book reviews in the *The Journal of Transport History*: 3rd series, 16, 1995, p. 201; 15, 1994, p. 92; 17, 1996, p. 84. See also Michael Robbins, 'The progress of transport history', *Journal of Transport History*, 3rd series, 12, 1991, p. 83; Jack Simmons, 'Literature of railways', in Jack Simmons and Gordon Biddle (eds), *The Oxford Companion to British Railway History*, Oxford, Oxford University Press, 1997, pp. 268–70.

16   Simmons and Robbins, 'Forty years on', p. vi.

17   Asa Briggs, 'The imaginative response of the Victorians to new technology: the case of the railway', in Chris Wrigley and John Shepherd (eds), *On the Move: Essays in Labour and Transport History Presented to Philip Bagwell*, London, Hambledon, 1991, p. 74.

18   Bryan Morgan, 'Introduction', to Morgan (ed.), *The Railway-Lover's Companion*, London, Eyre & Spottiswoode, 1963, p. 15. Original emphasis. J. C. Bourne was a fine topographical artist, setting down enduring images of the Great Western and the London and Birmingham railways' pioneer days. Francis Frith's oil painting *The Railway Station* (1863) was greatly appreciated in its day. After decades drifting in the critical doldrums, today its stock is rising once more. As vice-chairman of the London Passenger Transport Board, Frank Pick oversaw design on the London Underground system, hiring major artists for poster work and establishing an immensely influential house style throughout the system. Often dubbed 'the Father of Railways', George Stephenson (together with his son Robert, and Robert's close friend I. K. Brunel) dominated early British railway engineering. With their eight-foot driving wheels, Patrick Stirling's 'Singles' for the Great Northern Railway were, in many railway aesthetes' view, the loveliest locomotives ever built for a British railway. The Midland Railway, LMS and British Railways were successive owners for a particularly widespread section of the national railway network before and after the 1923 Grouping, and after nationalisation in 1947. The English Electric Company built pioneer diesel locomotives for the LMS, then for British Railways.

19   Jack Simmons, *Southey*, London, Collins, 1945. Three years earlier, he had been junior author to Margery Perham on her well-known *African Adventure*.

20   Jack Simmons (ed.), *Journeys in England: an Anthology*, London, Odhams, 1951.

21   Jack Simmons, *The Railways of Britain: an Historical Introduction*, second edition, London, Macmillan, 1968; (ed.), *Rail 150: the Stockton and Darlington Railway and what Followed*, London, Eyre Methuen, 1975; *Railway in England and Wales; Railway in Town and Country*. It is possible that his own literary sensibilities inhibited

Simmons from writing about imaginative work. 'A collection of railway fiction would be a thing of rags and patches', Bryan Morgan ruminated, 'with the pattern of each fragment lost through having been torn out of context' ('Introduction', to Morgan (ed.), *Railway-Lover's Companion*, 16). Not good practice: literary and visual texts are more than quarries from which to hack illustrative examples.

22 Jack Simmons, *Railways: an Anthology*, London, Collins, 1991. Reviewing this book in *The Journal of Transport History* (3rd series, 13, 1992, p. 92), Philip Bagwell pulled out an unexpected plum – 'Poisson d'Avril'. First published in *Further Reminiscences of An Irish R. M.* [1908], reprinted in Charles Irving (ed.), *Sixteen On*, London, Macmillan, 1957, pp. 87–100 and in L. T. C. Rolt (ed.), *Best Railway Stories*, London, Faber, 1969, pp. 106–18, Somerville and Ross' story is scarcely recondite. Could one seek a clearer illustration for transport historians' trained indifference to imaginative fiction? This is no new problem. *The Railway Magazine*'s anonymous reviewer (74, 1934, p. 389) found Graham Greene 'uncertain on his technical details' in *Stamboul Train*. Other errors were so egregious that 'his talk of signal boxes in Hungary, where they do not exist, is a minor fault'. Greene's ignorance of Hungarian signalling arrangements is easily explained. Trying to kick-start a literary career, he sat in Chipping Campden sweating over a conventional thriller set on the Orient Express. Arthur Honegger's *Pacific 231* revolved ceaselessly on his gramophone's turntable, providing mood music. (Erroneously, as it happens. Honegger's piece was pure music: only later did the railways-obsessed composer realise that a railway programme could be attached.) Back in Chipping Campden, Greene's funds were so slight that in researching his thriller he could afford no more than one third-class trip on the Orient Express – from Paris to Cologne. See Humphrey Carpenter, *The Brideshead Generation: Evelyn Waugh and his Friends*, Boston, Houghton Mifflin, 1990, p. 227.

23 Simmons, *Victorian Railway*, p. 195. Elsewhere, he ascribes this lack of interest to contemporary literary market signals, with technical matters deemed no fit subject for serious fiction: Jack Simmons, 'Literature, railways in English', in Simmons and Biddle (eds), *Oxford Companion*, p. 267.

24 Richard Boston, 'Prose and poetry of the railways', *The Guardian*, 4 May 1986.

25 Russell McDougall, 'The railway in Australian literature', *World Literature Written in English*, 28, 1988, p. 75. For some other cases, see Frank P. Donovan Jr, *The Railroad in Literature*, Boston, Railway and Locomotive Historical Society, 1940; Merton M. Sealts Jr, '"Pulse of the continent": the railroad in American literature', *Wisconsin Academy Review*, 36, 1990, pp. 27–32; George H. Douglas, *All Aboard: the Railroad in American Life*, New York, Paragon House, 1992, pp. 329–44; Alfred C. Heinimann, *Technische Innovation und Literarische Aneignung: diie Eisenbahn in der Deutschen und Englischen Literatur des 19. Jahrhunderts*, Bern, Francke, 1992.

26 Richard D. Altick, *The Presence of the Past: Topics of the Day in the Victorian Novel*, Columbus, Ohio State University Press, 1991, chapter 6; Asa Briggs, *The Power of Steam: an Illustrated History of the Steam Age*, London, Joseph, 1982, pp. 70–147; Briggs, 'Imaginative response'; M. F. Brightfield, *Victorian England in its Novels, 1840–1870*, Los Angeles, University of California Library, 1968, chapter 3; F. P.

Donovan, *The Railroad in Fiction: a Brief Survey of Railroad Fiction, Songs, Biography, Essays, Travel, and Drama in the English Language*, Boston, Railway and Locomotive Historical Society, 1940; D. A. Peart, 'Literature and the railway in the nineteenth and twentieth centuries', Unpublished M. A. Thesis, Liverpool University, 1964; Herbert L. Sussman, *Victorians and the Machine: the Literary Response to Technology*, Cambridge, Mass., Harvard University Press, 1968; Gillian Tindall, *Countries of the Mind: the Meaning of Place to Writers*, London, Hogarth Press, 1991, chapter 4.

27 A generation ago, Michael Robbins listed five elements which must be present for a railway to count as modern: a specialised track, accommodating public traffic, conveying passengers, conveying goods, mechanical traction, and some measure of public control (*The Railway Age*, London, Routledge & Kegan Paul, 1962, pp. 13–14). That only two of these elements are mechanical should warn us that changed social relations are no less fundamental to modernity than is novel physical machinery. One recent definition expands Robbins' definition by an order of magnitude. Stephen Hughes (*The Brecon Forest Tramroads: the Archaeology of an Early Railway System*, Aberystwyth, The Royal Commission on Ancient and Historical Monuments in Wales, 1990, pp. 104–5) needs 51 categories to distinguish modern railways from primitive and hybrid forms. Again, technical elements blend intimately with social. Flag-bearer for a mathematicised new economic history of railways in the 1960s, Gary Hawke recently argued that 'It is ... possible to disaggregate the notion of a railway and trace an earlier history of wheel-and-track technology and of steam engines so that the final step of putting a steam engine with flanged wheels on an iron track seems less than momentous': Gary R. Hawke, 'The impact of high speed trains: an historic comparison', in John Whitelegg, Staffan Hultén and Torbjörn Flink (eds), *High Speed Trains: Fast Tracks to the Future*, Hawes, Leading Edge, 1993, p. 220. Which sardonic historian of modern France said that enough historians hammering away at enough typewriters for enough years could dissolve any revolution into smoke? Of course, disaggregation will destroy the modern railway's epochal significance. The machine ensemble's importance lies in the way it aggregated many separate elements.

28 Some critics seek to deflate modernity, explaining it away as no more than another western trick to ignore the historical experience of non-western peoples. For recent surveys of such positions see Ted Benton, 'Radical politics – neither left nor right?', in Martin O'Brien, Sue Penna and Colin Hay (eds), *Theorising Modernity: Reflexivity, Environment and Identity in Giddens' Social Theory*, London, Longmans, 1999, pp. 53–5; Jack Goody, *Food and Love: a Cultural History of East and West*, London, Verso, 1998, pp. 1–26. These arguments' ramifications lie beyond my compass in this book; but Thomas Osborne's suggestion (in his *Aspects of Enlightenment: Social Theory and the Ethics of Truth*, London, UCL Press, 1998) that sociologists should stop haring after modernity on all occasions and engage in 'on-going fieldwork in our existing practices of enlightenment' (p. xii) is seductive.

29 'A web of common references to acceleration and evolution, primitive and progressive, an historical consciousness shaped by political rivalry, scientific ideology and

global capitalism which I have called "modern":' Matt K. Matsuda, *The Memory of the Modern*, New York, Oxford University Press, 1996, p. 206. As a young man, Herbert Spencer worked for ten years as a railway engineer, helping to build the London and Birmingham Railway and the Birmingham and Gloucester Railway as well as helping to plan several Railway Mania whimsies. Only with hindsight's benefit did he appreciate railways' tremendous significance for British society – and for his own social theory. See J. D. Y. Peel, *Herbert Spencer: the Evolution of a Sociologist*, London, Heinemann, 1971, pp. 10, 218–19; David Wiltshire, *The Social and Political Thought of Herbert Spencer*, Oxford, Oxford University Press, 1978, pp. 24–9, 41–5.

30 Alan Swingewood, *Cultural Theory and the Problem of Modernity*, London, Macmillan, 1998, p. 136.

31 This list comes from Trevor K. Snowdon, 'Railways, rationality and modernity', Unpublished PhD thesis, Department of Sociology, The University of Auckland, 1992, pp. 29–30; a thesis centred on ideas from Max Weber and Erving Goffman. Other lists exist, of course – with each covering different (if partially overlapping) ranges of issues. Thus Roger Friedland and Deidre Boden ('NowHere: an introduction', in Friedland and Boden (eds), *NowHere: Space, Time and Modernity*, Berkeley, University of California Press, 1994, pp. 9–12) focus modernity on 'the controlling centre and the reasoning subject, around city, state and firm and the active participation of residents, citizens and capitalists'. For yet other formulations see John Frow, 'What was post-modernism?', in Ian Adam and Helen Tiffin (eds), *Past the Last Post: Theorizing Post-Colonialism and Post-Modernism*, Calgary, University of Calgary Press, 1990, p. 140, and Stuart Hall, 'Introduction', to Stuart Hall *et al.* (eds), *Modernity: an Introduction to Modern Societies*, Oxford, Blackwell, 1996, p. 8.

32 H. G. Wells, *Anticipations*, London, Methuen, 1902, p. 4. 'There has never been any sustained attack on the idea that the steam railway was the most significant invention or innovation in the rise of industrial society', the American historian Albro Martin insists (Martin, *Railroads Triumphant: the Growth, Rejection and Rebirth of a Vital American Force*, New York, Oxford University Press, 1992, p. 12). 'The nineteenth century European, at once capitalist and revolutionary, had a dynamic conception of society', the French sociologist Alain Touraine reminds us. 'Lévi-Strauss was right to see the the steam-engine as the symbol of a social mechanism functioning between poles of heat and cold, between the capitalist entrepreneur and proletarianised workers': Touraine, 'The idea of a revolution', in Mike Featherstone (ed.), *Global Culture*, London, Sage, 1990, p. 129. Ah, structuralist's chaste binary delights! – but strip away Lévi-Strauss' verbiage and a *real* revolutionary would concur. 'Marx was right', Leon Trotsky told his readers, 'when he said that revolution is the locomotive of history': Trotsky, *The Revolution Betrayed: What is the Soviet Union and Where is it Going?*, New York, Pathfinder Press, 1972, p. 172.

33 Karl Marx, *Grundrisse* [1857–58], translated by Martin Nicolaus, New York, Random House, 1973, p. 539.

34 Leo Marx, 'The idea of "technology" and postmodern pessimism', in Yaron Ezrahi, Everett Mendelsohn and Howard Segal (eds), *Technology, Pessimism and Postmodernism*, Dordrecht, Kluwer, 1994, p. 13. See also Leo Marx, 'Closely watched trains', *New York Review of Books*, 15 March, 1984. Jonathan Carrick lives in Joan Brady's *Theory of War* (London, Abacus, 1994, p. 57). Railroads crowd this novel about post-bellum America.

35 Leo Marx, 'Idea of technology', p. 16, parsing Alfred D. Chandler, *The Visible Hand: the Managerial Revolution in American Business*, Cambridge, Mass., Harvard University Press, 1977; Jacques Ellul, *The Technological System*, translated by Joachim Neugroschel, New York, Continuum, 1980; and Wiebe E. Bijker, Thomas P. Hughes and Trevor Pinch (eds), *The Social Construction of Technological Systems*, Cambridge, Mass., MIT Press, 1989.

36 Wolfgang Schivelbusch, *The Railway Journey: Trains and Travel in the Nineteenth Century*, translated by Anselm Hollo, New York, Urizen, 1979, pp. 19–40.

37 Paul Jennings, 'Label by Appointment', in Jennings, *The Jenguin Pennings*, Harmondsworth, Penguin, 1963, p. 133.

38 L. T. C. Rolt and P. B. Whitehouse, *Lines of Character*, London, Constable, 1962, p. 11.

39 Charles Dickens, 'Master Humphrey's visitor' [1840] in Dickens, *Master Humphrey's Clock, and a Child's History of England*, Oxford, Oxford University Press, 1958, pp. 79–80. Mr Weller was no dispassionate observer. A coach driver made redundant by railways' spreading network, he has just suffered a journey locked in a train's compartment with 'a living widder' who, he feared, entertained matrimonial designs on his person.

40 H. G. Wells, *The War of the Worlds* [1898], edited by David Y. Hughes and Harry M. Geduld, Bloomington, Indiana University Press, 1993, p. 55. In context, this passage is an elegy. Within a couple of days the narrator's comfortably disciplined Surrey will collapse under a Martian invasion; he will not see his wife again until the novel's final page. Peart ('Literature and the railway', pp.122–3) makes the London and South Western Railway a symbol of normality in this invasion – with its trains chugging, strictly to timetable, among tripod fighting machines. An odd reading. A wrecked train blocks Woking station within thirty-six hours of the Martians' first cylinder landing (p. 88). By the next morning 'ordinary traffic had been stopped, I believe, in order to allow of the passage of troops and guns to Chertsey' (p. 96). As invasion develops, the narrator's complacent faith in modernity's oiled facticity collapses not only before his own terrible experience in Surrey but also before his brother's account of railway companies' puny helplessness in evacuating citizens from London, the world's greatest city. Outside Liverpool Street station 'revolvers were fired, people stabbed, and the policemen who had been sent to direct the traffic, exhausted and infuriated, were breaking the heads of the people they were called out to protect'. At Chalk Farm – London and North Western authorities had given up even trying to run trains down the Camden bank to Euston – 'the engines of the trains that had loaded in the goods yard there *ploughed* through shrieking people, and a dozen stalwart men fought to

keep the crowd from crushing the driver against his furnace' (p. 121: original emphasis).

41 *Quarterly Review*, quoted in Simmons, *Railways: an Anthology*, p. 9.

42 J. R. Kellett, *The Impact of Railways on Victorian Cities*, London Routledge & Kegan Paul, 1963; Simmons, *Railway in Town and Country*, Harold Perkin, *The Age of the Railway*, London, Panther, 1970, pp. 156–7.

43 'The Duke of Wellington was quite right in fearing that railways would encourage the wrong people to travel', Anthony Lejeune (*Professor in Peril*, London, Macmillan, 1987, p. 227) tells us. Is this a social myth? 'I could not find chapter and verse for this, and indeed turned up some speeches by the Iron Duke very much in favour of the iron horse', Roger Green reports in his introduction to Green (ed.), *The Train*, Oxford, Oxford University Press, 1982, p. vii.

44 Agatha Christie, 'The four suspects', in Christie, *Miss Marple and the Thirteen Problems* [1932], Harmondsworth, Penguin, 1953, p. 136. In the 1880s the Dells 'settled down in their marshland fastness twenty miles from a railway station', Margery Allingham recalls ('The correspondents', in Allingham, *Mr Campion's Lucky Day, and Other Stories* [1973], Harmondsworth, Penguin, 1993, p. 72), 'and as far from the world as if they had gone missioning to China'. In suburban Kent, 'the little self-important train was leaving Inching Round on its momentous journey to the Capital. To Firth the departing train was a symbol of his abandonment. London was only a few hours away even by that crawling little train, but it might as well have been a thousand miles away': Max Murray, *The Voice of the Corpse* [1948], Harmondsworth, Penguin, 1956, p. 82.

45 Perkin, *Age of the Railway*, pp. 96–121.

46 Of course, this distinction ignored the vast majority. They walked.

47 David Cannadine, *Class in Britain*, New Haven, Yale University Press, 1998, p. 89; Perkin, *Age of the Railway*, pp. 169–70; Jack Simmons, 'Class distinctions', in Simmons and Biddle (eds), *Oxford Companion*, pp. 84–7. E. Nesbit's *The Railway Children*, London, Wells Gardner 1906, and Lionel Jeffries' faithful movie version (1970) – see Keith C. Odom, 'Children, daffodils and railways', in Douglas Street (ed.), *Children's Novels and the Movies*, New York, Ungar, 1995, pp. 111–20 – shows class intersecting with railways and politics. Nesbit builds her novel around a middle-class father's unjust imprisonment and release. She shows us only one significant working-class character – Perks, a railway porter. Largely treated as comic relief, at one point the children insult him. Their author chides them for this lapse in manners: working people have feelings, too. But her socialism – Edith Nesbit was an active Fabian – does not spring her plot. Father's release comes not through class struggle, but through string-pulling by The Old Gentleman, a railway director to whom the children wave each morning as his train passes their country cottage. Old Gentlemen – railway company directors and officers – proved to be less than monolithic in their attitude to class. Rooted in sturdy midland Nonconformity (and seeking to dish the LNWR and the Great Northern in competition for traffic to the midlands and the north), in 1872 the Midland Railway's board outraged competitors by admitting third-class passengers to all express trains. Two years later they went

further, abolishing second-class and providing cushioned comfort for all third-class passengers (Frederick S. Williams, *The Midland Railway: its Rise and Progress* [1876], Newton Abbot, David & Charles, 1968, pp. 230–4). However much this irked other lines' directors, the Great Western's 'crass conservatism' made this resemble the worst excesses of the French Revolution. Forced by competitive pressures from the London and South Western to admit third-class passengers to one up and one down secondary express each day between Paddington and Exeter, 'To the August G. W. R. Waterloo [the L. & S. W. R'.s headquarters] seemed ever jacobinic and entirely lacking in decorum. It positively encouraged third class business! How the Paddington hierarchy hated the changes in the social order effected largely by the railways themselves' (David St J. Thomas, *A Regional History of the Railways of Great Britain. Vol 1: the West Country*, fourth edition, Newton Abbot, David & Charles, 1974, pp. 219–20). Heading for Blandings Castle, that imaginative sponger Lord Ickenham understood just how GWR directors felt. Usually obliged to enter London through Waterloo – '"all hustle and bustle, and the society tends to be mixed"' – he appreciates Paddington's languidly patrician aura. '"Here a leisured peace prevails",' he tells Pongo Twistleton; '"and you get only the best people – cultured men accustomed to mingling with basset hounds and women in tailored suits who look like horses"' (P. G. Wodehouse, *Uncle Fred in the Springtime* [1939], in Wodehouse, *Uncle Fred: an Omnibus*, Harmondsworth, Penguin, 1992, p. 74.

48   A dispute over time divides customers in a barber's shop off the Edgeware Road. '"Wait", commanded the fat man, heaving himself up and accomplishing vasty manoeuvres under his shrouding cape. '"This is the right time. This is the real time. Railway time, that's wot this is:"' Margery Allingham, *Hide My Eyes* [1958], Harmondsworth, Penguin, 1960, 51. Like other forms of modernising discipline, rigid timekeeping could generate resentment. A Piedmontese countryman explains why few people take the local diesel *automotrice* today. '"I can still remember my mother running to catch a train to town – this was before the war,"' he tells Aurelio Zen. '"She was a minute or two late, but people like us didn't have clocks. The guard saw her coming, waving and calling out, but he held his flag out just the same and the train took off, leaving her standing there. Her grandfather died that night, before she'd had a chance to see him for the last time. People round here have long memories, and they don't have much use for the train:"' Michael Dibdin, *A Long Finish*, London, Faber, 1998, p. 76. E. P. Thompson's classic essay on 'Time, work discipline and industrial capitalism' (*Past and Present*, 1967, 38, pp. 56–97) cemented studies of time in British industrial history; for one attempt to edge round this commanding edifice see Paul Glennie and Nigel Thrift, 'Reworking E. P. Thompson's "Time, work-discipline and industrial capitalism",' *Time and Society*, 5, 1996, pp. 275–99. See also Eviatur Zerubavel, 'The standardisation of time: a sociohistorical perspective', *American Journal of Sociology*, 1982, 88, pp. 1–23. Even Michel Foucault gets in on this act. In *Discipline and Punish*, translated by Alan Sheridan, New York, Pantheon, 1977, p. 149 he takes time standardisation to be a precondition for regulating rhythms of industrial production, in a thoroughly Thompsonian manner. Grouching about looming denationalisation, Iain

Sinclair (*Downriver*, London, Pimlico, 1991, p. 171) suggested that different local times might recrudesce as each of John Major's Mickey Mouse railway companies danced to its own time-clock.

49 Gordon Biddle, *The Railway Surveyors: the Story of Railway Property Management, 1800–1990*, London, Ian Allan and the British Railways Property Board, 1990, pp. 58–72; M. C. Reed, 'Accounting', R. B. Schofield, 'Civil engineering', and Rodney Weaver, 'Mechanical engineering', in Simmons and Biddle (eds), *Oxford Companion*, pp. 5–6, 83, 317–8; Simmons, *Victorian Railway*, pp. 102–19.

50 'Companies such as the London and North Western and, later, the North Eastern led the way in developing line and staff procedures, a delegation of authority to salaried managers, and a more comprehensive understanding of the complexities of accounting and costing in the modern business sense': T. R. Gourvish, *Railways and the British Economy, 1830–1914*, London, Macmillan, 1980, p. 10.

51 Quoted in Matsuda, *Memory of the Modern*, p. 49.

52 Simmons, *Railway in England and Wales*, pp. 74, 241; Richard Bartlett, 'Of trains and torts: a study of the interaction between technology and tort law during the late 19th and early 20th centuries', *Technology in Society* 3, 1981, pp. 337–47; S. A. Broadbridge, *Studies in Railway Expansion and the Capital Market in England, 1825–1875*, London, Cass, 1970; Henry Grote Lewin, *The Railway Mania and its Aftermath*, London, Railway Gazette, 1936; Perkin, *Age of the Railway*, pp. 176–80, 195–6. The 1844 Joint Stock Companies Act began this process: M. C. Reed, *Investment in Railways in Britain, 1820–1844: a Study in the Development of the Capital Market*, Oxford, Oxford University Press, 1975, p. 89; R. W. Kostal, *Law and English Railway Capitalism, 1825–1875*, revised edition, Oxford, Clarendon Press, 1997, pp. 25–9. A healthy tranche of fictions examine the local social and economic effects resulting from nineteenth-century railway construction: Gillian Avery, *The Lost Railway*, London, Collins, 1980 (Radnorshire); Walter Barker, *The Llangoch Chronicles*, London, Avon, 1993 (Wales); Brian Clarke, *The Slate Railway to Churchwater*, Llanfair Caereinion, Buddle, 1981 (Herefordshire); Alexander Cordell, *Tunnel Tigers*, London, Weidenfeld & Nicolson, 1986 (south Wales); John Downie, *The Celestial Railway*, Bristol, Sustrans, 1995 (County Durham); C. Hamilton Ellis, *Dandy Hart*, London, Gollancz, 1947 (Sussex); J. Farrimond, *The Unending Track*, London, Harrap, 1970 (Lancashire); Emmeline Garnett, *Hills of Sheep*, London, Hodder & Stoughton, 1955 (Westmoreland); Mary Ann Gibbs, *The Tulip Tree*, London, Hurst & Blackett, 1979 (East Anglia); James Kenward, *The Manewood Line*, London, Paul, 1937 (Hampshire); Charles Lowrie, *Level Crossing*, London, Ward Lock, 1950 (Lincolnshire); Malcolm Macdonald, *World From Rough Stones*, London, Hodder & Stoughton, 1974 (west Lancashire); Elizabeth McNeill, *A Bridge in Time*, London, Orion, 1994 (Scottish Borders); Michael Pollard, *Silver's Way*, Norwich, Rampant Horse, 1994 (southern England); L. T. C. Rolt, *Winterstoke*, London, Constable, 1954 (English midlands); Jean Stubbs, *The Vivian Inheritance*, London, Macmillan, 1982 (Lancashire); G. Sutton, *Fleming of Honister*, London, Hodder & Stoughton, 1953 (Westmoreland).

53 Until the First World War, the London and North Western Railway was the world's largest joint stock company. For accounts of Huish, Moon and Webb, the extremely tough eggs who established this company's intransigently modern management style, see Ellis, *British Railway History*, vol. 2, pp. 18–20; T. R. Gourvish, 'Captain Mark Huish: a pioneer in railway management', *Business History*, 12, 1970, pp. 46–58; Gourvish, *Mark Huish and the London and North Western Railway: a Study of Management*, Leicester, Leicester University Press, 1972; B. Reed, *Crewe Locomotive Works and its Men*, Newton Abbot, David & Charles, 1982, pp. 46–51, 83–127; M. C. Reed, *The London and North Western Railway*, Penryn, Atlantic, 1996.

54 P. W. Kingsford, *Victorian Railwaymen*, London, Cass, 1970, pp. 13–34; Frank McKenna, *The Railway Workers*, London, Faber, 1980; R. S. Joby, *The Railwaymen*, Newton Abbot, David & Charles, 1984, pp. 9–18; David Howell, 'Railway safety and labour unrest: the Aisgill railway disaster of 1913', in Wrigley and Shepherd (eds), *On the Move*, pp. 123–54.

55 *Punch* suggested that Parliament should require a railway company director to ride on the buffer beam of each passenger train's engine. Then, Mr Punch felt sure, accidents would cease (Charles L. Graves, *Mr Punch's History of Modern England*, vol 1: 1841–1857, London, Cassell, 1921, p. 63). In a letter to the *Morning Chronicle* Sydney Smith proposed a different solution. Burn but one bishop in a railway accident, he urged, and Parliament would legislate for safety. Even Sodor and Man would be an adequate human sacrifice. See Stuart Legg (ed.), *The Railway Book*, London, Hart-Davis, 1952, pp. 95–8.

56 Edward Cleveland-Stevens, *English Railways: their Development and their Relation to the State*, London, Routledge, 1915; Eric Hobsbawm, *Industry and Empire*, London, Weidenfeld & Nicolson, 1968, p. 128. For Friedland and Boden ('NowHere', pp. 9–10) modernity always looks to the future, not the present.

57 R. A. Buchanan, *The Power of the Machine: the Impact of Technology from 1700 to the Present*, London, Penguin, 1994.

58 Scott McQuire, *Visions of Modernity: Representation, Memory, Time and Space in the Age of the Camera*, London, Sage, 1998, pp. 183–5. Mach numbers, those *echt*-modern velocity measures, were born as a Prague professor mused on his railway carriage's transit round a steeply banked curve. See Everdell, *First Moderns*, p. 16. Margaret Bonham's short story sets transport acceleration against Old Adam's moral atavism. A boy fascinated with guns watches an express train crash horribly on a coastal track between two tunnels. (Shakespeare Cliff, perhaps?) He makes desultory efforts to help injured passengers, then drifts into a daydream. 'He began to remember the exquisite pleasure and ecstacy of the moment when the train, before it reached the tunnel, had smashed and disintegrated into ruin': Bonham, 'The train and the gun', in Bonham, *The Casino, and Other Stories*, London, Phoenix, 1942, pp. 42–8. This half-sexualised structure of feeling recalls the mannered sadism of Edward Upward's 'The railway accident' [1928], in Christopher Isherwood and Edward Upward, *The Mortmere Stories*, London, Enitharmon Press, 1994, pp. 125–59, that weird blend of Vorticism, surrealism and Communist Party chiliasm.

59 Having rubbished Francis Fukuyama's triumphalist arguments about a post-Cold War 'end of history', Zygmunt Bauman then declares acceleration finished now we float in cyberspace: Bauman, *Globalization*, pp. 12, 15. That's roughly what pioneer modern railway passengers thought as they rushed from Liverpool to Manchester in 1830 – at twenty miles an hour. Those with a taste for whimsy will appreciate Paul Jennings' bemused discovery of a British Railways timetable which appeared to show that all trains between Corwen and Barmouth Junction left Bala fifteen minutes before they arrived. See Jennings, 'Bala likely', in Jennings, *Iddly Oddly*, London, Parrish, 1959, pp. 96–7. Take that, Einstein!

60 Patrick Bair, *Faster! Faster!*, London, Eyre & Spottiswoode, 1950.

61 Eric Hobsbawm, 'Victorian values', in Hobsbawm, *Uncommon People: Resistance, Rebellion and Jazz*, London, Weidenfeld & Nicolson, 1998, p. 86. Diane K. Drummond, *Crewe: Railway Town, Company and People, 1840–1914*, Aldershot, Scolar, 1995 offers a nuanced account of how far this managerial onslaught succeeded in different workshops in the London and North Western Railway's huge plant. If most workers in a shop were time-served men, and if few trades were represented in that shop, then craft control in the labour process was likely to survive. More generally, struggle in the labour process was mediated and inflected by a multitude of variable factors, from company policy (not always monolithic, nor immune to change) to the trade cycle's state and broad labour market conditions. Mouthpiece for directors and officers with a penchant for paternal oppression, in January 1916 *The Great Western Railway Magazine* published a scathing review of *Life in a Railway Factory* [1915] (Gloucester, Alan Sutton, 1986), Alfred Williams' largely uncritical account of life and labour in Swindon Works. While accounts of life and labour under F. W. Webb's autocratic rule at Crewe make dismal reading for a democrat, conditions were much less oppressive for late-nineteenth-century shopmen in the Atchison, Topeka and Santa Fe Railroad's workshops. This railroad company's directors and officers did not set out to be lenient employers; they had little choice. With labour scarce and expensive (the reverse of British conditions), high transiency rates required the Santa Fe to handle its workforce lightly and deftly. See James H. Ducker, *Men of the Steel Rails: Workers on the Atchison, Topeka and Santa Fe Railroad, 1869–1900*, Lincoln, University of Nebraska Press, 1983. Detailed study of industrial relations in New Zealand Railways' Hillside works in Dunedin reveals patterns lying midway between these cases, as American-style labour market conditions collided with workshop cultures transferred very directly from Britain: see Erik Olssen and Jeremy Brecher, 'The power of shop culture: the labour process in the New Zealand Railway Workshops, 1890–1930', *International Review of Social History*, 37, 1992, pp. 350–75; Olssen, *Building the New World: Work, Politics and Society in Caversham, 1880s–1920s*, Auckland, Auckland University Press, 1995, pp. 123–54.

62 The quotation comes from McKenna, *Railway Workers*, p. 52. For detailed studies of this company town see W. H. Chaloner, *The Social and Economic History of Crewe*, Manchester, Manchester University Press, 1950; Drummond, *Crewe*; Reed, *Crewe Locomotive Works*; Rodney Weaver, 'Francis William Webb', *The Railway*

Magazine, 47, 1986, pp. 538–43, 606–11. Czar of the world's largest company-owned railway works, the LNWR's chief mechanical engineer, F. W. Webb, entertained no democratic nonsense. Hand-picked Conservative shop foremen coerced predominantly Liberal and Nonconformist craftsmen and labourers. Political intimidation was taken for granted. When Webb's brother was appointed to a local Anglican church in the railway company's gift, foremen ensured that workers' attendance at services improved dramatically.

63 Frank R. Dobbin, 'Vive la différence! Public policy and the development of high speed trains in France and the U. S. A.', in Whitlegg, Hultén and Flink (eds), *High Speed Trains*, pp. 124–44.

64 Lucius Beebe, *20th Century: the Greatest Train in the World*, Berkeley, CA, Howell-North, 1962, pp. 9–11. Beebe is forced into circumlocutions about Pullman porters because these men had black skins.

65 Democratic simplicity never excluded north American discrimination on grounds other than class, of course. Martin Chuzzlewit suffered an agonisingly slow and bumpy journey in eastern parts of the Great Republic. His locomotive headed 'three great caravans or cars … The ladies' car, the gentlemen's car, and the car for negroes, painted black' (Charles Dickens, *Martin Chuzzlewit* [1844], London, Everyman, 1994, p. 342). A gently sardonic poem traces the treatment which Chinese travellers suffered on early Canadian trains. At first they were obliged to ride in designated carriages at the train's rear. Then folk in head-end carriages were killed in a derailment, so Chinese carriages were marshalled directly behind the locomotive's tender. Then a collision saw white folk killed in rear-end carriages. Railway officials threw in the towel: 'after much debate / common sense prevailed / the Chinese are now allowed / to sit anywhere / on any train' (Jim Wong-Chu, 'Equal opportunity' [c1980], in Michael Rosen and David Widgery (eds), *The Vintage Book of Dissent*, London, Vintage, 1996, pp. 302–3).

66 C. Hamilton Ellis, *The Beauty of Old Trains*, London, Allen & Unwin, 1952, p. 105.

67 William Haggard, *The Arena* [1961], Harmondsworth, Penguin, 1963, p. 80.

68 Gladstone's 1844 Cheap Trains Act (7 & 8 Vict., cap. 86) contained a permissive nationalisation clause. It never was activated.

69 This had long-term consequences. Dobbin ('Vive la différence!') argues that to understand why France was able to develop its spectacularly successful TGV programme in recent decades, firmly grasping opportunities which always have been fumbled in the USA, one must explore state/capital relations undergirding the two nation states' nineteenth-century railway development. For a derisive account of leading Parisian intellectuals' overweening confidence that railways would remake French social life, see Camille Flammarion, *The Unknown*, New York, Harper, 1902, pp. 7–8.

70 Jack Simmons, 'Nationalisation: the concept of', in Simmons and Biddle (eds), *Oxford Companion*, p. 339. Robert Lynd's pleasantly insipid short story offers oblique support: '"Muncipalisation means jobbery",' his young spark in a bowler hat insists. '"Look at the County Council tramways"' (Lynd, 'In the train', in Lynd, *The Pleasures of Ignorance*, London, Richards, 1921, pp. 147–8).

71 The best summary will be found in Briggs, *Power of Steam*, pp. 104–47.

72 E. Foxwell and T. C. Farrer, *Express Trains*, London, Smith, Elder, 1889, p. 71. Original emphasis. Penny a mile 'Parliamentary trains' were forced on reluctant railway companies by Gladstone's 1844 Cheap Trains Act. In arguing that railways extinguished feudalism, Foxwell and Farrer echoed Thomas Arnold's paean to a London and Birmingham train passing Rugby School: 'I rejoice to see it, and to think that feudality is gone for ever; it is a great blessing to think that any one evil is really extinct' (quoted in Legg, *Railway Book*, p. 55).

73 Kingsford, *Victorian Railwaymen*, pp. 13–34; McKenna, *Railway Workers*, pp. 21–40; Philip S. Bagwell, *The Railwaymen*, London, Allen & Unwin, 1963, pp. 19–23.

74 As Frank McKenna noted (*Railway Workers*, pp. 37–9), striking work was not the only shot tucked away in railway workers' lockers. Dangers inherent in the steam railway's machine ensemble, and state authorities' concern to assure passengers' safety, meant that railwaymen's work routines were minutely specified in 'the almighty *Rule Book*'. Fair enough; except that railways worked through tacit agreement between workers and managers to lay less stress on some of this tome's more arduous prescriptions. This was not mere sloppiness. If the Rule Book's provisions were applied strictly, then the railway ground to a halt. For employees, 'working to rule' was a powerful sanction – and one which employers found it hard to denounce.

75 Patrick Renshaw, *The General Strike*, London, Eyre Methuen, 1975, pp. 215–25. Thomas buckled, not those he led and was supposed to represent: fewer than 2 per cent of footplate staff reported for work on 12 May 1926, one day before the strike was called off. See Julian Symons, *The General Strike*, London, Cresset, 1957, p. 209.

76 Remember Chou En-lai's dictum that we cannot yet judge the 1789 French Revolution's consequences.

77 Daniel R. Headrick, *The Tools of Empire: Technology and European Imperialism in the Nineteenth Century*, New York, Oxford University Press, 1981, p. 187. For more on railways and imperialism see Nicholas Faith, *The World the Railways Made*, London, Bodley Head, 1990, pp. 144–82; Faith, *Locomotion: the Railway Revolution*, London, BBC, 1993, pp. 96–115; and Clarence B. Davis (ed.), *Railway Imperialism*, Westport, Conn., Greenwood, 1991.

78 H. H. Johnston, quoted in Michael Adas, *Machines as the Measure of Man: Science, Technology, and Ideologies of Western Dominance*, Ithaca, Cornell University Press, 1989, p. 229.

79 Karl Marx, 'The future results of British rule in India' [1853], in Robert C. Tucker (ed.), *The Marx-Engels Reader*, second edition, New York, Norton, 1978, p. 662. As with some other predictions from this pen, history has played theory false. For some reasons why Marx's sanguine expectations failed – Indian railways' continued reliance on British and American equipment, and the careful reservation of skilled, supervisory and administrative positions to British men – see Daniel R. Headrick, *The Tentacles of Progress: Technology Transfer in the Age of Imperialism, 1850–1940*,

New York, Oxford University Press, 1988, pp. 84–5, 321–4; John M. Hurd, 'Railways', in Dharma Kumar (ed.), *The Cambridge Economic History of India. Volume 2: c1757–c1970*, Cambridge, Cambridge University Press, 1983, pp. 748–51; Ian J. Kerr, *Building the Railways of the Raj, 1850–1900*, Delhi, Oxford University Press, 1997.

80 For detailed accounts of particular projects, from broad-gauge main lines to wispy aerial ropeways, see Fred A. Talbot, *Cassell's Railways of the World*, three volumes, London, Waverley, 1924 and Clarence Winchester (ed.), *Railway Wonders of the World*, two volumes, Amalgamated Press, 1935. Given their publication dates we might excuse a triumphalist tone here; but it strikes oddly in Anthony Burton's *The Railway Builders*, London, Murray, 1994, p. 1: (This is a story of great adventures, of men in solar topees hacking their way through the jungles of uncharted lands. ... Somehow it seems to sum up much of what one thinks of as the great railway empire: the old giving way to the new, the splendours of British manufacture looking down, literally and metaphorically, on the crudities of an older world.)

81 G. O. Trevelyan, *The Competition Wallah* [1864], quoted in Adas, *Machines as the Measure*, p. 228.

82 Headrick, *Tentacles of Progress*, p. 12.

83 Quoted in Daniel Thorner, *Investment in Empire: British Railway and Steam Shipping Enterprise in India, 1825–1849*, New York, Arno, 1977, p. 96.

84 Ian Jack, 'Serendip', *Granta 61*, 1998, pp. 52–6.

85 Most notably in Beethoven's music: the ninth symphony's finale and *Fidelio*'s final chorus in big, public works; late piano sonatas and string quartets in more intimate forms.

86 Zygmunt Bauman, *Postmodernity and its Discontents*, Cambridge, Polity, 1997, p. 71.

87 W. A. Armstrong, 'The countryside', in F. M. L. Thompson (ed.), *The Cambridge Social History of Britain, 1750–1950: vol. 1, Regions and Communities*, Cambridge, Cambridge University Press, 1990, p. 115.

88 For the most famous cases see J. Mulvihill, 'Consuming nature: Wordsworth and the Kendal and Windermere Railway controversy', *Modern Languages Quarterly*, 56, 1995, pp. 305–26; Jeffrey Richards, 'The role of the railways', in Michael Wheeler (ed.), *Ruskin and Environment: the Storm-Cloud of the Nineteenth Century*, Manchester, Manchester University Press, 1995, pp. 123–43.

89 Schivelbusch, *Railway Journey*, p. 73. Or, as a recent novel set in 1855 tells us, 'Of all the proofs of progress, the most visible and striking were the railways. In less than a quarter of a century, they had altered every aspect of English life and commerce.' Michael Crichton, 'Introduction', to Crichton, *The Great Train Robbery*, London, Cape, 1975, p. 9. For a snapshot of less enchanted British public attitudes in the later 1870s, with railway travel taken for granted by another generation of British people, see Ellis, *British Railway History*, vol. 2, pp. 13–22.

90 For railways and modern war see Faith, *World the Railways Made*, pp. 312–32; E. Pratt, *The Rise of Rail Power in War and Conquest, 1833–1914*, London, King, 1915; M. Van Creveld, *Technology and War: from 2000 B. C. To the Present*, New York, Free Press, 1989; J. A. Van Fleet, *Rail Transport and the Winning of Wars*,

Washington DC, US Government, 1956. For technology on the Western Front see W. J. K. Davies, *Light Railways of the First World War*, Newton Abbott, David & Charles, 1967.

91 Voltaire offers an example. Fiercely anticlerical for his own part – and for those of his friends, able to stand, free but lonely, aloof from priestly superstition – he still recognised a need for some 'rational religion' to sustain servants and women, those weaker vessels.

92 Gregor von Rezzori, *The Orient-Express*, London, Vintage, 1994, pp. 154–5.

93 Jennings, *Jenguin Pennings*, p. 37. Charles Keene (1823–1891) and Rowland Emett (1906–1989) were celebrated *Punch* cartoonists; for Emett's railway life world see below, pp. 278–83.

94 For manifestations in particular non-European locations, see Davis (ed.), *Railway Imperialism*.

95 Ford Madox Ford, *Some Do Not...* [1924], London, Sphere, 1969, p. 11.

96 B. R. Mitchell, *British Historical Statistics*, Cambridge, Cambridge University Press, 1988, pp. 541–50; T. R. Smith, 'Coal traffic', in Simmons and Biddle (eds), *Oxford Companion*, pp. 92–4.

97 Lynd, 'In the train', p. 141.

98 Graham Greene, *Travels with my Aunt* [1969], London, Vintage, 1999, p. 114.

99 Theroux, *Riding the Red Rooster*, p. 93.

100 George Sims, *The Last Best Friend* [1967], Harmondsworth, Penguin, 1971, p. 47.

101 Notably in postwar American structural-functionalism. For the clearest exposition by the most significant figure see Talcott Parsons, *Societies: Evolutionary and Comparative Perspectives*, Englewood Cliffs, NJ, Prentice-Hall, 1966.

102 Norbert Elias, *The Civilizing Process: the History of Manners* [1939], translated by Edmund Jephcott, Oxford, Blackwell, 1978.

103 Even here, we must not fall into technological determinism: social technology mattered. As so many writers have insisted, from Erving Goffman in *Asylums: Essays on the Social Situation of Mental Patients and Other Inmates* ([1959], Harmondsworth, Penguin, 1961) to Primo Levi's ghost-haunted testimonies to the death camps' enduring legacy (notably *If This is a Man*, London, Orion, 1960; *The Periodic Table*, translated by Raymond Rosenthal, New York, Schoken, 1984; and *The Drowned and the Saved*, translated by Paul Bailey, London, Joseph, 1988), camp social organisation and control were no less significant for the final solution's fleeting triumph than Xyklon B or crematorium ovens.

104 Donald M. Miller, *City of the Century: the Epic of Chicago and the Making of America*, New York, Simon and Schuster, 1996, pp. 200–4. Note this sub-chapter's title: 'Empires of order and blood'.

105 F. Muller, *Auschwitz Inferno: the Testimony of a Sonderkommando*, London, Routledge & Kegan Paul, 1979, p. 143.

106 See Martin Gilbert's diary of his railway-based field trip with a group of students enrolled for a Holocaust Studies course, where every station and stopping-place resonates with echoes from monstrous events fifty years dead: Gilbert, *Holocaust Journey: Travelling in Search of the Past*, London, Phoenix, 1997.

107 Parallel maps could be drawn for other death camps, of course. Appalled by
    Nazism's crimes, we should not ignore the Gulag's horrors; nor that railways played
    an essential part in this system's vile machine ensemble, too. As Alexander
    Solzhenitsyn showed in *The Gulag Archipelago* (translated by T. P. Whitney,
    London, Collins, 1973), prison labour played an essential role in extending the
    USSR's railway network under Stalin. (For a broad account see Bryn Thomas,
    Trans-Siberian Handbook, Brentford, Lascelles, 1988, p. 98; for the most famous
    single case, blending heavy death rates with an outcome fatuous even for Stalin's
    imperial designs, see Athol Yates, *Siberian BAM Railway Guide: the Second Trans-
    Siberian Railway*, Hindhead, Trailblazer, 1995, pp. 20–3.) In the mid-1930s the
    diplomat Fitzroy Maclean was attached to the British Embassy in Moscow.
    Returning to that city from summer leave travel (and a little light spying) in central
    Asia, 'we passed a long prison train, eastward bound. It was composed of reinforced
    trucks. At the end of each truck was a guard of N.K.V.D. troops with fixed bayo-
    nets. Through cracks in the sides one could see the prisoners' faces, peering out. It
    served as a reminder that travel in regions from which I was returning is not always
    undertaken at the traveller's own wish': (Maclean, *Eastern Approaches*, London,
    Cape, 1949, p. 79). As with Nazi camp sites, physical remains from some Stalin-era
    camps have been commodified as gruesome tourist sights. Western rail travellers
    now find themselves advised that 'The highlight of a visit to North Baikal is the
    Akikan gulag': Yates, *Siberian BAM Guide*, p. 166.
108 Muller, *Auschwitz Inferno*, pp. 133, 135, 143.
109 A recent jeremiad traces four current world-scale horrors: environmental destruc-
    tion, growing poverty, weapons of mass destruction, and repressed democratic
    rights (Anthony Giddens, 'The social revolutions of our time', in Giddens, *Beyond
    Left and Right: the Future of Radical Politics*, Cambridge, 1994, pp. 97–100). All
    four, we are told, represent 'manufactured uncertainties' flowing directly from the
    Enlightenment project. It is difficult to take this last claim seriously: the last
    horseman in Giddens' apocalypse can show no descent from Enlightenment writers
    celebrating liberty. In this *mélange* of journalism masquerading as Grand Theory,
    only weapons of mass destruction display the lineage which Giddens' argument
    requires.
110 Quoted in Ludovic Kennedy (ed.) *A Book of Railway Journeys*, London, Collins,
    1980, p. 4.
111 Even at the century's turn Jan Morris (*Fifty Years of Europe: an Album*, London,
    Penguin, 1998, p. 250) confesses that she cannot see those double tracked main
    lines crossing the postwar German-Polish border without imagining the dreadful
    freights which travelled their metals fifty years earlier, bound for the death camps.
112 H. G. Wells, 'A story of the days to come', in Wells, *The Complete Short Stories of
    H.G. Wells*, London, Benn, 1927, p. 752.
113 Richard D. Altick, *The Presence of the Past: Topics of the Day in the Victorian Novel*,
    Columbus, Ohio, Ohio State University Press, 1991, pp. 783, 192. Altick's final
    simile leads him astray. Early American railroads ran on flat-bottomed rails spiked
    directly to cross-ties. With some eccentric exceptions (notably Brunel's broad-gauge

Great Western, with its bridge rail derived from Charles Vignoles' original pattern), Victorian British trains ran on bullhead rails carried in iron chairs. These chairs, not the rail, were spiked or bolted to cross sleepers.

114 Bryan Morgan, *Express Journey, 1864–1964: a Centenary History of the Express Dairy Company*, London, Express Dairy Company, 1964.

115 Simmons, *Railway in Town and Country*, pp. 245–8. 'Tis well from far to hear the railway scream / And watch the curling lingering clouds of steam', an 1882 meeting learned; 'but let not Bournemouth – health's approved abode / Court the near presence of the iron road': quoted in Charles H. Mate and Charles Riddle, *Bournemouth, 1810–1910*, Bournemouth, Mate, 1910, p. 135.

116 Benjamin Disraeli, *Endymion* [1880], London, Bodley Head, 1927, 12:45.

117 Jerome Blum, *In the Beginning: the Advent of the Modern Age: Europe in the 1840s*, New York, Scribners, 1994, pp. 3–4.

118 Quoted in Simmonds (ed.), *Railways: an Anthology*, pp. 231–2.

119 Wells, *Anticipations*, p. 12.

120 Wells, *Anticipations*, pp. 1–32. We should not write off Wells' travelators too quickly. Remembering Bulwer Lytton's scientific romance *The Coming Race*, J. B. Priestley insisted that 'nothing in that story was as fantastic as this journey from Hampstead to Oxford Circus by tube railway and escalator': Priestley, 'Man underground', in Priestley, *Self-Selected Essays*, London, Heinemann, 1932, p. 77. Wells ridiculed the notion of human flight in *Anticipations*, but not elsewhere. In 'The argonauts of the air' [1897] (in Wells, *Complete Short Stories*, pp. 346–58) the first man-carrying aircraft soars away from a five-mile elevated railway constructed alongside the London and South Western Railway's line between Wimbledon and Worcester Park.

121 Fanny Kemble, *Record of a Girlhood*, London, Beccles, 1878. For fuller versions of this famous account see, among many other places, Legg (ed.), *Railway Book*, pp. 18–21.

122 Anon. (attrib. W. S. Hayward), 'The mysterious countess', in Anon., *Revelations of a Lady Detective*, [c1864], reprinted in Laura Marcus (ed.), *Twelve Women Detective Stories*, Oxford, Oxford University Press, 1997, p. 22. In her introduction (*Twelve Women Detectives*, p. viii) Laura Marcus notes that here 'one of the technologies of modernity, the railway, speeds Mrs Paschal [the detective] to the archaic Gothic gloom of a Yorkshire abbey. The anachronism is surely deliberate: the railway, intimately bound up with the new form of the detective novel, will cut through the conventions of the most popular fiction of the late eighteenth and early nineteenth centuries, the Gothic novel'. Basil Copper's pastiche (*Necropolis: a Novel of Gothic Mystery*, Sauk City, Wisconsin, Arkham House, 1980) tries to heal that cut, as gothic horror blends with The London Necropolis and National Mausoleum Company's railway facilities in a white-painted Ghost Train. For less lurid details about this railway's liveries see J. M. Clarke, *The Brookwood Necropolis Railway*, Headington, Oakwood Press, 1983. For more on Gothic see Richard Davenport-Hines, *Gothic: Four Hundred Years of Excess, Horror, Evil and Ruins*, London, Fourth Estate, 1998.

123 See note 88 above.

124 Vitali Vitaliev, 'Foreword', to Michael Cordell, *Red Express: the Greatest Rail Journey from the Berlin Wall to the Great Wall of China*, Brookvale, Simon & Schuster Australia, 1990, p. 5. Surprisingly, the railway journey as a metaphor for spiritual salvation was no British invention, but introduced by American missionaries: Martha Vicinus, *The Industrial Muse: a Study of Nineteenth Century British Working-Class Literature*, London, Croom Helm, 1974, p. 39.

125 E. F. Benson, 'The Superannuation Department, AD 1945', in Benson, *Desirable Residences and Other Stories*, Oxford, Oxford University Press, 1992, p. 205. Jaan Kross' distinguished novel *Professor Martens' Departure* [1984], translated by Anselm Hollo, London, Harvill, 1994 turns this cliché into serious art. Undertaking the railway journey which he will not survive, Martens ponders his life's tensions. An Estonian covert social democrat, he has given a lifetime's diplomatic service to a Czarist state which denied both his ethnic identity and his politics. Like so much postwar eastern European historical fiction this novel is double-coded, speaking both to the present and the past.

126 McQuire, *Visions of Modernity*, p. 124.

127 Altick, *Presence of the Past*, p. 136.

128 Tindall, *Countries of the Mind*, p. 23. The London and South Western Railway reached Dorchester in 1847. For his description of railway-bereft Casterbridge see Thomas Hardy, *The Mayor of Casterbridge* [1886], London, Macmillan, 1958, pp. 31–4; for a penetrating analysis of the difference between Henchard's and Farfrae's social worlds see E. P. Thompson, 'Anthropology and the discipline of historical context', *Midland History*, 1/3, 1972, pp. 41–55.

129 Bernard Miles, 'Over the gate' [1941]. EMI CDP 7 99257 4.

130 Jerry Palmer, *Potboilers: Methods, Concepts and Case Studies in Popular Fiction*, London, Routledge, 1991, p. 1.

131 Harriett Hawkins, *Classics and Trash: Traditions and Taboos in High Literature and Popular Modern Genres*, New York, Harvester Wheatsheaf, 1990, p. xiv.

132 Gore Vidal, 'Dawn Powell: the American writer', *New York Review of Books*, 17 November 1987, p. 52.

133 Harriet Hawkins (*Classics and Trash*, p. 12) adds Chaucer, Shakespeare, Marlowe and Poe to the list of now literary authors whose words many 'ordinary' people once paid good money to read or hear.

134 Writing for a popular market rather than a coterie; writing comedy; untroubled by itches to formal novelty; refusing to retreat from plot; concerned that his readers should understand and appreciate what he wrote: Laura Mooneyham ('Comedy among the modernists: P. G. Wodehouse and the anachronism of comic form', *Twentieth Century Literature*, 40, 1994, pp. 114–38) shows precisely why Wodehouse cannot be taken seriously in today's academy. But whose loss is that?

135 'Such is the current general snobbery that scholars and critics ashamed to own ignorance of the jottings of Wyndham Lewis or William Burroughs are satisfied never to have heard of it, for it seems not be be a fiction': Paul Fussell, *Abroad: British Literary Travelling Between the Wars*, New York, Oxford University Press, 1980, p. 95.

136 Peart, 'Literature and the railway', p. 98.

137 Umberto Eco, *Reflections on 'The Name of the Rose'*, translated by William Weaver, London, Secker & Warburg, 1985, p. 25.

138 For generals in the blue bunker, see Allan Bloom, *The Closing of the American Mind: How Higher Education Has Failed Democracy and Impoverished the Souls of Today's Students*, New York, Simon & Schuster, 1987; and Harold Bloom, *The Western Canon: the Books and the Schools of Ages*, New York, Harcourt Brace, 1995. For generals in the red bunker see Leslie Fiedler and Houston A. Baker (eds), *English Literature: Opening Up the Canon*, Baltimore, Johns Hopkins University Press, 1981; and Paul Lauter, *Canons and Contexts*, New York, Oxford University Press, 1991. Lars Ole Sauerberg, *Versions of the Past – Visions of the Future*, New York, Macmillan, 1997 provides a useful guide to this battlefield, as culture wars become simply another engagement in long-running debates about how (or, perhaps, about whether) to assimilate migrant populations in a coherent and stable 'American' identity – with different critics' literary positions reflecting their political positions on the wider issue (p. 17). Sauerberg's insight is compelling, meshing comfortably with the culinary argument in Harvey Levenstein's splendid *Revolution at the Table: the Transformation of the American Diet*, New York, Oxford University Press, 1988.

139 Jan Gorak, *The Making of the Modern Canon: Genesis and Crisis of a Literary Idea*, London, Athlone Press, 1991, pp. 221–60 summarises these arguments cogently and concisely. It is particularly engaging to watch him (on p. 245) excavate the buried personal canon from which that arch anti-canonist Michel Foucault cast his bullets.

140 Gorak, *Making of the Modern Canon*, pp. 224–5; Jere Paul Stauber, *Culture and Critique: an Introduction to the Critical Discourse of Cultural Studies*, Boulder, Col., Westview, 1998, pp. 19–20. How valuable Williams' route has proved in avoiding the sound and fury of American debates is revealed unwittingly by Annabel Patterson's *Reading Between the Lines*, London, Routledge, 1993, proposing a middle road between zealous defenders of the traditional Western canon and their radical opponents. Urging moderate English common sense in the middle of an essentially contested debate is about as wise as inviting Haig and Ludendorff to discuss their differences like gentlemen on the slope below Passchendaele. Litterateurs aggrieved at having a sociologist probe their disciplinary politics may take heart from the garbled mess that the culture wars have made of American sociology: see Dan Clawson and Robert Zussman, 'Canon and anti-canon for a fragmented discipline', in Dan Clawson (ed.), *Required Reading: Sociology's Most Influential Books*, Amherst, University of Massechusetts Press, 1998, pp. 3–18.

Part I

In the Canon

2

Rain, steam and what?

Largely disparaged when exhibited for the first time at the Royal Academy in 1844, J. M. W. Turner's *Rain, Steam and Speed: the Great Western Railway* has matured into the exemplary visual image of early railway years in Britain. Indeed, one recent essay makes this the first significant railway painting in the history of art.[1] Intensively discussed by critics, John Gage even gave *Rain, Steam and Speed* its own monograph.[2] What else can one say about this supremely familiar painting? Only that, as Gerald Finley noted recently, existing criticism does not exhaust the image's meaning: it remains 'a particularly interesting work, though it is difficult to understand and appreciate'.[3] As a way to open up a more extended discussion of relations between railways and culture, this chapter peels a few more layers of meaning from this remarkable painting.

An experiential account blurred by the idosyncracies of his late style, Turner gives us more than straight description in *Rain, Steam and Speed*. One might cavil at some details, but Gage gives the quietus to the idea – still repeated remarkably frequently – that this is a simple record of what Turner saw when he stuck his head out of a Great Western Railway first-class carriage's window one wet day in 1843.[4] This painter meant us to draw lessons from his image. But which lessons? That is where arguments start. One camp suggests that *Rain, Steam and Speed* is about loss: a threnody for Old England crushed by steam power.[5] Here we are shown Turner's puns on speed: the hare (later painted out but now restored) which he set running before the racing locomotive; the ploughman afield, whose presence George Dunlop Leslie thought referred to an old English country dance tune, *Speed the Plough*.[6] The railway writer Hamilton Ellis, himself trained as a painter, makes *Rain, Steam and Speed* 'the vision of an old man confronting the forces of a new age'[7] – and fearing what he saw. A contrary view sees not supersession and loss, but progress: 'Very few Victorian works of art capture the present with the glowing heart of Turner's *Rain, Steam*

2.1   J. M. W. Turner, *Rain Steam and Speed: the Great Western Railway,* 1843–44

and Speed, Robin Gilmour tells us. Michael Adas concurs. Words do not convey the Victorians' exhilaration at the power of the railway as wonderfully as this picture manages, he claims. 'The locomotive racing unimpeded through a swirling storm proclaims that the Europeans have devised a machine that allows them to challenge the elements themselves.'[8] I shall suggest that both these warring camps are right, and both wrong. *Rain, Steam and Speed* is about loss, but also about progress. To be more precise, it is about the casualties of progress and the impossibility of not changing. The radical instability of Turner's image is its most enduring feature. In Raymond Williams' terms, residual tendencies collide fiercely with emergent,[9] generating unresolved tension in a fluid structure of feeling. For that reason, over a century and a half later we still find this picture enigmatic and disturbing.

By focussing on the painting's colouring – those richly brooding and threatening reds, browns and blacks – John Gage makes *Rain, Steam and Speed* a genuflection to the Baroque. The pattern for Turner's painting, he suggests, is Rembrandt van Rijn's *Landscape with a Coach* (1641).[10] But only the railway's property – train, track formation, bridge – is rendered in Rembrandt's ochrous palette. The landscape which Turner's train traverses is rendered in very different tones, with golds, creams and watery blues predominating. This looks remarkably unlike that thunderstorm which many critics think Turner was trying to paint. Tonally it resembles Claude Lorrain; and Turner's general debt to him has been recognised often enough. Andrew Wilton finds formal models for *Rain, Steam and Speed* not in Rembrandt, but in Poussin's classicism.[11]

Abstract the railway elements, and *Rain, Steam and Speed* becomes a highly conventional classical landscape. The elegant road bridge at the picture's left margin displays an almost Roman symmetry.[12] Landscape forms wend gently, river-rounded. View the painting this way, and Turner's once-obliterated hare becomes a nod to Aesop. The white-clad people on the riverbank at the image's bottom left – merely a 'crowd of waving figures' for Gage, noting (correctly) that watching trains pass was a popular adult pastime in early Victorian Britain, not yet vilified as train spotting – is for Wilton a group of 'dancing maidens'.[13] But within a classical frame these people accrete another meaning, transformed into naiads – nymphs of the flowing Thames. Turner's almost invisible ploughman becomes a reference to Virgil and Horace; and, through them, to routine pastoral conventions.

It is to these conventions that we now must direct some attention. Human action, pastoralism requires us to accept, is set in a tamed, a cultivated natural world. Nature is a garden; but this is a threatened garden. Classical writers assumed that readers would recognise 'a tension with other kinds of experience: summer with winter; pleasure with loss; harvest with labour; singing with a journey; past or future with the present'.[14] In his pioneering work on pictorial representations of north American railway subjects – work curiously ignored by Turner scholars – Leo Marx suggests that these counter-states to the garden were generalised as wild nature, signifying death. When we look at a pastoral image we are to appreciate this ordered idyll's *fragility*, with disorder ramping just beyond the picture's frame.[15] In England from the late seventeenth-century pastoral conventions were recruited to defend specific material interests through a neo-pastoral celebration of the new – but assertedly 'natural' and timeless – agrarian capitalist estate dominated by its country house.[16] Somewhat later in time, but in a cognate social formation, both the construction and operation of railways laid cherished neo-pastoral interpretations of physical and social landscape open to rampant disorder. 'When the straight new [rail] roads were laid across the fields', Christian Barman tells us, exemplifying this patrician objection, 'they slashed through the delicate tissue of a settled rural civilisation'.[17] Writing just after Turner exhibited *Rain, Steam and Speed*, for C. J. Lever 'Although the steam-engine itself is more naturalised amongst us than with any other nation of Europe, railroad traveling has unquestionably outraged more of the associations we once cherished, and were proud of, than it could possibly effect in countries of less rural and picturesque beauty than England.'[18] Tropes drawn from European fine art could be pressed into service to placate gentle allegations like these. One painterly response, in America as in Europe, was to disarm the threat through landscape conventions: to harmonise the railway with its setting, to snuggle the machine *in* the garden. As Leo Marx notes in a recent essay, this happens in *Starucca Viaduct, Pennsylvania* (1865), where Francis Cropsey

> adapts some of the stock devices of the pastoral mode in landscape painting: the placid reflecting surface of the river; the conformity of the curving railroad right of way with the matching curves of the river and the hills; the location of the machine at a great distance, its small scale making it seem, for all its prominence, toylike and wholly in accord with the sublime, panoramic landscape that surrounds it.[19]

'Probably the greatest of all American railroad paintings' for George Douglas, George Inness' *The Lackawanna Valley* (1865) contrives a similar effect: 'the railroad seems to be in harmony with its environment, as if it had verily created it, which in a sense it had' – though Nicolai Cikovsky suggests that this painting's prominent middle-grounded tree stumps disrupt straightforward pastoral readings.[20]

In analysing Cropsey's painting Leo Marx used the term 'sublime' in its general eighteenth century neoclassical sense, to signify awe, reverence or lofty emotion evoked through contemplating beauty, vastness or grandeur. Wilton makes *Rain, Steam and Speed* 'the supreme example of Turner's recreation of the Sublime', in just this sense.[21] Finley agrees that sublimity is central to this painting, but in a more limited sense. Now, Edmund Burke's definition becomes central: 'Whatever therefore is terrible, with regard to sight, is sublime'.[22] Transformed into the rampant Other threatening this rural idyll, sublimity no longer buttresses the pastoral order. Viewed thus, Turner's painting shocks us today, as his idealised Thames-side garden landscape, with its rounded shapes and pastel palate, is ruptured by the ochrous railway's single diagonal knife thrust. While other landscape features wend, the Great Western Railway's property penetrates the picture space, brutally. Turner's painting assumes and asserts a gendered distinction between female nature and male culture. Leslie reported that he was in high good humour while putting the finishing touches to *Rain, Steam and Speed* at the Royal Academy's varnishing days

George Inness, *The Lackawanna Valley*, c. 1855 **2.2**

in 1844. One reason may be his quiet pun on speed, as Leslie suggested. But the way his train penetrates the picture's space suggests a crueller joke. Eighty years earlier, in his first systematic work on aesthetics Kant had urged that sublimity was a male phenomenon, beauty a female.[23] Why has nobody thought it worth commenting on the fact that Turner's train forces its way through *Maidenhead*? Those dancing figures might be naiads. They might equally well be vestal virgins enjoying their last fling as the Great Western's express violates their temple. Even distanced by classical references, rape is not a pretty topic; but Ruskin reported that Turner painted *Rain, Steam and Speed* to show what he could do with an ugly subject.[24] His virile machine is enveloped fully by his fecund female garden, but none could call it tamed.

And yet, of course, under normal conditions a steam locomotive's vast energy was tamed. One reason why contemporaries were fascinated by early railways was their sense – dulled for us today, jaded chidren of yet more elaborate and powerful mechanical contrivances – of unprecedentedly huge kinetic forces held in check, guided, by delicate control mechanisms: a deft human hand on regulator or brake lever, a one-inch flange guiding an eight-foot driving wheel. Here, too, order was fragile. A broken rail or axle, a boiler explosion, a failure in rudimentary signalling systems, and large-scale calamity could – and did – follow. Hence travellers' characteristic response to early railway journeys; excitement at moving, for the first time in human history, faster than a galloping horse, but mixed with fear for the dreadful consequences which an accident might bring.[25] This, too, is in *Rain, Steam and Speed*. Turner exults in the machine's power, recalling his life-long interest in gadgets and novelty. Hence, John Gage urges, his decision to illustrate a Great Western train. With its seven-foot gauge and (for 1843) huge extent, this was the most ambitiously engineered, the most Protean railway line in its time. That is all true, but it raises a puzzle. For contemporaries one place on the GWR was best adapted to Turner's purposes, evoking the frisson which he sought. This was the vast and famous Box tunnel near Bath; a construction denounced as an inexorable passenger-killer, long before any trains ran, by Oxford's Dr William Buckland. For the railway's designer – I. K. Brunel, 'perhaps the greatest romantic of the early railway age, but fortunately also an engineering genius'[26] – this tunnel's western portal was a special place, where past met present and classicism collided with modernity. As his biographer notes,

> To Brunel, his great tunnel at Box must be something more than a mere hole in the ground, it must be a triumphal gateway to the Roman city. It was for this reason that he crowned Box with that huge Classic portico which towered high above Gooch's flying locomotives, *Lord of the Isles*, *Tornado* or *Typhoon*, as they shot from shadow into sunlight and swept down on their imperial way to Bath.[27]

Nobody seems to know whether Turner knew Brunel personally, but his close friend John Martin certainly did; and we may believe that he told Turner how Brunel's understanding of Box tunnel went beyond the utilitarian.[28] Here, of all places on the GWR, the romantic Turner could capitalise the romantic Brunel, setting cultural allusions bouncing around in mingled delight and terror. Here, more than anywhere else on the Great Western's line between London and Bristol, Burkeian sublimity incorporates in stone and gloom. [29]

What led Turner to spurn this golden chance? Since his important earlier series of Thames paintings, produced between 1806 and 1810, shows Turner acutely sensitive to symbolic and historical resonances evoked by particular riverine locations,[30] why did he opt here to paint a mundane bridge in mundane Maidenhead?

We have suggested one reason: a brutal pun on maidenhead. There are other answers, centring on the fact that neither bridge nor location was mundane. To appreciate the point about the bridge we must consider a railway image created twelve years before Turner picked up his brush in 1843. This is no oil painting, but a topographical print.

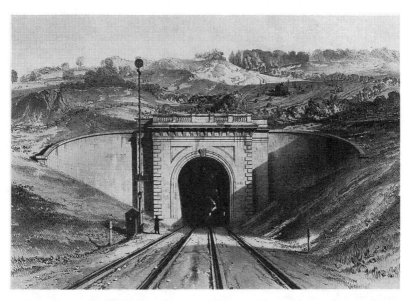

J. C. Bourne, *Box Tunnel, West Front, Great Western Railway*, 1846 **2.3**

T. T. Bury, *View of the Railway Across Chat Moss*, 1831 **2.4**

John Gage prints this image in his monograph on *Rain, Steam and Speed*, but tells the reader only that Turner's painting 'can certainly be related to some of the illustrations of T. T. Bury'.[31] There is more to it than that. Turner had a good deal to do with printmakers in his youth, and we may assume that he knew Bury's well-known lithograph.[32] Here, too, we look down from a high view-point as a train drives towards us on a long, straight track. Early printmakers emphasised railways' Euclidian nature: tangents and flat planes driven where surveyors and profit determined, regardless of local topography. This sense – the triumph of hard, engineered culture over soft undulating nature – is very clear in Bury's lithograph.

Viewpoint, train direction and division of the picture space: in all these ways Bury's and Turner's images show striking similarities. But there are deeper connections than these. As Bury's tiny locomotive trundles slowly across unculti-vated waste land it 'creates' pastoral, constructs order from natural waste. Turner's painting inflects this optimism, counterposing an engineered triumph against the destruction of a fragile rural idyll. His palate is important here: that light, blue-golden background pierced by a blackish-brown railway. R. L. Stevenson's *The Amateur Emigrant* (1895) has been plundered by railway historians for its description of vile living conditions aboard a Union Pacific emigrant train crossing the high plains west from Chicago, but none has noted his later comparison between Europe and America. Greece, Rome and Judea are gone, he tells us, and England declined. The USA is 'yet undeveloped, full of dark possibilities'. This parses George Berkeley's *On the Prospect of Planting Arts and Learning in America* (1683):

> Westward the course of empire takes its way;
> The first four acts already past,
> A fifth shall close the drama with the day;
> Time's noblest offspring is the last.

Stevenson makes his Spenglerian point through colour, comparing mornings at home and abroad.

> There is more clear gold and scarlet in our old country mornings; more purple, brown, and smoky orange in those of the new ... [In the United States] it has a duskier glory, and more nearly resembles sunset; it seems to fit some subsequential, evening epoch of the world, as though America were in fact, and not merely in fancy, further from the orient of Aurora and the springs of day.[33]

This model of historical decline, of sequential ages – gold, silver, bronze and iron – reaches back through Berkeley (and many other writers, of course) to Hesiod. Stevenson assumed that his readers would enjoy that command of classic authors necessary to recognise this reference. So does Turner. He shows us a golden age ravished by a train, the iron age's harbinger and embodiment. A cosmic judgement precipitates in tonal difference. As a recent editor notes, Hesiod's 'account of the Iron race [of men] turns into an apocalyptic prophecy of complete moral breakdown'.[34] For classically-trained early Victorians, Daniel Gooch's locomotive running freely on Isambard Brunel's railway was, indeed, the end of civilisation as they knew it. It may be to push this point too far, but Turner chose to depict a *down* train.[35]

Contemporaries read T. T. Bury's lithograph as a generalised celebration of 'the Enlightenment project', the triumph of (male) scientific reason over unreflecting (female) nature. At a more concrete level they also read a particular message as the pioneer modern railway struck, straight as an arrow, five and a half miles across Chat Moss, a twelve-square-mile bog near Manchester. This moss presented the Liverpool and Manchester Railway's engineer, George Stephenson, with his most difficult technical challenge. In evidence to Parliament, a competent civil engineer asserted that all Chat Moss would have to be drained, then a deep cutting excavated and backfilled before the railway could be constructed.[36] This procedure would have been insufferably expensive in time and money. Discounting this advice, Stephenson determined to build an embankment by tipping. Day after day, cart loads of hardcore sank into the spongy morass, and still he could find no firm road bed. At last Stephenson resorted to a corduroy, floating his embankment on a vast mass of faggotted tree branches. 'When the bank was finished', Anthony Burton tells us, 'it was estimated that 670,000 cubic yards of material had been tipped on to Chat Moss of which less than half appeared above the surface … [This] bleak, dark, seemingly featureless expanse of flat bog saw Stephenson enjoy his triumph.'[37] Bury illustrates this largely invisible 'triumph of practical ingenuity over theory'.[38] Contemplating his image, contemporaries would recognise the achievement – because their newspapers had been full of it. A generation later Samuel Smiles, Stephenson's first biographer, renewed the celebration.[39] For Smiles, George Stephenson's rise from humble Northumbrian stoker to worldwide fame (and considerable fortune) as Britain's pre-eminent railway engineer was a moral tale. Stephenson's resolute defiance of Chat Moss exemplified that complex of personal virtues – 'the capacity for strenuous application, diligence, industriousness, perseverence, patience, cheerfulness, determination, punctuality, the orderly employment of time, sedulous attention to detail, purposefulness, resoluteness, conscientiousness, courage, promptitude, decisiveness, method, honesty, thrift, self-denial, accuracy, good habits, cleanliness, chastity, integrity, orderliness, concentration … self-discipline and self-control' – which any ambitious working man must cultivate: virtues summarised in Smiles' influential *self-help* creed.[40] In 1871, more than forty years after the event to which it referred, R. M. Ballantyne's improving novel of railway life still could assume that young readers would understand (in the context of personal relationships) the problem of 'bridging over this difficulty – this Chat Moss, to speak professionally'.[41]

If I. K. Brunel's social origins were less modest than George Stephenson's, then his engineering was yet more audacious. Bury reminds his viewers of an invisible triumph as that antique train tootles across Stephenson's buried corduroy; but so does Turner as Gooch's locomotive scorches westward. Like Stephenson's buried embankment, Brunel's Maidenhead bridge is invisible from a train; merely one section of his billiard-table-flat line along the Thames valley. Some art historians note the novel length of this bridge's arches,[42] but none notices the outrageous ambition of Brunel's design. These remain the flattest brick arches ever constructed,[43] leading timorous contemporary engineers to claim that the bridge must collapse under load. When the eastern arch distorted after timber centring was removed in February 1838, these fears seemed vindicated. The contractor admitted that the failure was his – for having removed centring before the arch's cement had cured – but seeds of doubt were sown in the public mind. Faced with a rising moral panic, Great Western Railway directors ordered Brunel not to remove the replaced wooden centring. He complied, but secretly arranged for the timbers to be dropped a few inches. His bridge appeared to rest on solid centring, but its arches rested on air. Thus when his directors at last got round to asking Brunel whether Maidenhead bridge was safe for traffic after a storm blew down the centring late in 1839, he could reply that their trains had been running a regular service across it, in perfect safety, for nine months.[44] His biographer makes this an example of Brunel's 'impish humour':[45] and so it was. But, like Stephenson's victory at Chat Moss, this episode also exemplified the engineer as romantic hero, taming nature by throwing technical skill in a doubting world's teeth. This Promethean impulse is celebrated openly in Bury's lithograph. Rather more heavily cloaked, it also infuses Turner's painting.

The impulse is cloaked by its negative: a profound fear for the objective consequences of an engineered triumph. In 1847 *Punch* gave its readers a parody of the objections to railway development held by Colonel Sibthorpe, a diehard Tory member of Parliament. '"I have the greatest dislike against directors, guards, policemen, and everyone connected with railways",' Sibthorpe is made to fume. '"I think a stoker will go any lengths to attain his end; and I am of opinion that every railway engine is more or less an engine of destruction, and that nothing will stop it when once it has made up its boiler to go a certain distance."'[46] This sketch also illuminates Turner's painting. The slur on stokers takes us back to rape; but the insistence on mechanical relentlessness suggests something new. Jack Lindsay sees how, in *Rain, Steam and Speed*, 'The forward rush of the engine is expressed by making the engine darker in tone and sharper in edge than any other object, so that it shoots out in aerial perspective ahead of its place in linear perspective.' This 'mingling or superimposition of different moments' gives Turner's painting its disruptive formal character, Lindsay thinks: 'a direction in time as well as a pattern of tensional movements in space'.[47] We see another reason why this picture continues to disturb audiences. Glimpsed from the corner of one's eye in the National Gallery, Turner's train seems almost to leap from its frame, threatening to violate the viewer's personal space.

But the most pregnant phrase in *Punch*'s squib is the notion of the steam locomotive as 'an engine of destruction'. This takes us back to that printmaking world which the young Turner knew well: but to caricature rather than topographical illustration. John Gage suggests that *Rain, Steam and Speed* is a comment on the 1844–7 Railway Mania's fevered financial speculation.[48] This is perceptive.

John Leech's cartoon shows a steam locomotive named *Speculation* destroying family life in households where papa invested in fraudulent railway schemes. Not all British families would interest crooked railway financiers, of course. The Mania infected people from a wide range of social settings, but bore particularly hard on families burdened with large lumps of disposable income and wealth, from which gullible fathers could be separated. A second Leech cartoon has an alarmed Victoria pressing her distraught consort. '"Tell me, oh tell me, dearest Albert",' she pleads, '"have *you* any Railway Shares?"'[49]

This social perspective infuses Turner's *Rain, Steam and Speed*, that collision between celebration and regret. We can appreciate the point by punning the word *metropolitan*. 'In its heyday, from about 1880 to 1930', the landscape historian John Stilgoe tells us of America (and, with modified dates, his statement holds for Britain) 'the metropolitan corridor objectified the ordered life, the life of the engineered future'.[50] The railway's right of way drove a narrow, ultra- modern corridor through the most retired districts. Heading for Bristol, the Great Western Railway's main line from London crossed the Thames, England's metropolitan river, for the first time at Maidenhead. The capital city

2.5   John Leech, *The Railway Juggernaut of 1845*

lies downstream from this bridge. Upstream lies Oxford, one of England's two ancient university towns. Turner was fond of the Thames valley, and often painted there;[51] but this river's metropolitan associations added another resonance to his brutally playful use of pastoral and neo-pastoral conventions. In 1843 Oxford and Cambridge were modest county towns, far removed physically from the metropolis. But at much this time John Henry Newman argued that, culturally speaking, these towns' universities were fully metropolitan, devoted to educating those few young men who would rule the nation and its growing empire.[52] One went *up* to these places, just as one went *up* to London; and just as any train travelling towards London was moving in the *up* direction. In early-Victorian years one still went to Oxford or to Cambridge for an education rooted in the study of classical languages and classical authors. Those who controlled this university culture, and the major public schools which fed it, largely shared Sibthorpe's judgements on railway development. Neither the GWR (at Oxford) nor the Eastern Counties Railway (at Cambridge) was permitted to build a station close to the town centre. The liberal Dr Arnold might rejoice that feudalism was dead as a capitalist joint-stock company's trains thundered past Rugby School on the London and Birmingham Railway, but in 1835 the Provost and Fellows of Eton College prevented the Great Western from building any station at Slough, and required the company to employ special policemen to keep pupils from the trains' corruption over the next decade.[53] Thirty years later, furious University lobbying prevented the GWR from constructing a carriage works at Oxford.[54] By this date, and ever more threatened by rising mercantile and commercial interests, the defenders of patrician classics-based culture found themselves succoured by Dr Arnold's son. Matthew Arnold's 'Oxfordesque' *Culture and Anarchy* (1869) is a key text in liberal Victorian social criticism. No citadel could be constructed, he thought, to keep patrician culture safe from all-out assault. The only chance was to keep 'the Playful Giant' (working people) politically anaesthetised, and to educate 'Philistines' (members of the middle classes) to appreciate – and then to defend – 'the best that has been thought and said'. Failing that, all was lost. All would be lost for Oxford, but also for England: following the cultural conventions of his time, Matthew Arnold conflated the two entities.[55] At the deepest level that is what *Rain, Steam and Speed* shows us. Turner exults in the power and novelty of Daniel Gooch's engine, even as it rapes a classics-based culture and destroys a landscape crammed with classical allusions. Through this action it also destroys national political control by a landed aristocracy living off its rent roll.[56] Big issues are at stake, we see, as this train pounds westward.

The menacing black locomotive heading the train is the focal point of Turner's painting. Like so much else in this complicated work, it reveals unexpected dimensions. Some commentators treat it cursorily. For Stephen Daniels, *Rain, Steam and Speed* simply 'shows a locomotive of the Firefly class pulling a train across Brunel's Maidenhead's Bridge'.[57] He must have spent many youthful summers spotting trains to make such a confident identification from Turner's blurred projectile. Return once more to contemporary caricature, however, and different connections emerge.

In John Leech's *A Dangerous Character* the funnel's crooked crown is a sardonic reference to the Railway King, George Hudson, as a criminal locomotive is arrested by 'Policeman Sibthorpe'. The cartoon conflates early locomotives' notable potential for mechanical mayhem with contemporary gentle concerns over dangerous classes' envy for their betters' property. But steam locomotives' warm, trembling, half-animate nature also encouraged caricaturists to pun a connection between animals and machines. George Cruikshank's *The Railway Dragon* was a machine turned monstrous animal.

In *Rain, Steam and Speed* a cherished local world dies before Turner's train, headed by its monstrous black locomotive. Commentators puzzle over details in this machine. The reddish glare from firebox door and grate is comprehensible enough, but what is that big splodge of flake white on the smokebox front?[58] Stephen Daniels suggests, thoroughly unconvincingly, that this white patch represents the engine's furnace, 'which we see analytically, not realistically, *through* the front of its boiler'.[59] Once again, contemporary caricatures offer a better route forward. Cruikshank's *Railway Dragon* reverses over its

2.6   John Leech, *A Dangerous Character*, 1847

George Cruikshank, *The Railway Dragon, c.* 1845 **2.7**

prey, with steam gauges for eyes and firebox door for ravening mouth. The shape of this locomotive backhead precisely recalls Cruikshank's earlier stocking-capped and fire-belching Jacobin monster.

The front elevation of Turner's locomotive echoes these caricatures. No more than another little joke, perhaps? But accept this similarity and that white splodge becomes the key to Turner's entire painting: the modest space into which a doomed old world must place its head so that Dr Guillotin's machine – that epitome of enlighted rationality, invented to supplant the ancien régime's haphazard axework – may do its fatal work. Form follows function. This rational machine, this Jacobin machine will, indeed, mean the end of civilisation as those who viewed Turner's painting at the 1844 Royal Academy exhibition had known it. No wonder, perhaps, that *Rain, Steam and Speed* disturbed that audience, fifty years after the Terror. Turner shuddered with them at the prospect of that old world's supersession, but he also celebrated technical novelties in the new world that was symbolised by his rushing railway train. That *Rain, Steam and Speed* continues to disturb viewers a century and a half after it was painted is a tribute to Turner's ability to bring two attitudes to the onset of modernity face to face: and to hold them in tension, allowing his audience no comfortable resolution. We can forgive this old man if, at the last, his structure of feeling just tips towards regret for the past and away from celebrating novelty. The space which he opened between these attitudes would soon be explored by Charles Dickens – another man born into the coaching world, another man forced to confront new railways' relentless modernity.

2.8   George Cruikshank, *A Radical Reformer*, 1819

Notes

1 J.–O. Majastre, 'Était une fois la locomotive', *Sociologie de l'Art*, 5, 1992, p. 83.

2 John Gage, *Rain, Steam and Speed*, London, Allen Lane, 1972. Other discussions of railway art gravitate to a trinity of 'great works': William Frith's *The Railway Station* (1863), Claude Monet's *La Gare St Lazare* series (1877), and – overtopping these – *Rain, Steam and Speed*. See Stephen Daniels, 'Images of the railway in nineteenth century paintings and prints', in Anon (ed.), *Train Spotting: Images of the Railway in Art*, Nottingham, City Art Gallery, 1985, pp. 8, 17–18; C. Hamilton Ellis, *Railway Art*, Boston, New York Graphic Society, 1977, pp. 18, 80–1, 96–7; Jack Lindsay, *J. M. W. Turner: his Life and Work*, New York, New York Graphic Society, 1966, pp. 201–2; A. W. V. Mace, 'Exposure!', in H. A. Vallance (ed.), *The Railway Enthusiast's Bedside Book*, London, Batsford, 1966, p. 71; A. Noakes, *William Frith: an Extraordinary Victorian Painter*, London, Jupiter, 1978, pp. 70–5; Jeffrey Richards and John M. Mackenzie, *The Railway Station: a Social History*, Oxford, Oxford University Press, 1986, pp. 318–19, 327–8; Jack Simmons, *The Victorian Railway*, London, Thames & Hudson, 1991, pp. 127–145.

3 Gerald Finley, 'Turner and the steam revolution', *Gazette des Beaux-Arts*, 6th series, 112, 7/8, 1988, p. 24.

4 Gage, *Rain, Steam and Speed*, pp. 16–19. Critics who argue that Turner took a blurred photograph include M. Butlin and E. Joll, *The Paintings of J. M. W. Turner*, New Haven, Yale University Press, 1977, p. 232; Francis Klingender, *Art and the Industrial Revolution*, revised by Arthur Elton, London, Paladin, 1968, p. 134; and Lindsay, *Turner: Life and Work*, p. 14.

5 Finley, 'Turner and the steam revolution'.

6 Butlin and Joll, *Paintings*, p. 233; Gage, *Rain, Steam and Speed*, p. 19. Not only Turner's hare appears and disappears like the Cheshire Cat. When first exhibited, his locomotive's rushing progress was indicated by three prominent puffs of steamy smoke streaming from the funnel. Time faded these puffs to oblivion; but now they are back, good as new. Interesting questions about restorations ethics and aesthetics arise here, but they lie beyond our compass.

7 Ellis, *Railway Art*, p. 18.

8 Robin Gilmour, *The Victorian Period: the Intellectual and Cultural Context of English Literature, 1830–1890*, London, Longmans, 1993, p. 207; Michael Adas, *Machines as the Measure of Men: Science, Technology and Ideologies of Western Dominance*, Ithaca, Cornell University Press, 1989, pp. 222–3. See also Klingender, *Art and the Industrial Revolution*, pp. 90, 134. A less exalted source than these, (a whodunnit, in fact) lends support: '*Rain, Steam and Speed* ... had been painted in 1844 when railways and the power of steam seemed to offer England a future of limitless prosperity', we learn; 'there was a confidence about the picture that late twentieth-century man could only envy'. See J. R. L. Anderson, *A Sprig of Sea Lavender*, London, Gollancz, 1978, p. 43.

9 Raymond Williams, *Marxism and Literature*, Oxford, Oxford University Press, 1977, pp. 121–35.

10 Gage, *Rain, Steam and Speed*, pp. 45–64. He repeats the general reference to Rembrandt's influence in John Gage, *J. M. W. Turner: 'a Wonderful Range of Mind'*, New Haven, Yale University Press, 1987, p. 105.

11 Andrew Wilton, *The Life and Work of J. M. W. Turner*, London, Academy Editions, 1979, p. 220.

12 Though it could also be argued that this bridge breaks open the composition's picturesque, intruding the modern topographical print's anti-picturesque vocabulary at the margin of a classic landscape. This, we shall see, opens a space for more significant intrusion from topographical prints' disparaged discourse. It also signals connections between *Rain, Steam and Speed* and Constable's *Beach at Brighton: Chain Pier in the Distance* (1826–7), another apparently unsaleable work which, in building out from topographical illustration to high art, counterposed engineered modernity's hard line with nature's curves. See Andrew Hemingway, *Landscape Imagery and Urban Culture in Early Nineteenth-Century Britain*, Cambridge, Cambridge University Press, 1992, pp. 184–6.

13 Gage, *Rain, Steam and Speed*, 33; Andrew Wilton, *Turner in his Lifetime*, London, Thames & Hudson, 1987, p. 216.

14 Raymond Williams, *The Country and the City*, London, Faber & Faber, 1973, p. 18.

15 Leo Marx, *The Machine in the Garden: Technology and the Pastoral Ideal in America*, New York, Oxford University Press, 1964.

16 Williams, *Country and City*, pp. 22–34.

17 Christian Barman, *Early British Railways*, Harmondsworth, Penguin, 1950, p. 25.

18 C. J. Lever, *Tales of the Trains*, London, Orr, 1845, pp. 105–6. He supports this picayune judgement with slighting references to France, Belgium and Prussia.

19 Leo Marx, 'The railroad-in-the-landscape: an iconological reading of a theme in American art', in Susan Danly and Leo Marx (eds), *The Railroad in American Art: Representations of Technological Change*, Cambridge, Mass., MIT Press, 1988, p. 200.

20 George H. Douglas, *All Aboard: the Railroad in American Life*, New York, Paragon, 1992, p. 345. For uncertainty over whether Inness painted the Lackawanna Railroad's physical effects on native woodlands, or made a personal or symbolic statement, see Nicholas Cikovsky, '"The ravages of the ax": the meaning of the tree stump in nineteenth century American art', *The Art Bulletin*, 61, 1979, pp. 619–20; for the Delaware, Lackawanna and Western Railroad's presumed sponsoring of this painting see Nicholas Cikovsky, 'George Inness's *The Lackawanna Valley*. "type of the modern",' in Danly and Marx (eds), *Railroad in American Art*, p. 73.

21 Wilton, *Life and Work*, p. 220. 'This is another celebration of travel', he continues; 'no one can have been more alive than Turner to the fact that railways represented a fresh departure for the old tradition of landscape, offering a new vocabulary with which to describe that heightening of emotional tension associated with impressive natural phenomena which is the essence of 'Sublime' experience. Speed especially was a very novel factor of life, with the power to alter our apprehension of nature;

while the steam of railway locomotives was a new ingredient in the atmosphere which Turner loved to render'.

22 Edmund Burke, *A Philosophical Enquiry into the Origin of Our Ideas of the Sublime and Beautiful* [1757], quoted in Finley, 'Turner and the steam revolution', p. 19.

23 Immanuel Kant, *Observations on the Feeling of the Beautiful and Sublime* [1763], translated by John T. Goldthwait, Berkeley, University of California Press, 1960, pp. 76–96.

24 John Ruskin, *Works*, New York, Crowell, 1903–1912, volume xxxv, p. 601.

25 This structure of feeling's most interesting treatment is to be found in Wolfgang Schivelbusch, *The Railway Journey: Trains and Travel in the Nineteenth Century*, New York, Urizen, 1979, pp. 131–51.

26 John van Riemsdijk, 'Locomotives', in David Jenkinson (ed.), *The National Railway Collection*, London, Collins, 1988, p. 46.

27 L. T. C. Rolt, *Isambard Kingdom Brunel*, Harmondsworth, Penguin, 1970, p. 188.

28 This special status is encapsulated in the claim that on Brunel's birthday the rising sun shines straight through Box tunnel's long straight bore.

29 Gage, *Rain, Steam and Speed*, pp. 22–4.

30 Hemingway, *Landscape Imagery*, pp. 224–45.

31 Gage, *Rain, Steam and Speed*, p. 11.

32 Klingender, *Art and the Industrial Revolution*, p. 62. For an excellent treatment of Bury and his competitors see Gareth Rees, *Early Railway Prints: a Social History of the Railway from 1825 to 1850*, London, Phaidon, 1980.

33 Robert Louis Stevenson, *The Amateur Emigrant* [1895], London, Hogarth Press, 1984, pp. 80–1, 97.

34 Hesiod, *Works & Days*, edited by M. L. West, Oxford, Oxford University Press, 1978, p. 49.

35 In railway parlance, any train travelling away from London is running 'down'. This is an example of the Victorian convention (treated more fully below) that one went 'up' to any metropolitan location or metropolitan institution.

36 I. Shaw, *Views of the Most Interesting Scenery on the Line of the Liverpool and Manchester Railway* [1831], Oldham, Broadbent, 1980, pp. 13–14.

37 Anthony Burton, *The Railway Builders*, London, Murray, 1992, p. 65.

38 T. T. Bury, *Coloured Views on the Liverpool and Manchester Railway*, London, Ackermann, 1831, p. 5.

39 Samuel Smiles, *The Life of George Stephenson*, London, Murray, 1857. Smiles' celebration of old George's triumph over Chat Moss occupies chapter 10 of his later *Lives of George and Robert Stephenson*, London, Murray, 1874. In turn, this book originally appeared as volume 3 in Smiles' *Lives of the Engineers*, that work of 'pure hagiography … Smiles' canon of industrious saints': Eric de Maré, 'Introduction' to Smiles, *The Lives of George and Robert Stephenson*, London, Folio Society, 1975, p. 8.

40 Samuel Smiles, *Self Help* [1859], third edition, London, Murray, 1879. This list of Smilesian virtues comes from Miles Fairburn, *Nearly Out of Heart and Hope: the Puzzle of a Colonial Labourer's Diary*, Auckland, Auckland University Press, 1995, p. 164.

41 R. M. Ballantyne, *The Iron Horse: or Life on the Line*, London, Nisbet, 1871, p. 267.

42 D. Hill, *Turner on the Thames: River Journeys in the Year 1805*, New Haven, Yale University Press, 1993, p. 156. See also Butlin and Joll, *Paintings*, p. 232.

43 Gordon Biddle and O. S. Nock, *The Railway Heritage of Britain: 150 Years of Railway Architecture and Engineering*, London, Joseph, 1983, p. 216.

44 E. T. Macdermott, *History of the Great Western Railway: vol. 1, 1833–1863*, Paddington, GWR, 1927, pp. 89–91.

45 Rolt, *Brunel*, pp. 171–2.

46 *Punch*, 19 June 1847.

47 Lindsay, *Turner: Life and Work*, p. 202.

48 Gage, *Rain, Steam and Speed*, pp. 11–13, 22–6.

49 *Punch*, 1845, vol. ix, p. 183. One year later, this magazine offered its readers a satirical example of a fraudulent railway enterprise: 'The Great North Pole Railway. Capital £2,000,000. Deposit three-pence'. Many real schemes in the Railway Mania were scarcely less improbable than this. See C. L. Graves, 'The railway centenary', supplement to *Punch*, 1 July 1925, p. 1. The Mania's standard treatment is Henry Grote Lewin, *The Railway Mania and its Aftermath*, London, Railway Gazette, 1936.

50 John Stilgoe, *The Metropolitan Corridor: Railroads and the American Scene*, New Haven, Yale University Press, 1983, p. 339.

51 Hemingway, *Landscape Imagery*, Hill, *Turner on the Thames*. One Turner Thameside image is a fine study of Maidenhead bridge, emphasising Brunel's audaciously flat bridge arches.

52 John Henry Newman, *The Idea of a University* [1852], new edition, edited by C. F. Harrold, London, Longmans Green, 1947.

53 Dr Arnold's enthusiasm for modern trains did not survive proposals to build a railway line adjacent to his Lake District holiday home: Nicholas Faith, *The World the Railways Made*, London, Bodley Head, 1990, p. 55. For Etonian obduracy see J. R. Whitbread, *The Railway Policeman: the Story of the Constable on the Track*, London, Harrap, 1961, p. 33.

54 Simmons, *Victorian Railway*, p. 169.

55 Ian Carter, *Ancient Cultures of Conceit: British University Fiction in the Postwar Years*, London, Routledge, 1990, pp. 76–99.

56 The argument is contested, but most historians take the 1846 repeal of the Corn Laws to be one key date in the landed interest's decline.

57 Daniels, 'Images of the railway', p. 8.

58 'The fiery blaze on the front … has never been explained'. C. Hamilton Ellis, *A Picture History of Railways*, London, Hulton Press, 1956, plate 37.

59 Daniels, 'Images of the railway', p. 8.

3

Eight great pages:
Dombey and Son

On the (Rail)Road?

J. M. W. Turner's *Rain, Steam and Speed* shares features with Mary Anne Evans' ("George Eliot"'s) fiction. Both yielded their richest meanings to a learned and educated, to a polite world. Excluded from full membership by her gender, in middle age Evans moved comfortably in Cambridge college gardens. Her fiction suited places which claimed to value 'criteria of seriousness – the slow building of rounded characters, the intricacy of developing relationships, a certain tact and indication matched by the sobriety and subtlety of the novelist's direct language'.[1] Writing her sober texts, she pays little attention to railway development.[2] That is not true for her great Victorian competitor, Charles Dickens. He wrote not from cloistered comfort, but as a working journalist furiously engaged in a rapidly changing world. George Eliot looks forward (a good distance, to be sure) to Bloomsbury's cool complacency, to its superior literary modernism. Dickens built on existing demotic cultural forms. At the centre of his literary achievement lies 'that [pre-industrial folk] tradition altered, sharpened, by the experience of industrial life and cities; a popular culture, part of what it both expresses and opposes'.[3] Matching his image's viewpoint, Turner shows us the relationship between railways and culture viewed severely from above. Dickens sets our feet firmly on the ground. Looking at the new modern railways in their day, both men blended exhilaration with fear – but for interestingly different reasons.

When travelling by land, moneyed characters in Dickens' early novels always take the stage coach.[4] Sarah Gamp heralds new things in *Martin Chuzzlewit*. Brandishing her fearsome umbrella, she insists that new technology complicates her midwifery by inducing premature births. She anathematises steam engines, "'with your hammering and roaring and hissing and lamp-iling, you brute!"'[5] Ten years after that, respectable characters in *Hard Times* take train travel for granted: 'the railway has been as it were absorbed into the landscape, as well as into the pattern of the industrial society depicted'.[6] Most modern commentators mark divisions in Dickens' work between coach and rail travel not by a character (Mrs Gamp) but a novel. Telling us that *Dombey and Son* was published in 1841, the social historian Asa Briggs reports that here Dickens 'brilliantly noted many of the most important social events of the coming of the railway'.[7] This novel was published in eighteen monthly parts between 1 October 1846 and 1 April 1848, then in a single volume on 12 April 1848. If a distinguished historian gets a date badly wrong, what faith can we place in his other arguments? Is *Dombey and Son* a major railway novel?

Anthologists entertain no doubt. Every modern collection of general 'railway writing' except one prints excerpts from railway set pieces in *Dombey*;[8] the exception prints Patricia Beer's poetic cogitation on Mr Dombey's gloomy train ride.[9] Social and railway historians are equally convinced, mining this novel's railway set pieces for descriptive colour.[10] Literary critics concur. 'The most celebrated railway passages in Victorian fiction are the four in *Dombey and Son*', Richard Altick tells us. For Humphry House, Dickens 'had the railway mood spasmodically: he did not live and create in it, except perhaps in *Dombey*'; but this novel 'is full of it'. For Ivor Brown this is 'the most railway-minded of all his long books'. For Jeremy Tambling, 'railways and railway-power ... are central to *Dombey and Son*'. For Gail Cunningham, 'A particular interest of [*Dombey*] is that railways play an important part in it just at the time when they were transforming English life.'[11] For Kathleen Tillotson, the railway

> links high and low, devastates Camden Town, uproots Stagg's Gardens, provides employment for Mr Toodle, bears Mr Dombey from grim past to grimmer future, and finally obliterates Carker. Its appearance on each of the four carefully spaced and placed occasions (chs 6, 15, 20, 55) is emphasised by a volcanic upsurge in the style, by description much overflowing its narrative function. In these descriptions may be discerned the fascination of the new as well as the horror of the strange; but the tone is mainly that of dread. Twice the railway is used to highlight the darker thoughts of hero and villain, thoughts of fear and hate and death (chs 20, 55).[12]

A bleak picture. Against earlier critics, disparaging Dickens as a conjuror of comic grotesques, Tillotson centres the railway, and its effects, in a much less cheerful author. 'This colouring of gloom and and horror may derive from the over-riding mood of the novel', she tells us. 'It may be a picturesque reflection of contemporary doubts; but more probably, from the evidence of the later novels, it represents a persistent shade in Dickens' own social view, which contains at least as much pessimism as optimism, and always more of the visionary than of the reformer.'[13]

This is a standard move in most Dickens criticism: locate fiction's well-spring in the author's personal experience.[14] Charles Dickens was born in 1812. He came to manhood in years when the stage coach, not the railway train, exemplified distance crushed by speed.[15] His early fiction is stuffed with flying coach journeys, and with drivers' raffish banter. Running to accelerated schedules on macadamised turnpikes, stage coaches in the 1820s – those gaudy, delicate cockles – riveted small boys' attention. Living on the Mississippi's banks at Hannibal, Missouri, young Sam Clemens dreamed of being a steamboat pilot should God not grant his first wish and make him a pirate.[16] In Dickens' youth, British boys yearned to succeed hard-driving, hard-drinking and hard-swearing coachmen like Mr Weller, encased in his many-caped greatcoat and top-boots.[17] Leaving the editor's chair on *Bentley's Miscellany* in 1839, twenty-seven-year-old Dickens anticipated 'those days to-come when mail-coach guards shall no longer be judges of horse-flesh – when a mail-coach guard shall never even have seen a horse – when stations shall have superceded stables, and corn shall have given place to coke. "In those dawning times," thought I, "exhibition rooms shall teem with portraits of Her Majesty's favourite engine, with boilers after Nature by future Landseers…"'[18] All too soon for boys (of greater or lesser age) who idolised dashing coachmen, Mr Weller had to hang up his whip. Stage horses, it was claimed, went to grass or the knacker, superceded by the railway's iron horse.[19]

Dickens seems first to have travelled by train in 1838, from London to Birmingham. 'One of the earliest Victorian writers to seize the railway imaginatively',[20] he soon joined other British scribblers in taking railway travel for granted.[21] From the 1840s, trains seep insistently through his published work. Much of this lies almost forgotten today, buried among shorter fiction and journalism. Treated seriously or humorously, railway material surfaces in *Household Words* (1850–9) and *All the Year Round* (1859–70), Dickens' own magazines.[22] Much of this was written by him, though one may not always identify his hand precisely.[23] Among less fugitive work, *The Lazy Tour of the Two Idle Apprentices*, Dickens' Christmas book for 1857, contains sharp sketches of railway life and working between London and Carlisle. Eight years later, he wrote four chapters in *Mugby Junction*, the 1866 Christmas book. Railway catering and insolent boy porters are excoriated in one chapter. A second gave us the first important railway ghost story, still routinely anthologised.

Dealings with the Firm...

Dombey and Son is a much less genial book than *Sketches by Boz* or *Pickwick Papers*. Harbinger for his later 'dark' novels, and longer than Dickens' earlier books, here the plot is tightly integrated through 'a deeply considered plan'.[24] Dickens told John Forster that his plan pivots on Pride.[25] More specifically, it turns on *hubris*. As the novel opens, Mr Dombey's pride centres on two things. One is the large-scale merchant's business which he inherited from his father: the book's full title reads *Dealings with the Firm of Dombey and Son, Wholesale, Retail and for Exportation*. First readers bought shilling monthly parts wrapped in green paper. Designed by Hablôt Browne, this wrapper carried the novel's title in a framed cartouche. A great ledger supports this cartouche's bottom edge. Its left-hand edge is supported by that confident merchant prince, Mr Dombey. Above him, a rising pile of cash books and ledgers frames the title's left side. His chair resting on a cash box and a pay book, Dombey sits enthroned at the top among cartoons illustrating key scenes from the novel. To the right, a house of cards collapses on a bowed and defeated Dombey. This frame summarises Dickens' story competently enough: a tale of pride humbled, as a great merchant's House falls to the ground.

Dombey's pride in the business which he inherited from his father looks backwards. His second prideful instance looks forward. We meet him first at forty eight, a family man equipped with a wife and one young daughter, Florence. He needs a male heir. In a letter to John Forster dated 25–6 July 1846, Dickens explained that his new novel would treat a particular obsession, 'that one idea of the Son, taking firmer and firmer possession of him, and swelling and bloating his pride to a prodigious extent'.[26] This son, Paul, has just been born as the novel opens. '"The House will once again, Mrs Dombey ... be not only in name but in fact Dombey and Son,"' Paul's father exults. Since Mrs Dombey dies at the end of chapter one, her relict must invest all his hopes for patrilineal inheritance in this son. Poor loving, slighted Florence holds no place in her father's plans: this is 'a patriarchal narrative of regular succession and linearity'.[27] But Paul dies in chapter 16 (of 62). After many vicissitudes, not the least of them his business's total collapse, humbled Dombey learns to appreciate steadfast Florence, long despised and rejected by her cold, hard father. Married to Walter Gay, near the novel's end Florence herself produces a son, young Paul; but now there is no Dombey and Son for this grandSon to inherit. Teaching Dombey to value Florence as he had valued the elder Paul, forcing pride to yield to love,[28] forms a central plank in Dickens' narrative. Miss Tox's exclamation after Paul's death – "'To think … that Dombey and Son should be a Daughter after all!'" (p. 225) – rings against his father's proud outburst at Mrs Dombey's bedside. Miss Tox's prescient comment already exists, fully developed, in Dickens' detailed plan for his novel.[29]

It is quite possible to discuss *Dombey and Son* without ever noticing trains.[30] Blink, and you miss them. Significant railway matters emerge in only four chapters. Within those chapters, treatment is terse. One episode, 'The most celebrated description in English of any railway being built',[31] shows us the new London and Birmingham Railway's smashing progress through Stagg's Gardens, Camden Town. This takes no more than one page and twenty four lines to describe (pp. 65–6).[32] Our return journey, to see Stagg's Gardens reconstructed as a railway settlement, occupies one page and eight lines (pp. 217–19). The third episode, with Dombey travelling the line from London to Birmingham,[33] occupies at most five pages and thirteen lines (for Dickens' text does not mark the precise point at which this journey ends). The famous passage in this episode, as distraught Dombey mourns his dead son, fills no more than one page and nineteen lines (pp. 275–7). The final episode – showing James Carker, Dombey's villainous manager, ripped apart by an express train's wheels – occupies only twenty-four lines (p. 743). Direct railway interest in *Dombey and Son*, we see, occupies from four-and-a-half to eight-and-a-half pages – in a novel running to 833 pages. A slender base, we might think, on which to erect claims that this is Victorian Britain's 'railway novel'. Can detailed investigation calm these doubts?

Four vignettes

Accident, or suicide?

Let us begin at the end, with Carker's death. Like the three other railway episodes, this vignette is woven tightly in the plot's texture. Carker is doomed: 'Death was on him', Dickens tells us. 'He was marked from the living world, and going down into the grave' (p. 743). With this fatal fact revealed, all that piques our interest is how this villain will die. Dickens sends him off to a railway station.[34] He has to wait until a quarter past four for his train: "'Express coming through at four, Sir,'" the ticket clerk tells him. "'Don't stop.'" Nor does it. Thundering through, this express train extinguishes Carker. We know that he must die; but any fire, runaway wagon or cliff fall would suit Dickens' purpose just as well.[35] Why does his novel's plan indicate a railway death? Chapter 55 bears the 'brilliantly half-revealing'[36] title 'Rob the Grinder loses his place'; but the plan's detail specifies 'Carker's progress-/journey/death'. Dickens even roughs out a key passage which, like Miss Tox's outburst after Paul's death, appears – slightly tidied up – in the finished text. In draft this passage reads '"while others drove some dogs away, that sniffed upon the road, and < p> soaked his blood up, with < > a train of ashes."' We see Dickens' point. He wants to play with puns. Echoing the Anglican burial service, his train of ashes conducts readers to a strong connection between railways and death.

It is the *experience* of death by railway which interests Dickens in this episode; even if, with Nelson, we take him to suggest that Carker demonstrates early railway travel's disorienting influence.[37] Briefly abandoning the Victorian novelist's third-person omniscience,[38] here Dickens moves inside Carker's head as he staggers backward into the express train's path. Transcribed by his author, life's last sense impressions strike James Carker.

> He heard a shout – another – saw the face [of Dombey, on the platform] change from its vindictive passion to a faint sickness and terror – felt the earth tremble - knew in a moment that the rush was come – uttered a shriek – looked round – saw the red eyes, bleared and dim, in the daylight, close upon him – was beaten down, caught up, and whirled away upon a jagged mill, that spun him round and round, and struck him limb from limb, and licked his stream of life up in its fiery heat, and cast his mutilated fragments in the air. (p. 743)

Like fast cutting in a movie, short phrases conjure Carker's last crowded seconds – as rushing sensations (and then the rushing train) overwhelm him. With life extinguished, phrases lengthen. Like the tempo of carriage wheels clicking over rail joints as a train slows for a station, prose rhythms ease. *Rallentando*, a space for reflection opens. Metaphor intrudes: a mill, evoking individual human puniness before modern mechanical intractability; a demon from hell, evoking older Christian iconography. As so often in other fictions, here Dickens displays his striking ability to convey subtle ideas through rhythm.[39]

Disabling grief

All this recalls Dombey's train ride in chapter 20. Dickens' plan for this chapter merely states its title: 'Mr Dombey goes upon a journey'. A memorandum notes that this chapter will be concerned with '*The Railroad Ride*'. Emphasis tells us that Dickens intended some important purpose for this third railway episode. . His purpose is not far to seek. Chapter 20 turns the novel's plot.[40] With Dombey's Son dead in London, Major Bagstock bullies the grieving father to leave London. They travel by train and coach to Leamington, to meet new people in a place not drenched with memories of Paul. Dashing Miss Tox's trembling matrimonial hopes, one of these new acquaintances will become Dombey's second wife. For a time it seems conceivable that Edith, this second wife, might refresh the novel's patriarchal narrative by giving her husband a second son. But Carker seduces Edith, and elopes with her to France. Sitting beside Major Bagstock in the Birmingham train, Dombey travels towards new possibilities, good and bad. With his senses overwhelmed by grief for the dead son in whose person he placed such hopes, Dombey realises none of this. 'The railway carries him to his doom', Schwarzbach tells us, 'far faster than he could move to it himself'.[41]

Some commentators take this episode's famous passage, that 'classic fictional account of a railway journey'[42] in which Dickens shows us what Dombey sees as he stares out of his carriage window, to be simple description. 'Dickens' account of the journey is no confused phantasmagoria', Jack Simmons tells us. 'It is quite precise, showing the passage of the train "through the chalk, through the mould, through the clay, through the rock".'[43] This recalls Humphry House, linking these phrases to a new public interest in stratiographic geology spurred by railway construction.[44] More generally, House argues, 'the amount of observation [Dickens] compresses into a few paragraphs is amazing'.[45] He invites us to admire Dickens the empirical journalist, not Dickens the creative novelist. This invitation is seductive – rapid cutting from one passing scene to another conjures precisely how landscape appears to an observer looking sideways from a railway carriage[46] – but the argument is too simple. Read this passage through Carker's death, and a different picture emerges. Again Dickens enters a character's head, showing us the flickering pictures generated by Dombey's 'stunted imagination'.[47] Locked in grief for dead Paul, he sees little, hears nothing, feels desolate. He pays no attention to other characters; we might not know that Major Bagstock, that dunning toady, shares Dombey's carriage. Through his eyes we traverse widely varied local scenes.[48] In six paragraphs, linked one to another like engine and carriages in a railway train, his attention drifts away from immediate sense impressions, settling on deeper questions. Two concluding sentences in the first paragraph establish a dominant metaphor: Paul's life as a trammelled journey towards a terminus which arrived too soon. 'The very speed at which the train was whirled along, mocked the swift course of the young life that had been borne away so steadily and so inexorably to its foredoomed end', he introspects. 'The power that forced itself upon its iron way – its own – defiant of all paths and roads, piercing through the heart of every obstacle, and dragging living creatures of all classes, ages, and degrees behind it, was a type of the triumphant monster, Death'. *Dragging* these varied folk: this inexorable power is the locomotive engine.[49] Behind come five paragraphs, five carriages. This is the second of them:

> Through the hollow, on the height, by the heath, by the orchard, by the park, by the garden, over the canal, across the river, where the sheep are feeding, where the mill is going, where the barge is floating, where the dead are lying, where the factory is smoking, where the stream is running, where the village clusters, where the great cathedral rises, where the bleak moor lies, and the wild breeze smooths or ruffles it at its inconsistent will; away with a shriek and a roar and a rattle, and no trace to leave behind but dust and vapour: like as in the track of the remorseless monster, Death! (p. 276)

Stanzas in a prose poem, one sentence fills each paragraph, each carriage in this stylised train. As with James Carker's death – but now so insistently that every critic notices the fact – each sentence is controlled by rhythm, by the noise of carriage wheels clicking across rail breaks.[50] Like railway carriages, the first three of these five paragraphs have much the same length: ten, nine and nine text lines. Like railway carriages, they have much the same form: a rapid succession of short verses as changing vistas slide past Dombey's eyes. These vistas reveal many particular local worlds, each marked by its own history. Local particularity is flattened by the modern train's relentless progress.[51] Phrases lengthen and rhythm loosens as Dombey's eye turns inward. His earlier cogitation on the locomotive's deadly progress had ended with the engine, 'that type of the triumphant monster, Death'. These three paragraph/carriages follow 'in the track of the remorseless monster, Death!/in the track of the remorseless monster, Death!/in the track of the indomitable monster, Death!' A fourth paragraph repeats the general form of those before, but omits the fiery monster at the train's head. It appears again at the beginning of the fifth, as Dombey's train approaches Birmingham: 'Louder and louder yet, it shrieks and cries as it comes tearing on resistless to the goal: and now its way, still like the way of Death, is strewn with ashes thickly'. There it is: an open pre-echo for Carker's death, with its carefully planned train of ashes, four hundred and fifty pages before the villain dies.

Social disruption

> The first shock of a great earthquake had, just at that period, rent the whole neighbourhood. Traces of its course were visible on every side. Houses were knocked down; streets broken through and stopped; deep pits and trenches dug in the ground; enormous heaps of earth and clay thrown up; buildings that were undermined and shaking, propped by great beams of wood. Here, a chaos of

carts, overthrown and jumbled together, lay topsy-turvy at the bottom of an unnatural hill; there, confused treasures of iron soaked and rusted in something that had accidentally become a pond. (p. 65)

The London and Birmingham Railway is a-building, smashing its way towards Euston through Camden Town in north London. As with Dombey's ride, many commentators take this passage to be no more than 'brilliant description';[52] take Dickens, that 'incomparable reporter of the contemporary scene',[53] to be no more than a working journalist. Again, this is an ingenuous reading. Dickens' description generates very different readings. For some commentators he is venially tender-hearted: 'Horrified by the turmoil and confusion, he found the sight almost unbearable.'[54] Others find Dickens unmoved by displaced inhabitants' plight, gazing stonily as vile houses tumble down.[55] These differences might indicate authorial confusion – or they might signal textual complexities deeper than is commonly recognised.

In Dickens' plan for *Dombey and Son*, 'Stagg's Gardens' is the first among six topics noted for chapter 5. (In the event, this topic was shifted to chapter 6.) Stagg's Gardens matters for Dickens' plot. With his mother dead in childbirth, infant Paul needs a wet nurse. In chapter 2 a married woman, Polly Toodle, is hired for this task. With Polly away from home, her unmarried younger sister, Jemima, will run the Toodle household. Lodged in Dombey's house and missing her own children, in chapter 6 Polly takes Paul, Florence and Susan Nipper, Florence's sardonically protective maid-companion, to visit her own family. As they walk there, Dickens shows us the profound disruption caused by smashing the London and Birmingham Railway towards London. Playing with Polly's children, Florence first learns what loving family life can mean. Warm but poor, in this episode the Toodle family first indicts rich Dombey's cold household.

The Toodles live in Stagg's Gardens. Michael Freeman locates this place very precisely: J. C. Bourne's lithograph of the new cutting and retaining wall at Park Street, Camden Town represents, he insists, 'the scene immortalised by Dickens in *Dombey and Son*'.[56] This is too confident. Bourne's image records respectable streets – look at those rows of solid, modern houses. But an engineer involved in building the London and Birmingham recalled that

with the exception of crossing Park Street and the Hampstead Road …, hardly a single house of any respectable size was touched by the extension [of the railway from Kilburn towards Euston]. To Park Street, the line ran southward through fields of stiff clay pasture; from Park Street to Hampstead Road, its site was chiefly occupied by small and not very well tended market-gardens, and a little colony of firework makers had their cottages or rather huts in this intramural desert'.[57]

3.1 J. C. Bourne, *Park Street, Camden*, 1836

Staggs Gardens enjoys little kinship with respectable Park Street. This literary space lies in F. R. Conder's intramural desert between Park Street and Hampstead Road – that district of 'frowzy fields, and cow-houses, and dunghills, and dustheaps, and ditches, and gardens, and summer-houses, and carpet-beating grounds, at the very door of the Railway'.

> It was a little row of houses, with little squalid patches of ground before them, fenced off with old doors, barrel staves, scraps of tarpaulin, and dead bushes; with bottomless tin kettles and exhausted iron fenders, thrust into the gaps. Here the Stagg's Gardeners trained scarlet beans, kept fowls and rabbits, erected rotten summer-houses (one was an old boat), dried clothes, and smoked pipes. (p. 66)

Since Toodles show Dombeys how family life should be lived, we might expect pathetic fallacy here, with proto-industrial Stagg's Gardens displaying social virtues extinguished by the new railway's thoroughgoing capitalist industrialisation.[58] But consider those adjectives: little, squalid, dead, bottomless, exhausted, rotten. Can Dickens want us to admire this place? Consider the name he gave the district, and remember that Dickens chose that name well before he started writing his novel. He tells us that local etymologists traced 'Stagg's Gardens' to a deceased capitalist, one Stagg, who once lived there; or to the deer who once might have roamed the district. (p. 66) An innocent soul,

Jeremy Tambling concludes that Dickens 'created the name with total arbitrariness'.[59] This would have surprised contemporaries familiar with that Radical rag *Punch*, edited by Dickens' friend Mark Lemon. Readers would remember Thackeray's feuilleton '"The Railway Speculator at Home;" or, Mr Jeames Plush in his Celebrated "Stagging Character,"' and Richard Doyle's cartoon '"Stag" Stalking in Capel Court'. They would recall that pastiche of Jacques' speech from *As You Like It*:

> All the world are stags!
> Yea, all the men and women merely jobbers!
> They have their brokers and their share-accounts,
> And one man in his time tries many lines,
> The end being total ruin ...[60]

Dickens knew this very well. His etymology for Stagg's Gardens is ironic, knowingly spurious. Initially a slang term for share traders dealing in large lots, 'stag' soon came to mean any share speculator. Dickens despised speculators. He planned and largely wrote *Dombey and Son* while the Railway Mania gripped respectable Britain.[61] *Little Dorrit* (1857) portrays a crooked financier, Merdle. This portrait was based on a defaulting financier, John Sadleir; a man ruined by collapsing Irish banks. Dickens turned him into that mid-century folk devil for propertied classes, a railway speculator. Stagg's Gardens is his natural habitat; the place where stags gambol and gamble.

Dickens tells us that its inhabitants regard this little district 'as a sacred grove not to be withered by railroads' (p. 66). Not all of them. The leading local politician, a master chimney sweep, might trumpet that the new railway never would open; but other petty entrepreneurs prove keen as any Merdle to turn a rapid profit.

> One or two bold speculators had projected streets; and one had built a little, but had stopped among the mud and ashes to consider farther of it. A bran-new Tavern, redolent of fresh mortar and size, and fronting nothing at all, had taken for its sign The Railway Arms; but that might be rash enterprise – and then it hoped to sell drink to the workmen.[62] So, the Excavator's House of Call had sprung up from a beer shop; and the old-established Ham and Beef Shop had become The Railway Eating House, with a roast leg of pork daily, through interested motives of a similar and immediate and popular description. Lodging-house keepers were favourable in like manner; and for the like reasons were not to be trusted. (pp. 65-6)

Key phrases in this passage – 'rash enterprise', 'interested motives', 'not to be trusted' – set the reader against Stagg's Gardens' petty entrepreneurs. Reading Dickens' fiction through his life, this might not surprise us. Living in Camden

Town as a boy, in 'a small, mean tenement' at 16 Bayham Street, he knew this district very well. He loathed it.[63] Preferring life to death on general grounds, Dickens declines to mourn as the London and Birmingham Railway destroys this exiguous Eden.

Social improvement

One sub-heading (from three) in Dickens' plan for chapter 15 reads 'Stagg's Gardens after the Railroad'. This is misdirection. As Florence and Susan Nipper discover when, at ailing Paul's urgent request, they try to find his old nurse, 'There was no such place as Stagg's Gardens'.

> Where the old rotten summer-houses once had stood, palaces now reared their heads, and granite columns of gigantic girth opened a vista to the Railway world beyond. The miserable waste ground, where the refuse-matter had been heaped of yore, was swallowed up and gone; and in its frowsy stead were tiers of warehouses, crammed with rich goods and costly merchandise. The old by-streets now swarmed with passengers and vehicles of every kind; the new streets that had stopped disheartened in the mud and waggon-ruts, formed towns within them-selves, originating wholesome comforts and conveniences, belonging to them-selves, and never tried or thought of until they sprung into existence. Bridges that had led to nothing, led to villas, gardens, churches, healthy public walks. The carcasses of houses, and beginnings of new thoroughfares, had started off upon the line at steam's own speed, and shot away into the country in a monster train. (pp. 217–18)

Dickens revisits his picture of destruction from chapter 6, showing in precise detail how former infelicities – rotten summer-houses, miserable waste ground, old by-streets – have been transformed and improved. Adjectives describing this new world – gigantic, rich, costly, wholesome, healthy – invite our admiration. Looking forward to Dombey's ride, only that 'monster train' disturbs this hymn to progress.

We see that Kathleen Tillotson was unwise to conflate the four railway vignettes in *Dombey and Son* through a common 'volcanic upsurge' in Dickens' writing style. They would be read differently by contemporaries who had or had not travelled by train, who had or had not witnessed the physical disruption caused by railway building, who had or had not plunged on railway shares in the Mania.[64] Thematically, these four episodes sort into two pairs. The return to Stagg's Gardens mates with our first visit there, as Dombey's ride mates with Carker's death. The first two episodes treat broad changes, with omniscient Dickens riding high above his landscape. The second pair treat personal experi-ence, with Dickens sitting in particular characters' skulls. Differences in register split these four episodes differently, three against one. Governed by whirling Nemesis, Carker's death is unreservedly gloomy. For most of its length, the third vignette matches that mood. Seen from the train, industrial Birmingham echoes Dombey's depressed mood.

> Everything around is blackened. There are dark pools of water, muddy lanes, and miserable habitations far below. There are jagged walls and falling houses close at hand, and through the battered roofs and broken windows, wretched rooms are seen, where want and fever hide themselves in many wretched shapes, while smoke, and crowded gables, and distorted chimneys, and deformity of brick and mortar penning up deformity of mind and body, choke the murky distance. (pp. 276–7)

Artisanal Birmingham is conjured as a fully urban Stagg's Gardens. Dickens now distinguishes the author's attitude from his character's. 'As Mr Dombey looks out of his carriage window', he tells us, 'it is never in his thoughts that the monster who has brought him there has let the light of day in on these things: not made or caused them'. The railway is part of Birmingham's solution, not part of that unlovely city's problem.[65] This recalls our first visit to Stagg's Gardens. For twenty-three lines Dickens piles up details about 'wildly mingled' confusion on and around the railway's construction site. Then he turns this minute description on its head: 'In short, the yet unfinished and unopened Railroad was in progress; and from the very core of all this dire disorder, trailed smoothly away, upon its mighty course of civilisation and improvement.' Chapter 15 puts flesh on this broad generalisation, piling up improvement's particular detail. Where frowsty Stagg's Gardens once stood, now we find a larger, cleaner, better organised and more prosperous place. Doubters have been routed. Embraced fully by local people, the railway now rules every aspect of local social and economic life: 'There was even railway time observed in clocks, as if the sun itself had given in.' Much more affluent than ever before, that pessimistic master sweep now profits from cleaning railway chimneys by machinery.

Stance

How does Dickens invite his readers to judge the railway in *Dombey and Son*? Opinions differ. Some think him an enthusiast. For F. R. and Q. D. Leavis 'the railway is the triumphant manifestation of benificent energy'; for Schwarzenbach it 'benefit[s] all social classes by making mere change into progress'.[66] Hesketh Pearson is less convinced. He makes Dickens neutral, a working journalist churning out what his readers want to read: 'Railways and engines were novelties in the decade that first read *Dombey and Son*, and so we hear a lot about the iron monsters rushing through the countryside, belching flame and steam.'[67] Can iron monsters be that insipid? Many think not. 'Dickens keeps returning to railways and railway journeys', Nicholas Faith insists, 'as symbols of death and destruction, of landscapes as of people.'[68] 'The train is seen only as destructive, ruthless', Kathleen Tillotson reports, 'an "impetuous monster," a "fiery devil." There is no suggestion of hope, of social progress.'[69] Badri Raina builds a train-hating syllogism: 'Polly Toodle suckles Paul; Polly Toodle lives in Stagg's Gardens; the railways uproot Stagg's Gardens; the railways cannot be good'.[70] Faced by differences among *Dombey and Son*'s four railway episodes, and by unsettling irony in two of those four, many commentators conclude that here a weakly ambivalent Dickens entertained no clear attitude to the railway. This might signify sloth.[71] Occupying less than 1 per cent of his text, why should the author exert himself over an insignificant railway motif?

But, to repeat, Dickens planned *Dombey and Son* very carefully. His four railway vignettes mark plot cruxes. Like trains themselves, they carry a heavy narrative weight. 'In the world of this novel', Steven Marcus asserts, 'the railroad exists … as a impersonal and ironic comment upon the grim, doomed and determined lives of its principal characters'.[72] Most commentators agree that in *Dombey and Son* the railway stands for more than itself; it is a symbol, an emblem. A symbol of what? An emblem for what? Many things, it has been suggested. Power and ruthlessness.[73] Death and progress.[74] Reconfigured time and space.[75] The new industrial city, 'which had made the railways possible'.[76] Simple death.[77] More complicated death – for an old England 'with all its vices and virtues, [with the train] ruthlessly bridging through into a new era'.[78] Along with his merchant House, the railway may be seen to exemplify Mr Dombey. Embodying male culture, he stands for the railway's firm road-bed against the sea, natural Florence's realm. As Nina Auerbach notes,

> Like Mr Dombey, the railroad is an artifact of civilisation, the sphere of the mechanical and masculine rather than the organic, the feminine. It too is part of a closed and regulated system, without flowing and diffusing beyond it. Like Dombey on a grand scale, the railroad embodies phallic force; and like clock-time's, its progress is implacably linear.[79]

At the place which used to be Stagg's Gardens, 'To and fro from the heart of this great change, all day and night, throbbing currents rushed and returned incessantly like its life blood'.

Crowds of people and mountains of goods, departing and arriving scores of times in every four-and-twenty hours, produced a fermentation in the place that was always in action. … Night and day the conquering engines rumbled at their distant work, or, advancing smoothly to their journey's end, and gliding like tame dragons into the allotted corners grooved out to the inch for their reception, stood bubbling and trembling there, making the walls quake, as if they were dilating with the secret knowledge of great powers yet unsuspected in them, and strong purposes not yet achieved. (pp. 218–19)

If we wish to interpret *Dombey and Son* as a serious 'railway novel', then we should pay close attention to this passage. Shown to us in later episodes (for precise plot purposes) as death-dealing monsters, steam locomotives here are half-magical animals; fully domesticated, gently trembling tame dragons. Echoing Nina Auerbach's critique of Mr Dombey's world as a male public domain, these 'conquering' locomotives drag passengers and goods inexorably in their trains, accelerating the movement of people and things over long distances along linear tracks. Their great powers and strong purposes are controlled by skilled drivers, bringing them gliding to rest at just the proper place. That Dickens 'grooved' this place 'out to the inch' was no accident. He well knew that modern railway trains ran on edge rails. Here he nods to that famously optimistic passage in Tennyson's *Locksley Hall* (1842): 'Forward, forward let us range,/Let the great world spin for ever down the ringing grooves of change'.

Dombey and Son's setting in time is important. As Stagg's Gardens reminds us, Dickens wrote with the Railway Mania fresh in his readers' minds. He started writing his novel in Lausanne on 27 June 1846, one day after the bill repealing the Corn Laws was read a third time at Westminster. A significant conjuncture: liberal Dickens puts pen to paper as a key liberal reform cements rising urban manufacturers' triumph over a declining landed interest. Commentators debate what this means for *Dombey and Son.* Dombey's firm trades 'for exportation' as well as within Britain. Does Dickens' picture of that firm's collapse constitute a critique of economic colonialism?[80] When read against *laissez-faire* liberalism's rising tide, is Dombey a progressive free trader or a declining mercantilist?[81] But now note phrases in the passage quoted above, as we return to Camden Town in chapter 15. We see 'crowds of people and mountains of goods'; we see 'fermentation'; we see 'a place that is always in action', 'secret knowledge of great powers yet unsuspected', 'strong purposes not yet achieved'. As A. E. Dyson points out, *Dombey and Son* was still being written in 1848, the year when 'the *Communist Manifesto* came into its at first obscure existence, an analysis of capitalism hardly bleaker than Dickens' in its force'.[82]

Dyson suggests that Dickens' surface analysis is close to Marx and Engels', but that their underlying explanations and prescriptions diverge radically. The former point certainly is true. We should place less confidence in Dyson's assurance that Dickens's deep explanations differed greatly from Marx's. Stagg's Gardens after the railway recalls the *Manifesto* celebrating nineteenth-century capitalism as liberation from constraint ('what earlier century had even a presentiment that such productive forces slumbered in the lap of social labour?'[83]), creating – for the first time in human history – material conditions sufficient to sustain abundance. Now, the earth's plenty can satisfy all humankind's demands. Utopia fails to bloom for reasons that have to do with distribution, not production – because dominant social classes bleed surplus value from productive workers. 'The railway is at once the "life's blood" and "the triumphant monster, Death,"' reports marxisant Raymond Williams of *Dombey and Son*. 'And in this dramatic enactment Dickens is responding to the real contradictions – the power for life or death; for disintegration, order and false order – of the new social forces of his time'.[84] Like Marx, Dickens probed social changes, looking for ways to facilitate individual human betterment. 'There is ... a choice of the human shape of the new social and physical environment', Williams takes Dickens to be urging, 'if we see, physically and morally, what is happening to people in this time of unprecedented change'.[85]

One of these people is Polly's husband, Toodle (we never learn his first name). Toodle is mere stage dressing for D. A. Peart, 'one of Dickens' improbable honest bumpkins':

> He plays too small a part in the story to affect its progress and we feel that he is there because the author wished to provide a railway background for certain scenes in his latest novel and could do this through the medium of the Toodles, and also because he required a respectable, hard-working husband for Polly.[86]

This judgement is both ungenerous and misleading. As F. R and Q. D. Leavis note, Dickens explores possibilities for human betterment by comparing Mr Dombey with Engine Fireman Toodle. For the Leavises, the Toodles 'stand for that which is repressed and denied by the Dombey code: human kindness, natural human feeling, thriving human life'. This is all true. They then renege on this insight by making Polly and her family into wallpaper, a background against which developments in Dombey's character can be projected: 'The Toodles are, we don't question, just a working-class family belonging to the workaday Victorian world'.[87] Certainly, Polly and her family show few signs of aspiring to class mobility. That does not make them dopes, passive instruments for measuring more dynamic characters' development. Dickens shows us the Toodles as a warm and united family – but an *active* family. When Polly takes Paul and Florence to visit Stagg's Gardens in chapter 6, Jemima reports to her sister that Mr Toodle is at work. '"But he's always talking of you, Polly, and telling the children about you; and is the peacablest, patientest, best-tempered soul in the world, as he always was and will be!"' (p. 68). A model father, the judgement which damns Dombey. Polly brings joy to Dombey's house. Blasting everything which he touches, Dombey brings pain to the Toodles. Intending to reward Polly for the care she gives Paul, Dombey nominates her eldest son for a place in an endowed school, the Charitable Grinders (p. 62). Dressed in that school's uniform and pewter badge, he becomes a target for every young vagabond around Stagg's Gardens: 'His social existence had been more like that of an early Christian, than an innocent child of the nineteenth century' (p. 69). Revolting against this treatment, Rob turns delinquent.

Miss Tox recruits Polly to be Paul's wet nurse through a gloriously Dickensian recruitment agency, Queen Charlotte's Royal Married Females. This requires positive vetting. Toodle is dragged along to Dombey's house, to be inspected. Miss Tox asks him how he earns his living: '"Stoker," said the man, "Steaminjin"' (p. 16). From the novel's earliest chapters, inarticulate Toodle represents the steam age artisan. His eldest son Rob, fated so soon to be persecuted as a Charitable Grinder, is 'known in the family by the name of Biler, in remembrance of the steam engine' (p. 23). Learning that Toodle worked underground[88] before marrying Polly, Dombey doubts this family's respectability; and hence doubts Polly's suitability for the sacred charge of suckling infant Paul. His pride rescues him. The vast social distance separating vulgar Toodles from the respectable Dombey household ensures, he thinks, that his precious son can develop no attachment to Polly. This miscalculation sets up a running comparison between Mr Dombey and Mr Toodle. The father of five children ('"Four hims and a her. All alive!"') Toodle's life experience counterpoints Dombey's. (One him physically dead. One her socially dead.) Their appearance differs. In chapter 2 Toodle

was a strong, loose, round-shouldered, shuffling, shaggy fellow, on whom his clothes sat negligently: with a good deal of hair and whisker, deepened in its natural tint, perhaps, by smoke and coal-dust: hard, knotty hands: and a square forehead, as coarse in grain as the bark of an oak. A thorough contrast in all respects to Mr Dombey, who was one of those close-shaved close-cut monied gentlemen who are glossy and crisp like new bank notes, and who seem to be artificially braced and tightened as by the stimulating action of golden shower-baths. (pp. 18–19)

Dombey exemplifies aetiolated bourgeois civilisation, monied culture. With his knotty hands and oak-like complexion, illiterate Toodle is half tree. He straddles culture's boundary with nature, with savagery.[89] Swaddled by pride, Dombey is content to stay where he is. Not so Toodle. He intends to improve himself. He will remedy his illiteracy: "'One of my little boys is a-going to learn me, when he's old enough, and been to school himself'" (p. 19). He will find a better job: "'I'm a-going on one of these here railroads,'" he tells Dombey, "'when they comes into full play'" (p. 20). So he does, making the short occupational journey from stationary steam engine stoker to locomotive fireman.

When Dombey hears about Polly's outing to Stagg's Gardens he dismisses her "'for taking my son – my Son … into haunts and into society which are not to be thought of without a shudder.'" Florence clings to Polly as she leaves. 'It was a dagger in the haughty father's heart, an arrow in his brain, to see how the flesh and blood he could not disown clung to this obscure stranger' (p. 84). Bereft of his loved nurse, infant Paul howls lustily in the night. With his wife disgraced, Toodle disappears from Dickens' text for more than a hundred pages. He reappears in chapter 15 as Engine Fireman Toodle, living in 'the Company's own Buildings, second turning to the right, down the yard, cross over, and take the second on the right again. It was number eleven; they couldn't mistake it' (p. 219). Just returned from Birmingham, Toodle is busy eating his dinner when Susan Nipper and Florence rush in to fetch Polly to Paul's deathbed. He 'laid down his knife and fork, and put on his wife's bonnet and shawl for her, which were hanging up behind the door; then tapped her on the back; and said, with more fatherly feeling than eloquence, "Polly! cut away!"' (p. 220). This warm family feeling continues later. In a passage often overlooked by commentators looking for railway content in *Dombey and Son*, Miss Tox revisits the Toodle household in chapter 38. She finds father contentedly feeding himself and sundry older children with great wedges of bread and butter, while 'conveying the two young Toodles on his knees to Birmingham by special engine' (p. 513).

Ten years after writing *Dombey and Son*, and wanting information about the engine driver's craft, Dickens arranged a footplate pass for a young journalist colleague, John Hollingshead.[90] His report infused Dickens' picture of a trip from London Bridge to Dover and back with 'steady Tom Jones. … As he stands there before me in the glare of the coke oven [the locomotive's firebox], or the flickering light of the station in the middle of the night, carefully oiling the joints of his engine, he is the model of an honest, conscientious workman, dutiful, orderly and regular.'[91] Good for Tom Jones. Good for Mr Toodle, that self-improved and railway-improved working man; the poor but loving father whose example damns rich, proud Mr Dombey. For Kathleen Tillotson, the new railway simply gave Toodle a job.[92] It did much more than that, we see. Railway employment transformed his existence. Engine Fireman Toodle views his life, and his social world, wholly through occupational metaphors. "'Polly, old 'ooman,'" he tells his wife, "'I don't know as I said in partickler along o' Rob, I'm sure. I starts light with Rob only; I comes to a branch; I takes on what I finds there; and a whole train of ideas gets coupled on to him, afore I knows where I am, or where they comes from. What a Junction a man's thoughts is," said Mr Toodle, "to-be-sure!"'" (pp. 512–13). Chapter 2's illiterate stoker has grown into an articulate railway philosopher. Demotic language apart, we might be listening to Herbert Spencer.

Toodle plays no more than a minor part in *Dombey and Son*'s first two railway episodes. He is more prominent in the third. Arrived at Euston, Dombey and Major Bagstock walk up and down the station's platform while waiting for their train to start. Dombey is accosted by a diffident man, a 'coarse churl'. 'He was dressed in a canvass suit abundantly besmeared with coal-dust and oil', Dickens reports, 'and had cinders in his whiskers, and a smell of half-slaked ashes all over him. He was not a bad-looking fellow, nor even what could be fairly called a dirty-looking fellow, in spite of this; and, in short, he was Mr Toodle, professionally clothed' (p. 273). Dombey instantly suspects that Polly has sent her husband to wheedle money from her former employer. Twisting a crêpe-swathed cap in his hand, Toodle denies this calumny. Polly and he have had four more children, he reports, and they have lost one. His surviving sons 'made a wery tolerable scholar of me', but Rob has 'gone rather wrong'. "'Polly's dreadful down about it, genelmen,'" he tells Dombey and the Major. (p. 274). Gazing across a class chasm, Toodle seeks sympathy, seeks advice about how to help his son. He gets none.

> 'A son of this man's whom I caused to be educated, Major,' said Mr Dombey, giving him his arm. 'The usual return.'
> 'Take advice from plain old Joe, and never educate that sort of people, Sir,' returned the Major. 'Damme, Sir, it never does! It always fails!' (p. 274)

Incapable of sympathy for others' plights, Dombey persuades himself that the crêpe in Toodle's cap is for Paul, not for Polly's dead child. He persuades himself that Toodle wants to steal Dombey's most precious property, grief for his dead heir. Clutching this property to his breast, off they all go to Birmingham with Dombey's 'triumphant monster, Death' stoked by 'this presumptuous raker among coal and ashes' – this poor man who, could he but see it, shows rich Dombey how a proper father should behave.

Lessons

Critics tell us that *Dombey and Son* was Dickens' first social novel, the decisive break between early and mid-period Dickens. Compared with earlier novels' spasmodic attacks on particular evils – denouncing the New Poor Law's harsh workhouse system in *Oliver Twist* [1838], for instance – here 'a pervasive uneasiness about contemporary society takes the place of an intermittent concern with specific social wrongs'.[93] Unlike his later dark novels – *Hard Times* [1854] offers the clearest example – in *Dombey and Son* Dickens does not despair when weighing the risks of rapid social change against brighter possibilities. Here, agency enjoys some latitude among structural constraints. 'The railroad is the great symbol of social transformation',[94] but it does not always override character. A train kills Carker, but stoking trains improves Toodle. New technology can foster good personal outcomes, or it can foster evil. Each character gets his just deserts from the railway. Carker deserves to die, Toodle to prosper modestly, Dombey to be racked by impotent grief.

In *Dombey and Son*, 'across the social picture are ruled the ruthless lines of the new order, symbolised by the railway'.[95] Focussing on the four railway vignettes, different critics make Kathleen Tillotson's ruthless lines carry different messages. Death; progress; urban growth; rationalisation (of time, to take one crucial instance); tighter work discipline; capitalist industrialisation: we have seen that different commentators find different messages in *Dombey and Son*'s railway episodes. But each element in the modern railway is less significant than their combination in Wolfgang Schivelbusch's *machine ensemble*. In similar fashion, each feature identified in Dickens' railway vignettes is less significant than their combination. They blend in *modernity*: that portmanteau term, jumbling together (not always in comfortable proximity) the many shifts in material conditions and consciousness which Victorian social critics identified as they struggled to make sense of a world changing its contours before their eyes. These commentators made railways the exemplary modern institution. It is no accident that the railway should be woven so intimately into the texture of this, Dickens' 'business novel'. 'In *Dombey and Son*', Humphry House asserts, 'the new style is so far developed as to be unmistakable. The people, places and things become "modern".'[96] So they do. Three of Dickens' railway vignettes include elements identified by Schivelbusch as characteristic of modern consciousness born on the railway: *shock* resulting from *accident* (Carker's death); *panoramic travel* (Dombey's ride); and *circulation* (Stagg's Gardens after the railroad). More than any of his other fictions, *Dombey and Son* merits John Ruskin's sniffy judgement that 'Dickens was a pure modernist – a leader of the steam-whistle party *par excellence*'.[97]

Ruskin's slight was an epitaph. Dickens came to manhood in coaching days, then transferred easily to rail travel. Until 9 June 1865, that is. Returning from Paris to London on the South Eastern Railway's 2.38 tidal train from Folkestone, Dickens was caught up in the Staplehurst disaster. With great coolness and considerable courage, he assisted injured fellow passengers; but then severely edited his part in the crash and its aftermath to hide the fact that he was accompanied on this train by his mistress, Ellen Ternan, and her mother. Initially, he seemed shaken but not seriously disturbed by this major accident. Ominous signs soon appeared, as post-traumatic shock emerged. Committed to a strenuous reading tour, Dickens found himself unable to travel by express train. Slow trains reduced anxiety, but increased boredom.[98] On his son's testimony, Dickens 'may be said never to have altogether recovered' from the shock which he received in the 1865 Staplehurst railway crash. He died five years later, to the day.[99]

We have seen that most critics read Dickens' fiction through his life. In an early attempt at psychobiography, Jack Lindsay used *Dombey and Son* to reverse this process:

> This train image is profoundly important for Dickens, and indeed is in the end to kill him, as the imagined train killed Carker. Carker as the guilt-self of Dickens is run over, crushed; and if we think back we shall recall that when Dickens revisits the key places of his childhood he finds the ravaging train has smashed things up. He goes back to Chatham, and the playing grounds are ruined and turned into smutty deserts, and the tunnel maw gapes for its victim. He goes back to Camden Town, and finds that Euston has smashed up the haunts from which he first looked fascinatedly over towards London. He goes back to his school, and finds that the Birmingham railway has driven right across and shorn an end off the school house. When the frontispiece of *Dombey* was drawn, there appeared in it a monster train with demon eyes; and this was in very truth the nightmare train which ran the guilt-self down in the lifelong pursuit.[100]

Post hoc ergo propter hoc is a dangerous argument. Dickens was less consistently fearful for railway development's consequences than Lindsay suggests. But this critic does capture how, in *Dombey and Son*, railways act as the standard-bearer for that on-rushing, multifaceted modernity which intrigued – and, in part, horrified – Dickens: 'the real contradiction – the power for life or death; for disintegration, order and false order – of the new social and economic forces of his time'. Like the Circumlocution Office and Bleeding Heart Yard in *Little Dorrit*, the railway in *Dombey* exemplifies Dickens' general method, 'to grasp certain social forces almost as if they were characters'.[101] Jack Simmmons claims that 'Among the great Victorian writers the railways never found one staunch admirer or sympathetic defender; none seemed grateful for the the resultant benefits, which simply came to be accepted, without remark, as part of the machinery of "progress."'[102] Dickens was no mouthpiece for the railway interest, but our return trip to Staggs Gardens denies Simmons' generalisation. Fewer than ten pages in *Dombey and Son* might describe trains, stations or permanent way; but this handful of pages forms a brilliant lightning sketch of what a developed railway novel might look like. It would be other English writers' task to block in Dickens' sketch. What a scandal it is that so few serious authors took up that challenge.

Notes

1 Raymond Williams, 'Introduction', to Charles Dickens, *Dombey and Son*, Harmondsworth, Penguin, 1970, p. 13.
2 *Middlemarch* (1872) contains some recollection about surveying the London and Birmingham Railway's line in Warwickshire; *Daniel Deronda* (1876) fleetingly considers railways' effects on polite English language and consciousness. See Jack Simmons, 'Literature, railways in English', in Jack Simmons and Gordon Biddle (eds), *The Oxford Companion to British Railway History*, Oxford, Oxford University Press, 1997, p. 267. In the introduction to *Felix Holt* (1866) a coachman takes William Huskisson's death on the Liverpool and Manchester Railway's opening day to be 'a proof of God's anger against Stephenson'.
3 Williams, 'Introduction', to Dickens, *Dombey and Son*, p. 15.
4 Michael Wheeler, *English Fiction of the Victorian Period*, second edition, London, Longmans, 1994, pp. 26–31.
5 Charles Dickens, *Martin Chuzzlewit* (1844), London, Everyman's, 1994, p. 626. Jack Simmons (*The Victorian Railway*, London, Thames & Hudson, 1991, p. 198) makes this an anathema on railway engines. Mrs Gamp's did work herself up to attacking '"the Ingeins…them screeching railroad ones;"' but in these earlier words she 'indignantly apostrophised' a steamship, '"the Ankworks package"' [Antwerp packet].
6 Robin Atthil, 'Dickens and the railway', in Bryan Morgan (ed.), *The Railway-Lover's Companion*, London, Eyre and Spottiswoode, 1963, p. 505.
7 Asa Briggs, *The Age of Improvement*, London, Longmans, 1959, p. 288.
8 Roger Green (ed.), *The Train*, Oxford, Oxford University Press, 1982, pp. 1–2, 14–15, 53–4, 99–100; Paul Jennings (ed.), *My Favourite Railway Stories*,

Guildford, Lutterworth, 1982, pp. 54–7; Stuart Legg (ed.), *The Railway Book*, London, Hart-Davis, pp. 29–31; Morgan (ed.), *The Railway-Lover's Companion*, pp. 213–14; Jack Simmons (ed.), *Railways: an Anthology*, London, Collins, 1991, pp. 14–16.

9 Ludovic Kennedy (ed.), *A Book of Railway Journeys*, London, Collins, 1980, p. 34.

10 W. G. Hoskins, *The Making of the English Landscape* [1955], London, Hodder & Stoughton, 1977, pp. 258–62; Francis D. Klingender, *Art and the Industrial Revolution* [1947], edited and revised by Arthur Elton, London, Paladin, 1968, p. 134; John Marshall, *The Guinness Railway Book*, Enfield, Guinness, 1990, pp. 64–5; Jeffrey Richards and John M. McKenzie, *The Railway Station: a Social History*, Oxford, Oxford University Press, 1986, p. 352.

11 Richard D. Altick, *The Presence of the Past: Topics of the Day in the Victorian Novel*, Columbus, Ohio State University Press, 1991, p. 190; Humphry House, *The Dickens World*, second edition, London, Oxford University Press, 1942, pp. 145, 139; Ivor Brown, *Dickens in his Time*, London, Nelson, 1963, p. 119; Jeremy Tambling, 'Death and modernity in *Dombey and Son*', *Essays in Criticism*, 43, 1993, p. 308; Gail Cunningham, 'Dombey and Son', in Andrew Michael Roberts (ed.), *The Novel: a Guide to the Novel from its Origins to the Present Day*, London, Bloomsbury, 1994, pp. 134–5.

12 Kathleen Tillotson, 'Dombey and Son', in A. E. Dyson (ed.), *Dickens: Modern Judgments*, London, Macmillan, 1968, p. 182.

13 Tillotson, 'Dombey and Son', p. 182.

14 Or, as David Musselwhite argues (in *Partings Welded Together: Politics and Desire in the Nineteenth Century English Novel*, London, Methuen, 1987, pp. 143–226), by a Dickens who glides backwards and forwards between 'Boz' and 'Dickens' personae, contriving to simulate developing personal experience. Harland S. Nelson ('Stagg's Gardens: the railway through Dickens' world', *Dickens Studies Annual*, 3, 1974, pp. 41–53) seeks to sediment Dickens' imputed distaste at the confusion caused by railway building in his fastidious neatness in living arrangements.

15 This point is embroidered in Michael and Molly Hardwick, *Dickens' England*, London, Dent, 1970, pp. 45–8.

16 Mark Twain, *Life on the Mississippi*, Boston, Osgood, 1883, pp. 62–3.

17 'Boys were ambitious to be coachmen, as later to be engine-drivers. They haunted the White Horse Cellar in Piccadilly and the General Post Office to see the coaches, as they afterwards hung about King's Cross to see the streamlined engine of the Flying Scotsman': House, *Dickens World*, p. 25.

18 Quoted in House, *Dickens World*, p. 139. We should mourn these never-painted masterpieces by Landseer and others, no less than John Betjeman's much later fancy: 'that exhibition of the etchings of the insides of railway engines by Frank Brangwyn'. See Betjeman, 'Lord Mount Prospect' [1929], in Dorothy L. Sayers (ed.), *Great Short Stories of Detection, Mystery and Horror: Third Series*, London, Gollancz, 1934, pp. 538–51.

19 This claim was false. Horse numbers rose through the steam railway age, as carters carried ever more traffic to and from goods yards. Dickens noted this fact obliquely

in *The Uncommercial Traveller*, railling that the old coach office in Dullborough (Rochester) had turned into one from Mr Pickford's many carting depots.

20 Tillotson, 'Dombey and Son', p. 176.

21 'Many writers quickly perceived and started to deal with some of the broader issues raised by the existence of railways', Roger Green (*The Train*, p. 1) reports. 'But only one seems to have understood immediately all the implications – Charles Dickens. Once he had become comfortable with rail travel, Dickens did not hanker for coaching inns' rapacity and extortion'. Quite true: dispatching a character from London to Yorkshire in *The Holly Tree Inn*, Dickens reminded his readers that 'There was no Northern Railway at that time, and in its place there were stage-coaches; which I occasionally find myself, in common with some other people, affecting to lament now, but which everybody dreaded as a very serious penance then'.

22 Note how often railway material appears in Michael Slater (ed.), *Dickens' Journalism. Vol. 2: 'The Amusements of the People' and Other Papers*, London, Dent, 1996. See also Ewald Mengel (ed.), *The Railway Through Dickens' World: from Household Words and All the Year Round*, Frankfurt, Lang, 1989; Simmons, *Victorian Railway*, pp. 199–201; Atthil, 'Dickens and the railway'; Brown, *Dickens in his Time*, pp. 113–30.

23 See for example 'By rail to Parnassus' [1855] in Harry Stone (ed.), *Charles Dickens' Uncollected Writings from 'Household Words', 1850–1859*, Bloomington, Indiana University Press, 1968, pp. 530–6.

24 Julian Moynahan, 'Dealing with the firm of Dombey and Son: firmness *versus* wet-ness', in John Gross and Gabriel Pearson (eds), *Dickens and the Twentieth Century*, London, Routledge & Kegan Paul, 1962, p. 121. For an analysis of Dickens' plan see John Butt and Kathleen Tillotson, *Dickens at Work*, London, Methuen, 1957, pp. 90–113. This plan is printed in Charles Dickens, *Dombey and Son*, edited by Alan Horsman, Oxford, Clarendon Press, 1974, pp. 835–55. All page references in this chapter come from this edition.

25 John Forster, *The Life of Charles Dickens* [1872–4], edited by J. W. T. Ley, London, Palmer, 1928, vol. 3, p. 2. Of course, we need not privilege Dickens' own account. We shall see that feminist critics read his text in ways which might well puzzle the author. In a different manner, Susan R. Horton (*Interpreting Interpreting: Interpreting Dickens' Dombey*, Baltimore, Johns Hopkins University Press, 1977) uses this novel as a hermeneutic stalking horse, demonstrating that readings cannot be limited.

26 Kathleen Tillotson (ed.), *The Letters of Charles Dickens*, vol. 4, Oxford, Clarendon Press, 1977, p. 589.

27 Tambling, 'Death and modernity', p. 315.

28 Butt and Tillotson, *Dickens at Work*, p. 96.

29 Miss Tox's comment rings down the years, but transformed by social change. Richard Green ('Dombey and daughter', *Forbes*, 5 September 1988, pp. 114–15) notes how frequently daughters now are recruited to managerial positions in family firms, compared with their mothers' and earlier generations. In Dickens' view no

less than Dombey's, Florence could look forward to no future spent bossing Dombey and Son.

30 See for example Audrey Jaffe, *Vanishing Points: Dickens, Narrative and the Subject of Omniscience*, Berkeley, University of California Press, 1991, pp. 71–111; Musselwhite, *Partings Welded Together*, pp. 143–50. In letters to John Forster outlining *Dombey*'s plot, Dickens never mentioned the railway.

31 Simmons, *Victorian Railway*, p. 14.

32 The Clarendon Edition of *Dombey* prints forty text lines to each page. Intriguingly, one of the surveyors who set pegs to guide this smashing destruction was young Herbert Spencer, putting his shoulder firmly to social evolution's wheel. See David Withshore, *The Social and Political Thought of Herbert Spencer*, Oxford, Oxford University Press, 1978, p. 25.

33 Not all the way to Leamington, as Hardwick and Hardwick (*Dickens' England*, p. 97) suggest.

34 This station has long been identified as Paddock Wood, between Tunbridge and Ashford in Kent. When Dickens executed Carker on the track he influenced other Victorian authors. The clearest influence is to be found in Lopez' suicide under an express train's wheels in Anthony Trollope's *The Prime Minister* (1876); but there are other cases. Having murdered Mrs Main on the 4 p.m. express from London, Valentine Santon was executed in a thoroughly Carkerish manner by the same train while fleeing a hue and cry on a later date: Fergus Hume, *The 4 p.m. Express* [1914], London, Mellifont, n. d., p. 145. In Eden Philpotts' 'My adventure in the Flying Scotsman' [1888] (reprinted in William Pattrick (ed.), *Mysterious Railway Stories*, London, Star, 1984, pp. 39–84) another murderer, Beakbane, is squashed by a locomotive leaving its shed.

35 'Clearly, Carker is not destined for a peaceful end, but there are no half-measures with Dickens…Carker might have been a publisher in disguise': Hesketh Pearson, *Dickens: his Character, Comedy and Career*, London, Methuen, 1949, p. 154.

36 Butt and Tillotson, *Dickens at Work*, p. 109.

37 Nelson, 'Stagg's Gardens', pp. 41–2.

38 Jaffe, *Vanishing Points*, pp. 71–111.

39 John Gross, 'Dickens: some recent approaches', in Gross and Pearson (eds), *Dickens and the Twentieth Century*, p. xv.

40 Kathleen Tillotson, *Novels of the Eighteen-Forties*, Oxford, Clarendon Press, 1954, p. 185.

41 F. S. Schwartzbach, *Dickens and the City*, London, Athlone Press, 1979, p. 107.

42 Robin Gilmour, *The Novel in the Victorian Age*, London, Arnold, 1986, p. 36.

43 Simmons, *Victorian Railway*, p. 198.

44 For this interest see Christian Barman, *Early British Railways*, Harmondsworth, Penguin, 1950, pp. 24–5 and Michael Freeman, *Railways and the Victorian Imagination*, New Haven, Yale University Press, 1999, pp. 53–5.

45 House, *Dickens World*, p. 141.

46 Wolfgang Schivelbusch, *The Railway Journey: Trains and Travel in the 19th Century*, New York, Urizen, 1980, pp. 57–72. Like many other first-class travellers in early

railway days, Dombey travels in his own closed carriage, strapped on a flat truck. This form of transport lasted longer than one might imagine. The last passenger so to travel, 'a most unpleasant English eccentric, Mrs Caroline Prodger ... was observed, *en route*, covered with dust, at Chesterfield in the English Midlands, as late as the 1880s': C. Hamilton Ellis, *The Lore of Steam*, London, Hamlyn, 1984, p. 70. Dombey's view of the passing scene would have been no different if he had sat in a London and Birmingham Railway first-class carriage, of course.

47 Murray Baumgarten, 'Railway/reading/time: *Dombey and Son* and the industrial world', *Dickens Studies Annual*, 19, 1990, p. 70.

48 It has been suggested that these gimpses evoke scenes from Mr. Dombey's past (Gillian Tindall, *Countries of the Mind: the Meaning of Place to Writers*, London, Hogarth Press, 1991, p. 61). This seems excessively ingenious. Humphry House's suggestion in *The Dickens World*, p. 142 – that these fleeting views of varied little social worlds connect with contemporary 'condition of England' debates – seems more persuasive.

49 Removed from demotic speech to elevated description, this echoes Sam Weller senior's complaint in an earlier book:

> And as to the ingein – a nasty, wheezin', creakin', gaspin', puffin', bustin' monster, alvays out o' breath, with a shiny green-and-gold back, like a unpleasant beetle in that 'ere gas magnifier, – as to the ingein as is alvays a pourin' out red-hot coals at night, and black smoke in the day, the sensiblest thing it does, in my opinion, is ven there's somethin' in the vay, and it sets up that 'ere frightful scream vich seems to say, 'Now here's two hundred and forty passengers in the wery greatest extremity o' danger, and here's their two hundred and forty screams in vain!': Charles Dickens, 'Master Humphrey's visitor', in Dickens, *Master Humphrey's Clock,* and *A Child's History of England* [1840–41], Oxford, Oxford University Press, 1958, p. 80.

50 Expanding Steven Marcus' point that in this novel Dickens imports the sights and rhythms of the industrial revolution into 'the living language', Baumgarten ('Railway/reading/time', p. 70) puts this argument well: 'Perhaps that is why Dickens, the virtuoso of English, makes his *Dombey* prose so clearly do the work of painting and of music. His railroad scenes include onomapoetic passages that punctuate the novel.'

51 As Altick notes (*Presence of the Past*, p. 184), railways erased 'the provincial immobility that had tied most English people to the neighbourhood where they had been born as long as travel by coach was expensive, uncomfortable, and slow'.

52 Simmons, *Victorian Railway*, p. 14. 'The description of the driving-through of the railway that was to have Euston for its terminus is in its vigour, vividness and clear authenticity, a magnificent document of the early Victorian era': F. R. Leavis and Q. D. Leavis, *Dickens the Novelist*, London, Chatto & Windus, 1970, p. 11. See also C. Hamilton Ellis, *Railway Art*, Boston, New York Graphic Society, 1977, p. 30.

53 Hoskins, *Making of the English Landscape*, p. 258. See also Nicholas Faith, *The World the Railways Made*, London, Bodley Head, 1990, p. 287.

54 Jack Simmons, *The Railway in Town and Country, 1830–1914*, Newton Abbot, David and Charles, 1986, p. 32. Nelson, 'Stagg's Gardens' offers the strongest case for Dickens' Camden Town as a lost Eden.

55 See Schwartzbach, *Dickens and the City*, p. 110; Jonathan Arac, 'The house and the railroad: *Dombey and Son* and *The House of the Seven Gables*', *New England Quarterly*, 51, 1978, p. 17.

56 Freeman, *Railways and the Victorian Imagination*, p. 234.

57 F. R. Conder, *Personal Recollections of English Engineers* [1868], facsimile editon (as *The Men Who Built Railways*), edited by Jack Simmons, London, Telford, 1983, pp. 18–19. How could Dickens stop himself from slotting those firework makers into *Dombey and Son*? This was just the kind of occupational oddity he savoured – remember *Our Mutual Friend*'s Golden Dustman and riverine scavengers. Perhaps fireworks were too closely connected with match factories for Dickens' psychic comfort.

58 For Humphry House (*The Dickens World*, p. 150), Dickens'picture of unreconstructed Stagg's Gardens illustrates 'plain delight'.

59 Tambling, 'Death and modernity', p. 322.

60 Quoted in Richard D. Altick, *Punch: the Lively Youth of a British Institution, 1841–1851*, Columbus, Ohio State University Press, 1997, p. 457. Note the pun on 'lines'.

61 Michael Steig, 'Dombey and Son and the Railway Panic of 1845', *The Dickensian*, 1971, 67, pp. 145–8.

62 A delicate nod to railway navvies' contemporary reputation for drink and mayhem: see Terry Coleman, *The Railway Navvies*, London, Hutchinson, 1965.

63 Hardwick and Hardwick, *Dickens' England*, p. 20; Peter Ackroyd, *Dickens*, London, Sinclair-Stevenson, 1990, pp. 58–60; Michael Allen, *Charles Dickens' Childhood*, London, Macmillan, 1988, pp. 71–9. Dickens' own account of this district (in his essay 'An unsettled neighbourhood', *Household Words*, 11 December 1854), described an unlovely place on 'the outskirts of the fields…as shabby, dingy, damp and mean a neighbourhood as one would desire not to see…quiet and dismal [with] crazily built houses.'

64 Altick, *Presence of the Past*, p. 191.

65 In his *Victorians and the Machine: the Literary Response to Technology*, Cambridge, Harvard University Press, 1968, pp. 55–6) Herbert L. Sussman disagrees: 'the industrial wasteland through which the train runs is not merely an objective correlative for the emotional blight of Dombey's mind but suggests also in its destruction of an older way of life that the machine is in some way responsible for this emotional dissication'. This makes sense in Sussman's larger theme, but travesties Dickens' argument.

66 Leavis and Leavis, *Dickens the Novelist*, p. 11; Schwartzenbach, *Dickens and the City*, p. 110.

67 Pearson, *Dickens*, p. 154.

68 Nicholas Faith, *Locomotion: the Railway Revolution*, London, BBC Books, 1993, p. 188.

69 Tillotson, 'Dombey and Son', p. 182.

70 Badri Raina, *Dickens and the Dialectic of Growth*, Madison, University of Wisconsin Press, 1986, p. 69.

71 Or, with stern Raina (*Dickens and the Dialectic of Growth*, p. 69) it might indicate ideological confusion.

72 Steven Marcus, *Dickens: From Pickwick to Dombey*, London, Chatto & Windus, 1965, pp. 356–7.

73 Athill, 'Dickens and the railway', p. 502.

74 Marcus, *Dickens*, p. 323; Raymond Williams, *The Country and the City*, London, Chatto & Windus, 1973, p. 163.

75 Tambling, 'Death and modernity', p. 319.

76 Schwartzenbach, *Dickens and the City*, p. 105.

77 Asa Briggs, *The Power of Steam: an Illustrated History of the World's Steam Age*, London, Joseph, 1982, p. 93.

78 Jack Lindsay, *Charles Dickens: a Biographical and Critical Study*, London, Dakers, 1950, p. 284.

79 Nina Auerbach, 'Dickens and Dombey: a daughter after all' [1979], in Alan Shelston (ed.), *Dombey and Son and Little Dorrit: a Casebook*, London, Macmillan, 1985, p. 105. Given the broad outlines of Dickens' plot, with Dombey forced to appreciate steadfast Florence, it is no surprise that feminist critics have enjoyed a field day here. Dickens would recognise interpretions built on a gendered dichotomy between public and private worlds, between the *firm* and the *wet* in Julian Moynahan's ('Dealings with the firm', pp. 121–31) felicitous formulation: see also Robert Clark, 'Riddling the family firm: the sexual economy in *Dombey and Son*', *ELH*, 51, 1984, pp. 69–84; Louise Yelin, 'Strategies for survival: Florence and Edith in *Dombey and Son*', *Victorian Studies*, 22, 1979, pp. 297–319; Lynda Zwinger, 'The fear of the father: Dombey and daughter', *Nineteenth-Century Fiction*, 1985, pp. 420–40. One would give a good deal to read Dickens' astounded response to Mary Armstrong, 'Pursuing perfection: *Dombey and Son*, female homo-erotic desire, and the sentimental heroine', *Studies in the Novel*, 1996, pp. 281–302.

80 Suvendrini Perera, 'Wholesale, retail and for exportation: empire and the family business in *Dombey and Son*', *Victorian Studies*, 33, 1990, pp. 603–20; Schwarzbach, *Dickens and the City*, pp. 104–5. The strongest evidence that Dickens does not intend this critique concerns Walter Gay's career. After being shipped around the world at Dombey's (and Dickens' plot's) behest, he ends the novel happily married to Florence – and building a new mercantile empire.

81 For this debate see Tambling, 'Death and modernity', pp. 309–10.

82 A. E. Dyson, *The Inimitable Dickens: a Reading of the Novels*, London, Macmillan, 1970, p. 103.

83 Karl Marx and Friedrich Engels, 'Manifesto of the Communist Party' [1848], in Robert C. Tucker (ed.), *The Marx–Engels Reader*, second edition, New York, Norton, 1978, p. 477.

84 Williams, *Country and City*, p. 163. Less analytically, this judgement is supported in D. A. Peart, 'Literature and the railway in the nineteenth and twentieth centuries', Unpublished MA thesis, Liverpool University, 1964, p. 66.

85 Williams, *Country and City*, p. 161.

86 Peart, 'Literature and the railway', p. 76.

87 Leavis and Leavis, *Dickens the Novelist*, pp. 10–11. Sussman, *Victorians and the Machine*, pp. 58–60 manages to be less patronising than this.

88 Signifying low status, through the geological metaphor which will appear again in Dombey's ride.

89 For the shifting boundary between culture and nature in *Dombey and Son*, see Elizabeth Deeds Ernath, *The English Novel in History, 1840–1895*, London, Routledge, 1997, pp. 31–5.

90 Athill, 'Dickens and the railway', p. 507.

91 *Household Words*, 12 December 1857.

92 Tillotson, 'Dombey and Son', p. 182.

93 *Ibid.*, p. 158.

94 Marcus, *Dickens*, p. 306.

95 Tillotson, 'Dombey and Son', p. 182.

96 House, *Dickens' World*, p. 136.

97 Quoted in Philip Collins (ed.), *Dickens: the Critical Heritage*, London, Routledge & Kegan Paul, 1971, p. 443.

98 Hardwick and Hardwick, *Dickens' England*, p. 147.

99 Ackroyd, *Dickens*, p. 964.

100 Lindsay, *Charles Dickens*, p. 284.

101 Williams, Introduction', to *Dombey and Son*, pp. 34, 30.

102 Simmons, 'Literature, railways in English', p. 267.

4

'Death by the railroad':
Anna Karenina

Anna Karenina's principle(s)

'Domesticable animals are all alike; every undomesticable animal is undo-mesticable in its own way.' This is Jared Diamond's *Anna Karenina principle*, central to his lauded account of human cultural growth and social differentiation over thirteen millenia. He takes his principle from the first sentence in Tolstoy's novel *Anna Karenina*: 'Happy families are all alike; every unhappy family is unhappy in its own way.' 'By that sentence', Diamond tells us,

> Tolstoy meant that, in order to be happy, a marriage must succeed in many different respects: sexual attraction, agreement about money, child discipline, religion, in-laws, and other vital issues. Failure in any one of those essential respects can doom a marriage even if it has all the other ingredients for success.[1]

So that's what *Anna Karenina* is: a self-help pamphlet on how to keep your husband contented. A remarkably odd conclusion, given Tolstoy's recent conversion to marital sexual abstinence when he wrote this novel, and the remarkably unhappy relations with his wife which conversion brought in its train. But Diamond does get one thing right. Tolstoy was a didactic novelist. Diamond's error lies in excavating such a peculiar principle from *Anna Karenina*. It can sustain others.[2]

Today's dominant principle flows from Anna's experience as a woman. The Moravian composer Leoš Janácek introduces it. On 17 October 1924 he heard his first string quartet's premier public performance, in Prague. 'Inspired by Tolstoy's *Kreutzer Sonata*' as its subtitle insists, this work tells what happened on a long railway journey as the social pariah Pozdnyshev explained why he slaughtered his wife. This was Janácek's third attempt to set Leo Tolstoy's fiction to music. In 1907 he started composing an opera based on *Anna Karenina*, but abandoned the project. Next year he tried to conjure *The Kreutzer Sonata* in a piano trio. This piece was completed, but did not satisfy the composer. Material from this suppressed trio reappeared fifteen years later, in his first string quartet.[3] What fascinated Janáček in these Tolstoy fictions? That both *Anna Karenina* and *The Kreutzer Sonata* indicted 'man's despotic attitude to women'.[4] 'I had in mind an unhappy, tortured, beaten woman', he wrote to Kamila Stössel about the string quartet, 'beaten to death as Tolstoy described her in his *Kreutzer Sonata*'.[5] Four days after finishing that piece he started work on *Jenůfa*, a powerful opera centred on a wronged woman. Sadly enough, none of these principled concerns about women's oppression influenced Janáček's own practice. After his two children died he treated his wife like a skivvy, cruelly taunting her with a string of younger mistresses.[6]

We see that for Leos Janáček the Anna Karenina principle states that men abuse women, but – in theory, if not in one's own practice – should not.[7] Anna will abandon her husband and children for another man, but she bears no guilt. This reading enjoys second-hand authoritative warrant. Tolstoy's wife confided to her diary that 'He told me that he had imagined a type of married woman from the highest society, but who lost herself. He said that the problem was to make this woman only pitiful and not guilty.'[8] For Vladimir Nabokov, Anna was 'a young, handsome, and fundamentally good woman, and a fundamentally doomed woman'.[9] Like Thomas Hardy's *Tess of the d'Urbervilles* (1891) (subtitled *A Pure Woman*) and Charles Dickens' *Dombey and Son*, Tolstoy's *Anna Karenina* proves grist for feminist mills.[10] Anna is conjured as patriarchy's victim, an undomesticable woman. In all three novels we are to appreciate how a male author challenges his time's conventions, struggling (however dimly) toward denouncing women's oppression. Like Tess Durbeyfield, like the wife in *The Kreutzer Sonata* (her identity defined so completely by her marriage that we never learn her first name), Anna Karenina dies violently in the course of the fiction which gave her life. We know who killed Tess Durbeyfield: British state authorities. We know who killed Pozdnysheva: her husband. Who killed Anna Karenina?

Three vignettes

Tolstoy tells us that she killed herself. Committing suicide under a train's wheels, Anna Karenina enters European literature's canon as 'the most famous train traveller in nineteenth-century fiction'.[11] This judgement comes in an article about Dickens, not Tolstoy. 'The best books all are English', Tolstoy said in 1877; 'Whenever I take some English books home with me, I always find they contain something new and strange'.[12] Critics find some echoes from Anthony Trollope in Tolstoy, but the strongest threads lead to Mary Anne Evans and to Charles Dickens.[13] A link to Dickens should not surprise us. As many commentators recognise, Tolstoy's *Childhood, Boyhood, Youth* and *What is Art?*, and many letters, reveal strong and open influences on his work and thought from early 'sentimental' Dickens works: *A Christmas Carol, The Chimes, David Copperfield.* Brian Rosenberg stalks bigger game than this, suggesting that Tolstoy's most religious and least patrician major novel, *Resurrection*, owes deep debts to *Little Dorrit*, Dickens' darkest critique of his own society. 'The central institution in both *Resurrection* and *Little Dorrit* is clearly the prison', Rosenberg urges, 'and the most striking similarity between the two novels is their comparable treatment of the prison as both an actual, intolerably abusive enforcer of the law and a complex metaphor for social relations and individual psychological life.'[14] London's Marshalsea and Tolstoy's unnamed provincial prison are vivified, become important characters in the novels which they inhabit. That, we saw, happens to the railway in *Dombey and Son*: the novel where, for the first time, railways emerge as 'a vital presence in European literature'.[15] So what about *Anna Karenina*? As in *Dombey*, here a major character hurls herself under a moving train from an insignificant railway platform.[16] Why does Tolstoy slaughter Anna under that train?

For George Steiner, an essay could be written on the role of railway platforms in Tolstoy's and Dostoyevsky's novels and lives.[17] Railways appear at least thirty two times in *Anna Karenina*,[18] but significant passages are much fewer. As in *Dombey*, a handful of passages magnetise critical interest. In book 1, six pages bridging chapters 17 and 18 describe a train arriving from St Petersburg at Moscow. Relatives greet each other, then a railway worker is killed in an accident. Five pages in chapters 29 and 30 treat a railway journey from Moscow to St Petersburg. In book 7, five pages in chapter 31 show us a railway journey ending in suicide at a wayside station. These three passages occupy no more than sixteen pages from 807, a proportion scarcely less insignificant than *Dombey and Son*'s eight pages from 864: yet, as in *Dombey*, these slim pillars support disproportionate narrative weight. Plot cruxes, here we first meet Anna Karenina, watch as she prepares to abandon her husband and family for a lover, and watch her die.

Notoriously, Anna Karenina takes a long time to appear in her novel, and then absents herself for long periods. With audacious architectural skill Tolstoy builds two largely independent plots. One centres on Levin, a landowner articulating Tolstoy's own opinions on a host of socio-political issues. The second

centres on Anna, a woman married to Karenin, that coldly intellectual bureau-
crat; a woman who will be seduced and ruined by Vronsky, officer and rotter.[19]
Tolstoy allows sixteen chapters to pass before setting this second plot in motion.
At the Moscow terminus Vronsky arrives to collect his mother from the St
Petersburg train. He bumps into his friend Stiva Oblonsky. Oblonsky is waiting
to meet his sister Anna Karenina, coming to Moscow for an extended visit by
the same train. The station platform vibrates, 'and puffing out steam driven
downward by the frosty air, the engine rolled past, the piston[20] of the middle
wheel rising and extending slowly and rhythmically, the bent, muffled figure of
the engine driver all covered with hoarfrost'. The train stops. Passengers disem-
bark. Tolstoy draws our attention to a Guards officer, a tradesman, a peasant
with a sack over his shoulder. Vronsky looks for his mother. Finding her, he
learns that she shared her compartment with a woman 'of the best society'. This
is Anna. She meets Vronsky. He is attracted to her; she returns some interest.
Oblonsky finds them all, and begins escorting Anna from the station. Public
commotion draws their attention: 'A guard, either drunk or too much muffled
up against the bitter frost, had not heard the train being shunted back and had
been run over.'[21] '"It's an omen,"' Anna comments.

So, of course, it is. The guard's death prefigures Anna's suicide in book 7.
Tired of her charms, Vronsky is set to abandon Anna. With her reputation
ruined, and scarcely aware of her own actions, she travels along the Moscow to
Nizhnii Novgorod (now Gorki) railway to Vronsky's local station at Obiralovka
(now Zheleznodorozhnaia). As her train prepares to leave Moscow, 'a grimy,
deformed peasant' passes her compartment window, tapping carriage wheels.
Arrived at Obiralovka, Anna is met by Vronsky's coachman. He hands her a
slighting note. The station platform shakes as a lumbering goods train
approaches. 'And suddenly remembering the man who had been run over on
the day she first met Vronsky, she realised what she had to do'.[22] Choosing the
precise set of wheels for her purpose, she throws herself under the goods train.
With well-signalled connections – that trembling platform, that passing
peasant – Anna's omen has been fulfilled. The novel graced by her name has
almost fifty pages to run, but henceforth she will appear only in other
characters' memory.

These two railway episodes give us our first and last views of Anna Karenina.
Clearly enough, they bear heavy structural weight in Tolstoy's plan. So does the
third episode. Anna's visit to Moscow has run its course. Pursued by Vronsky
and by other testosterone-charged young men, she has not succumbed. On a
wild winter's night Oblonsky puts her in a luxurious sleeping carriage for her

return journey to St Petersburg. Reading an English novel of domestic manners, she ponders the morality of her behaviour in Moscow. A 'lean peasant' checks the thermometer in her heated carriage. At a minor wayside station she disembarks in a 'terrible blizzard', to stretch her legs. She is astonished to find Vronsky waiting on the platform.

> 'I did not know that you were travelling too. Why?' she said, letting fall the hand with which she was about to take hold of the handrail. And her face shone with irrepressible joy and admiration.
> 'Why?' he repeated, looking straight into her eyes. 'You know that I am going in order to be where you are', he said. 'I can't help it.'[23]

Fiercely buffetting wind and snow echoes Anna's emotional state. Back in her compartment, she cannot sleep. Terrified but exalted, she lies on the cusp of the event which will destroy her: her decision to yield to Vronsky. In this railway carriage she succumbs, in mind if not yet in body, to disastrous passion.

Each of these three railway episodes can generate an Anna Karenina principle. Each is rooted in a different academic discipline. Each can be used as a key to unlock a profoundly different meaning for Anna's plot. Her night journey to St Petersburg, Gary Browning argues, exposes 'her fundamental frailties: a tendency to indulge her romantic (even suicidal) fantasies and a propensity to resort to deception rather than confront unpleasant reality. This results in an ever greater and, finally, an essentially permanent disintegration (bifurcation) of her personality.'[24] This Anna Karenina principle insists that illicit sex maddens those who yield to it. Abandoning psychology for philosophy, Gary Saul Morson urges that in the third episode Anna is rescued from nihilistic vengeance – '"There, right in the middle [of a goods truck's wheelbase], and I shall punish him and get rid of them all and of myself"' – when, almost involuntarily, she crosses herself.[25] Lying between the wagon's wheels, 'she was horror-struck at what she was doing. "Where am I? What am I doing? Why?"' A familiar figure appears for the last time: 'The little peasant, muttering something, was working over the iron.[26] And the candle, by the light of which she had been reading the book filled with anxieties, deceits, grief and evil, flared up with a brighter light than before, lit up for her all that hitherto had been shrouded in darkness, flickered, began to grow dim, and went out forever'. Given Tolstoy's religious beliefs, this little peasant might have muttered a prayer as Anna met her maker. In Morson's secular reading, her last thoughts celebrate free will as she realises – at last, one might say – that she could have chosen not to do 'what she had to do'. This principle is existential, urging that Being-to-Death gives human life its spice and meaning, its true humanity.

Proffering a sociological key, Robert Louis Jackson's Anna Karenina principle tells us that accelerating social change can outrun individuals' capacity to adapt. The first episode, he claims, 'may be regarded as constituting in microcosm the action of the novel as a whole as it pertains to Anna'.[27] It exemplifies Tolstoy's method. Chance meetings build into structural relations, as the novelist slowly reveals his minutely planned architecture. Anna's destiny springs directly from what happens in her first meeting with Vronsky. Character governs fate: an old idea. Tolstoy exploits it, then transcends it. Vronsky first hears Anna's voice offstage, as she talks to a servant on Moscow's station platform before re-entering her compartment for their fateful meeting.

> 'I don't agree with you all the same', said the lady's voice.
> 'That's the Petersburg way of looking at things, ma'am.'
> 'No it isn't the Petersburg way, it's simply a woman's way', she replied.

With his quivering station platforms and repetitive peasants, Tolstoy never writes at random.[28] What part could counterpointing 'the Petersburg way' with 'a woman's way' play in the grand design he is busy constructing? Immediately, nothing: Tolstoy leaves this exchange hanging in the air. But it does matter. After the railway guard has been mangled, Stiva takes Anna to his home. In book 1 chapter 19 Stiva's wife Dolly, Tolstoy's pattern for how a genteel Moscow woman should behave, greets her sister-in-law as a being radically different from herself, 'a Petersburg *grande dame*'. In the next chapter Dolly's sister Kitty meets Anna for the first time. She knows Anna only by reputation, as a 'Petersburg society woman'. Recalling the overheard conversation on that station platform, we understand that Anna Karenina's life moves in the space between a woman's way and 'the Petersburg way'. In Tolstoy's early draft 'the Petersburg way' signifies nihilism,[29] his shorthand for modernity. Clearly enough, to understand Anna's biography we must attend not only to what Tolstoy tells us about this particular woman but also to what he reports about broader relations between men and women, and about broader relations between St Petersburg and Russia. We must vacate the narrow territory which much *Anna Karenina* criticism occupies, 'the common isolation of characters from their context, as if the tragedy of Anna could be considered apart from the actual relationships with Karenin and Vronsky, and without reference to the society in which these are lived out'. That is Raymond Williams, comparing Tolstoy with D. H. Lawrence.[30] He develops the point in a later book, urging that *Anna Karenina* and *Women in Love* show how a personal relationship can spawn death. Both novels, he argues, entangle one central tragic relationship in a web of other personal connections.

But again, in each novel, it is more than this. It is impossible to read either novel without feeling the pressure of other experiences and other questions: sharply contrasted ways of living; questions of the nature of work and of its relation to how a man lives; questions, finally, about the inward nature of a given civilisation, which the form of each novel seems designed to dramatise.[31]

In *Anna Karenina*, many of these framing social questions emerge in Levin's plot, to which we pay no attention here. In Anna's plot social questions turn on the nexus between the Petersburg way and a woman's way. We meet this crux on a railway platform for very good reasons. The 'Moscow-Petersburg express train' is 'a central character in *Anna Karenina*',[32] playing a pivotal role in the action. Whether or not Tolstoy knew Dickens' novel, *Dombey and Son* casts its aura over *Anna Karenina*.

Real foundations

In 1834 Russia had no railways. Sniffing profits, von Gerstner, a Viennese professor who built the first continental European public railway, dangled economic and strategic bait before the tsar and his advisers. He offered to construct two new railways from Moscow: one north to St Petersburg, the other east to Nizhnii Novgorod and Kazan. These are the lines which Anna Karenina travels in Tolstoy's novel.[33] In return for his labour and capital, von Gerstner demanded a twenty year monopoly over Russian railways. His offer was declined, but he was granted generous conditions to construct a short line from St Petersburg to the tsar's summer residence at Tsarskoye Selo. This line would establish whether steam railways could operate efficiently in Russian winters.[34] With that matter settled satisfactorily, bureaucratic planning began for new construction. The first line, in Russia's western borderlands, helped link Warsaw with Vienna. Its significance was dwarfed by the second.

On 1 February 1842 Nicholas I announced that to 'unite the two capitals as if they were one, we have decreed the construction of a railroad from St Petersburg to Moscow'.[35] Quite what Nicholas thought would follow in his decree's train is sharply disputed. In 1845 he told a French visitor that 'the improvements in the means of communication will change everything and the dregs that rested in the depths will rise to the top'.[36] Against that, a modern specialist historian of Russia reports that 'The tsar himself was something of a supporter of the iron horse'. 'According to unsubstantiated anecdote, Nicholas took a hand in this line', Paul Dukes continues, 'fixing its route with a bold stroke on the map'.[37] John Pendleton elaborates this anecdote:

When the Emperor Nicholas was asked to decide upon the route of the line between St Petersburg and Moscow he contemptuously tossed aside the plans placed before him, ordered a map to be unrolled on the table, put his sword across the map, and drawing a straight line from one city to the other, regardless alike of rights of way and rights of property, flung his inexorable plan to the astounded surveyor, saying, 'Voilà votre chemin de fer'.[38]

This is the 'ruler legend' (other accounts substituted a straight-edge for Nicholas' sword). Richard Mowbray Hayward traces the myth back to an 1864 article in a British technical magazine, *The Engineer*.[39] It is entirely fallacious. Scholarship exposes how minutely this railway's route was planned through a string of commissions, and demonstrates that 'the tsar's decision was reached after a thorough examination of the problem and accorded with the wishes of the merchants of the two capitals, all of the tsar's most competent engineers led by Mel'nikov, and a majority of high officials'.[40]

Myths' significance is not destroyed by demonstrating that they lie. Hayward shows how the ruler legend was rooted in long debates among officials, merchants and others over whether the projected railway line should link Moscow with St Petersburg along the shortest possible route, or link population centres along a more circuitous route. As conventional wisdom shifted over time, so did the legend. From the 1840s to the 1860s educated European opinion held that railways should link population centres. Coloured thus, the tsar's line symbolised an autocrat's refusal to recognise economic realities, as 'the Gendarme of Europe' rode rough-shod over his suffering people. From the later 1860s politics trumped economics, and opinion shifted. Nicholas now gained credit for refusing to sanction a meandering line which would have advantaged powerful officials' personal or local interests. He might have been less than an ideal monarch, this suggested, but at least Nicholas inhibited greedy court lackeys from lining their own pockets as fully as they wished.[41]

If economic and political debates about early local railways resonated in Tolstoy's first Russian readers' minds, then so did the general notion of the train. As elsewhere in Europe, and beyond, the train symbolised irresistable progress – remember Pendleton's phrases about Nicholas I's 'straight line', his 'inexorable plan'. Railways carried progress in their train. Whether one thought that good or bad turned on one's attitude to the cities where Anna got on and off her trains. Nicholas' 1842 edict promised to eradicate contrasts between the two capitals: but Moscow and St Petersburg resonated very differently in educated nineteenth-century Russians' minds. Moscow was the old capital, heartland for a historically grounded sense of the nation's identity. Constructed from nothing after 1703, St Petersburg exemplified enlightened absolutism. This was Peter the Great's new city, erected at uncounted human cost on a muddy estuarial archipelago. In Marshall Berman's judgement, 'The building of St Petersburg is probably the most dramatic instance in world history of modernisation conceived and imposed draconially from above'. 'Throughout the nineteenth century', he continues, 'the clearest expression of modernity on Russian soil was the imperial capital of St Petersburg'.[42] In *Anna Karenina* as in other Russian literature, the two capitals 'symbolise the conflict between old pieties and modern pressures'.[43] Anna travelled essentially contested territory as her trains trundled between Moscow and St Petersburg.

After completing *War and Peace* Tolstoy attempted, and abandoned, a novel about Peter the Great. On 11 May 1873 he wrote to N. N. Strakov that 'I am writing a novel that has no connection with Peter.'[44] This was *Anna Karenina*; but we should not assume that the bronze horseman plays no part here. Peter's new capital symbolised his fierce determination to make Russia a European country, to import modern European ideas and modern European technology, to modernise Russia from above against any opposition. That ambition did not die with Peter I, in 1725. Refracted, and always contested, it dominated Russian social and political debate through the nineteenth century, and beyond. Telling their stories, historians cheerfully carve time into distinct periods, contriving that post-Petrovian enlightenment should yield to reactionary absolutism under Alexander I and Nicholas I between 1801 and 1861.[45] But railways were the nineteenth century's central modern symbol, and Nicholas ordered that Russia's first railways be built. Periodisation isolates *tendencies*, not discrete categories. Debates about how far and how fast to push Russian modernisation have gridlocked intellectual and official discussions from Peter I's time down to our own.[46]

Stance

Andrew Baruch Wachtel tells us that nineteenth-century western European writers' sharp division into historians and litterateurs never happened in Russia. There, writers continued an older practice: the 'man of letters' mingled fictional and historical narratives. For this and other reasons (largely to do with Russia's location on Europe's geographical and cultural margin, offering possibilities for autonomous social and political development), he argues, Russian novels always have been didactic.[47] This itch to insert social and historical comment in fiction does not guarantee political clarity. Tolstoy's own position on his time's major issues never proved easy to pin down. A deeply contradictory man, on many large matters he changed his position over time. Even when one finds more consistency, his attitudes did not locate Tolstoy comfortably on mid- and late-nineteenth-century Russian political terrain.[48] His Rousseauian faith in human goodness, his trust in the Russian peasantry, and his antagonism to the Tsarist state apparatus made him look like a radical, standing shoulder to shoulder with populists and nihilists. Against that, Christian pacificism led him to reject many radicals' willingness to countenance violence in pursuing political ends, and to denounce those radicals' materialist schemes for social reform.[49] This confusion does not mean that *Anna Karenina* stands bereft of social ideas. On two issues which matter for this novel Tolstoy held clear and consistent beliefs. The first was railways, which he hated and feared.[50] The second was marriage, which he took to be disastrously decayed in his time. Both signalled a deeper change against which Tolstoy always railed: Russia's modernisation, her shift (however slow and halting) from what he believed once to have been a stable rural patriarchalism to urban-industrial license.

'For Russia', James Billington argues, 'the new railroads brought the first massive intrusion of mechanical force into the timeless, vegetating world of rural Russia, and a great increase in social and thus class mobility throughout the empire'.[51] For Anna, 'Her misfortunes and the railroad are linked'.[52] As she trundles along chatting to Vronsky's mother just before the first railway episode opens, Anna rides in modernity's symbol (the train) along modernity's symbol (Nicholas' railway) from modernity's symbol (Peter's city). Arrived in the terminal station at Moscow (capital of, and emblem for, old Russia) she meets Vronsky. Tragedy lurches into motion. Moving inexorably, as if guided by rails, 'Anna finds death by the railroad, that most powerful nineteenth-century symbol of urbanisation, Westernisation and secular society'.[53] Expanding this argument, Robert Louis Jackson notes that the guard's death in this episode

> is a symbol and an embodiment … not of some irrational, metaphysical factor in existence that may at any moment strike us down, but of the rational disorder of modern social and economic existence. It is of cardinal importance that two or three of the most traumatic moments of Anna's existence are played out in interaction with the harsh and discordant rhythms of the railroad. The iron railroad, or jarring train, as a symbol of dislocation of life, as an embodiment of new forces ruthlessly destroying the old patterns of patriarchal existence, becomes in *Anna Karenina* (as it does later, in a more didactic way, in *The Kreutzer Sonata*), a kind of symbol for the disorders of individual and family existence.

Anna's suicide, he argues, is rooted in 'the dislocations and contradictions that the railroads bring to Russian life, dislocations which somehow acquire a unique and terrifying embodiment (in all its abstraction and senselessness and brutality) in the accident or suicide of the guard'.[54] And, one might add, in that symbol of old Russia – the peasant who pops up so persistently whenever anything important happens on a railway.[55]

Peter Ulf Møller tells us that Tolstoy entertained two purposes in *The Kreutzer Sonata* (1889). One was to express aesthetic arguments later collected in his tract *What is Art?* (1897–8); the other was to intervene in contemporary Russian debates about 'contagious morality' and about conjugal relations.[56] Again, we should urge that individual factors carry too much weight in this judgement. As railways transformed Russian conceptions of space, time and structured social relations, so (Tolstoy believed, through all his personal gyrations about marital sex) modernity's dislocations eroded proper conjugal patterns. Jolted in his train for hour after hour, Pozdnyshev railed not just against the condition of his own marriage, but also against decayed relations between all genteel Russian husbands and their wives. Aping European manners and fashions – 'the Petersburg way' – meant introducing lascivious Romantic music to Russian salons. Society wives now yearned to play musical instruments. Music masters must be engaged. This placed wives in acute moral danger. '"A couple are occupied with the noblest of arts, music," Tolstoy tells us. '"This demands a certain nearness, and there is nothing reprehensible in that, and only a stupid, jealous husband can see anything undesirable in it. Yet everybody know that it is by means of those very pursuits, especially of music, that the greater part of the adulteries in our society occur."'[57] No less than musical practice, musical performance inflames licentiousness:

> 'They played Beethoven's Kreutzer Sonata', he continued. 'Do you know the first presto? You do?' he cried. 'Ugh! Ugh! It is a terrible thing, that sonata. And especially that part. … [H]ow can that first presto be played in a drawing-room among ladies in low-necked dresses? To hear that played, to clap a little, and then to eat ices and talk of the latest scandal?'[58]

Pozdnysheva is taught by the sleek Trukhachevski, 'a musician, a violinist; not a professional, but a semi-professional semi-society man'.[59] Previously watertight social membranes leak, bringing women from good society into close contact with men from whom they would have been protected in better days. Other social mores decay. When Trukhachevshi starts his music lessons, Pozdnyshev starts beating his wife. On a trip to his estate's Zemstvo Meeting, Pozdnyshev is driven wild by images of his wife's musical infidelity. He catches a train back to Moscow, finds her at table with her teacher, and stabs her. She dies a victim to Beethoven,[60] and to modernity.

'Then we came to the Kreutzer Sonata', George Ponderovo reports. 'It is queer how Tolstoy has loaded that with suggestions, debauched it, made it a scandalous and intimate symbol'.[61] Reading *Anna Karenina* through *The Kreutzer Sonata*, we appreciate this scandalous symbolism. Anna's tragedy is not wholly her fault. A complicated mixture of willed choice and social compulsion drove her to take her own life. Levin's principled excellence measures Vronsky's and Karenin's inadequacy. Other married women (Dolly, Kitty) show us that, in less troubled personal and social circumstances, it is possible to lead good lives in metropolitan Russian society. Tolstoy roots these differences in politics, in assertions about what desirable social arrangements might look like. As hostile contemporary liberal and radical reviewers were quick to note, *Anna Karenina* proposes that improvement can come only if modernisation reverses direction and a mythical 'Merrie Russia' congeals: if urban and industrial society withers and rural virtues flourish under paternal landlords; if flashy Petersburg fashions yield before older Moscow certainties; if wives defer to their husbands' authority. We see why Turgenev thought *Anna Karenina* 'burdened by the sti-fling influences of Moscow, the Slavophiles, aristocrats, and old spinsters'.[62]

And yet, and yet … For F. R. Leavis, stern critic of modernity's oppressive 'technologico-Benthamism', *Anna Karenina* is '*the* European novel'.[63] Through and against his intentions, in sixteen pages Tolstoy welds together Anna's fate, Russia's fate, and the railway. As with Dickens' *Dombey and Son*, this weld has resisted all subsequent corrosion. In each novel a railway metaphor links social experience with psychological experience, ties biography to history. In each novel this metaphor is fuelled by powerful covert arguments about modernity. But if eight pages are not enough to make *Dombey* a railway novel, can sixteen pages in *Anna Karenina* suffice?

Notes

1   Jared Diamond, *Guns, Germs and Steel: a Short History of Everybody for the Last 13,000 Years*, London, Cape, 1997, p. 157.
2   Martha M. Flint, 'The epigraph of *Anna Karenina*', *Proceedings of the Modern Language Association*, 80, 1965, pp. 461–2; Malcolm V. Jones, 'Problems of communication in *Anna Karenina*', in Malcolm Jones (ed.), *New Essays on Tolstoy*, Cambridge, Cambridge University Press, 1978, p. 89.
3   Jaroslav Vogel, *Leos Janácek: a Biography*, second edition, London, Orbis, 1981, pp. 19, 291–2.
4   Vogel, *Leos Janácek*, p. 294. Vogel puts these words into Josef Suk's mouth. Suk played in the Bohemian Quartet, which premiered Janácek's first quartet.

5 Bohumír Stedron, *Leos Janácek: Letters and Reminiscences*, translated by Geraldine Thomas, Prague, Artia, 1955, p. 171.

6 Zdenka Janáckova, *My Life With Janácek*, translated by John Tyrell, London, Faber, 1998. On a shared holiday one year, Leos forced his wife to share his mistress' bed while he slept on a sofa. This bizarre action made Zdenka physically sick.

7 This principle extends beyond Europe's boundaries. "'It's very old with us that the man is more important,'" a young Chinese woman told Colin Thubron in post-Mao Guangzhou: "'some husbands still beat their wives.'" She fingered the pages of *Anna Karenina* in embarrassment. "Perhaps women don't end up well anywhere'": Thubron, *Behind the Wall*, London, Penguin, 1988, p. 188.

8 Quoted in C. J. G. Turner, *A Karenina Companion*, Waterloo, Ontario, Wilfrid Laurier University Press, 1993, p. 47.

9 Vladimir Nabukov, *Lectures on Russian Literature*, edited by Fredson Bowers, New York, Harcourt Brace Jovanovich, 1981, p. 144. For Anthony Thorlby (*Leo Tolstoy: Anna Karenina*, Cambridge, Cambridge University Press, 1987, p. 21), 'By social standards, she is guilty of nothing more than a refusal to compromise and conform'.

10 Gayle Green, 'Women, character and society in Tolstoy's *Anna Karenina*', *Frontiers*, 2, 1977, pp. 106–25; Abby H. P. Werlock, 'Tolstoy's *Anna Karenina*: a palindrome, a paradox, a beginning as she ends', in Mickey Pearlman (ed.), *The Anna Book: Searching for Anna in Literary History*, Westport, Conn., Greenwood, 1992, pp. 59–69; Amy Mandelker, 'Feminist criticism and *Anna Karenina*', *Tolstoy Studies Journal*, 3, 1990, pp. 82–105. In *Framing Anna Karenina: Tolstoy, the Woman Question and the Victorian Novel*, Columbus, Ohio, Ohio State University Press, 1993, p. 122 Amy Mandelker makes Anna exemplify Nancy Miller's nostrum that Victorian novels's phallocentric (or, in Miller's ugly coining, 'phallagocentric' – 'alien-centred') discourse allowed a heroine to choose only between marriage and death. Having discarded the first, Anna must meet the second. Structural arguments as crude as this used to be called overdetermined.

11 Murray Baumgarten, 'Railway/reading/time: *Dombey and Son* and the industrial world', *Dickens Studies Annual 19*, 1990, p. 81.

12 Quoted in R. F. Christian, *Tolstoy: a Critical Introduction*, Cambridge, Cambridge University Press, 1969, p. 165.

13 George Watson, 'Tolstoy's master: the case of Trollope', *Virginia Quarterly Review*, 69, 1993, pp. 666–75; Edwina J. Blumberg, 'Tolstoy and the English novel: a note on *Middlemarch* and *Anna Karenina*', *Slavic Review*, 30, 1971, pp. 561–9; Tom Cain, 'Tolstoy's use of *David Copperfield*', *Critical Quarterly*, 15, 1973, pp. 237–46; W. Gareth Jones, 'George Eliot's *Adam Bede* and Tolstoy's conception of *Anna Karenina*', *Modern Languages Review*, 61, 1966, pp. 473–81; Shoshona Knapp, 'Tolshoj's reading of George Eliot: visions and revisions', *Slavic and East European Journal*, 27, 1983, pp. 318–26; Philip Rogers, 'Scrooge on the Neva: Dickens and Tolstoy's *Ivan Il'ič*', *Comparative Literature*, 40, 1988, pp. 193–218; Brian Rosenberg, '*Resurrection* and *Little Dorrit*: Tolstoy and Dickens reconsidered', *Studies in the Novel*, 17, 1985, pp. 27–37. For details of what Tolstoy read while he planned and wrote *Anna Karenina* see Turner, *Karenina Companion*, pp. 99–122.

14 Rosenberg, '*Resurrection* and *Little Dorrit*', p. 32.

15 Marshall Berman, *All That is Solid Melts into Air: the Experience of Modernity*, New York, Simon & Schuster, 1983, p. 159.

16 As we saw, Carker died beneath a train in *Dombey*. Tolstoy read a great deal of Dickens' work, but I can find no direct evidence that he read this novel. Jack Simmons (*Railways: an Anthology*, London, Collins, 1991, p. 78) suggests that Tolstoy read and admired Trollope's *The Prime Minister* (1876) while he was writing *Anna Karenina*. Hence, he suggests, Anna's suicide seems to have been influenced by Lopez' death at Tenways Junction [Willesden] in Trollope's novel. Russian specialists suggest a different debt. Mistress to Tolstoy's neighbour A. H. Bibikov, in January 1872 Anna Piragova threw herself under a train after learning that Bibikov was to marry another woman. Tolstoy took the trouble to view her mangled corpse. See Turner, *Karenina Companion*, p. 4.

17 George Steiner, *Tolstoy or Dostoevsky: an Essay in Contrast*, London, Faber, 1959, p. 63. On 20 November (7 November, Old Style) 1910 Tolstoy died from pneumonia at the remote Astapovo railway junction, in Ryazan Province. For a fictional treatment of his death see Jay Parina, *The Last Station: a Novel of Tolstoy's Last Year*, London, HarperCollins, 1992. Railways loom in Tolstoy's and Dostoevsky's fictions, but that presence fades against Boris Pasternak's *Doctor Zhivago* (1958). *War and Peace* for the Bolshevik revolution, railway travel saturates *Zhivago*'s pages. See Elliot Mossman, 'Metaphors of history in *War and Peace* and *Doctor Zhivago*', in Gary Saul Morson (ed.), *Literature and History: Theoretical Problems and Russian Case Studies*, Palo Alto, CA, Stanford University Press, 1986, pp. 247–62; Roger B. Anderson, 'The railroad in *Doctor Zhivago*', *Slavic and East European Journal*, 31, 1987, pp. 503–19.

18 Sydney Schultze, 'Anna Karenina: a Structural Analysis', PhD dissertation, Indiana University, 1974; quoted in Gary R. Jahn, 'The image of the railroad in *Anna Karenina*', *Slavic and East European Journal*, 25, 1981, p. 1.

19 Nicholas Gogol's *Nevsky Prospect* (1835) established 'the primal scene in Petersburg literature and life: the confrontation between officer and clerk' (Berman, *All That Is Solid Melts Into Air*, p. 204). In Max Weber's terms the officer symbolised traditional domination, the clerk legal-rational domination. Embodied as Vronsky and Karenin, Anna is torn between these archetypes.

20 Tolstoy means 'connecting rod': mechanical engineering was not his strong point.

21 Leo Tolstoy, *Anna Karenina* [1877], translated by David Magarshack, New York, New American Library, 1961, p. 79. All quotations refer to this edition.

22 Tolstoy, *Anna Karenina*, p. 759.

23 *Ibid.*, p. 116.

24 Gary L. Browning, 'The death of Anna Karenina: Anna's share of the blame', *Slavic and East European Journal*, 30, 1986, p. 328.

25 Gary Saul Morson, 'Anna Karenina's omens', in Elizabeth Allen and Gary Saul Morson (eds), *Freedom and Responsibility: Essays in Honor of Robert Louis Jackson*, New Haven, Yale University Press, 1994, pp. 149–50.

26 While continuing Tolstoy's railway/peasant *leitmotif,* here Anna recalls a specific event – the dream about which she told Vronsky in book 4, chapter 3: '"And that something turned round and I saw that it was a peasant with a tousled beard, small and terrible. … He kept fumbling around, and muttering in French …': 'Il faut le battre le fer, le broyer, le pétrir …'"' For more on this dream see Morson, 'Anna Karenina's omens', pp. 146–8.

27 Robert Louis Jackson, 'Chance and design in *Anna Karenina*', in Peter Demetz, Thomas Greene and Lowry Nelson Jr (eds), *The Disciplines of Criticism*, New Haven, Yale University Press, 1968, p. 325.

28 See Turner, *Karenina Companion*, pp. 13–35 for the intense planning, drafting, redrafting and writing that produced the novel we read.

29 Turner, *Karenina Companion*, p. 134.

30 Raymond Williams, 'Lawrence and Tolstoy', *Critical Quarterly*, 2, 1960, p. 34. His argument runs parallel with F. R. Leavis' undated talk to the Cambridge University Slavonic Society: 'Anna Karenina: thought and significance in a great creative work', printed in Leavis, *Anna Karenina, and Other Essays*, London, Chatto & Windus, 1967, pp. 9–32. For a recent example of what Williams sought to bury see that exercise in limp Freudian psychotherapy, David Holbrook's *Tolstoy, Woman and Death: a Study of War and Peace and Anna Karenina*, Madison and Teaneck, Fairleigh Dickinson University Press, 1997. Both Williams and Holbrook were much influenced by Leavis.

31 Raymond Williams, *Modern Tragedy*, London, Chatto & Windus, 1966, p. 122.

32 Berman, *All That is Solid Melts into Air*, p. 193.

33 As built, separate lines linked Moscow with Kazan and with Nizhnii Novgorod.

34 J. N. Westwood, *A History of Russian Railways*, London, Allen & Unwin, 1964, pp. 21–5.

35 George Vernadsky *et al.* (eds), *A Source Book for Russian History from Early Times to 1917*, volume 2, New Haven and London, Yale University Press, 1972, p. 551.

36 Quoted in Jerome Blum, *In the Beginning: the Advent of the Modern Age: Europe in the 1840s*, New York, Scribners, 1994, p. 3.

37 Paul Dukes, *A History of Russia: Medieval, Modern, Contemporary, c882–1996*, third edition, Durham, NC, Duke University Press, 1998, p. 137. Not only Russian historians are at fault here. The railway historian C. Hamilton Ellis applauds (in *The Lore of Steam*, London, Hamlyn, 1984, p. 86) 'that Emperor of All the Russias, who is supposed to have decided a disputed survey by using his sword as a ruler for the line from St Petersburg to Moscow'.

38 John Pendleton, *Our Railways* [1894], quoted in Stuart Legg (ed.), *The Railway Book*, London, Hart-Davis, 1952, p. 66.

39 Richard Mowbray Haywood, 'The "ruler legend:" Tsar Nicholas I and the route of the St Petersburg/Moscow railway, 1842–3', *Slavic Review*, 37, 1978, p. 640.

40 Haywood, 'Ruler legend', p. 649; see also Westwood, *Russian Railways*, pp. 26–30. Mel'nikov was a military engineer who had been sent abroad to study American railway construction. Together with another soldier, Kraft, he oversaw detailed surveys, and technical aspects of the railway's construction.

41 Haywood, 'Ruler legend', p. 641.

42 Berman, *All That is Solid Melts into Air*, pp. 175–6.

43 Henry Gifford, 'Anna, Lawrence and "The Law"', *Critical Quarterly*, 1, 1959, p. 205.

44 Turner, *Karenina Companion*, p. 38.

45 For Marshall Berman (*All That Is Solid Melts Into Air*, p. 190), Nicholas I busied himself slamming shut the window to the west which Peter I struggled to open.

46 Dukes, *History of Russia*, pp. 63–7; Lindsey Hughes, *Russia in the Age of Peter the Great*, New Haven, Yale University Press, 1998.

47 Andrew Baruch Wachtel, *An Obsession With History: Russian Writers Confront the Past*, Palo Alto, CA, Stanford University Press, 1994, pp. 1–18.

48 'Actually, his ideology was so tame and so vague and so far from politics and, on the other hand, his art was so powerful, so tiger bright, so original and universal that it easily transcends the sermon. In the long run what interested him as a thinker were Life and Death, and after all no artist can avoid treating these themes': Nabukov, *Lectures*, pp. 137–8.

49 Thorlby, *Leo Tolstoy*, p. 3.

50 Like so many other mid- and late-nineteenth-century Russian intellectuals. 'How rich a treasure awaits the composer in the speech of the people', the populist Mussorgsky mused; 'so long that is, as any corner of the land remains to which the railway has not penetrated.' (Quoted in James H, Billington, *The Icon and the Axe: an Interpretive History of Russian Culture*, London, Weidenfeld & Nicolson, 1966, p. 407).

51 Billington, *Icon and Axe*, p. 384.

52 Baumgarten, 'Railway/reading/time', p. 81.

53 Andrew Wachtel, 'Death and resurrection in *Anna Karenina*', in Hugh McLean (ed.), *In the Shade of the Giant: Essays on Tolstoy*, Berkeley, University of California Press, 1989, p. 108. Berman (*All That is Solid Melts into Air*, p. 230) makes the Moscow–St Petersburg train 'a vivid symbol of dynamic modernity'.

54 Jackson, 'Change and design', pp. 326–7.

55 '[Peasants] are different from other Russians because they still retain what other Russians lost at the time of Peter', Donna Tussing Orwin tells us (in 'Children and peasant in Anna Karenina: from nature to culture', in Leo Tolstoy, *Anna Karenina: the Maude Translation*, edited by George Gibian, second edition, New York, Norton, 1995, p. 848). Back to Peter I, and his enthusiasm for western enlightenment. Orwin writes with specific reference to Orthodox Christianity, but her argument resonates more widely.

56 Peter Ulf Møller, *Postlude to The Kreutzer Sonata: Tolstoy and the Debate on Sexual Morality in Russian Literature in the 1890s*, Leiden, Brill, 1988. The connection with *What is Art?* is developed further in David Herman, 'Stricken by infection: art and adultery in *Anna Karenina* and *The Kreutzer Sonata*', *Slavic Review*, 56, 1997, pp. 15–36. Arguing that these three Tolstoy fictions offer ever more elaborate accounts of issues about art and adultery first raised in Pushkin's story 'Egyptian nights', Herman totally ignores railway motifs.

57   Leo Tolstoy, 'The Kreutzer sonata' [1899], in Tolstoy, *The Kreutzer Sonata, and Other Stories*, edited by Aylmer Maude, London, Oxford University Press, 1924, p. 299.

58   Tolstoy, 'Kreutzer Sonata', pp. 306–7.

59   Tolstoy, 'Kreutzer Sonata', p. 285.

60   In one persuasive account, Tolstoy's 'mean-spirited and inattentive' account of Beethoven's music in *The Kreutzer Sonata* combines an old European cultural belief that music (and, notably, violin music) was the devil's work, with Tolstoy's particular belief that Beethoven's romanticism opened the door to Richard Wagner. Tolstoy loathed Wagner's music, as he despised Wagner's personal licentiousness. See Ruth Rischin, '*Allegro tumultuosissimamente*: Beethoven in Tolstoy's fiction', in McLean, *Shade of the Giant*, pp. 43–51.

61   H. G. Wells, *Tono-Bungay* [1909], London, Collins, n.d., p. 338.

62   Quoted in A. V. Knowles, 'Russian views of *Anna Karenina*', *Slavic and East European Journal*, 22, 1978, p. 302; for a more recent statement of Turgenev's complaint see A. L. French, '*Anna Karenina*: Tolstoy's "Toryism",' *The Critical Review*, 22, 1980, pp. 21–31. Marshall Berman (*All That is Solid Melts into Air*, p. 192) argues that under Nicholas I's repression Petersburg 'acquired a reputation, which it never lost, as a strange, weird, spectral place', well expressed in Gogol's and Dostoevsky's fiction. Tolstoy rejects this metropolitan weirdness, among much else.

63   Leavis, 'Anna Karenina', p. 32. For his anathema on technologico-Benthamism see F. R. Leavis, *Nor Shall My Sword: Discourses on Pluralism, Compassion and Social Hope*, London, Chatto & Windus, 1972.

5

Railway life:
La Bête Humaine

Setting the scene

Writing in 1901, George Brandes declared that *The Kreutzer Sonata* treated 'the animal in Man'.[1] This phrase directs our attention not to Tolstoy's novella, but to a deeply scandalous novel written in another language: Émile Zola's *La Bête Humaine* [1890]. By general agreement among railway historians, this is the greatest railway novel ever written.[2] Unlike *Dombey* or *Anna Karenina*, here we are saved from having minutely to examine a handful of pages. Zola word-paints some set pieces – a train vainly fighting snow drifts, a driver taking his engine out of the Paris engine yard, the same driver stabling his engine at Havre, a big railway smash, a runaway train – but this entire 'train novel' treats 'railroad life'.[3] All major characters are firmly trammelled by this 'living organism stretching over northwestern France' as they travel up and down the Ouest Railway Company's main line.[4]

As was his practice, Zola prepared meticulously before writing this novel: his text renders down many thousand preliminary notes, now preserved at the Bibliothèque Nationale in three huge volumes. For almost ten years he collected newspaper clippings about railway accidents, paying particular attention to a terrible 1886 crash between two trains near Monte Carlo. He carefully studied police records for three murders. In the first, in 1860, a senior judge, Poinsot, was found dead in his compartment on a Bâle to Paris train. In the second, in 1886, the Prefect of Police for Eure, Barrême, was murdered on a Cherbourg to Paris express. The third case had no direct railway connection. In 1882 a jealous husband, Fenayrou, persuaded his wife to entice her lover to a retired country house, then forced her to help him murder that lover.[5] Unusually for a novelist writing about railways, Zola was careful to get technical details correct.[6] With official permission, he examined a wide range of Ouest railway facilities between Paris and Havre, noting floor plans from three stations. With clearance from the line's chief engineer, on 15 April 1889 he rode an express locomotive's footplate from the Gare Saint-Lazare to Mantes and back, noting precisely what happened on that bucketing, lurching platform.[7] Anatole France later might charge him with seeing what an engine driver sees, not seeing through an engine driver's eyes;[8] but, more than any other author, Zola depicts a life world immediately recognisable by railway staff.

La Bête Humaine is translated into English both as 'the human beast' and as 'the beast in Man'. Adopting the first sense, one English commentator confidently identified *la bête humaine* as 'Lison, Jacques' pet locomotive'.[9] That is an odd reading, but it has the virtue of pointing up Zola's appreciation for the close attachment which drivers and firemen forged with particular steam locomotives.[10] Jacques Lantier and Pecqueux, his fireman, care deeply for Lison, their beautiful express engine: just as skilled ploughmen care deeply for their work horses.[11] Lison becomes a real character, an iron horse. 'Galloping how she liked, gone crazy', she belts towards Paris one winter's morning. As snow thickens, she grows 'winded' and 'out of breath'. Charging drifted snow, 'she seemed to catch her breath in little gasps, like a nervous horse. She was shaken by violent gasps and reared, only kept going by the firm hand of her driver'. When snow-buried sleepers knock one of Lison's cylinders out of alignment, Lantier feels over her body as a horseman would feel his animal's flanks, noticing that 'she was wounded there'.[12] This wound proves serious. A spavined iron horse, Lison never recovers her full strength. Contriving that Lantier's train should crash, lovelorn Flore murders not only fifteen passengers but also this mechanical thoroughbred.

> Lison had heeled right over, and was losing steam through her open belly, through taps ripped off and broken tubes, in roaring blasts like the desperate gasps of a dying giant. A continuous mass of white vapour billowed forth from her in dense clouds along the ground, while the red-hot coals falling like the life-blood from her vitals added their black smoke. In the violence of the impact the chimney had been forced into the ground; at the point where it had taken the weight the frame was broken and both the frame-plates were bent. Like some monstrous steed ripped open by a gigantic horn, Lison lay with her wheels in the air, displaying her twisted coupling-rods, broken cylinders, smashed valve-gear with its eccentrics in one fearful wound gaping to the sky, through which her life was still issuing with a hiss of rage and despair'.[13]

No besotted railway enthusiast, Zola deploys precise knowledge about mechanical engineering for precise imaginative purposes.[14] Poor, beautiful Lison lies mortally wounded. No human character's death in this blood-soaked book shocks Jacques Lantier more than his iron horse's murder.

Pictures

'I remember having noticed a man in the Gare Saint-Lazare perched with his easel on a pile of crates', Hugues Le Roux recalled in 1889, twelve years after the event he described.

> I moved closer because I wanted to know who couldn't wait till he got to the first stop before hauling out his paints and putting up his umbrella. It was Claude Monet. He was doggedly painting the departing locomotives. He wanted to show how they looked as they moved through the hot air that shimmered around them. Though the station workers were in his way, he sat there patiently, like a hunter, brush at the ready, waiting for the moment when he could put paint to canvas. That's the way he always worked: clouds aren't any more obliging sitters than locomotives.[15]

Monet was busy working on one of the twelve railway paintings which he completed in early 1877. With permission from the Ouest Company's officers, he set up his easel on the Gare Saint-Lazare's cross platform, then moved down the line, passing under the Pont de l'Europe toward the Batignolles tunnel's multiple bore.[16] The Gare Saint-Lazare resonated with personal meanings for Monet. Here he had arrived in Paris as a boy, from Havre. Trains from here carried him, and his painter friends, to places (Bougival, Louveciennes, Argenteuil, Vétheuil, Giverny) where they painted and, intermittently, lived.[17]

Monet exhibited many Saint-Lazare paintings at the third Impressionist exhibition in April 1877; his image of the Auteil platform greeted visitors as they arrived.[18] Most visitors were impressed with his work. Among these was Émile Zola. A schoolfellow of Cézanne's in Aix-en-Provence, and later a friend to many of the Impressionists and other artists who used the Café Guerbois as their meeting place and watering hole,[19] Zola understood shifting Parisian art fashions intimately.[20] He was stunned by Monet's 'terrific views of train stations. You can hear the trains rumbling in, see the smoke billow up under the huge roofs'.[21] Prophetic words. Twelve years later, in the year when Le Roux recalled seeing Monet working at his easel, Zola described the view greeting Roubaud, an under station master at Havre, from a window in the Ouest Company's Parisian apartment block in the Impasse d'Amsterdam.

> Opposite, in this vapoury sunlight, the buildings in the rue de Rome seemed hazy, as though fading into air. To the left yawned the huge roofs spanning the station

5.1   Claude Monet, *Interior View of the Gare Saint-Lazare: the Auteuil Line,* 1877

with their sooty glass; the eye could see under the enormous main-line span, which was separated from the smaller ones, those of the Argenteuil, Versailles and Circle lines, by the buildings of the foot-warmer depot and the mails. To the right the Europe bridge straddled the cutting with its star of girders, and the lines could be seen emerging beyond and going on as far as the Batignolle tunnel. And right below the window, filling the whole space, the three double lines from under the bridge fanned out into innumerable branches of steel and disappeared under the station roofs. In front of the arches the three pointsman's posts looked like bare little gardens. Amid the confusion of carriages and engines crowding the lines, one big red signal shone through the thin daylight.[22]

Zola set his novel in the late 1860s, almost a decade before Monet set to work; but Roubaud's conspectus covers a scene remarkably similar to those recorded on Monet's canvases.[23]

According to Auguste Renoir, Monet's Gare Saint-Lazare paintings were designed to outface a critic's complaint that fog was no suitable subject for a painter. Defiantly, he set out to out-fog his earlier efforts. Abandoning early ideas – notably 'a scene of negroes fighting in a tunnel' – he settled on views of the Gare Saint-Lazare 'with smoke from the engines so that you can hardly see a thing'.[24] This anecdote suggests that atmosphere is the real subject in Monet's paintings. Smoke, steam and clouds drift across the picture space as the artist struggles to freeze evanescence. These paintings are vehicles 'for the study of light and shade, smoke and shape: an evocation of station atmosphere'.[25] Impression is all.

Railway life: illicit sex, bungled violence

Just like Zola's *plein air* word picture, perhaps? Many think so: but remember that 'big red signal' shining 'through the thin daylight'. Monet's *Gare Saint-Lazare: the Normandy Line Viewed from a Vantage Point Under the Pont de l'Europe* (1877) depicts Roubaud's Impasse d'Amsterdam building looming above the railway, with resting engines snoozing peacefully in the locomotive yard. Just below and to the right of this apartment block, a stark blob of solid red colour burns through the painting's brown/grey palette.

Claude Monet, *Gare Saint-Lazare: the Normandy Line Viewed from a Vantage Point under the Pont de l'Europe*, 1877   **5.2**

The impressionist picturesque is where we start in Zola's novel, not where we finish. Red for danger; red for blood.[26] Roubaud's peaceful conspectus is the last repose which this author allows his readers. Beautiful Séverine Roubaud soon arrives in the Impasse d'Amsterdam apartment, and lets slips to her husband that, some years earlier, she was seduced by her godfather (and, perhaps, her natural father) Grandmorin, an Ouest Company director and president of the Rouen law court. Maddened by jealousy and by masculine outrage at having been sold soiled goods, Roubaud forces Séverine to help him murder Grandmorin in a Havre train that evening. An off-duty engine driver, Jacques Lantier, witnesses this murder. He demands Séverine's sexual favours as his price for silence. Maddened by jealousy at this liaison, Flore Misard – a Normandy crossing-keeper's beefy daughter who mutely adores Lantier, her cousin – plans to destroy Lantier and Séverine in a train crash. She recruits Cabuche, a local ox-like carter, as her unwitting tool. Though the lovers survive this crash, fifteen passengers and lovely Lison die, and thirty-two passengers are injured. Contrite Flore kills herself beneath a train's wheels. Cabuche is jailed for Grandmorin's murder. Lantier and Séverine plan to kill Roubaud in a retired country house; but maddened Lantier kills Séverine instead. Accused of murdering his unfaithful wife, at last Roubaud confesses to Grandmorin's murder. This confession does not wash. Suspected of seeking public sympathy as a husband avenging his wife's adolescent seduction, Roubaud is sentenced to penal servitude for killing Séverine. Fighting over the sexual favours of his fireman Pecqueux's slatternly mistress, Philomène, the novel's last pages show Lantier tumbling Pecqueaux off their speeding locomotive's footplate. They unite in headless mateship under their train's wheels. The driverless express thunders onward, with railway staff scrambling to clear a path through ever more crowded suburban stations and goods yards. The novel stops; but readers appreciate that a huge and bloody crash lies beyond this book's back cover.

Summarised thus, Zola's novel seems melodramatic: a shilling shocker. Certainly he courted public outrage in *La Bête Humaine*, as in much else that he wrote. His translator's son recalled that 'such was the state of public opinion that it seemed impossible to produce even a bowdlerized version of that work in England'.[27] It was not just the violence that shocked English sensibilities in *La Bête Humaine*; it was Zola's insistence on mingling violence with sex. For Matthew Josephson, 'the book is drenched with blood and sexual aberrations.'[28] *Anna Karenina* linked railways with sex and death, but decorously. *La Bête Humaine* flaunted twisted connections. Lantier, Séverine, Roubaud, Pecqueax, Grandmorin, Philomène; all these characters display sexual habits sharply different, as that anonymous British matron said after seeing Sarah Bernhardt play Cleopatra, 'from the home life of our own dear Queen'. Even poor, frustrated Flore meets death in violent sex, striding composedly towards a speeding locomotive.

> Then, through some unexplained compulsion…[she] took off the scarf around her neck and opened her blouse until it was half off. The eye was turning into a blaze, an open furnace-door vomiting forth fire, the monster's breath could already be felt, steamy and hot, and the rumble of thunder was ever more deafening. Still she strode on, making straight for this blaze so as not to miss the engine, fascinated like a moth drawn to a flame. Even at the moment of the terrible impact, the very embrace, she drew herself up again as though, rising in a final urge to fight, she meant to seize the colossus and strike it down.[29]

Anna Karenina threw herself under a train at a wayside station. Flore chooses a tunnel. Schooled by post-Freudian commentators (who have a field day with *La Bête Humaine*[30]) we have no difficulty in understanding her end. Among other characters' orgasms, their *petits morts*, Flore's death stands out as murderous rape, with Flore a complicit victim.[31]

Stance

Focussing on Zola's characters' manifold sexual tics and peccadillos turns his novel into grist for Kraft-Ebbing's monographs. But morbid psychology fixes our attention on individual motivations. This meshes with much literary criticism's determination to make individual character delineation and development the measure for a novelist's excellence. *La Bête Humaine* cannot succeed on that criterion. Even Zola's major characters are flat and lifeless, no more than cardboard figures. Rutting and dying, these marionettes exist; they do not grow. But Zola was not trying to emulate George Eliot. His characters stand for broader groupings in a novel which, like its companions in the huge Rougon-Macquart cycle, seeks to turn fiction into social scientific investigations. Liberal humanists like F. W. J. Hemmings entirely miss Zola's point by turning *La Bête Humaine*'s aspersions on Second Empire justice into 'gentle irony'.[32] Twenty years after that regime collapsed, Zola's first French readers would remember that Monsieur Poinsot's murder on his Paris-bound train was rumoured to be connected with the mysterious disappearance of certain state papers in his possession. They would remember that Prefect Barrême, defenestrated from his Paris-bound train, was rumoured to be carrying a large sum in Secret Service money, and to enjoy a scandalous private life. For reasons of state, many cynics suggested, full explanations for neither railway murder could be tolerated in official circles.[33] Just, we see, like Président Grandmorin's death. A senior judge, a railway director, a man with excellent political connections, his private life could stand close investigation no better than Barrême's. Denizet, the Rouen examining judge, explores Grandmorin's murder competently enough; but political chicanery then intervenes. Determined to avoid scandal, Camy-Lamotte suppresses crucial evidence. Anticipating George Orwell's doubles-peak, the Ministry of Justice's secretary-general connives at flagrant injustice. Innocent Cabuche[34] carries the can for Grandmorin's death (and later, jointly with Roubaud, for Séverine's). Roubaud is brought to justice, but for killing his wife – which he did not do – rather than for killing Grandmorin. Subverted by money and by covert influence, the vaunted French legal system gets everything wrong. This may be irony, but of no gentle kind.

Inspired by contemporary medico-criminological paradigms (notably Lucas' *L'Hérédité Naturelle* (1850) and Cesare Lombroso's *The Criminal Man* (1876)[35]), Zola's Rougon-Macquart novel cycle requires readers to accept that moral taint can be inherited. Hence the reason why, for most commentators, Jacques Lantier is prime suspect for 'the beast in man'.[36] His rotten Macquart blood, not willed choice, generates Jacques' rising sexual frenzy as he stalks unknown women around northern French towns before murdering Séverine Roubaud under maddened genetic compulsion. Beyond this, Zola's novels explored major social issues on a vastly ambitious scale. Talking to Balzac's ear-lier *Comédie humaine* novel cycle, Zola gives us a panoptical survey of Second Empire French society under Notable rule. Industrialisation's widening gulf separates these two novel cycles. Contrasting Dostoevsky with Baudelaire, Marshall Berman distinguishes Russian 'modernism of underdevelopment … forced to build on fantasies and dreams of modernity' from progressive mod-ernisation in Britain and, after 1840, in France: 'Marx's factories and railways, Baudelaire's boulevards'.[37] Anatomising French modernity, Zola explored Marx's and Baudelaire's world. In novels like *L'Assommoir* and *La Terre* he studied down the social scale. *Germinal* forced bourgeois readers to watch coal miners struggling to defend and assert proletarian rights against limited liability joint-stock mining companies: that classic modern corporate form, refined to facilitate railway companies' vast appetite for capital. Elsewhere, Zola cast his sardonic eye upward to other modern institutions: in *L'Argent* to the Bourse, male racetrack for bulls and bears, for innocents and crooks; in *Au Bonheur des Dames* to the department store, novel temple for female consumers gripped by commodity fetishism.[38]

'Show all the time the stream of passengers on their travels', Zola reminded himself in his preliminary notes for *La Bête Humaine*.

> Not only the increase of trade, but the exchange of ideas, the transformation of nations, the mingling of races, the advance towards a world-wide unification. And against this background, this mechanical to-and-fro of the trains and its social and intellectual outcome, show, by my mysterious and agonising drama, the *status quo* of emotions, man fundamentally a savage.[39]

Berg and Martin suggest that Zola's 'fascination with systems, machines and movement' made it inevitable that he would write this novel.[40] This is half correct. Writing a crime novel and a railway novel had been in Zola's mind for many years.[41] Sitting down to plan his saga in 1868, Zola decided that twenty books would form a canvas sufficiently broad to accommodate the many topics which he wished to tackle. A detailed family tree entwined clean Rougons with tainted Macquarts, providing a structure from which he could select major characters for each book. But by the time when Zola started writing *La Bête Humaine*, over twenty years later, this plan was fraying. Zola had almost exhausted his stock of mad Macquarts. Freshly minted for this book, Jacques Lantier had to be grafted on an existing family tree, messing up details in earlier works. More urgently, Zola was running short of novel slots. After spreading himself expansively in earlier years, he found himself approaching his saga's conclusion bearing more topics than spaces. He could have expanded beyond twenty novels, of course; but that would have been such an *un-French* solution, offending the decimal system's formal purity. Instead, Zola chose to conflate his planned crime and railway novels. For Philip Walker this solution works beautifully: 'Its two main subjects, crimes of passion, the railroads, go perfectly together'.[42] Others are less convinced. For F. W. J. Hemmings, *La Bête Humaine*'s preliminary sketches promised a major work, with relentless technical progress crashing against obdurate human imperfectability: 'But his main theme became overgrown by a tangle of collateral ones, through which it rises to view only in occasional episodes and tableaux'.[43] In this 'bivalent, oppositional, almost hybrid text'[44] crime gets in the railway novel's way. Blood clogs the main line.

Scraping away the crime novel's crusted gore, again and again in *La Bête Humaine* we watch personal troubles collide with social issues, as imperfect humanity crashes against technical progress. Planning his novel, Zola centred most action in three sites: terminal railway complexes at Havre and at Saint-Lazare, Paris; and, between them, the Misard family's La Croix-de-Maufras crossing-keeper's house. The railway line is no less important metaphorically, linking his major interests to plot details.[45] Insistently disciplining human action, 'railway time' obtrudes persistently through the finished work's texture.[46] Clearly enough, Zola's interest in the railway lay deeper than a concern for striking local colour. As he was perfectly well aware, the Second Empire, like Victorian Britain, installed the railway as modernity's central symbol. Behind only Britain as a European economic power in 1770, the 1789 Revolution and its aftermath greatly disrupted France's economy. Not until around 1840 was this deficit restored, permitting French industrialisation to gather pace. The conventional measure for this mid-century acceleration is the railway network's spread.[47] When Napoleon III proclaimed the Second Empire in 1852, France boasted 3,992 km of railway line. When he abdicated eighteen years later, after the military débâcle at Sedan, this figure had multiplied more than six-fold, to 25,494 km. State policy governing British railway promotion always had been resolutely liberal: companies could build which lines they chose, subject to parliamentary oversight protecting private property rights. Things were different across the Channel. There, central state authorities determined the proper shape for France's railway network, then licensed private companies to construct and operate particular network segments.[48] State direction and articulation made French railways much more directly political creatures than in Britain, important nodes in a web of power and influence extending from Paris to enmesh every settlement and every citizen in patron-client relations. Hence, of course, disreputable events following from Grandmorin's murder. Zola shows us mid-century French public life hollowed out through rottenness, with Notables' money and influence corrupting democratic political rights and legal due process. The Second Empire (but not corruption in French public and economic life) died in the Franco- Prussian War, destroyed by ruthlessly modern Prussian military efficiency. As Lantier's and Pecqueux's mutilated corpses lie in each other's arms on the four-foot way, their abandoned train roars onward. Heavily laden with drunken soldiery, cattle trucks echo to patriotic songs. These songs rise louder as engine no. 608, its firebox loaded with fresh coal by drunken Pecqueaux, accelerates this troop train towards disaster. *Élan* will not suffice. Should they escape death in a messy railway accident, these soldiers will meet their Waterloo at Sedan. Like that runaway train, France's Second Empire is doomed.[49]

More pictures

Claude Monet's Gare Saint-Lazare paintings might have impressed many visitors to the third Impressionist exhibition in 1877, but the loudest plaudits went to a couple of Gustave Caillebotte's oils: *Paris Street, Rainy Day*, and *The*

Pont de l'Europe. As a minor counterpoint to the main figures in this latter work – a bourgeois man half turning to a woman who might be his wife, his mistress, or a trawling prostitute – a working man lounges against a huge lattice truss supporting the four-armed Europe bridge as it spans Saint-Lazare's station throat. He stares downward, fascinated by this mechanical world laid out for his delectation. Caillebotte's later *On the Pont de l'Europe* (c 1876-1880) shifts the viewpoint, but concentrates our attention more firmly on the railway's male, engineered world. Now a top-hatted bourgeois joins a blue-coated artisan in gazing, entranced, through the bridge's girders. Clearly enough, Monet was not the only male 'Batignolles group' artist who liked painting the railway's machine ensemble.[50]

Prominent among these was Edouard Manet. Like other local artists, he knew Émile Zola well. When Manet's work faced widespead public derision it was Zola, in 1867, who sprang most effectively to his defence in print. Manet expressed his gratitude by painting Zola's portrait the following year. Like Claude Monet, Manet painted a picture usually known today as *La Gare Saint-Lazare* (1873). That was not the artist's title: he preferred *Le Chemin de Fer*. One might expect this title to draw intense interest from critics interested in railway painting. Not a bit of it. Hamilton Ellis' survey prints images of far more railway paintings than most people would imagine ever existed, but he does not reproduce Manet's oil: 'The passage of a train behind a mother and child in the foreground', his text sniffs, 'is indicated only by billowing clouds of steam.'[51] How crass to produce a railway painting without a single visible train to seduce the eye!

As we saw earlier, most art historians assume that Monet sought to capture evanescence in his Saint-Lazare paintings, as smoke, steam and clouds drifted across the picture space. For Hamilton Ellis all impressionist painters scorned the railway as 'a source of drama or incident; for them it remained a purely objective visual phenomenon'.[52] Narrowing the focus, John Rewald insists that Monet 'discovered and probed the pictorial aspects of machinery but did not comment on its ugliness or usefulness or beauty, nor upon its relationship to man'.[53] But, like Zola, Monet was a keen amateur photographer. Both men often turned their camera lenses toward railway subjects; both liked simply to watch trains pass their lineside homes.[54] Zola was quite clear that railways' significance ruptured his own time's aesthetic categories: 'You modern poet, you detest the modern life', he wrote to Paul Bourget. 'You go against your gods, you do not accept frankly your age. Why do you find a *gare* ugly? It is very beautiful, a *gare*'.[55]

5.3   Edouard Manet, *Le Chemin de Fer*, 1873

Just like Edouard Manet's *Le Chemin de Fer*, the work which baffled visitors to the 1874 Salon. Writing with benefit from a century's hindsight, Peter Gay found this bafflement puzzling. He makes this a simple painting:

> The young woman, the little girl and the little dog are a commentary on [modernity's] pleasures and its possibilities. The puppy sleeps, oblivious to the noise, the smell, the smoke of the train. The girl is rivetted to her spot; she is watching the passing train, possibly with interest or, more probably, with the calm indifference that habituation brings. The young woman sits like a monument to serenity, looking at the world with her clear dark eyes.[56]

Why should this idyll outrage Manet's contemporaries? Because it is no idyll. Stuffed with contemporary references, *Le Chemin de Fer* is much more complicated than Gay realised. 'One day, on my way back from Versailles, I climbed into the locomotive beside the driver and the fireman', Manet told Georges Jeanniot. 'Those two men were a magnificent sight, so calm and collected, so staunch! It's an appalling job, and they and men like them are the real heroes of our time.'[57] Approach it through this anecdote, and Manet's painting echoes

Zola's praise (in *Germinal*, *La Bête Humaine* and other places) for industrial workers' disciplined labour. At one time Manet intended to honour this labour by straighforwardly painting a locomotive and its footplate crew, 'to illustrate the theme of man and machine':[58] one major element in *La Bête Humaine*, of course. Instead, he gave us the enigmatic *La Chemin de Fer*. Juliet Wilson-Barreau guides us to buried issues in this image.[59] That billowing locomotive steam in the picture's 'blank centre' forces us to concentrate on two fore-grounded figures, on the bars constraining them, and on three background vignettes: a railway pointsman's hut to the lower right, one of the Pont de l'Europe's many buttresses to the upper right, and – enjambed in the top left-hand corner – the doorway to Manet's new studio. Facing the viewer sits Victorine Meurent, the beautiful professional model who Manet painted so many times (most scandalously in two Salon pictures where she appears nude: *Le Déjeuner sur l'Herbe* (1863) and *Olympia* (1865)). Persuasively, Wilson-Barreau suggests that the young girl standing alongside Victorine evokes the vir-ginal female figure in Pierre Puvis de Chavannes' *Hope* (1871–2) and its many imitators. Facing the viewer, Chavanne's maiden symbolised French civilisation rising, Phoenix-like, from the ashes of the Franco-Prussian War and the Commune. In Manet's painting her broad blue, bow-tied sash threatens to lift her from the ground, like an angel's wings. She, Victorine and we share a common space, railled off by thick black iron bars from the railway and its furious, steamy energy.[60] Settled against those formidable railings, experienced Victorine[61] looks at us – and, beyond us, to the past: this is the last time Manet will paint her. In company with Manet and his maiden we look forward to France's new world, symbolised by the modern railway's machine ensemble. Getting there will not be easy: those thick bars represent a real challenge. But Manet nails his colours to the future's mast. France will rise again, in a new and better world. Just like his angelic maiden reaching out to embrace the railway's modernity, Manet will embrace the modern world in his new studio behind that enjambed door at 4 rue Saint-Pétersbourg. Less stridently, we see that this enigmatic painting anticipates Marinetti's Futurist manifesto. Expressing a single idea in extravagant words, Marinetti's technological commitment thrusts forward like a speeding bullet. Mingling regret for an old, dead France with enthusiasm for the new France gestating as he sets brush to canvas, Manet speaks both to loss and to gain in this, the first painting which he completed after 1870–1's traumatic events. Zola's *La Bête Humaine* allegorised the old Second Empire rushing to destruction at Sedan. Manet's *Le Chemin de Fer* alle-gorises hope budding under the new Third Republic. Details in his account might be over- simple, but Peter Gay's broad assessment is sure footed: this painting is 'Manet's manifesto in behalf of modernity … I know of no nine-teenth-century painting that celebrates modernity more unreservedly than this.'[62]

Moving pictures

Like so many other Dickens works, *Dombey and Son* was turned into a stage play in his time; but it seems never to have attracted practitioners from the twentieth-century's novel art form, movies. For sound commercial reasons, Anna's story from *Anna Karenina* has been filmed again and again (with Levin's story usually getting short shrift). As sex coupled to death on those Russian railway lines, Anna's decision to choose illicit passion over marital fidelity always was warranted to soak at least three handkerchiefs per female cinema patron. And in any 'chick flick' (as my daughters disparage them), tears equal profits. The latest movie version – Bernard Rose's *Anna Karenina* (1997), with Sophie Marceau playing feisty Anna as a droopy victim – exemplifies Hollywood's current idea of what a bankable women's movie looks like. The standard by which film history will judge it inadequate reaches back to Julian Duvivier's 1947 British film with Vivien Leigh and Ralph Richardson; and, overtopping that, to Clarence Brown's 1935 Hollywood movie with Greta Garbo and Frederic March.[63] With northern ice barely melting under passion's heat, Garbo might have been born to play Anna Karenina.[64] Female leads made or ruined these movies.[65] Who remembers Duvivier or Brown today? That Sean Bean's Vronsky lingers longer in the memory than Sophie Marceau's Anna damns Rose's movie.

La Bête Humaine has fared better than this. In 1954 Fritz Lang gave Zola's novel the Hollywood treatment. Played by Glenn Ford, here the Lantier-figure becomes a railroad engineer newly returned from war service in Korea. Unable to settle easily back in civilian life, he conducts a disastrous affair with Gloria Grahame around the Southern Pacific Railroad's yards and stations.[66] Since diesels have supplanted steam locomotives on this line, railway machinery no longer evokes organic emotions: a throbbing diesel locomotive is a soulless beast when compared with Lison's quivering iron horse. Zola's sardonic social analysis cannot survive shifting the movie's setting from Second Empire France to 1950s California. These matters apart, Lang cleaves rather closely to the novel's spirit. His movie opens 'with a long sequence documenting the inflexible itineraries of trains on their strict metal tracks – a diagram of predestining fate'.[67] Convinced that Zola's title invited them to market bestiality (they had not read the novel, of course), Lang's producers proposed a weak pun: *The End of the Line*.[68] He roared that '"Zola wanted to show that every human being is a beast"',[69] but Lang's protest was hopeless. Hollywood moguls branded his movie with a pruriently titillating title, *Human Desire*.

Views differ on this movie's excellence. Other directors liked it. On first release, Lindsay Anderson and François Truffaut (on at least three different occasions) reviewed *Human Desire* warmly.[70] Modern critics divide. For Tony Bilbow this is 'Fritz Lang at his most detached and unsentimental – in other words, at his best. His examination of the characters is almost clinical, as cold and impersonal as the railway yards against which this chilling story is set.'[71] Leslie Halliwell demurs, making Lang's movie 'A drab and unattractive remake of *La Bête Humaine*.'[72] A remake of Zola's novel? No: Halliwell judges Lang against Jean Renoir's 1938 movie. Echoing liberal humanist literary critics' complaints about Zola's cardboard characters, Halliwell does not rate Renoir's film highly. 'Curious melodrama with strong visual sequences', he complains, 'flawed by its ambivalent attitude to its hero-villain.'[73] That is not a common view. Fritz Lang admired Renoir's movie, preferring it to his own version.[74] For Leo Braudy, among more than sixty attempts to film Zola's fiction up to 1969, only Renoir's movies (*Nana* in 1926, *La Bête Humaine* twelve years later) can stand alongside the original fiction – because only he understands and appreciates important ambiguities in Zola's naturalism.[75] Today, Renoir's *La Bête Humaine* would find a place in every critic's list of the top half dozen railway movies ever made.[76] It also figures in broader evaluations of Renoir's career as a director. These discussions have as much to do with politics as with aesthetics.

A famous anecdote insists that Jean Gabin – contemporary French cinema's leading man, whose raffish accent and calculatedly rough demeanour made him an ideal Jacques Lantier – badgered Jean Renoir to make this movie because he, Gabin, ached to drive a steam locomotive.[77] In an unguarded moment Renoir confessed that he had been no less keen to play trains.[78] Certainly his movie's astonishing thirty-one-shot opening sequence – as Lison rockets towards Havre, and thunderous footplate noise forces Lantier to communicates with Pecqueaux almost entirely through gestures – suggests that everybody involved in making this film thoroughly enjoyed playing trains. Nothing here comes from the studio. Instead, hair-raisingly dangerous location camera work offers movie patrons a gripping sense of the exhilaration and expertise, the dirt, danger, noise and fatigue, that came with driving and stoking a hard-running steam locomotive.[79] But providing industrial *frisson* for comfortably circumstanced cinema patrons was not the only thing on Jean Renoir's mind. In the thirties his movies – including *La Grande Illusion* (1937) and *La Règle du Jeu* (1939), cinematic monuments revered today in regular art-house showings – always dragged a political undertow against surface narratives. Renoir firmly supported the French Popular Front, uniting socialists with communists against a common fascist threat. This Front died in 1938, just as he prepared to direct *La Bête Humaine*. Following Louis Althusser's method, Christopher Faulkner claims that this movie shows Renoir trimming his personal politics as French high politics shifted. In this reading, with his trust for progressive class action evaporated, Renoir falls back on bourgeois romantic fatalism: 'Lantier's class definition and his occupation as an engine-driver are socially irrelevant to his psychological state. The film's principal setting, the railway yards at Le Havre, is atmospheric rather than exemplary of a social condition.'[80] Back to impressionism and bourgeois mystification. Back to fog. For Faulkner, against its' *auteur*'s intentions, *La Bête Humaine* shows a window of opportunity to press for social change closing in 1938.[81] That is its only significance.

This is facile. All Renoir's movies from the late 1930s pivot on a murder.[82] In *La Bête Humaine* he mutes Zola's scabrous attack on judicial corruption, boiling down the 'judicial novel' to thirteen linked shots. Other things are reduced, too: Flore's part in the movie's action withers to a twenty-shot sequence.[83] One effect of this condensation is to highlight the Roubaud/Séverine/Lantier triangle. Set against Simone Simon's sensuous fragility as Séverine, Jean Gabin's louche sex appeal underscores the screenplay's attention to this emotional triangle. But condensation's second effect, signalled in Renoir's bravura opening sequence on that bucking locomotive's footplate, is to rivet our attention on the railway and its servants.[84] If, as Hemmings suggests, Zola's weakness for extraneous subplots seduced him from writing a great, spare novel which smashed engineered perfection four-square against human imperfectibility, then one might argue that Renoir's movie set Zola back on the right (rail)road.

Like Manet in *Le Chemin de Fer*, Zola believed that a less unsatisfactory new world would arise from the old world's smash. Comfortably manipulating grand abstractions, preening themselves *en fête*, modern French notables appropriated Zola – once they could be confident that his historical project had expired. As the 1955 Modernisation Plan anticipated that railways in Britain would move from steam to diesel traction, Paul Jennings suggested that British Railways would establish a Romance Department to keep steam's cultural memory green. 'Over the centuries there will develop, at Euston, a sort of Tabernacle of Steam', he predicted, where one holy, splendid, symbolic National Steam Train will be kept. On special occasions it will roll through the streets of London on special lines. It will go to Buckingham Palace for the Changing of the Guard; it will take conventions of foreign scholars to the British Museum and guests to the Royal Academy for the annual dinner; and it will lead the Lord Mayor's Show, that the plumes of steam may add their tradition to the ancient stones of London'.[85]

Life imitates whimsy, but hyperreally. Paul Jennings' National Steam Train provided the climax for a procession far grander that any which he expected, but not in London. 'Since history likes great men', Ginette Vincendeau tells us (and, given his unflattering portrait of Napoleon Bonaparte in *War and Peace*, she will be in big trouble if Leo Tolstoy is listening),

> it is not surprising that *La Bête Humaine*, in which three of the greatest names in French literature and cinema joined forces, has become emblematic in French culture. A lifelike wooden replica of *La Lison*, Jacques Lantier's steam engine, was the final exhibit in the three hours parade down the Champs Elysée that marked the 200th anniversary of the French Revolution. Driven by a Gabin lookalike, the model was called upon to evoke an idea of the French proletariat visualised by Renoir in 1938, dramatically shaped by Zola in 1890, but clearly born on Bastille Day in 1789.[86]

That last phrase is remarkably confident, cutting like Alexander's sword through ever-thickening historical dispute about who did what to whom, and why, on 14 July 1789 – if that's when some of it (or all of it) really happened. Goodbye, as Fritz Lang's diesel-powered *Human Desire* suggested, to the steam railway. Goodbye, as Andre Gorz and the bicentenary's wooden Lison suggested, to the proletariat as history's agent.[87] Goodbye to the railway as modernity's epitome? That is a question which we will not be equipped to answer until this book's conclusion. Before that, we must track relationships between texts, railways and modernity in some very different British locations.

Notes

1 Quoted in Peter Ulf Møller, *Postlude to The Kreutzer Sonata: Tolstoj and the Debate on Sexual Morality in Russian Literature in the 1890s*, Leiden, Brill, 1988, p. 1.

2 Jeffrey Richards and John M. MacKenzie, *The Railway Station: a Social History*, Oxford, Oxford University Press, 1986, p. 340; Nicholas Faith, *The World the Railways Made*, London, Bodley Head, 1990, p. 49; Jack Simmons, *The Victorian Railway*, London, Thames & Hudson, 1991, pp. 217–18.

3 Marian S. Robinson, 'Zola and Monet: the poetry of the railway', *Journal of Modern Literature*, 10, 1983, p. 64; Matthew Josephson, *Zola and his Time*, London, Gollancz, 1929, p. 344.

4 William J. Berg and Laurey K. Martin, *Émile Zola Revisited*, New York, Twayne, 1992, p. 31; J. W. Scott, 'Realisme et realité dans *La Bête Humaine*: Zola et les chemins de fer', *Revue d'Histoire Litteraire de la France*, 63, 1963, pp. 635–43. The Ouest Line from Paris to Havre was surveyed by Joseph Locke, once George Stephenson's assistant. It was constructed by the greatest Victorian civil engineering contractor, Thomas Brassey. (See Arthur Helps, *Life and Labours of Mr Brassey*, fourth edition, London, Bell and Daldy, 1873, pp. 54–73.) Locke arranged that drivers on this line should work from the left side of the locomotive's cab, in the usual British manner. Other French railways drove from the right. This made the Ouest line interestingly ambiguous as a symbol for the French nation. No literary critic notices this point, but Julian Barnes exploits it adroitly in his short story 'Junction'. See Barnes, *Cross Channel*, London, Cape, 1996, pp. 21–42.

5 Martin Kanes, *Zola's La Bête Humaine: a Study in Literary Creation*, Berkeley and Los Angeles, University of California Press, 1962, pp. 12–13, 21–3.

6 One tiny example: twenty years before Zola wrote, in the period when *La Bête Humaine* is set, Ouest engines 'still used such Heath Robinsonish devices as the Furness lubricator, by which oil in a container on the upper side of each single out-side cylinder is drawn through a small valve in the cylinder wall which during the exhaust stroke opens about 1/16", closing automatically again on compression. On *Lison*, which Jacques Lantier drove with such artistry, the valve-gear (apparently that devised by the Belgian engineer Walschaert) happened to be peculiarly suscep-tible to fine adjustment, though – as Lantier was never tired of lamenting – *Lison* was "heavy on oil". (Of course, the Furness lubricator was partly responsible for that:)' Alec Brown, translator's 'Introduction' to Émile Zola, *The Beast in Man*, London, Elek, 1969, pp. vi–vii. Brown does not explain why Lantier should find Lison's thirst for oil so lamentable: the brute material fact that many nineteenth-century railway companies calculated how much coal and oil a particular journey should consume, then deducted excess charges from drivers' wages.

7 Alan Schom, *Émile Zola: a Bourgeois Rebel*, London, Macdonald and Queen Anne Press, 1987, pp. 122–3. For details about Zola's technical preparation see Kanes, *Zola's La Bête Humaine*, pp. 237–48.

8 Quoted in F. W. J. Hemmings, *Émile Zola*, Oxford, Clarendon Press, 1953, p. 220.

9 Josephson, *Zola and his Time*, p. 344.

10 Thus Max Carrados notes a driver's 'bulldog-like devotion to his favourite 538': Ernest Bramah, 'The Knight's Cross signal problem', in Peter Haining (ed.), *Murder on the Railways*, London, Orion, 1996, p. 184.

11 George Ewart Evans, *The Horse in the Furrow*, London, Faber & Faber, 1960; Ian Carter, *Farm Life in North East Scotland, 1840–1914: the Poor Man's Country*, second edition, Edinburgh, John Donald, 1997; Stephen Caunce, *Amongst Farm Horses: the Horselads of East Yorkshire*, Stroud, Sutton, 1991.

12 Émile Zola, *La Bête Humaine* [1890], translated by Leonard Tancock, Harmondsworth, Penguin, 1977, pp. 189–202, pp. 215–16. All quotations are taken from this edition.

13 Zola, *La Bête Humaine*, p. 293.

14 André Possot, 'Thèmes et fantasmes de la machine dans *La Bête Humaine*', *Les Cahiers Naturalistes*, 57, 1983, pp. 104–15 explores Zola's mechanical analogies in considerable detail.

15 Hugues Le Roux, 'Silhouettes parisiennes. L'exposition de Claude Monet', *Gil Blas*, 3 March 1889, pp. 1–2, quoted in John House, *Monet: Nature into Art*, New Haven, Yale University Press, 1986, p. 137.

16 Robinson, 'Zola and Monet', pp. 57–62 treats the cross-platform paintings in detail; Juliet Wilson-Bareau, *Manet, Monet and the Gare Saint-Lazare*, New Haven, Yale University Press, 1998, pp. 106–25 escorts us all the way to the Batignolles tunnel.

17 Stephan Koja, *Claude Monet*, Munich, Prestel, 1996, pp. 66–7. Getting that right, Koja then gets other things wrong. The Pont de l'Europe straddled the Gare Saint-Lazare's main lines, not (as he claims) 'a siding'. He prints a photograph purporting to show the main station; actually it shows the goods shed flanking the Normandy line's arrival platform.

18 Wilson-Barreau, *Manet, Monet*, p. 105. The number of Saint-Lazare views exhibited at this exhibition is contested, ranging between five and ten. See Wilson-Barreau, *Manet, Monet*, p. 188, note 83.

19 Kanes, *Zola's La Bête Humaine*, p. 43.

20 Set in the Parisian art world, Zola's novel *L'Oeuvre* (1886) deftly anatomises contemporary styles and trends. See the conference papers collected in Jean-Max Gisieu and Alison Hilton (eds), *Émile Zola and the Arts*, Washington, Georgetown University Press, 1988.

21 Émile Zola in *La Sémaphore de Marseille*, 19 April 1877.

22 Zola, *La Bête Humaine*, p. 19.

23 The Gare Saint-Lazare changed little in these years. Rebuilt for the third time in 1867, the next major rebuild would not come until 1886. See Wilson-Bareau, *Manet, Monet*, pp. 70, 111.

24 Jean Renoir, *Renoir, My Father*, Boston, Little Brown, 1962, pp. 174–5; C. Hamilton Ellis, *Railway Art*, Boston, New York Graphic Society, 1977, p. 96.

25 Richards and MacKenzie, *Railway Station*, pp. 327–8. See also Simmons, *Victorian Railway*, p. 217; Koja, *Claude Monet*, p. 67. For Rev A. W. V. Mace (in H. A. Vallance (ed.), *The Railway Enthusiast's Bedside Book*, London, Batsford, 1966, p. 72). 'No great detail is to be found in his paintings … but they are full of railway atmosphere'.

26 Much later, another character looks at this view one winter's night. From the window she watches the Havre express arrive, 'a dark, crawling mass, with the bright flame of its headlight cutting a swathe through the darkness, and she watched it disappear under the bridge, its three rear lights staining the snow with blood'. Zola, *La Bête Humaine*, p. 220.

27 Ernest A. Vizetelly, *Émile Zola: Novelist and Reformer*, London, Bodley Head, 1934, p. 315.

28 Josephson, *Zola and his Times*, p. 344.

29 Zola, *La Bête Humaine*, p. 306.

30 For Gilles Deleuze ('Introduction à *La Bête Humaine*', in Zola, *Les Oeuvres Complèts d'Émile Zola*, Paris, Denöel, edited by Henri Mitterand, vol 6, pp. 13–21), Zola sets eros struggling with thanatos. Philippe Bonnefis, 'L'inénerrable même', *CN*, 48, 1974, pp. 125–40, prefers scotophilia. James J. Barron, 'On the track(s) of desire in Zola's *La Bête Humaine*: riding the rails with Jacques Lacan', *Degre Second: Studies in French Literature*, 10, 1986, pp. 31–8, vigorously tops and tails Zola's first chapter to make it fit Lacan's mirror stage.

31 A simpler explanation exists for this suicide's tunnel setting: Zola always was scared of dark, enclosed spaces. See Kanes, *Zola's La Bête Humaine*, pp. 9–10; William J. Berg and Laurey K. Martin, *Emile Zola Revisited*, New York, Twayne, 1992, p. 32. In this century, mundane Freudian interpretations turn train and tunnel into phallus and vagina with suspicious facility. Ludovic Kennedy ('Introduction', to Kennedy (ed.), *A Book of Railway Journeys*, London, Collins, 1988, p. xx), finds 'affinity between the womb and the [train's] steel cylinder'. Donovan Grant prepares to assassinate James Bond as the Paris-bound Orient Express enters the Simplon tunnel. Fellow passengers ride the train comfortably, oblivious to this drama. 'And, all the while, just down the corridor, death was riding with them down the same dark hole, behind the same great Diesel, on the same hot rails' (Ian Fleming, *From Russia With Love* [1957], London, Pan, 1959, p. 198). Which *hot rails*? We must imagine Fleming cooling off under his cold shower after writing this passage. Whenever Trevor Howard and Celia Johnson meet on a railway platform or in a railway buffet as they conduct their remarkably constipated English affair in David Lean's movie *Brief Encounter* (1946), a West Coast main line express thunders through the station. Not subtle. Much later, in late 1993, a television commercial advertising a young person's railcard was banned after strong public protest. This ad's voiceover enjoined young folk to travel by train to meet those whom they loved. Its fast-cutting visuals showed nothing but diesel multiple unit trains shooting rapidly in and out of tunnels. Backbench Conservative members roared that licentious British Rail exploited vulnerable adolescents here, encouraging premarital sex for corporate profit. Curiously enough, these train/penis and tunnel/vagina connections draw no warrant from Freud himself. His earliest discussions of railway travel had to do with 'railway brain' and 'railway spine', those forgotten nineteenth-century post-traumatic ailments: see Sigmund Freud, *The Standard Edition of the Complete Psychological Works of Sigmund Freud*, edited by James Strachey and Anna Freud, London, Hogarth Press, 1953–1974, vol. 1, pp. 12, 51–3; Wolfgang Schivelbusch, *The Railway Journey: Trains and Travel in the Nineteenth Century*, New York, Urizen, 1977, pp. 135–6; Michael Trimble, *Post-Traumatic Neurosis: from Railway Spine to Whiplash*, New York, Wiley, 1981; Ralph Harrington, 'The neuroses of the railway', *History Today*, 44/7, July 1994, pp. 15–21. Railways find no place in the book where Tory testosterone theory would suggest that we must find them: Freud's *On the Interpretation of Dreams* (1900). Havelock Ellis (*The World of Dreams*, second edition, London, Constable, 1926, p. 81) does describe one railway dream, but roots it in a rattling bedroom window and slight indigestion, not the Oedipus complex. In *The Psychopathology of Everyday Life* (1901) Freud explored three cases where people

missed trains, or caught the right train on the wrong day, because they unconsciously wished not to meet obligations to which their conscious minds were committed (Freud, *Works*, vol. 8, pp. 226–8. His famous case study of 'Little Hans', so central to Freud's developing ideas about infantile sexuality, returned him to earlier work on railway spine. Here, too, trains' psychological significance lies in motion, not symbolism: 'The shaking produced by driving in carriages and later by railway-travel exercises such a fascinating effect upon older children that every boy, at any rate, has at one time or other in his life wanted to be an engine driver or a coachman. It is a puzzling fact that boys take such an extraordinarily intense interest in things associated with railways, and, at the age at which the production of phantasies is most active (shortly before puberty) use those things as the nucleus of a symbolism that is peculiarly sexual. A compulsive link of this kind between railway-travel and sexuality is clearly derived from the pleasurable character of the sensation of movement' (Freud, *Works*, vol. 7, p. 202). Dread for railway travel here signifies repression, that blockage on the psychological journey to satisfactorily adult sexuality. Freud himself entertained lifelong fears about missing trains, and about being caught up in railway accidents. Interestingly, Sander L. Gilman (*Freud, Race and Gender*, Princeton, NJ, Princeton University Press, 1993, pp. 125–130 ascribes these fears to status anxiety, to Freud's marginality in imperial Vienna as a child from eastern Jewry's declassé social world. When he interpreted Frau Emma von M's railway phobia as a manifestation of her unconscious desire to escape Freud's therapeutic clutches (Freud, *Works*, vol. 2, p. 84), may we not diagnose a bad case of transference?

32 Hemmings, *Émile Zola*, p. 217.

33 Kanes, *Zola's La Bête Humaine*, pp. 22–3. J. J. Connington's excellent *The Two Tickets Puzzle* (London, Gollancz, 1930, p. 96) shows us a British malefactor mugging up famous train murders for tips about how to dispose of his own victim in a railway carriage. He is fully aware that the Barrême investigation was bungled for high political reasons.

34 Cabuche has other blood on his hands, of course, as Flore's unwitting accomplice in crashing Lantier's express train.

35 Joseph Conrad gives us a sardonic railway-borne footnote to Lombroso's ideas. In the decades when these ideas were taken seriously, criminologists and policemen were interested less in the heritability of moral taint than in Lombroso's claim to have isolated criminal (and other) human 'types', using anthropometric measurement. Fleeing justice (or, at least, the singularly dilatory Metropolitan Police force) with Winnie Verloc, Ossipon took the 10.30 boat train to Southampton (for St Malo). With his professed anarchist beliefs covering unprincipled egotism and sensuality, 'He gazed scientifically. He gazed at her cheeks, at her nose, at her ears. Bad! Fatal! Mrs Verloc's pale lips parting, slightly relaxed, under his attentive gaze, he gazed also at her teeth … Not a doubt remained … A murdering type …' (Conrad, *The Secret Agent* [1907], Harmondsworth, Penguin, 1963, p. 259; original punctuation). Persuading himself that he stood in mortal peril from this dangerous woman, and with all her money now resting comfortably in his pocket, Ossipon hurled himself from this boat train as it left Waterloo. Winnie Verloc was carried on

to Southampton, and mid-Channel suicide. For Conrad this is self-fulfilling prophecy, not a triumph for Lombroso's exploded system.

36 Renée Bonneau, *La Bête Humaine, Zola*, Paris, Hatier, 1986, pp. 24–30 proffers a wide range of candidates for *la bête humaine*: Jacques Lantier, primitive man, Roubaud, Cabuche, Flore, Misard (Flore's money-obsessed father); and railway locomotives, notably Lison. She is surely correct to suggest that Zola exploits the term's ambiguity. Thus Marian Robinson urges that while Roubaud's initial conspectus of Saint-Lazare welds together love, death and steam engineering (a view for which I can find little warrant in Zola's paragraph), as the novel proceeds 'The human beast – those dark and hidden impulses, sexual and violent, become the roaring, smoking, speeding locomotive whose benign façade is shattered like the veneer of civilisation masking the turmoil within the men and women who people this novel'. See Robinson, 'Zola and Monet', p. 65.

37 Marshall Berman, *All That is Solid Melts into Air: the Experience of Modernity*, New York, Simon & Schuster, 1984, p. 232.

38 Richard Lehan, *The City in Literature: an Intellectual and Cultural History*, Berkeley, University of California Press, 1998, pp. 66–8.

39 Quoted in Hemmings, *Émile Zola*, pp. 215–16.

40 Berg and Martin, *Émile Zola Revisited*, p. 30. Henri Mitterand ('The genesis of novelistic space: Zola's *La Bête Humaine*', translated by Anne C. Murch, in Brian Nelson (ed.), *Naturalism in the European Novel: New Critical Perspectives*, London, Berg, 1992, p. 66) asserts that Zola's is the first great French novel to explore compressed distance and accelerated speed.

41 The former since at least 1869, the latter since at least 1871. See Mitterand, 'Genesis of novelistic space', 69; Kanes, *Zola's La Bête Humaine*, pp. 7–8.

42 Philip Walker, *Zola*, London, Routledge & Kegan Paul, 1985, p. 196.

43 Hemmings, *Émile Zola*, p. 216.

44 Robert M. Viti, 'The cave, the clock and the railway: primitive and modern time in *La Bête Humaine*', *Nineteenth Century French Studies*, 19, 1990–91, p. 114.

45 Mitterand, 'Genesis of novelistic space', p. 73 argues that building out from this simple metaphor, Zola constructs an elaborate 'spatiographic semiotics and semantics' around railway workers' everyday technical vocabulary. Good point; pity about the language.

46 As Robert Viti notes ('The cave, the clock and the railway', pp. 114–19), *La Bête Humaine* resonates to 'the clockwork precision of the railroad'. Jacques Lantier's developing monomania goes critical when he buries his watch. As we saw in chapter 1, nineteenth century railways' codified timetables forced time regimes to be standardised by the state in Britain, by congregated railway companies in America. Viti grounded his argument in J. B. Priestley's distinction between primitive and modern time (in *Man and Time* (1964)). E. P. Thompson's famous contrast between task-oriented time and industrial time (in his essay 'Time, work discipline, and industrial capitalism', *Past and Present*, 38, 1967, pp. 56–97) better suits his purpose.

47 'The history of this century could be written around the rise of the railway, which dominated economic life as much as any other single invention': Theodore

Zeldin, *France 1848–1945: Volume Two: Intellect, Taste and Anxiety*, Oxford, Clarendon Press, 1977, p. 638. Despite this domination, France never became a railway-centred nation in the full British sense. At the peak, 794 million train journeys were made in France during 1924, against 1746 million in Britain: Zeldin, *France*, p. 99.

48   In 1835 a reluctant government granted Émile Péreire the concession to construct France's first modern railway, from Paris to Saint-Germain. When this line opened two years later, its technical and financial success confounded many private and offical detractors. Good Saint-Simonian that he was, Péreire never doubted that technical progress would triumph: Jerome Blum, *In the Beginning: the Advent of the Modern Age: Europe in the 1840s*, New York, Scribner, 1994, pp. 25–6. For a collection of material on railways, France and Saint-Simonism see Walter Benjamin, *The Arcades Project*, translated by Howard Eiland and Kevin McLaughlin, Cambridge, Harvard University Press, 1999, pp. 571–602.

49   Books talk to books. Milos Hrma's death on the last page of Bohumil Hrabal's tenderly whimsical novella *Closely Observed Trains* [1965] (translated by Edith Pargeter, London, Abacus, 1968, p. 91) inflects Jacques Lantier's death. Hrabal turns Zola's parable about the gathering Franco-Prussian War into a Prague Spring paean for Czech resistance to Soviet occupation. A minor official working at a Bohemian wayside station in early 1945, young Hrma loses his burdensome virginity to a resistance courier, the lovely (and significantly named) Viktoria Freie, while Dresden's blazing aura illuminates the horizon. Hated German troops learn that they 'should have sat at home on your arse'. Made a man by Viktoria Freie, Hrma uses the bomb she carried to destroy a German ammunition train. Shot by a sentry, he shoots the sentry in return. Echoing Lantier's and Pecqueaux's end, they die holding each other's hand, human victims of rail-centred geopolitical struggles.

50   For Caillebotte and others – Béraud, Goeneutte, Anquetin – see Wilson-Barreau, *Manet, Monet*, pp. 77–87, 92–101.

51   Ellis, *Railway Art*, p. 94. Art-school trained, like many of Manet's contemporaries Hamilton Ellis would be offended by the manner in which billowing steam created a 'blank centre' in Manet's painting. See Wilson-Barreau, *Manet, Monet*, p. 61. Stephan Koja (*Claude Monet*, p. 66) is very specific about what this picture shows: 'In 1873 Manet painted *Le Chemin de Fer* at the Gare Saint-Lazare (with his wife and daughter at the platform barrier.)' That is spectacularly mistaken. The figures represent neither Manet's wife nor his daughter. His easel stands in the rue de Rome, between the Pont de l'Europe and the Batignolle tunnel, several hundred metres from Saint-Lazare. Even more bizarrely, Nicholas Faith (*The World the Railways Made*, London, Bodley Head, 1990, p. 51) ascribes Monet's Gare Saint-Lazare series to Manet. Appreciating "Edouard Monet"'s paintings showing 'the harsh solidity of the railway bridge at Charing Cross', Jack Simmons (*Victorian Railway*, p. 153) returns this twisted compliment.

52   Ellis, *Railway Art*, p. 95.

53   John Rewald, *The History of Impressionism*, fourth edition, New York, Metropolitan Museum of Art, 1973, p. 380.

54 Robinson, 'Zola and Monet', 56; François Émile-Zola et Massin (ed.) *Zola Photographe: 480 Documents*, Paris, Denoël, 1979.

55 Quoted in Robinson, 'Zola and Monet', p. 66. This was no novel suggestion. Somewhat earlier, Thomas Couture (Edouard Manet's teacher) exhorted French artists to celebrate the modern railway's machine ensemble in paint (Couture, *Méthode et Entretiens d'Atelier* [1867], quoted in Peter Gay, *Art and Act: On Causes in History – Manet, Gropius, Mondrian*, New York, Harper & Row, 1976, pp. 87–8).

56 Gay, *Art and Act*, p. 107.

57 Quoted in Wilson-Barreau, *Manet, Monet*, pp. 128–9.

58 Françoise Cachin, *Manet*, translated by Emily Read, London, Barrie & Jenkins, n.d., p. 106.

59 Wilson-Barreau, *Manet, Monet*, pp. 9–49.

60 As a hostile critic, Cham, noted: 'These unfortunate women, seeing themselves painted in this way, wanted to escape, but he has foreseen this and placed a railing to cut off their escape' (quoted in Cachin, *Manet*, p 106.

61 'Manet liked to paint this girl looking at men looking at her' (Gay, *Art and Act*, p. 43). Here, as Victorine returns the male gaze so brazenly, Manet counterposes familiar (and straightjacketed) Western painterly perceptions of woman as virgin or as whore.

62 Gay, *Art and Act*, pp. 105, 107.

63 Richards and MacKenzie, *The Railway Station* p. 354; John Huntley, *Railways on the Screen*, Shepperton, Ian Allan, 1993, p. 5. With railway enthusiasm coded as a resolutely male activity, few female moviegoers would recognise Huntley's strictures on authenticity. He complains that a strictly 'studio' locomotive runs down poor Anna in Duvivier's film. MGM feebly disguised the local Californian machine ensemble for Brown's movie, sticking a vaguely Russian superstructure on an American steam locomotive. Studio bosses made no attempt to cover even the most glaring technical discrepancy – clear visual differences between American standard and Russian broad gauge tracks. For more on railways, movies and authenticity, see Jonathan D. Spence, 'Shanghai Express', in Ted Mico, John Miller-Monzon and David Rubel (eds), *Past Imperfect: History According to the Movies*, New York, Holt, 1995, pp. 208–11.

64 Garbo had played Anna once before, with John Gilbert in a 1928 silent movie. Its title – *Love* – stripped Tolstoy's complicated argument down to the lowest commercial denominator.

65 Hence James Agee's waspish judgement that in the 1947 film 'Vivien Leigh is lashed about by the tremendous role of Anna like a pussy cat with a tigress by the tail. She is not helped by a script which insists on sentimentally ennobling one of fiction's most vehemently average women'. (Quoted in Leslie Halliwell, *Halliwell's Film Guide*, eighth edition, edited by John Walker, London, HarperCollins, 1991, p. 45).

66 Robert A. Armour, *Fritz Lang*, Boston, Twayne, 1977, pp. 162–4 and E. Ann Kaplan, *Fritz Lang: a Guide to References and Resources*, Boston, Hall, 1981, pp. 116–18 provide brisk plot summaries. Lang's first producer, Jerry Wald, failed to

interest the Santa Fe Railroad in this project. 'For a long time Jerry couldn't understand that it was not good publicity for the Santa Fe to show a sex maniac who kills people in their sleeping cars' (Peter Bogdanovich, *Fritz Lang in America*, London, Studio Vista, 1967, p. 93).

67 Peter Conrad, 'The man with the X-ray eye', *Times Literary Supplement*, 22 August 1997, p. 18.
68 Bogdanovich, *Fritz Lang in America*, p. 138.
69 Conrad, 'Man with the X-ray eye', p. 198.
70 Kaplan, *Fritz Lang*, pp. 200–1, 203.
71 Quoted in Huntley, *Railways on the Screen*, p. 74.
72 Halliwell, *Film Guide*, p. 532.
73 *Ibid.*, p. 102.
74 *Cahiers du Cinéma*, 99, September 1959, pp. 1–10; Patrick McGilligan, *Fritz Lang: the Nature of the Beast*, New York, St Martins Press, 1997, pp. 407–10, 500.
75 Leo Braudy, 'Zola on film: the ambiguities of naturalism', *Yale French Studies*, 42, 1969, pp. 68–88. For the most recent survey of attempts to film some Zola fiction (but not *La Bête Humaine*) see Paul Warren (ed.), *Zola et la Cinéma*, Sainte-Foy, Les Presses de l'Université Laval, 1995.
76 For what it is worth, my list also would include Buster Keaton's *The General* (1927), Alfred Hitchcock's *The Lady Vanishes* (1938), David Lean's *Brief Encounter*, Charles Crichton's *The Titfield Thunderbolt* (1952) and Lars von Trier's *Zentropa* (1991). Criteria for excellence can differ, of course. Trailing behind the *Guide Michelin*, mainstream film guides award stars for cinematic significance, artistic effort or whatever. John Huntley's *Railways on the Screen* rates movies using up to five ancient tank locomotive symbols. These indicate how much railway content each movie displays. Which true railway enthusiast cares about art?
77 Ginette Vincendeau, 'The beauty of the beast', *Sight and Sound*, new series, 1, 1991, no. 3, pp. 13–14.
78 John Anzalone, 'Sound/tracks: Zola, Renoir and *La Bête Humaine*', *The French Review*, 62, 1989, p. 584.
79 Limited clearances in tunnels and bridges gave the greatest danger. It is hard to understand how several cameramen's heads were not lost in capturing long forward shots, filmed outside the locomotive cab's side-sheets.
80 Christopher Faulker, *The Social Cinema of Jean Renoir*, Princeton, Princeton University Press, 1986, p. 101.
81 Faulker, *Social Cinema*, p. 103. On the previous page Faulkner sneers at Renoir's claim that he had made a film about 'a revolutionary subject, since it leads to the conclusion that individuals living in better conditions would act better'. One wonders what this critic thinks today, with Althusser's theoretical practice lying, thoroughly rusted, on History's scrapheap.
82 Faulkner, *Social Cinema*, p. 66.
83 Anzalone, 'Sound/tracks', pp. 584–5.
84 Alexander Sekonse, *Jean Renoir: the French Films, 1924–1939*, Cambridge, Mass., Harvard University Press, 1980, p. 358. Anzalone, 'Train/tracks', pp. 585–8,

suggests that much material stripped from Zola's novel in Renoir's screenplay is smuggled back into the movie through Joseph Kosma's expertly contrived musical score. A nice point, showing difficulties involved in conveying a cinematic experience in words.

85 Paul Jennings, 'Dieselization', in Jennings, *The Jenguin Pennings*, Harmondsworth, Penguin, 1963, p. 82. Jennings' Tabernacle eventually was constructed – but at York's National Railway Museum, not at Euston. Given the style in which this station was reconstructed by British Rail seven years after Jennings wrote his piece, that is no surprise.

86 Vincendeau, 'Beauty of the beast'. p. 11.

87 Andre Gorz, *Adieu au Prolétariat: ou Delà du Socialisme*, Paris, Galilée, 1981.

6

Accident:
new English life?

'There is nothing in English', Jack Simmons tells us, 'to touch the sustained power of the depiction of a railway, as a mechanical organisation worked by men, in *La Bête Humaine*. Nor – looking a little beyond 1914 – has any English writer ever come to treat the railway with the intimate poetic affection bestowed on it by Proust, to convey his 'love of enchanted journeys by train'.[1] That judgement is true, but it is limited. Paying little direct attention to the machine ensemble or to travelling poetics, one English novelist does give us a now-forgotten book-length interrogation of the railway's entanglement with modernity. Arnold Bennett wrote two fiction streams. One stood rooted in the Potteries' provincial realism (the 'Five Towns' novels and stories). The other exhibited – to that world's habitués – a gauche and ingenuous delight in high life. 'Certain amusing traits of Arnold Bennett's odd but engaging character', J. B. Priestley reported in 1934,

> his knowing air, his passion for excessively smart cosmopolitan ways of life, his delight in being 'in the swim', were always explained by the fact that he was very much the provincial come to town. The explanation never entirely satisfied me because so many English authors, perhaps the majority of them, are also provincials who have arrived in town, and yet few of them shared Bennett's boyish enthusiasm for all that was metropolitan, fashionable, anything-but-provincial. The very first morning I spent in the Potteries gave me the clue. Coming from this part of the world, Bennett was not merely a provincial but a super-provincial. He came – perhaps, in reality, he fled – from a region that contains the very essence of remote provinciality'.[2]

'Unique in their remote, self-contained provincialism … Victorian industrialism in its dirtiest and most cynical aspect',[3] for Priestley the Potteries stand as Mayfair's negation. But not for Arnold Bennett. Unnoticed by almost all commentators, railways link his two worlds in a single structure of feeling –

intimately compounding North with South, province with metropolis, business with pleasure, production with consumption.

'"You should see the Flying Scotchman come through at half-past six!" said Leonard, whose father was a signalman. "Lads, but she doesn't half buzz!" and the little party looked up the lines one way, to London, and the other way, to Scotland, and they felt the touch of these two magical places'.[4] Scotland meant celtic Otherness for an Edwardian midland English lad: but London was the greatest city in the world, the Empire's metropolis. Provincial youths gawping at metropolitan splendour are common figures in modern English fiction. Waited with two siblings at a station in the Nottingham mining country's Erewash valley, Paul Morel 'was dying for the man to know they were expecting somebody from the London train: it sounded so grand ... They looked down the darkness of the railway. There was London! It seemed the uttermost of distance'.[5] Couterpointing grim local vistas, this London is a place different in kind, not just a city far away. Tragicomically mired in Stradhoughton, a rugged Yorkshire industrial town, young Billy Fisher escapes in his head to two utopias. One is Ambrosia, a kingdom where King Billy rules in pomp and epaulettes. The other is London, a no less magical place whose citizens enjoy lives liberated from Stradhoughton's hard constrictions.[6] Writing from close knowledge of his native Potteries, Arnold Bennett started his first novel in this tradition of provincial yearning. 'There grows in the North Country', he reports, 'a certain kind of youth of whom it may be said that he is born to be a Londoner'.

> The metropolis, and everything that appertains to it, that comes down from it, that goes up into it, has for him an imperious fascination. Long before schooldays are over he learns to take a doleful pleasure in watching the exit of the London train from the railway station. He stands by the hot engine and envies the very stoker. Gazing curiously into the carriages, he wonders that men and women who in a few hours will be treading streets called Piccadilly and the Strand can contemplate the immediate future with so much apparent calmness; some of them even have the audacity to look bored. He finds it difficult to keep from throwing himself in the guard's van as it glides past him; and not until the last coach is a speck in the distance does he turn away and, nodding absently to the ticket-clerk, who knows him well, go home to nurse a vague ambition and dream of Town.[7]

This infection roars right through the Five Towns' respectable citizenry, the group to which Bennett limits his attention. As the best London train approaches Knype-on-Trent, 'the main-line station for all the Five Towns, and the radiating centre of the local lines',[8]

> The worlds of pleasure and of business meet on that platform to await the great train with its two engines. The spacious pavement is crowded with the correctness

of travelling suits and suit-cases; it is alive with the spurious calm of those who are about to travel and to whom travelling is an everyday trifle. 'Going up to the village?' the wits ask, and are answered by nods in a fashion to indicate that going up to the village is a supreme bore. And yet beneath all this weary satiety there lurks in each demeanour a suppressed anticipatory eagerness, a consciousness of vast enterprise, that would not be unsuitable if the London train were a caravan setting out for Bagdad.[9]

Alicia Orgreave can find no *Bradshaw* in her prosperous architect father's house. 'In the Five Towns', Bennett tells us, 'the local time-table, showing the connections with London, suffices for the citizens, and the breast-pocket of no citizen is complete without it.'[10]

   Employing one of those connections, a passenger soon would know that she had left the Potteries: "We're fairly out of the smoke now', Hilda Lessways remarks to her companion as their train speeds south towards London.[11] Travelling there, and beyond, unsettles even the most confident provincial. In 1892 Edwin Clayhanger, sole proprietor in a prosperous Bursley printing business and Bennett's portrait of the man he might have become had he not escaped his native district, travels to rescue Hilda from penury in Brighton.

> The very character of Victoria Station and of this express was different from that of any other station and express in his experience. It was unstrenuous, soft; it had none of the busy harshness of the Midlands; it spoke of pleasure, relaxation, of spending free from all worry and humiliation of getting. Everybody who came towards this train came with an assured air of wealth and dominion. Everybody was well dressed; many if not most of the women were in furs; some had expensive and delicate dogs; some had pale, elegant footmen, being too august even to speak to porters. All the luggage was luxurious; hand-bags could be seen that were worth fifteen or twenty pounds apiece. There was no question of first, second, or third class; there was no class at all on this train. Edwin had the apologetic air of the provincial who is determined to be as good as anybody else.[12]

Edwin can well afford to pay a premium fare on the London, Brighton and South Coast Railway Company's super-first-class Pullman train: but, an outsider, he is not comfortable in this place. Productive relations – social class – play some part in his discomfort, but not all. Bennett's insistence on softness, on luxury, on southern England's shameless indolence, tells us that *consumption* patterns set this Five Towns bourgeois apart from all those be-furred dowagers prattling away round him. Complicated cultural consequences rooted in delicately-shaded social status, not stark cleavages between social classes, make Edwin squirm in his padded seat. Elsewhere, in a passage which directly anticipates Bennett's later attempt to write a major railway novel, Denry Machin, that prosperous Five Towns card, devoted to 'the great charge of cheering us all up', squirms just as uncomfortably in a first class carriage between Dieppe and Switzerland.[13]

Five Towns

'Extremely ugly', the 'ugliest town in Britain',[14] smoke from collieries, from iron works, from teeming pot banks, drifts across the Potteries' ravaged landscape. From Toft End, above Bleakridge,

> To the east is the wild grey-green moorland dotted with mining villages whose steeples are wreathed in smoke and fire. West and north and south are the Five Towns – Bursley and Turnhill to the north – Hanbridge, Knype and distant Longshaw to the south – Hanbridge and Bursley uniting their arms to the west. Here they have breathed for a thousand years; and here to-day they pant in the fever of a quickened evolution.[15]

Neither urban nor rural, a scatter of industrial settlements among blackened fields, this landscape lies closely pocked with working factories and ruined buildings. Character matches landscape. Against 'the soft and delicate South … in the Five Towns human nature is reported to be so hard that you can break stones on it'.[16] *Not* a nice place in which to live nice lives.

Showing us how respectable people do manage to survive in this bleak place, Bennett points again and again to railways' significance. He insists that the Five Towns are creatures of their history and their transport links. Walking the ridge separating the Five Towns from Oldcastle, their administrative centre, 'the exalted borough which draws its skirts away from the grimy contact of the Five Towns, and employs its vast leisure in brooding upon an ancient and exciting past',[17] in 1872 young Edwin Clayhanger wondered at the vast loads of Cornish china clay carried to Staffordshire.[18] When first practised, 'making pots' fired local clay with local coal to serve local markets. By mid-Victorian years the Potteries served national and international markets, first through canals and then through 'the Great Connector', railways. Fundamental to local economic prosperity, railways influenced local culture just as deeply. Oldcastle's 'relentless ignorance of its prejudices had blighted the district', Bennett tells us. 'Fifty years earlier, the fine and ancient borough had succeeded in forcing the greatest railway line in England to run through unpopulated country five miles off instead of through the Five Towns, because it loathed the mere conception of a railway. And now, people are inquiring why the Five Towns, with a railway system special to itself, is characterised by a perhaps excessive parochialism'.[19] With trains on the west coast main line pounding from London to Scotland through Crewe, the Five Towns had to make do with a connection to the metropolitan corridor at Stoke (Knype), as London and North Western Railway express trains to Manchester exercised running powers over the North Staffordshire Railway's metals from Norton Bridge to Macclesfield. Delivered to Knype by branch lines built by the intensely parochial North Staffordshire Railway Company,[20] here 'all voyagers for London, Birmingham and Manchester had to foregather in order to take the fast expresses that unwillingly halted there, and there alone, in their skimming flight across the district'.[21]

Bennett insists, we see, that railway history deeply marked 'the history of the two hundred thousand souls in the Five Towns. Oldcastle guessed not the vast influence of its sublime stupidity'.[22] This stupidity stunted social life through all the Potteries, but its strength varied with distance by rail from Knype. In 1878 the northernmost town represents 'the extremity of civilisation', because 'only within recent years had Turnhill got so much as a railway station – rail-head of a branch line'.[23] Distance signifies social as much as physical separation. Turnhill is a junior Oldcastle, the 'smallest and most conceited of the Five [Towns]'.[24] Compared with this local-genteel outpost, Bursley's wide Trafalgar Street 'had almost the feeling of being in a metropolis, if a local metropolis'.[25] Electric trams rumbled from Trafalgar Street over Bleakridge to Crown Square, Hanbridge, 'the metropolis of the Five Towns'.[26]

Important in inhabitants' quotidian lives, these fine distinctions pale against broader contrasts between the Potteries and London. A bounder soon to trap an innocent girl in bigamous marriage, a Frenchman's son bounced from fraudulent practice as a solicitor, George Cannon spits out an almost Parisian loathing for the Potteries' 'odious provincialism'.[27] Many later writers would echo his contempt. Like Arnold Bennett's hero in *A Man From the North*, like Billy Liar, they would stare in awe at the London train, seeing in it a means of escape to sundry freedoms, to cultural liberation. Bennett understood this; in his Grand Hotel manner he might even seem to succour it. What makes him an interesting writer is that, at bottom, he does nothing of the sort.[28] 'My knowledge of industrial districts amounted to nothing', status-proud Loring confides to us one day as he sits in a London to Manchester train.

> Born in Devonshire, educated at Cambridge, and fulfilling my destiny as curator of a certain department of antiquities at the British Museum, I had never been brought into contact with the vast constructive material activities of Lancashire, Yorkshire and Staffordshire. I had but passed through them occasionally on my

way to Scotland, scorning their necessary grime with the perhaps too facile disdain of the clean-faced southerner, who is apt to forget that coal cannot walk up unaided out of the mine, and that the basin in which he washes his beautiful purity can only be manufactured amid conditions highly repellent.[29]

Comfortably seated, Loring reads in his London newspaper that a great painter, the Five Towns-born Simon Fuge, has died. Yielding to a sudden impulse, he leaves his train at Knype and sets about exploring how this retired and ravaged district could produce such a celebrity. A risky enterprise: as the Manchester train leaves, 'I fancied that my last link with civilisation was broken'.[30] Ripped from his comfortable seat in the metropolitan corridor, Loring might be staring at north Borneo, not north Staffordshire. Simon Fuge moved from the Potteries to London, from province to metropolis. Moving in the other direction, Loring comes to appreciate the place and some residents' cultural resources.[31] In another story Myson, a Manchester man who had lived in London, 'was not provincial, and he beheld the Five Towns as part of the provinces; which no native of the Five Towns ever succeeds in doing'.[32] Bennett insists that local notables must resist metropolitan snobbery. '"Everybody knows,"' the Danish maiden Manna Höst tells a Bleakridge gathering, '"that the English are the finest nation, and I think the Five Towns are much more English than London. That is why I adore the Five Towns."'[33] Life in these settlements is validated by past events. So is life in Mayfair. But, unlike Mayfair, the Five Towns have a future. They are modern. 'All this seemed to me to be fine', Loring tells us on a later visit; it 'seemed to throw off the true romantic savour of life. I would have altered nothing in it. Mean, harsh, ugly, squalid, crude, barbaric – yes, but what an intoxicating sense in it of the organised vitality of a vast community unconscious of itself!'[34] The future lies with this unconscious provincial vitality, not with Mayfair's febrile self-absorption. Backward-looking metropolitan pretension chafes against thrusting industrial advance. Through his several visits north Loring learns that middle-class citizens may enjoy lives in the Potteries which differ from their London peers', but that these lives have their own logic and their own pleasures. They are not negligible. They are not to be despised. In balancing the condition of Edwardian England, history's scale pan need not fall decisively on the metropolitan side.

Bennett's fiction scrutinises personal experience modified through time. Again and again, his Five Towns novels show experience mediated by transport changes. In one of the best of these, *The Old Wives' Tale* (1908), Constance Baines, the elder of Bursley's premier draper's two daughters, stayed rooted in her native town for more than half a century. Marrying her father's shopman, she watched Bursley's slow eclipse as a commercial centre, with steam and then electric tram cars chugging and whisking citizens over Bleakridge to shop in Hanbridge's gaudy streets. Her sister Sophia would not bear this stupor. Suborned by a genteel Manchester rotter, Gerald Scales, she escaped the Five Towns' provincial monotony by train from Knype, fleeing to marriage in London and abandonment in France. Surviving and prospering in the Second Empire and the Third Republic, surviving the siege of Paris and the Commune, eventually Sophia retired home to Bursley. Her life, too, was framed by transport changes. Wooed by letter, in the mid-1850s she made her fatal assignation with Scales on a bridge over new works for the loop line which, when completed, would connect Bursley by rail to Knype – and thus to national and international rail networks.[35] Forty years later, the glamorously cosmopolitan Sophia returned to Bursley. Her dowdy stay-at-home sister met her at Knype station. 'The immense engine, gliding round the curve, dwarfed the carriages behind it, and Constance had a supreme tremor. The calmness of the platform was transformed into a mêlée'.[36] Here, in the mid-1890s, railways remain sublime, modernity's master symbol. Ten years after that, and long believing herself a widow, Sophia is disturbed to be called to Gerald Scales' deathbed in a Manchester slum pawnshop. She goes to him, but arrives too late. Returning home, Sophia dies near Congleton. Her last journey away from Bursley and back, in a life whose larger shape took her away from Bursley and back, could have been made by the loop railway to Knype and the North Staffordshire and LNWR's lines to Manchester. Instead she was whisked to Manchester by a go-ahead nephew, a pioneer motorist. Modernity's standard-bearer for almost a century, the railway yields to the motor car – just as Bursley's commercial supremacy yielded to Hanbridge's flashy attractions.

For Arnold Bennett these usurpations are neither to be applauded nor mourned: they are simply to be recorded. The Five Towns' particular provincial culture was created by a particular pattern of transport connections. That culture will change as transport patterns change.[37] Not all changes have fruited when Sophia dies. Abandoned by her unsatisfactory husband, around 1870 she tremulously entertained new romantic possibilities with his journalist friend Chirac. These perished in the first siege of Paris. Rendered reckless by patriotic fervour, Chirac made a desperate balloon flight, carrying political despatches over the Prussian blockade. Ascending (significantly) from the Gare du Nord's courtyard, Sophia's platonic lover disappeared into the ether and was presumed drowned in the English Channel.[38] Technological presumption claimed another Icarus. Hindsight's beneficiaries, modern readers know that air travel eventually destroyed railways' monopoly over long distance genteel passenger travel; but in 1871 that fate still lay generations ahead. Writing almost forty years after Chirac's doomed ascent, in *The Old Wives' Tale* Arnold Bennett still made human flight an adventure for dare-devil pioneers rather than a hum-drum experience for jaded travellers.

Accident

So it remained twenty years later. In a late Bennett novel Pearl Frith-Walter leaves her husband in Newcastle, fleeing by *train de luxe* to her mother on the Italian Riviera. Jack, her husband, overtakes her train by persuading a friend to fly him from Newcastle to Aix-les-Bains. Pearl is impressed by Jack's initiative, and by the risks which it involved. Sharing this attitude, Bennett wrote on the cusp when railways' monopoly for privileged long-distance travel began to be challenged by aviation.[39] Serialised in the *Daily Express* from July 1927 as *Train de Luxe* before book publication in January 1929, *Accident* never saw a second edition. Failing to please the public in its time, today it has been forgotten. No railway historian seems to have heard of the book.[40] Literary critics ignore it[41] or disparage it.[42]

These judgements are too hasty. *Accident* is a significant British railway novel. Its plot is deceptively simple. Alan Frith-Walter is a fiftyish partner in a major Tyneside engineering firm, and runs the firm's London office. Travelling to meet his wife Elaine, sojourning in Liguria, he anticipates a pleasant late December journey from London to Genoa, travelling in a Pullman coach on the Dover boat train from Victoria, then by a Wagons-Lit coach from Boulogne. This coach will be worked round Paris from the Gare du Nord to join the Rome Express at the Gare de Lyon. But delays in Kent, and persistent rumours about French railway disasters, disturb Alan and his fellow passengers. These alarms culminate in a moderately serious train crash just short of the Italian frontier. Surviving this crash, Alan arrives safely in Genoa. To his consid-erable surprise, he has shared the journey with his daughter-in-law Pearl; and, after Aix, with his son Jack. A retired Newcastle engineering competitor, Lucass, and his extraordinary wife, 'the hag beauty', also turn up on Alan's train. Tracking developments among these five characters occupies three quarters of the book's pages. Alan acts as the instrument recording violent fluctuations among two married couples divided by age: Lucass/hag beauty and Jack/Pearl. Elaine joins the plot in Genoa, and the Lucasses depart. The couples shuffle around, but contrasts between two generations persist. In his closing chapters Bennett measures Alan/Elaine (as age) against Jack/Pearl (as youth).

Contemporary reviewers took *Accident* to be about no more than character – 'a study of the conjugal relations of three couples running quietly across its vehemence of episode' for *Punch*'s anonymous reviewer; 'a study of family intimacy', for Cyril Connolly.[43] But we saw earlier that railways influence more than individual experience in Bennett's Five Towns fictions. On the Continent as in north Staffordshire, railways embody social messages. Here, too, standardised time (born from railway travel) governs human action. In an earlier story his concern to meet timetabled connections dominates Arthur Cotterill's comically desperate train journey from Bursley bachelorhood to marriage in London.[44] In his journey, too, Alan worries over timetables and connections in a narrative built around conjugal relations. Not until he arrives timeously at Paris' Gare de Lyon can he jump down 'impatiently, joyously' to the station platform. 'He had caught the Rome Express. On every carriage of his train shone the immortal name of Rome, and glittered in gold the impressive words: "Grands Express Européens."'[45] Unconsciously underpinning the parallel with Arthur Cotterill, Cyril Connolly urged that Alan's *train de luxe* is *Accident*'s chief comic character, 'clowning its way from the Channel to the Mediterranean'.[46]

Arnold Bennett does not tell us that Alan Frith-Walter ever visited the Potteries. His firm is based in Newcastle-on-Tyne, not Newcastle-under-Lyme (Oldcastle's real identity). Alan lives in London. But here, too, Bennett exploits distinctions between north and south, between production and consumption. Despite her love for luxury and her mother's enormous wealth, northern-born Pearl owes little to southern England: '"She is hard," thought Alan, "she is hard. She is surely capable of being very hard."' By contrast, 'Alan was of northern stock by his father and southern by his mother'.[47] This double inheritance allows him to appreciate both sides of that railway-linked distinction between metropolis and province which looms so insistently in Bennett's Five Towns novels. Pearl abandoned Jack, whom she still loves, when he told her that he intended to stand for Parliament as a Labour candidate. And not just for the comfortable, milk-and-water Ramsay Macdonaldish Labour Party. '"Independent Labour Party, in fact,"' a sneering Pearl tells Alan: '"He'll be communist next."'[48] For Pearl, Jack threatens class treachery; but her acute discomfort at this prospect raises other echoes. Jack's choice scouts respectability: that central, complicated, bourgeois fetish. Class always compounds with status in Five Towns novels and stories. This happens in *Accident*, too; but now Bennett stalks bigger game.

Divisions between province and metropolis modulate into wider differences. Again and again Alan disparages foreign travel – 'these awful French lines', 'the barbarism of continental trains … so absurdly labelled "de luxe"' – when compared with 'the superiority of English trains to all others'.[49] This is Alan Frith-Walter's 'pet topic'. It is Arnold Bennett's pet topic.[50] When first we meet him in a taxi heading for Victoria, Alan carries

> a slim volume, Wordsworth's *The Prelude*, at whose opening pages he had been glancing with agreeable anticipation. He was a business man of some culture, who, however, rarely meddled with poetry. But of late he had encountered Matthew Arnold and Arnold's solemn and convincing praise of the Wordsworth had directed him to the author of *The Prelude*.[51]

Matthew Arnold, mildly pessimistic defender of genteel Englishness in *Culture and Anarchy* (1869), recommends Wordsworth, archetypal English romantic poet, to Alan Frith-Walter, confused Englishman. Alan moves between approving and despising *The Prelude* as his journey unfolds, signifying changes in attitude to wider social questions. He goes by train from London to Genoa for the same reason that Edwin Clayhanger took train from Knype to Brighton: so that his author can show us a man better understanding where he came from. *Accident* is a profit-and-loss account for late-twenties Englishness, measured against Abroad. This is a 'condition of England' novel, written eighty years after Dickens, Disraeli and Elizabeth Gaskell.

Crisis

The germ for *La Bête Humaine* was Prefect Barrême's 1886 railway murder and defenestration.[52] *Accident*'s germ was no less specific and no less French. On 6 July 1911 Arnold Bennett visited T. B. Wells at Pont de l'Arche. He returned to Fontainebleau the next day, in 'a sort of large Pullmanesque compartment at the back of a first-class coach, two or three coaches from the engine'.[53] 'My train ran off the line at Mantes', he reported to Jane Wells. 'Front part of my coach telescoped & the whole coach smashed. For a few seconds I was in a storm of glass, flying doors, and hand-luggage. All over in ten seconds. A woman in front part of my coach had her leg broken'.[54] Inscribing this event in his journal, he produced something close to a novel's chapter draft. Expanded and polished, fifteen years later this draft became *Accident*'s central episode.[55]

As with Zola's interest in Barrême's messy death, Bennett's experience was the seed, not the flower. It is remotely possible that his interest in Rome Express sybarites was sparked by reading Arthur Griffiths' late Victorian thriller,[56] but Bennett started writing *Accident* only in November 1926. Six months earlier, Britain had been brought to a complete halt by a General Strike led by 'the Triple Alliance': unions representing miners, railwaymen, and other transport workers. On 4 May 1926, this strike's second day, only one percent of railway engine drivers, firemen and guards defied the TUC General Council's orders, and reported for work.[57] Transmuted by metaphor, a key passage in *Accident* conjures the general strike, as Alan's boat train shudders to an unscheduled stop in southern English countryside.

> The train was arrested and lay moveless as though under an enchantment. By leaning forth Alan could see the curve [sic] succession of coaches on the curved track, and the engine so nonchalantly smoking. He saw the bright steel up-line in a corresponding curve, wedged in fish plates that were nailed to sleepers; thousands of sleepers stretching all the way to London and all the way to Folkestone and Dover; and the tens of millions of road-metal pebbles, smoothed out, raked flat, combed! And in the misty distance a tall, frail, signal – at danger. No luxury here. Nothing but the naked bones and backbone and bottom foundation of a system. Here a train de luxe was no better than a common goods-train or a third-class excursion-train. All luxury seemed forlorn, pathetic, comic, fragile as a bride-cake; for ever under threat of destruction'.[58]

The machine stops,[59] its huge extent and minute division of labour (which army of unseen servants rakes all that ballast?) arrested 'under enchantment'. Changes in the economic 'bottom foundation of a system' induce changes elsewhere. Social distinctions melt; privilege decays. Class insurrection looms.[60] Intent on ensuring that carriage wheels should revolve smoothly, 'a slatternly greaser, … absorbed and humble' had crossed the Pullman passengers' roped-off private platform at Victoria.

> For Alan he became a symbolic figure representing all the humble who would be left behind when the trains with their thousand tons of luxury rolled off towards the south: the taxi-drivers, the porters, the minor-officials, the newsboys etc., etc. 'Why are we going, and why are they helping us to go?' thought Alan. 'And why do they not storm the trains and take our places by force?'[61]

For fearful bourgeois in 1926, Karl Marx's revolutionary prophecy – 'All that is solid melts into air' – had an uncomfortably solid feel. The general strike insinuated that firm social arrangements might evaporate. Bennett personalises this point. Grim Lucass (so grim, indeed, that we never hear his first name) 'was the former tyrant of the great Tyne firm, the legendary, pitiless protagonist of more than one colossal battle of industry in which workmen and their wives and children had starved – and the hardy despot had sworn that he would see them rot before he yielded one inch to their demands. And he had melted in fatigue beneath the solicitude of the terrible wife whom he adored!'[62] If this pitiless champion could capitulate before a nagging wife's raddled charms, what chance for a less single-minded bourgeois, for equivocating Alan, faced with social deliquescence? Symbolised by that Kentish train, England was prevented from moving forward by the TUC's frail signal. Standard-bearer for organised labour, the engine's driver would not disobey this signal's instruction. Sitting in their stalled train, respectable citizens could only wait and hope. The general strike collapsed after nine days. This railway signal will lift. English life moved forward again. This train will rumble towards Dover. Threats recede: but thoughtful citizens and passengers must ponder, like Arthur Wellesley on an earlier visit to the continent, that this was the nearest run thing you ever saw in your life. And what if the 1926 general strike should prove to be not the last episode in nationwide organised working-class action, but the first?[63]

British history makes the British general strike a British difficulty. Waiting for the Rome Express to depart from the Gare de Lyon, Alan Frith-Walter

> saw men and women hurrying into a train – a train with a common little locomotive and many narrow compartments marked with a '3'. They had no luggage bigger than handbags; they carried newpapers, some of them. Suburbans going home to-night and every night, to their simple evening soup, and their tiny enormous worries. The same lives were being lived here, in this city of romance and prestige, as were lived at Waterloo and Liverpool Street.[64]

And at Newcastle; and at Knype. The English Channel presents no barrier to class struggle. Expanded to continental scale, tensions between province and metropole, between England and Abroad, imbricate class with status. Should crisis deepen, then these intricate relationships will clarify. Status, region, religion, ethnicity: all will precipitate to class relations, just as Marx predicted all those years ago. With capital locked in titanic struggle against organised labour, class tensions will cross national borders. Later in *Accident*, Jack tells Alan that fourteen passengers were injured when their train crashed, but that nobody was killed. It is from a French worker, a waiter in Mondane's station restaurant, that Alan learns that his train's driver died. With his ideas already disturbed by Jack's political quarrel with Pearl, this news upsets Alan.

> The man had a home somewhere, hopes, regrets, ambitions, plans, a past, a future, good qualities, was of a certain experience and maturity, or he would not have been put in charge of a precious train de luxe, scores of lives entrusted to his good judgement and technical equipment. And he was entirely innocent, and he was dead. Simple! And his widow would soon know she was a widow, if she did not already know it. Alan could hear the woman telling her five children: 'Your father is dead', and the youngest children crying and not quite understanding why they cried.[65]

Alan is disturbed by the driver's double innocence: as a victim in a crash which he did not cause, and as a casualty in a half-declared class war. Throughout his journey Alan puzzles about what might justify the privilege which he enjoys so thoroughly. Leaving Victoria, he is repelled by his Pullman carriage's other passengers: 'What a cargo of opulent beings, of whom it might be said that for them the sensual world did indeed exist! What a cargo of fleshly ideals and aspirings!'[66] He buys two tickets for the Rome Express, so that he will not have to share his wagons-lit compartment. Challenged to explain this plutocratic exclusion, he worries that 'He, Alan, was becoming the weak victim of luxurious habits. Why should he refuse to accept conditions which were accepted by the majority of even wealthy people?'[67]

Alan recognises that Jack's decision to stand for Parliament in the ILP interest – 'Jack, his own son, a fanatic!'[68] – is calculated class treason. This decision will not go unnoticed.

> The news would resound throughout the continents. One day, soon, it would be the chief item on the front pages of newspapers. It would be in every mouth. A scion of the world-renowned firm of Frith, Walter & Co – known colloquially as 'Friths' – 'gone red!' The thousands of employees would grin. The partners would look askance. The directors and heads of department would look askance. The clerks would unconvincingly pretend that nothing on earth had happened. The official daily luncheons – such fine cooking! – on Tyneside and at the London offices where Alan reigned, would be scenes of mourning.[69]

Alan shudders at the prospect of social shame rippling through Friths' complex organisation; but he recognises that Jack must follow his conscience's dictates.

> He [Alan] had a superfluity of money, and he was squandering it on an inexcusable self-indulgence. Were his heart and brain in such a state that he could find no better use for riches? Were there not hospitals, educational schemes, the advancement of science? He was getting gross and ostentatious, after the style of a plutocrat who by chicane has made a fortune in a moment, and is too ignorant and coarse to employ it with dignity. He was ashamed of his compartment. Jack was right. But he could not instantly confess an error of taste to the beautiful superior creature.[70]

Ay, there's the rub. Pearl – that beautiful, superior, expensive creature – would not understand. She does not understand. In the novel's key chapters, titled 'Politics' and 'More politics', first Jack and then Pearl tries to persuade Alan – and, through him, to persuade the reader and each other – of violently opposed positions' truth. Cyril Connolly thought Alan a cipher, a weathercock registering every change in others' emotional attitudes; but that is just how Bennett must use him. Caught in their train 'like rats in a trap',[71] two historic enemies slug it out. Flint-hard capital (Pearl) confronts an insurgent labour movement (Jack) determined to ensure that workers receive a greater share of the wealth which they create. Equivocating Alan must decide which side gets history's nod.

This, of course, he cannot do. Persuaded first by one side's arguments and then by the other's, he swivels like Connolly's weathercock, driven by every wind-shift. Like any other troubled liberal, Alan hopes for compromise. Slowly, this begins to emerge. The French railway company provides a relief train to carry passengers from the crash site to Mondane. 'Composed exclusively of third-class compartments', this relief train is much less palatial than the Rome Express; though the Frith-Walter family still manages to commandeer an entire carriage.

> Alan sat on hard, yellow, unclean wood. The compartments were not properly compartments, but mere semi-enclosures. No privacy except the chill and draughty privacy of the entire coach! For there was no heating. 'Well', Alan had philosophically thought at first, 'this is how ninety percent of people have to travel, and it's just as well to be reminded of the fact.'[72]

In this neutral setting, entrenched attitudes begin to moderate. Alan is surprised to see Pearl and Jack talking quietly to each other at the other end of the coach, not shouting past each other. Flint-hard Pearl starts to soften. Earlier, she had accepted Alan's suggestion that she should stop smoking, signifying to the reader that she could accept reasoned argument. In the Italian customs shed at Mondane Pearl unexpectedly succours Mrs Lucass, absurdly ranting about her impounded luggage.[73] Jack, too, grows less intransigent. In Genoa he offers to abandon his socialist political career to save his marriage. Now fully softened, Pearl declines his offer: then declares that she will stick by him even if he does stand for the ILP. Capital and labour reach a historic compromise. Given good-will on both sides Labour's rights can be advanced, it appears, without upending the social apple cart. E. M. Forster's hunch from *Howards End* (1910) has turned out well. Working through railways, the great connector, 'Only connect' did the trick.

Judgements

Like Charles Dickens, Arnold Bennett's popularity with a wide novel-reading public damaged his literary reputation.[74] When *Accident* was published in January 1929, Bennett had twenty-six months left to live.[75] Declining a knighthood in 1918 failed to prevent his reputation among rising literary lions from fading to avuncular irrelevance. In 1924 Virginia Woolf wounded that reputation fatally, in her essay 'Mr Bennett and Mrs Brown'. Unlike insightful younger modernists (like, for example, to pick one name at random, Mrs Woolf herself) Arnold Bennett, she urged, would be unable to understand a particular woman's psychological inwardness as she sat, 'very clean, very small, rather queer, and suffering intensely' opposite beaky Virginia in a Southern Railway train travelling from Richmond to Waterloo.[76] Woolf's attack must seem fatuous to our eyes, grounded in its bald assertion that 'in or about December, 1910, human character changed'. Evidence for this striking lurch comes in a single reference 'to the character of one's cook'.[77] This fiend's leading characteristic, we learn, consists in bursting into the drawing room at all hours to borrow *The Daily Herald* (a Labour paper), and to demand information about hats. The lower orders are getting frightfully uppity. Jellylike, Bloomsbury's liberal privilege quivers.

Just the issue which Bennett addressed in *Accident*, of course; but no critic noticed this fact then, or later. With modernism's radical individualism privileging psychological insight beyond sociological oversight, Bennett's romantic realism crashed from grace. Writing in 1940s' austerity, for Walter Allen *The Strange Vanguard* and *Accident* 'represent, as they belong to, Bennett's world of luxury yachts and *wagons-lit*. They were conceived as commercial articles and are now unreadable'.[78] In the most extended modern discussion of this novel, John Lucas judges that *Accident* had the makings for 'a very fine, perhaps even great, novel'.[79] This promise collapsed after the train crash, he thinks, as Bennett lurched into a 'cheery resolution of all difficulties'.[80] *Accident* certainly does change gear after everybody leaves their train in Genoa. At this point, three quarters of the way to the last page, Bennett shifts completely into his 'Imperial Palace' writing mode, and starts counting bathrooms in luxury hotel suites. Alan Frith-Walter's world does end with a resoundingly comfy whimper. But Lucas' broader evaluation of *Accident* is instructive. Promisingly, he locates the novel in its time. 'Even more than the 1890s', he suggests, 'the spirit of the age at the end of the 1920s must have seemed *fin de siècle*'.[81] "Yes!" one wants to urge him. "Go on! Tell us about the general strike!" Lucas does not. He tells us about *The Waste Land* instead, about *Vile Bodies* and Edward Upward's 'The railway accident'. This literary turn robs Bennett's achievement of its proper context. *Accident* is measured against the wrong things. Quite against John Lucas' intentions, one suspects, the shade of Virginia Woolf, that supercilious prig, sports the laurel wreath.[82]

Do not mistake my argument. *Accident* is no masterpiece. That said, John Lucas' final judgement on the novel – 'a broken-backed affair'[83] – is ungenerous. This novel may be less satisfying than Arnold Bennett's best work – *Anna of the*

Five Towns say, or *Clayhanger*, or *The Old Wives' Tale*, or *Riceyman Steps* – but *Accident* is better than Lucas suggests. With 1920s' modernism looking no less quaintly historical today than the Five Towns novels, let us not constrain enthusiasm too fully. Bennett's handling of Pearl, of Jack, of grim Lucass' harridan wife, displays that compassionate objectivity which William Scheick admired in Anna Tellwright's portrait.[84] As in his major novels, here Bennett weaves personal and social threads, creating an entertaining and instructive design. Passengers' lapses into unreason – vague and formless fears when their boat train stops in Kent; wilder anxieties about French railway accidents always running in couples (and, after the first two events have happened, in threes); Mrs Lucass' superstitious terror when, convinced that her train is doomed, she forces her husband to bale out on a wayside station's darkened platform in the middle of the night – undercut railways' long-standing cultural status as exemplars for reliable mechanical reason. Dissolving railways' accepted status allows Bennett to insinuate other matters. The 1926 General Strike leached respectable British people's trust in public institutions' solidity. Arguing against Jack's red-blooded socialism, Pearl insists that British capitalism stands rock-solid. In 1927, two years before the Crash.

A thoroughgoing realist and a Francophile, Arnold Bennett learned many lessons from Émile Zola. *Accident* may stand in *La Bête Humaine*'s shadow, but it treats issues of similar scale. Nor is the manner in which it treats those issues wholly to be despised. In *Accident* Arnold Bennett wrote a more penetrating, and a more convincingly canonical, British 'railway novel' than any competitor ever managed. For that reason if for no other, this work ill-deserves oblivion.

Notes

1 Jack Simmons, *The Victorian Railway*, London, Thames & Hudson, 1991, p. 218, quoting Marcel Proust, *Remembrance of Things Past*, translated by C.K. Scott-Moncrieff, London, Faber, 1938, vol. 2, p. 1038.

2 J. B. Priestley, *English Journey*, London, Heinemann and Gollancz, 1934, pp. 211–12.

3 Priestley, *English Journey*, pp. 233, 211.

4 D. H. Lawrence, *Sons and Lovers* [1913], Harmondsworth, Penguin, 1948, p. 204. Always check a novelist's railway details. Leonard's 'Flying Scotchman' cannot be the 10.00 a.m. ex-Kings' Cross or ex-Waverley – for these lads are gawping at the Midland Railway's main line north from Trent. The time is wrong for the East Coast companies' trains, in any case; but so it is for Midland expresses pounding to or from the Settle and Carlisle line. April 1910's *Bradshaw* reveals no

up or down Scottish train passing Trent at any time remotely like half-past six in the morning or evening.

5 Lawrence, *Sons and Lovers*, pp. 102–3.
6 Keith Waterhouse, *Billy Liar*, London, Joseph, 1959.
7 Arnold Bennett, *A Man From the North* [1898], London, Hamish Hamilton, 1973, p. 1.
8 Arnold Bennett, *Whom God Hath Joined* [1906], London, Methuen, 1935, p. 20.
9 Bennett, *Whom God Hath Joined*, p. 45.
10 Arnold Bennett, *Hilda Lessways*, London, Methuen, 1911, p. 385. See also 'The matador of the Five Towns', in Arnold Bennett, *The Matador of the Five Towns, and Other Stories* [1912], London, Chatto & Windus, 1972, p. 2: 'Robert Brindley [an architect] drew a time-table from his breast-pocket with the rapid gesture of habit. All men of business in the Five Towns seem to carry that time-table in their breast-pocket'.
11 Bennett, *Hilda Lessways*, p. 224.
12 Arnold Bennett, *Clayhanger*, London, Methuen, 1910, pp. 474–5.
13 Arnold Bennett, *The Card: a Story of Adventure in the Five Towns* [1910], London, Methuen, 1950, pp. 256, 218–21. Earlier in this comic novel, Denry finds himself locked in a Palladian mansion's state rooms. He finds a striking measure against which to judge this august opulence: 'Denry had once seen a Pullman car, which had halted at Knype Station with a French actress on board … What he saw now presented itself to him as a train of Pullman cars, one opening into the other, constructed for giants': Bennett, *The Card*, p. 121.
14 Priestley, *English Journey*, p. 210; Mary Kelly, *The Spoilt Kill* [1961], Harmondsworth, Penguin, 1964, p. 19. The Surrey heathlands devastated by Martian heat-rays reminded another observer 'more than anything, of the Potteries at night': H. G. Wells, *The War of the Worlds* [1898], edited by David Y. Hughes and Harry M. Geduld, Bloomington, Indiana University Press, 1993, p. 88. Snarling in reply, Arnold Bennett reported himself pleased that Potteries scenery had impressed Wells: H. G. Wells, *An Experiment in Autobiography*, London, Macmillan, 1934, p. 533.
15 Bennett, *Whom God Hath Joined*, p. 13.
16 Arnold Bennett, *Helen with the High Hand* [1908], London, Nelson, n. d., p. 1.
17 Bennett, *Whom God Hath Joined*, pp. 176–7.
18 Bennett, *Clayhanger*, p. 7.
19 Bennett, *Clayhanger*, pp. 3–4. This 'greatest railway line in England' is the Grand Junction, opened in 1837 but soon incorporated in the London and North Western Railway's main line from Euston to Carlisle. 'Between Stafford and Warrington', Gordon Biddle tells us (in *The Railway Surveyors: the Story of Railway Property Management, 1800–1990*, London, Ian Allan and the British Rail Property Board, 1990, p. 112), '[Joseph] Locke's Grand Junction Railway passed through nowhere of importance (Crewe did not then exist) and completely missed the Potteries'. Missing the Potteries had little to do with borough prejudices for Biddle. Much more urgent was Joseph Locke's desire to avoid gradients taxing early steam locomotives' puny

power. For other diversions see V. A. Hatley, 'Northampton hoodwinked? How a main-line of railway missed the town a second time', *Journal of Transport History*, 1966, 1st series, 7, pp. 160–9 and J. R. Hepple, 'Abingdon and the G. W. R., or why the Oxford line missed the town', *Journal of Transport History*, 1974, 2nd series, 2, pp. 155–66; for fictional struggles see L. T. C. Rolt, *Winterstoke*, London, Constable, 1954, pp. 135–8.

20 Given its restrictive compass, 'the Knotty' (the North Staffordshire Railway) was a progressive company. 'Knype is no mean railway station', Bennett tells us, quite correctly. 'It is the headquarters of a local railway company with a capital of over ten millions of money, a gross income of nearly a million, and a permanent way of over two hundred miles – a steady four per cent line' (Bennett, *Clayhanger*, p. 44). Riding in 'a third-class railway carriage belonging to the North Staffordshire Railway Company', and rolling on that company's loop line between Longshaw and Hanbridge' Edward Till, a notably imprudent underaker, stows his gorgonzola in a baby's coffin, with comically grisly consequences (Arnold Bennett, 'In a new bottle', in Bennett, *The Grim Smile of the Five Towns* [1907], Harmondsworth, Penguin, 1946, p. 188). Returning to his native town after many years' residence elsewhere, Toby Hall notices that the Turnhill loop line's train service has not changed in decades. 'We return Radicals to Parliament', Toby's creator tells us, 'but we are proud of a railway which for English conservatism brooks no rival' (Arnold Bennett, 'Beginning the new year', in Bennett, *Grim Smile*, p. 113). Communal particularism binds while it supports, of course. '"What a ghastly line!"' Edwin Clayhanger winges, marooned on a Moorland branch. '"I remember Ingpen telling me there was one fairish train into Knype in the morning and one out in the afternoon. And there wouldn't be that if the Locomotive Superintendent didn't happen to live at Axe:"' Arnold Bennett, *These Twain*, London, Methuen, 1916, p. 469.

21 Bennett, *Hilda Lessways*, p. 221.

22 Bennett, *Clayhanger*, p. 4.

23 Bennett, *Hilda Lessways*, p. 23.

24 Bennett, *Helen with the High Hand*, p. 8.

25 Bennett, *Hilda Lessways*, p. 165.

26 Bennett, 'Matador of the Five Towns', p. 5.

27 Bennett, *Hilda Lessways*, pp. 228–9.

28 That does not make him a northern nationalist like the Newcastle-born Basil Bunting, informing his Berkshire Quaker school's headmaster in 1916 that 'I have utterly failed to be happy here. … I think there must be some great underlying difference between North & South which makes people with Northern manners comfortable & easy to deal with, but people with Southern manners are, for me utterly *impossible* and hateful. … I think it is your duty to give me my [train] fare to Newcastle'. Quoted in Keith Alldritt, *The Poet as Spy: the Life and Wild Times of Basil Bunting*, London, Aurum, 1998, 16. Original emphasis.

29 Arnold Bennett, 'The death of Simon Fuge', in Bennett, *Grim Smile*, pp. 136–7.

30 Bennett, 'Death of Simon Fuge', p. 137.

31 Linda R. Anderson, *Bennett, Wells and Conrad: Narrative in Transition*, London, Macmillan, 1988, pp. 59–62.

32 Bennett, *The Card*, pp. 177–8.

33 Bennett, *These Twain*, p. 524.

34 Bennett, 'Matador of the Five Towns', p. 40.

35 Arnold Bennett, *The Old Wives' Tale* [1908], London, Dent, 1936, p. 99. Bennett bends history here. The North Staffordshire Railway's Loop Line was projected in 1847, but building did not start before the 1860s and it was not completed until 1875. See Jack Simmons, *The Railway in England and Wales, 1930–1914. Volume 1: the System and its Working*, Leicester, Leicester University Press, 1978, p. 102.

36 Bennett, *Old Wives' Tale*, p. 414.

37 'The first thing he saw was an electric tram, and the second thing he saw was another electric tram. In Toby's time there were no trams at Turnhill, and the then recently-introduced steam-trams between Bursley and Longshaw, long since superceded, were regarded as the final marvel of science as applied to traction. And now there were electric trams at Turnhill! The railway renewed his youth, but this darting electricity showed him how old he was': Bennett, 'Beginning the new year', pp. 113–4.

38 Bennett, *Old Wives' Tale*, pp. 368–73.

39 This was no overnight change, of course. In *The 12.30 from Croydon* [1934], Harmondsworth, Penguin, 1953, Freeman Wills Croft contrived an alibi for a comfortably circumstanced murderer through scheduled air services between London and Paris. Five years later, in *Party Going*, London, Hogarth Press, 1939, Henry Green besieged a set of wealthy friends, bound for unspecified Continental delights, in fog-bound Victoria station.

40 Since drafting these words I have discovered that Graham Boyes, Matthew Searle and Donald Steggles (eds), *Ottley's Bibliography of British Railway History: Second Supplement*, York, National Railway Museum, 1998, p. 403 does list *Accident* – but to make it no more than 'A novel centred on a railway accident on a journey from London to Genoa'. By this measure *Hamlet* is just a play about high politics in the Danish court.

41 Anderson, *Bennett, Wells and Conrad*.

42 As 'his light novel' (Walter F. Wright, *Arnold Bennett: Romantic Realist*, Lincoln, University of Nebraska Press, 1971, p. 129), 'only a pot-boiler' (D. A. Peart, 'Literature and the railway in the nineteenth and twentieth centuries', Unpublished MA thesis, Liverpool University, 1964, p. 117), or 'competent and readable without significance' (Olga R. R. Broomfield, *Arnold Bennett*, Boston, Twayne, 1984, p. 117).

43 The *Punch* review is quoted in James Hepburn (ed.), *Arnold Bennett: the Critical Heritage*, London, Routledge & Kegan Paul, 1981, p. 107; Connolly's review from *The New Statesman*, 19 January 1929, is reprinted in Hepburn (ed.), *Arnold Bennett*, pp. 491–5.

44 Arnold Bennett, 'Catching the train', in Bennett, *Matador of the Five Towns*, pp. 150–64.

45 Arnold Bennett, *Accident*, London, Methuen, 1929, pp. 50, 52.

46 Hepburn (ed.), *Arnold Bennett*, p. 493.

47 Bennett, *Accident*, p. 93.

48 *Ibid*, pp. 74, 78.

49 *Ibid*, pp. 71–2, 126, 165–6.

50 On 4 December 1907 Bennett took train from Paris to London. 'The English side of the journey has improved', he noted. 'Better carriages: electric light, contrasted with oil in French train.[…]Permanent way much better in England than in France. Carriages quieter. Porters better and more agreeably man-like'. Newman Flower (ed.), *The Journals of Arnold Bennett, 1896–1910*, London, Cassell, 1932, p. 270.

51 Bennett, *Accident*, p. 1.

52 Martin Kanes, *Zola's La Bête Humaine: a Study in Literary Creation*, Berkeley, University of California Press, 1962, p. 22.

53 Newman Flower (ed.), *The Journals of Arnold Bennett, 1911–1921*, London, Cassell, 1932, p. 9.

54 Arnold Bennett, *Letters of Arnold Bennett*, ed. James Hepburn, vol. 2, London, Oxford University Press, 1968, pp. 285–6.

55 Bennett, *Accident*, pp. 164–71. Never one to waste good copy, Bennett also published an account of this accident in *New Age* on 20 July 1911 (reprinted as 'A book in a railway accident', in Bennett, *Books and Persons: Being Comments on a Past Epoch, 1908–1911*, London, Chatto & Windus, 1917, pp. 328–30). He told his journal that 'we had shaved a short goods train standing on the next line' (Flower (ed.), *Journals, 1911–1921*, p. 10). In *Accident* this humble, passive goods train becomes '"Some special train that two American bankers had had, for Turin. It was returning empty. An engine and two carriages. The engine's nearly upside-down. It left the track – some catch-points open or something, and hit our train"' (Bennett, *Accident*, p. 176). An interesting change. Bennett goes sharply upmarket, from a local goods train to a bankers' special. This is a hackneyed projectile, fired straight from *The Strand Magazine*. Special trains were whistled up with monotonous regularity by Sherlock Holmes and his competitors.

56 Arthur Griffiths, *The Rome Express*, London, Milne, 1896.

57 Henry Pelling, *A Short History of British Trade Unionism*, Harmondsworth, Penguin, 1963, p. 174.

58 Bennett, *Accident*, pp. 21–2. Bennett uses the railway's machine ensemble for metaphorical purposes, but he knows just a little less about it than one might wish. In his day British rails were wedged in chairs bolted to sleepers. Fish plates connected one rail to the next.

59 Cf Morgan Forster's short story 'The machine stops', satirising mechanised utopias contrived by H. G. Wells, Arnold Bennett's close friend. See E. M. Forster, *Collected Short Stories* [1947], Harmondsworth, Penguin, 1954, pp. 109–46.

60 As in Henry Green's *Party Going*, when Britain's notables have to barricade themselves against the mob behind the Grosvenor Hotel's stout doors on Victoria Station's concourse. Not a convincing episode: on the whole, Kent and Surrey commuters were not (and are not) colourable *sans-culottes*.

61 Bennett, *Accident,* p. 9.

62 *Ibid,* p. 43.

63 Douglas Browne's thriller countenanced this possibility. A second general strike paralyses Britain, a decade after the first. As then, transport is particularly hard-hit. "'It is curious the hold Communism has on the railways,'" one character muses: "'It is the same in every country'" (Douglas G. Browne, *The Stolen Boat-Train,* London, Collins, 1935, p. 255). British rail traffic dwindles almost to nothing, with the Southern Railway managing to run only one passenger service each day. For prestige reasons this service is the *Golden Arrow.* Bound for Dover, one day the down train disappears – only to chuff from an unexpected train ferry some time later. Its carriages stuffed with heavily-armed German soldiers, this train's passage to London is facilitated by Socialist League railwaymen-fanatics suborned by Berlin's gold. A far-fetched idea, of course; but which 1930s political pundit anticipated the Stalin-Ribbentrop pact?

64 Bennett, *Accident,* pp. 51–2.

65 *Ibid.,* p. 209.

66 *Ibid.,* p. 12.

67 *Ibid.,* pp. 72–3.

68 *Ibid.,* p. 76.

69 *Ibid.,* p. 76.

70 *Ibid.,* p. 73.

71 *Ibid.,* p. 61.

72 *Ibid.,* p. 197.

73 *Ibid.,* pp. 220–1.

74 John Gross, 'Dickens: some recent approaches', in John Gross and Gabriel Pearson (eds), *Dickens and the Twentieth Century,* London, Routledge & Kegan Paul, 1962, p. ix; Walter Allen, *Arnold Bennett,* London, Home & van Thal, 1948, pp. 9–10, 101–3.

75 Even Bennett's passing merits a footnote in British transport history. Having contracted typhoid from Parisian restaurant water (so much for high living!), in March 1931 he lay dying in his mansion flat above Baker Street underground station. His last days' trials were eased when straw was spread on the road outside to muffle traffic noise – the last occasion when this happened in London. See Ian Parker, 'Traffic', *Granta,* 65, 1999, p. 28.

76 Virginia Woolf, 'Mr Bennett and Mrs Brown' [1924], in Woolf, *Collected Essays,* volume 1, edited by Leonard Woolf, London, Hogarth Press, 1966, p. 323. Could Mrs Brown's suffering have been caused by Mrs Woolf's beady glare? We should be told. As it happens, Beverley Nichols (*Death to Slow Music,* London, Hutchinson, 1956, p. 7) spikes Woolf's gun, reporting how 'the sketch of an old woman's profile, hurriedly glimpsed in an bus' could set a novelist writing. 'Which', he continues, 'was all that was needed to set Arnold Bennett writing his long saga of *The Old Wives' Tale*'. How's that for inwardness?

77 Woolf, 'Mr Bennett and Mrs Brown', p. 320. Astonishingly, Woolf's claim is taken seriously in some literary nooks. 'On [*sic*] or about December 1910 human nature

changed, Virginia Woolf remarked, and well she might have', the blurb to Peter Stansky, *On or About December 1910: Studies in Cultural History*, Cambridge, Mass., Harvard University Press, 1996 tells us. 'The company she kept, the Bloomsbury circle, took shape before the coming World War I, and would have a lasting impact on English society and culture after the war'. Did no editor notice a yawning gulf between Stansky's vast claim and the limping evidence marshalled to support it?

78 Allen, *Arnold Bennett*, pp. 98–9.

79 John Lucas, *Arnold Bennett: a Study of his Fiction*, London, Methuen, 1974, p. 213.

80 *Ibid.,* p. 218.

81 *Ibid.,* pp. 217–18.

82 As literary modernism creaks towards its quietus, some judgements begin to favour Bennett over Woolf – or, at least, to recognise how unfair was Woolf's attack. For examples see Irving Howe, 'Mr Bennett and Mrs Woolf: late justice for one of modernism's victims', *New Republic*, 4 June 1990, pp. 26–9; and Wendy Lesser, 'Who's afraid of Arnold Bennett?', *New York Times Book Review*, 2 September 1997, p. 39.

83 Lucas, *Arnold Bennett*, p. 213.

84 William J. Scheick, 'Compassion and fictional structure: the example of Gissing and Bennett', *Studies in the Novel*, 15, 1983, p. 307.

Part II

Beyond the Canon

7

Crime on the line

Conjured illusions

'Seven o'clock in the evening on a chilly Monday in March', a routine who-dunnit begins. 'The boat train had left Dover twenty minutes ago, travel-ling slowly through the dense fog that blanketed the country'.[1] Sir Julian Sheriffe shares his compartment on this London-bound train with two crooks. One is French, the other Dutch. Put a bad baronet in company with foreign crooks, and we can be confident that this journey will not end well. Sure enough, seven pages later the boat train stands halted. It is then struck violently from behind by a train overrunning fog signals. Sixteen passengers die in this 'terrible accident on the Dover Express'. With his story launched with a satisfy-ingly loud bang, this author now guides us firmly away from railway travel. His novel's remaining pages engross us (or fail to engross us) in a mundane country house mystery. This is a wholly conventional action. 'There were times during my reading', the anthologist Bryan Morgan reports, 'when it seemed that half the crime short stories published before the first world war began, "The stranger in the astrakhan coat leaned towards me across the first-class compartment" and I read on avidly, not to realise until perhaps half the story had passed that its action could as well have taken place in a cathedral vestry or a bordello'.[2] He was disappointed at where these stories ended. We should be interested in where they started. 'All sorts of comedy, tragedy, gallantry and melodrama of real life were often enacted in very ordinary railway compartments', C. Hamilton Ellis insists, 'as many eminent novelists quickly discovered'.[3] Eminent novelists like Charles Dickens might have discovered this truth quickly, but most forgot it with equal expedition. It was left to writers working in popular genres to probe the railway's value for fiction. None of these genres has attracted significant crit-ical attention, but crime fiction has fared least badly. In this chapter we consider railways' broad treatment in whodunnits, thrillers and spy novels. Chapter 8 focusses more narrowly on the train as a site for dirty deeds.

With railways enjoying a monopoly in passenger land transport beyond the strictly local any British writer setting a crime story among travellers between 1830 and 1914 had little option but to describe railway travel. This was no less true for French, German or Italian writers, of course. It offers no explanation why 'British crime-writing and British railway-writing are of the highest world standards',[4] why detective fiction and British railways go together like bacon and eggs, forming 'one of the better sub-genres of crime fiction'.[5] Much of this excellent work appeared under *noms de plume.* Marketing reasons lay behind some disguises,[6] but protecting reputations as serious writers forced some authors to hide their real features. In common with other popular genres, canon-building literary critics stigmatised crime fiction as 'light', not worth critics' attention (except, of course, as bedtime reading to help the Senior Common Room's port and nuts go down). "'My name's Carver'", one man reports, "'and I certainly write books. But according to most of the critics I'm not an author – I write detective novels and they don't consider that that's being an author'". One mad critic goes so far (by train) as to murder a popular crime novelist, as "'a service to the literary craft'".[7] Even major figures found themselves excluded by this undiscriminating discrimination. Graham Greene acknowledged Eric Ambler as the master of their thrilling craft. Today, Greene's novels are standard university reading list fodder,[8] while Ambler's novels are out of print. These slights hurt. Binding up his wounds, twentieth-century British comic fiction's greatest writer (and a life-long crime fiction fan) guyed canonical judgements:

> He held rigid views on the art of the novel, and always maintained that an artist with a true reverence for his craft should not descend to goo-ey love stories, but should stick austerely to revolvers, cries in the night, missing pages, mysterious Chinamen and dead bodies – with or without gash in throat.[9]

"'I don't pretend to draw character'", one writer tells his friends. "'They tell me it's not necessary in detective stories'".[10] Privileging plot construction over character drawing, detective and crime fiction[11] damaged its academic reputation. Conventional literary criticism awards high marks for character development; but when we readers thirst to know who did what foulness to whom – and when, where and why – delicate Jamesian inwardness clogs the action.

Bundle all these factors together, and we see why chapters treating crime and comic literature must differ from what has gone before. In Part I of this book we probed particular texts rather closely. In this second part we must privilege breadth over depth, skimming many British texts. As with our discussion of canonical work, this does not require us to limit our attention entirely to British authors, nor prevent us from following some Britons abroad – if only to observe blackguardly Otherness among people unfortunate enough to have been born foreigners. 'There's any amount of frontier smuggling on Continental railways', Thorpe Hazell muses. 'I once saw half a hundredweight of tobacco fixed under a passenger coach on the St. Gotthard, and beautifully run through Chiasso'.[12] Wouldn't happen at Berwick on Tweed, of course: and, among Englishmen abroad, only farouche Mr Norris would stoop to smuggling objects past guards on the border between Holland and Germany.[13]

Birth and transfiguration

We might be less surprised that British railway crime fiction gathered few critical plaudits if we appreciated that early readers treated it no less lightly. 'The detective short story has never received its due', an anthologist mourned seven decades ago. 'You read it usually in a magazine, possibly on a train journey; you may be enthralled by it; then you lay it down or give away or lose your magazine and forget it'.[14] Context determined form. Today, long-haul airline passengers buy interminable novels to while away interminable journeys. They inherit this practice from habits born on the smoothly travelling railway train. A book was useless for jolting journeys on horseback or by coach, but 'The idea of reading while travelling on trains is as old as the railroad itself'.[15] When, from the mid-nineteenth century, newsagents and booksellers began to lease space for platform bookstalls, publishers rushed to issue *yellowbacks*: newly commissioned 'railway novels' and existing titles reissued in uniform 'railway libraries'.[16] Given a strong and growing market for exciting fiction, this was sound commercial sense. '"I never travel without my diary"', Gwendolen tells Cicely. '"One should always have something sensational to read in the train"'.[17] If one's own diary was less sensational than Gwendolen's, then Mr Smith or Mr Menzies could supply lurid substitutes. More and more of these volumes told stories about crime and detection – like the yellowback *Revelations of a Lady Detective* (1864). As the pioneer female sleuth sits watching the scenery pass, 'one of the technologies of modernity, the railway, speeds Mrs Paschal to the archaic Gothic gloom of a Yorkshire abbey. The anachronism is surely deliberate', a later editor tells us: 'the railway, intimately bound up with the new form of the detective novel, will cut through the conventions of the most popular fiction of the late eighteenth and early nineteenth centuries, the Gothic novel'.[18] As rail commuter traffic increased in the later nineteenth century, so new periodicals – *The Strand Magazine, Pearson's Magazine, Harmsworth's Magazine* and the rest – fed readers' demands for exciting short stories to hold attention on brief (if boring) railway journeys to and from the city office.[19] British detective fiction germinated in these periodicals' seedbed. It flowered in late Victorian and Edwardian years, just when a bloody corpse in the mansion's library came to be the whodunnit's indispensible adornment.[20] But Friday-to-Monday country house weekending itself emerged in these decades, born from spreading outer suburban railway networks.[21] Hence the abnegation shown by Sir Andrew, that late Victorian statesman who 'gave up his country house because when he journeyed to it in the train he would become so absorbed in his detective stories that he was invariably carried past his station'.[22] It is striking how these periodicals' decline from the First World War's end marched with railway passenger trains' waning patronage.[23] Railway station bookshops remained meccas for crime afficionados,[24] but detective fiction's form, content and scale shifted. Laconic hard-boiled stories found a ready market in American magazines like *Black Mask*, but Golden Age short stories' focus on a single surprise prevented their following longer crime fiction into psychological narratives.[25] Some stories continued to find publishers[26] – but as *cut-throats* (short, sharp fictions) yielded to drop-by-drop *poisoners*, so novels rose to be the dominant form.[27] By 1939 the publisher Wedge, a wafer-thin disguise for Victor Gollancz, drew comfortable profit not from periodicals stuffed with stories short enough to while away commuter trips but from cheap editions of crime novels purchased by passengers facing much longer train journeys – 'the boredom of the Flying Scotsman or the Blue Train'.[28] Plots for novel-length thrillers and crime novels remained exciting, but gained in sophistication and ingenuity.[29]

Constructed knowledge

What passes for fictional knowledge about railways in British crime fiction warrants attention. Take this fiction seriously, and interesting material springs to the eye. First, we can watch attitudes to foreign Otherness change. Early spy fiction is a fruitful field here, as German, French and Russian agents morph rapidly from cads to heroes (or vice versa), changing their sign value as Whitehall's foreign policy lurches around. Particular nations' citizens might move in or out of novelists' favour, but their substrate never shifted: foreignness always was a suspect quality in British popular culture. Not so class deference. Adjudicating platform quarrels, a railway guard's training 'led him to despise foreigners, and to respect and admire well-dressed gentlemen who travelled first class'.[30]

Second, we can examine the sense which authors make of railway's broad operating practice. John Dickson Carr set an important scene in a historical whodunnit at Paddington. His research went no deeper than examining 'a contemporary train-model in the Science Museum, South Kensington', and staring at 'Frith's once-famous painting *The Railway Station* (1883), whose background is Paddington'.[31] Frith finished his painting in 1863. When Carr gets that wrong, who can be surprised that little else convinces in his railway picture? Since he conjured a world ninety years dead, we might forgive him some errors. Less defensible are Arthur Conan Doyle's many railway mistakes in his Sherlock Holmes stories, set in and about contemporary London.[32]

Third, sex rears her alluring head in the railway's masculine life world. 'The sexual connotation of trains is well known', we were assured recently; 'particularly trains entering tunnels'.[33] Ever since Freud's ideas escaped from the psychiatric zoo, popular attitudes to railways have glided along this track. 'The south end of Sevenoaks Tunnel has agreeable memories for the writer', one unworldly vicar recalled.

> The grass-clothed cutting swept steeply up to the tree-covered hillside … Down trains could be heard when still some distance inside the tunnel, and the front of the locomotive seen a moment or so before the train burst into full view amidst a scurry of steam and smoke. It was a very satisfying spot.[34]

Ho, ho! we chortle. Passion recollected in tranquillity! Clerical consummations much to be desired! The unconscious mind in full flow! Leaching from analyst's couch to fiction, the train's sexual symbolism soon enthused novelists. Watching from her sleeping compartment's window in Virginia Woolf's last novel, Kitty studies preparations for a Scottish train's departure from a London terminus. 'She looked down the length of the train and saw the engine sucking water from a hose. It seemed all body, all muscle; even the neck had been consumed into the smooth barrel of the body'.[35] Contemplating succumbing to extra-marital infidelity, a timorous *fin de siècle* Minor Poet found his thoughts drifting from Bloomsbury to 'the Continental Express'.[36] Maddened by lust and envy, Simenon's villain determined to rape and murder his employer's mistress in an Amsterdam hotel. 'After that, with his five hundred florins, he'd take a train, a night-train, needless to say – why not the luxurious *Étoile du Nord*?'[37] Julia Starling, née Almond, shows us how firmly the train/sex nexus was rooted by the interwar years. One morning she climbed into fresh knickers, 'For her mother had always put her into clean underclothes for a railway journey "in case anything happened", by which Mrs Almond meant a railway accident'.[38] Julia does suffer an accident, but not on a train. Needing unofficially to abort a foetus, she is directed to a Camden Town tobacconist's shop near a railway arch: just where Stagg's Gardens once stood. Like couch grass, tough subterranean runners bind the modern railway to tropes about sexual excitement. They might weigh up to ninety tons, but British footplate staff always referred to warm and trembling steam locomotives (each marked by its individual if not always tractable character) as 'she'.[39] Coded as sublime rather than beautiful, the modern railway's machine ensemble always was a man's domain.

This should not surprise us. Centuries of European social theory embroidered the basic idea that men moved in reason's stern realm, women in misty domains of sentiment and emotion. Of course, from the nineteenth century the modern railway stood four-square for engineered reason. Hence the reason why, after the 1923 Grouping, the Great Western Railway published a series of books about its delectable machinery, 'for boys of all ages'.[40] Working in Walsall's Cottage Hospital from 1863 to 1878, Dorothy Pattison ('Sister Dora') 'nursed many railwaymen, and always expressed admiration for the masculine mysteries of gauges, boilers, signals, plates, and shunting'.[41] Men controlled women in this world, we see; and women entered it on men's suffrance. Propelled by fears about sexual molestation in physically isolated train compartments, respectable women soon took to the class differentiated ladies' compartments which Victorian railway companies began to supply after 1845.[42] With passenger trains' titillating potential to bring people from different social worlds into intimate but fleeting contact blending with prevailing male stereotypes of unmarried women as virgins or whores, any unaccompanied woman who declined the ladies' compartment's chaste delights risked being numbered in the other category. Certainly, popular fiction soon conjured many train-travelling bad girls. This had some slight basis in experience. Workers in well-established sex trades forged strong connections with the new railway. Large-scale traffic with soldiers barracked in Aldershot, and sailors on shore leave in Pompey, made the slums around the London and South Western Railway's terminus into Whoreterloo. Half feminine London was said to wait at night for its young man under the clock at Charing Cross, 'and the other half said that was who it was waiting for'.[43] For a few years after 1866, services between Charing Cross and Cannon Street drew a curious traffic: 'Some ladies of the street had found that the SER's first-class compartments, combined with the uninterrupted seven-minute run, provided ideal conditions for their activities at a rental that represented only a minute proportion of their income'.[44] Paris had a traffic to match this, with a special cohort of tarts working through carriages travelling the ceinture line between the Nord and Lyons termini.[45] Those stations, and the sparkling wagons-lit carriages which left their *quais* for other major cities and for luxurious watering places, attracted pricier sex workers: 'a new and specialised type of prostitute, who frequented the booking halls of railway stations, ready to relieve the tedium of a journey … for any gentleman with the wherewithal'.[46] With a string of fully consummated pre- and extra-marital affairs unsafely behind her, Connie Chatterley still disdained the Orient Express from Venice to Paris, denouncing 'the atmosphere of vulgar depravity on board *trains de luxe*'.[47]

The fourth factor which we can contemplate concerns the particular opportunities which trains offer authors. Characters from different social worlds can be jammed together to dramatic effect in a train's 'travelling incarceration', its 'isolation-cum-proximity'.[48] "'It lends itself to romance, my friend'", Hercule Poirot tells his friend the wagons-lit director as they survey browsers and sluicers in the Orient Express's dining car.

> All around us are people, of all classes, of all nationalities, of all ages. For three days these people, these strangers to one another, are brought together. They sleep and eat under one roof, they cannot get away from each other. At the end of three days they part, they go their several ways, never, perhaps to see each other again.[49]

Throwing different passengers together in a closed little society is a powerful card in the railway crime writer's hand, as we shall see in the next chapter; but it can be used in less murderous games than Agatha Christie and her peers play. Cecil Roberts' romance *Victoria Four-Thirty* (1937) interweaves fates among many passengers travelling by train from London to Athens. This idea underpinned a string of other novels. One shows us human lives entangled with the collapse of Bouch's first Tay Bridge on the last Sabbath day in 1879. Several passengers with whose life circumstances we have been invited to become interested die when a Victoria-bound Southern electric train is caught in a tunnel collapse under the North Downs. Moving in the other direction, we follow the experience of four passengers as they travel through time and Kent on the down *Golden Arrow*.[50] Bringing strangers together in brief conjuncture also infused an unusually serious late-1940s Ealing movie, *Train of Events* (1949). Three segments show us how four different groups of passengers came to be travelling on the 3.45 p.m. train from Euston to Liverpool. Our interest in these people is piqued by the movie's opening sequence – revealing that this train will crash, horribly. We spend the rest of the movie wondering who will survive.[51]

Trains offer the novelist other advantages beyond enforced contiguity. Station stops permit some passengers – perhaps physically dead; perhaps (for the plot's purpose) merely exhausted – to be unloaded, then replaced with fresh victims, villains and red herrings. With his social critique abstracted, Zola's project in *La Bête Humaine* – studying what happens when human imperfectibility collides with smooth technical perfection – enlivens narratives where we are to be entertained, not repelled, by bloody crime.[52] Railway tracks' iron inflexibility, and absolute block train control mechanisms decreed by state agencies pressed by public demands for improved passenger safety, makes railway operation highly predictable. This assists any detective seeking to apply Sherlock Holmes' nostrum that when all other explanations have been exploded, whatever remains must be the truth, however unlikely this might seem.[53] Since a particular wagon left Didcot marshalled in the middle of a goods train but never reached Newbury, the lost wagon must rest in a siding somewhere between those towns. This logic controls several other fictions. Setting his unconvincing story about a lost special train in east Lancashire, Conan Doyle is forced to invent a false industrial structure to explain how this train disappeared so completely. Among American crime magi, Ellery Queen sets Doyle's plot in a much more convincing New England setting – and Donald E. Westlake's caper thriller secretes a hijacked coffee train in a jungle-covered locomotive depot deep in Idi Amin's Uganda. Back in Edwardian Britain, understanding absolute block signalling principles allows Max Carrados to lift the blame for a terrible rail accident from an innocent engine driver.[54]

Finally, we should not disparage the value for imaginative writers of another aspect of railways' iron inflexibility: 'the Mussoliniesque precision of fictional timetables, handy for establishing time of death and for checking alibis'.[55] '"Come, Angela"', imperious Lancelot Mulliner insists. '"Let us read together in a book more moving than the Koran, more eloquent than Shakespeare, the book of books, the crown of all literature – Bradshaw's Railway Guide"'.[56] Supported with copious references to *Bradshaw* or the *A. B. C. Guide*, Golden Age crime novels pullulate with some characters' true – and others' mendacious – accounts of which train they sat in when some foulness happened somewhere else.[57] Unpicking these alibis can make tedious reading. 'Oh, yes! everything fitted in like the pieces of a puzzle', J. D. Beresford assures us.

> After that, nearly all I had to do was to discover if it had been possible for him to have left Fulford at 6.30 on the previous evening and be back there in time to get away again, as himself, by the next morning? And it was. The time-table showed me that he could have left Westbourne by the 7.10 for London; have got out at 7.50 at the first stop, Catbridge Junction, and have taken the 8.5 from there to St Edmund's in time to catch the 9.15 on the branch line back to Fulford.[58]

Elementary, my dear Watson. Once timetable conventions were firmly established, authors could beaver away subverting them. A female private detective in good practice outwits villains by pretending to retire defeated to London from a Riviera case. Then she returned to Paris on 'an *unfashionable* train'.[59] Nobody would think of looking for her there! Shards from a smashed watch-glass alert a sharp-eyed detective to an embezzling sorter's action in heaving his murdered mate's body above their travelling post office's roof, striking the victim's head against an overbridge to conceal where an iron pipe's blow actually killed him. Unnoticed on his wrist, the sorter's arrested watch tells our detective precisely what happened, and when. Recourse to the railway company's working timetable soon identifies the bridge involved, decorated with blood and hair.[60] Another case shows us a wristwatch set two hours fast, then deliberately smashed. The purpose behind this curious action was to insinuate false timing for a murderous attack. Unfortunately for the killer this watch's hands continued to rotate after it had been dashed to the ground. Penetrating the illusion, Hercule Poirot demonstrates that Paul Renaud's murderer could indeed have caught the last train from Merlinville-sur-Mer to Calais. Since this is Agatha Christie at her most perversely ingenious, Poirot then shows that she did nothing of the kind.[61] In spy fiction's *ur-text*, just reading the current Continental *Bradshaw* could not equip our hero to decipher Kaiser Bill's dastardly plan to invade Britain with troop-stuffed, steam tug-hauled barges chuffing across the North Sea from Frisia: railway timetables needed to be correlated with tide-tables.[62] To solve one case Freeman Wills Crofts' Inspector French not only must correlate *Bradshaw* with tide-tables, but also must scrutinise a photograph of moored yachts to check in which direction the tide flowed when murder was committed.[63] In another offbeat case, a signalman's log recorded precisely when trains closed a particular level crossing, rather than the times when the public timetable asserted that the crossing should have been closed. This log confirmed some suspects' alibis, directing attention to the murderer's less explicable movements.[64] In the most complicated case known to me, unpicking two brothers' attempts at establishing mutual alibis required that tightly timetabled journeys by train, plane and bus be correlated with less firmly trammelled trips by taxi and motorbike.[65]

Machine ensemble

Remarkably varied bits of the railway's equipment may be employed for murderous purposes. Rush hour crowds thronging platforms in London termini provide cover for slick stiletto work.[66] Pass from main line platforms to the underground and that old cliché, the shove in one's back on a crowded Tube platform, still looms.[67] The only *echt*-Sherlock Holmes story with significant railway content also is set on London's underground railways. When a corpse turns up beside the Metropolitan company's track, Holmes shows that it was lowered to a halted passenger carriage's roof from a house window further up the line, then fell to the ground when, approaching Aldgate station, the train rocked through pointwork.[68] A modern (if atavistically bloodthirsty) deity, the dynamo at the heart of steam-powered electric generating plant for London underground trains demands human sacrifice in one H. G. Wells story.[69] New technology blends with old evil elsewhere, too. A guard skirts death when his train leaves a country junction's platform just before one passenger's silver-plated bicycle (carried there in the guard's van) turns out to be a powerful grenade. Three platform saunterers die here, with another twelve injured.[70] Two 1920s' whodunnits peak with bomb outrages at major stations' refreshment rooms.[71] Beyond station limits, push your inebriated enemy over the parapet on a hundred-foot-high LNWR viaduct, and he will land with a satisfactorily final *splat!* at the bottom.[72] Having shoved his honest English art thief accomplice down a crevasse on the Rhone Glacier, a dastardly Italian criminal makes a dash for freedom in his own country, taking a train through the newly-electrified St Gotthard tunnel. Cornered on this train, he chooses to climb on the train's roof. As a laconic policeman notes later, "'He went off like a box of matches'".[73] Elsewhere, blithe complacency born from intricate train control systems can be turned to fiction's deadly account.[74] The police took Sir Aaron Armstrong's death to be a railway murder when his body was found close to the four-foot way in Hampstead. It needs Father Brown's commonsensical Catholic sensibility to show that, maddened by his atheistic life's empty philanthropy, Armstrong hurled himself from a window in his house, high above the line.[75] John Wain reverses that judgement. Arthur Geary's plunge through Paddington station's glass roof to death on the platform lines below might appear accidental, but Wain turns it into collective murder. Suffering a breakdown, for several weeks Geary abandoned his Oxford science job for nights in the Great Western Hotel and days spent wandering Brunel and Wyatt's station's womb-like enclosure. Just as his mental condition abated, he was hounded to death by intrusive television journalists.[76] Many plots see stunned, drugged or dead victims draped over running rails like Hollywood maidens, waiting for the next train to make murder resemble suicide or accident.[77] This device became so threadbare that fiction's dimmest policeman could see through it. Torrance's plan was much more ingenious. Contriving the appearance that a commuting city magnate had shot himself in his first class compartment on the 5.00 p.m. ex-Cannon Street service, Torrance planned to use a red hand lamp to stop the train in Blackdown Tunnel, then climb aboard and plug his victim. But how to reach the railway track, when both tunnel ends were guarded by manned signal boxes? Our murderer has a brainwave: he will enter and leave Blackdown Tunnel not horizontally but vertically, swarming down and up a rope dangling down a ventilation shaft. What a shame that this bright notion should unravel![78] At railway technology's recondite limit, north Devon bank robbers escaping up the hydraulic funicular connecting Lynmouth with Lynton find themselves foiled when a police marksman punctures the descending car's water tank. Victims of their own body weight, these robbers descend gracefully into the constabulary's waiting arms.[79] Some devices which might prove useful for criminally-inclined authors attract surprisingly little notice. When Michael Dibdin imprisons his victim in a locked railway goods van for a week in inland Sicily's baking summer heat, we realise that nobody ever thought of that trick in Britain.[80] (English summer heat might not discomfort a snowman, of course; but a good winter freeze could do the job.) More strikingly than this, 'It is a curious thing', urbane Mr Mulliner tells us, 'that in spite of the railway companies' sporting willingness to let their patrons have a tug at the extremely moderate price of five pounds a go, very few people have ever pulled a communication cord or seen one pulled.'[81] True, true. Howsoever threatened, stabbed, shot, bludgeoned, doped, poisoned, garrotted or smothered crime fiction's victims might be, rather few manage to tug that useful cord. Fruitlessly attempting to persuade conspirators that he had left the city, Hercule Poirot once paid a friend to do this on a (theoretically) non-stop boat train from Paris' Gare du Nord.[82] When a threatened passenger pulls the communication cord in another story, pantomime struggles must be mounted to prevent a tiffing lover from being hauled off to jail.[83]

We can study writers' attempts to use railway equipment to solve a perennial difficulty. '"That is, and has always been, the great stumbling-block to the murderer"', British crime fiction's first scientific detective lectures his friends: '"To get rid of the body"'.[84] Corpse-laden trunks may be hoisted into passenger trains' luggage vans if 'some dozen of tottering porters' rush to bear the weight.[85] Even this action may breed misdirection. That heavy coffin loaded on the night mail at Kings' Cross station in 1909 should have held Stephen Barr's mortal remains. Instead, it held lead ingots packed in cotton wool. The levanting Barr was arrested at Victoria, with a fortune in bearer bonds on his person.[86] Entire corpses concealed in barrels or packing cases for consignment by a freight train are best carted to the nearest railway goods shed.[87] Given solid forward planning, a railway strike then can delay murder's discovery for several days.[88] Needing to lose another inconvenient corpse, conspirators 'decided against leaving him in a trunk at the cloak-room of a railway station. It had been done before, several times, and inevitably it attracted the attention of Scotland Yard'.[89] Good thinking: this device had been done, one might say, to death. "'Bury … Cliff … Well … Acids'", a wife planning her husband's demise muses. "'Fire, quick-lime, *trunks in cloakrooms*, drowning. ...'" A severed head turns up in a suitcase in one London station's cloakroom. A slaughtered woman is discovered in Rudyard Kipling's misdirected new trunk in a station luggage office on the Brighton line. "'Do you see this grey suit I am wearing?'" a crime writer asks a fellow Bohemian party-goer in another novel: "'It was bought out of the blood of a dismembered heiress in a trunk at Waterloo Station'". "'One reads these horrid stories of corpses left in luggage'", one British archaeologist in Greece tells a formidably saurian female detective when another archaeologist's body turns up in a box. "'Ah, that's at Charing Cross", said Mrs Bradley. "Ephesus isn't a bit like Charing Cross, in spite of all that poets try to tell us'". All these grisly deposits recall forgetful Miss Prism's dereliction in leaving that capacious Ernest-stuffed handbag at Victoria's left luggage office. "'The Brighton side'", motherless Jack Worthing (a.k.a. Ernest) reports to his formidable mother-in-law-to-be. Lady Bracknell proves no railway enthusiast. "'The side is immaterial'", she thunders.[90]

As we saw in chapter 1, the modern railway's machine ensemble included social and economic elements alongside technical equipment. 'If Dukes had talked about his plans for the next robbery, on the train itself, to anyone but a *railway servant*', Nicholas Blake tells us, 'suspicion would have been incurred should they have been seen together'.[91] Blake appreciates how modern British railway workers laboured under master and servant legislation inherited from premodern days. Golden Age detective fiction's class conventions limited suspects to persons in good social standing: no servant may pull his master's shotgun trigger, or dope her mistress' bedtime cocoa.[92] It follows that no railway servant should commit fictional railway crime. This inhibits nobody. 'Jack the Wrecker', a malefactor who has caused five serious railway accidents in as many weeks, turns out to be a stationmaster maddened by the railway's machine ensemble. "'Noise! Trains! Sirens! Steam! Whistles!'" he screams, after failing to shoot the Great Trunk Railway's chairman. "'Engines that never run to time … chaos'".[93] Joseph Berch, a pre-grouping company's disgruntled ex-servant, tries to wreck several of the company's express trains by tying sleepers across the running rails.[94] In the early 1930s a London suburban station master kills himself (still a criminal act at that time) under the wheels of the long-distance train which seduced his bored wife to disastrous passion with a commercial traveller.[95] Oversleeping one morning, Old Sam Henniker fails to open the level-crossing gate for which he is responsible on a quiet branch line. The 7.01 branch train smashes through his gate and trundles on its way. Nobody is hurt – except Sam. A fiercely proud and upright man, he blames himself for derelict service. Neighbours watch his character soften as health and spirit ebb away. Eventually the railway company's letter arrives to inform him that his excellent previous service means that he will not be dismissed from his post; but by then he is comatose. He will not regain consciousness. Sam's death is some kind of suicide, born from his terror at the railway machine ensemble's ferocious labour discipline.[96] Finally, a very short story lays out a remarkably complicated murder (or, perhaps, manslaughter) involving a railway linesman. He missed catching a particular train: the 7.16. He was then given a lift by a freakish film director who was busy filming an evening paper's short story series concerning 'murder on the 7.16'. This director sat the linesman in the film company's fake railway compartment, then set the background diorama moving. As a somewhat laboured joke, he intended to make the befuddled linesman believe that he must jump from a fast-running train. Refusing to oblige, his victim clobbered the director with his sledgehammer.[97]

Conjurers

Professional

Freeman Wills Crofts (1879–1957) is the doyen of British railway crime writers. A Dublin-born Ulster protestant raised in comfortable circumstances, Crofts enjoyed a life-long fascination with transport technology. Extending to ships, cars and aircraft, this interest always remained rooted in railways. As a lad he constructed a huge model of the Forth Bridge for his garden railway.[98] In 1897 he started work as a civil engineering pupil on the Belfast Counties Railway (later the Northern Counties Committee of the Midland Railway: then, after 1923, of the LMS), rising to become chief assistant engineer. Already a part-time author, when illness forced him to retire from this post in 1929 he turned to writing crime fiction full-time. For our purposes, *Death of a Train* (1946) is his masterpiece. Concerning German spies' attempts to sabotage a crucial wartime consignment of radio valves, here he conducts the reader carefully through modern railways' operation and management, exploring remote regions in these large and complicated organisations. Novelists usually ignore these complexities. In a rare exception, J. R. L. Anderson draws our attention to 'inconspicuous little doors' at Liverpool Street station. 'You seldom notice them', he chides us, 'but they are the keys to the working life of the station, for they lead to the offices where the running of trains is controlled, freight organised, and the hundred and one things done, from arranging sleeper reservations to ensuring that trains connect with boats, that are required to move the public and its goods'.[99] With Crofts acknowledging help from a Southern Railway administrator 'advising me on points concerning which my own railway knowledge had grown out of date',[100] *Death of a Train* could be a textbook on how British 'Big Four' companies coped in wartime, with difficult operating conditions mitigated (or, some claimed, exacerbated) by close state control.[101]

This novel is his *tour de force*, but Crofts' expert railway knowledge slips into many novels which appear to be about other matters.[102] Determinedly, he explored standard 'railway crime' devices. Though he tried his hand at the locked room puzzle and the trunk murder, alibi-breaking was his *forte*. Dorothy Sayers imagined him doggedly trailing a suspect, *Bradshaw* in hand, from Stranraer to Saint Juan-les-Pins.[103] So primed were readers to discover Crofts' solutions turning on railway timetables that Agatha Christie could parody him in 'The unbreakable alibi'.[104] Much later, with Crofts safely dead, she judged him a deadly dull writer, but technically interesting as the alibi's finest conjuror. She noticed something else, as well. Christie glossed Crofts as Cyril Quain, 'sitting there with around him the A.B.Cs, the continental Bradshaws, the air-line brochures, the timetables of every kind. Even the movement of liners. Say what you will … there is order and method in Mr Cyril Quaid.'[105] Order and method: base virtues in detective fiction, as in capitalist industrialisation and Ulster presbyterianism. Crofts' relentless insistence on these virtues, codified and exemplified in rigid timetables, could be used to fool readers through misdirection. As its title suggests, 'The 8.12 from Waterloo'[106] is a London suburban train: but *The 12.30 from Croydon* (1934) is an aeroplane heading for Paris. Trying to solve the Ponson murder, dogged Inspector Tanner checks railway alibis. Some of these are London suburban services; others take him up the East Coast main line to Grantham, and to Montrose.[107] A Scottish laird's murder in a South African railway tunnel is solved when Inspector Ross breaks an alibi built around Anglo-Scottish and West Highland line train services.[108] Less exotically, smugglers use authentically timetabled trains on the Doncaster/Selby/Goole triangle to lead Inspector Willis (and Crofts' readers) astray while they break for their coaster at Hull, and freedom on the high seas.[109]

Inspector Willis tumbles that trick, of course. So would Crofts' great detective – Inspector (and later, in the fullness of time and persistence, Superintendent) French. The first British writer to follow a professional police detective through a case's twists and turns (with Inspector Burnley in *The Cask* (1920)), Crofts invented the British police procedural novel.[110] None among his coppers possessed the Golden Age amateur sleuth's imaginative flair.[111] 'Of all the jobs that fell to French', we learn in one book, 'the investigation of the life, habits and human relationships of a given individual was that which he found most tedious.'[112] Just like his maker. Crofts displays the engineer's marked distaste for human quiddities; his characters scarcely manage to rub together two dimensions, let alone three. Closely patterned on railway tracks, his fictions are resolutely linear. French is a relentless plodder, inching towards a distant goal. Like Theseus' thread, logic guides him through crime's labyrinth.

Two examples demonstrate his method. The first is a short story, 'The Suitcase'.[113] Albert Rank murders David Turner. Rank is porter to a small north London hotel, Turner a passenger guard on main line trains from King's Cross. One day Rank takes a ticket on Turner's train. He places his suitcase near the train's front, then locks himself in a lavatory near the rear, close to Turner's guard's van. At a predetermined place he leaves his lavatory, bludgeons Turner to death, steals his uniform and hides his body. Passing forward through the train disguised as Turner (to confuse witnesses), Rank collects his suitcase and slides into another lavatory to change back into his own clothes. Leaving the train at its next stop, he takes a bus to a nearby town and dumps the suitcase containing all incriminating evidence – the fatal cosh, Turner's uniform – in a convenient large river. From this town Rank takes a train back to London along a different line. Smugly, he congratulates himself that he is safe. Not from French. Deducing the uniform trick, French decides that the murderer must have taken precisely the route, and modes of transport, which Rank did take. He estimates that precisely this bridge on this river would be the best place from which to hurl incriminating evidence. He has the river dragged below that bridge, and the suitcase is recovered. Unwisely enough, Rank chose to weight it with a burnt-through firedoor from his hotel's stove. French traces new firedoor sales, identifies Rank's hotel through elimination, and collars him. Deductive reasoning has triumphed – as long as one does not inspect all those logical links too closely. His plot moves smoothly from here to there, with other routes excluded by points firmly controlled from signalman Crofts' cabin. Not for nothing do British railway workers call signalmen 'bobbies'.

Our second example is a novel, *The Sea Mystery* (1928). French is called to south Wales when a fisherman in the Loughor estuary hooks a submerged packing case containing a decomposed body. Using tide tables and *Molesworth's Pocket Book of Engineering Formulae*, French determines that this heavy case must have been tumbled into the Loughor from a particular road bridge. That would have required a portable crane. Tracing these machines' movements in the locality, he tracks the case's rail journey to Swansea (High Street) goods depot from Ashburton, in Devon. After much to-ing and fro-ing, he gets his man – as we knew he would. Crofts points the moral. 'Once again French experienced the keen delight of finding his deductions justified by the event', he crows. 'In this whole case he had really excelled himself. On several different points he had imagined what might have occurred, and on a test being made, his idea had been proved correct. Some work, that! As he did not fail to remind himself, it showed the highest type of ability'.[114] Governed by the Enlightenment project's metaphors, Freeman Wills Crofts' fictions live in a controlled, predictable, engineered world where trains run to time, positivist applied science is the royal route to knowledge and every problem has only one solution. Combined with properly employed technical knowledge (codified in *Molesworth*, tide tables and *Bradshaw*), dogged labour always will find the right answer.[115]

Amateurs – skilled and otherwise

'Your assistance will be most valuable', a military gent investigating a neighbour's death tells his friend, a solicitor. 'I know your hobby – railways. It might help us.'[116] We find ourselves less than astounded when it does. Freeman Wills Crofts stands peerless as a professional railwayman turned crime writer,[117] but several expert crime writers have been amateur railway fanatics. Finest among them is the Anglican cleric who wrote the words just quoted, Victor Whitechurch (1868–1933). Until recently this man's excellence was little recognised. In 1929 Dorothy L. Sayers saluted him as a specialist railway mystery writer, but as late as 1973 Hugh Greene complained that Whitechurch's only collection of railway mysteries between hard covers, *Thrilling Stories of the Railway* (1912), was so scarce that neither he nor any second-hand bookseller he knew ever had seen a copy for sale.[118] Facsimile reprinting solved that problem, and not before time. Resting on close knowledge – 'He knew how to scotch a point', Bryan Morgan tells us, 'what was the loading-gauge of the Great Northern and how long an engine took to rewater as well as how to play model-trains with an eccentric parishioner'[119] –

Whitechurch's railway crime stories are models of their kind. Given slick criminal work under Edwardian branch line operating conditions, the baffling disappearance of 'Sir Gilbert Murrell's picture' is technically feasible, and plays fair by the reader.[120] This piece often turns up in anthologies, but rarer gems exist. One of these, 'Donald Penstone's escape', tackles an inverted problem: not how to get off a racing express, but how to get on it. Whitechurch's solution is ingeniously expert, combining railway tail lamp codes with signalmens' standing orders.[121]

Victor Whitechurch overtops competing amateur railway crime writers, but some others enjoy good moments. A railway historian conducts us around forgotten tunnels beneath London while Michael Gilbert's Inspector Petrella hunts goods pilfered from railway yards.[122] John Creasey treats this matter sensationally. Opening with a signalman murdered because he hears a particular man's name mentioned in his box, his thriller about large-scale thefts from British Railways good yards closes with a determined attempt to wreck 'The Forest Express' near Winchester – merely in order to eliminate one witness.[123] This effect is out of scale with its cause: Creasey's melodrama shows us that not all writers can evoke the steam railway's everyday world convincingly. Elsewhere, too, errors creep in. Some can be fleabites, like seating bullhead rail in 'shoes' rather than chairs, making a poem scan 'with abominable precision, like a train clicking over the points' rather than over plain track's rail breaks, using 'granite sleepers' to hold the London and North Western's main line through Staggs' Gardens to gauge in the late 1840s, or spiriting a heavy main line express locomotive and train along the East Kent Light Railway's rusting little rails to a rotting train ferry wharf.[124] Some mistakes can be pleasantly recondite. John Ferguson's thriller turns on yet another German plot to invade Britain. Spies track Abercromby, the Mearns Scot into whose possession their coded plan's only copy has fallen, to his Auchenblae family home. This German invasion plan must reach Whitehall authorities: but all railway stations will be watched by ruthless Nazi assassins. Our hero has a bright idea.

> I remembered that some miles south there was a lonely spot that was once famous in the days when two great railway companies ran races between London and the North. This spot was the place where the two lines joined into one for the rest of the journey. There was nothing there but the signalman's cabin. In the years of which I speak that cabin was a famous place, for the signalman it was who decided which route won for the day, passing on the train which was 'belled' first, detaining its rival till the first was clear ahead. Yet though these exhilarating races were long ended, trains were still sometimes held up for either line to clear at such places – fish trains, mineral and goods, even the stately London train itself.[125]

Abercromby stows away on a fast fish train (doubtless stuffed with delectable Aberdeen haddock and Fraserburgh kippers bound for London's Billingsgate market) when it is halted at this box. Ferguson congratulates himself that he has explained why this happened; but he is wrong. The Caledonian Railway's signalman at Kinnaber Junction, furth of Montrose and Brechin, did decide whether the East Coast or West Coast train won each day's race to Aberdeen in 1895; but these races were run only by *down* trains, coming from London. Ferguson's hero needs to catch an *up* train, travelling towards London. Since two lines split to four at Kinnaber, there would be half as much reason for an up train to be checked there than at a signal box controlling any normal block section.

Errors can be worse than this. A 1950s English adventurer is suborned by Comintern agents to assassinate an American admiral arriving at Madrid's Norte station. Fair enough (for the plot, if not for the admiral); but this doomed old salt could be settled on his air-conditioned and diesel-powered Talgo luxury express without the author insisting that Spanish summers were too hot for 'coal locomotives' to cover long distances in daylight.[126] A thriller novelist disgorges a half-digested meal of railway history while setting the stage for his Trans-Siberian trainjack, then gets Russian railways' track gauge dramatically wrong.[127] In Northumberland, Ford Madox Ford persisted in routing East Coast main line expresses through Wooler ("'junction for Bamborough'");[128] no wonder that everybody got so confused. In Suffolk, Edgar Wallace entertained no sense of how closely the Board of Trade controlled railway operations when he allowed Augustus Tibbetts ('Bones' to his friends) to play around on his newly-purchased branch line. Without benefit of timetables, signals or much else in railways' machine ensemble, Bones cheerfully drives his one asthmatic locomotive, *Mary Louisa*, up and down – until the branch train almost collides with a thundering special carrying Chinese Commissioners past the main line junction.[129] Averting this near-accident requires an alert signalman to divert the runaway branch train across a facing crossover to the up main line, with the road already set and signalled for the speeding special. Couldn't be done, of course. Nor could a thief use his walking stick, hooked over telegraph wires, to swing from a fast-running train after chloroforming a city clerk and stealing his money-stuffed hand bag: clearances between train and wires would be far too great. For the same reason it is most improbable that a cow's horn protruding from a cattle wagon parked on a siding would have penetrated a woman's temple as she leaned from her compartment's window to watch a rick fire.[130] A female adventurer in a

Buchanesque chase novel could not have avoided hot pursuit by jumping in a box van parked in a Highland station's siding, then riding from that siding down the main line's steep gradient to stop in another station's goods yard. Shunting blocks, pinned wagon brakes, catch points, signals interlocked with pointwork: all would prevent her escape.[131] Much the same argument holds for that night-time special from Truro to St Blande which pitched so impetuously into a Cornish river. Even if Ted Holmes had not fallen dead on his station platform before he could close a swing bridge, this train would have been stopped at a home signal firmly interlocked with the bridge's operating lever.[132] And how could a Dorset branch line from Poxwell Regis to Krunte Abbas not be 'single-gauge'? Trains would fall off the rails if it were otherwise.[133]

In this chapter we have explored the modern railway's value for fictional crime, and considered how practitioners' played gruesome games with it. One matter we did not discuss – the train, that trundling locked room which attracted most crime writers to the railway in the first place. Our next chapter remedies this deficiency.

Notes

1 Christopher Reeve, *Murder Steps Out*, London, Ward, Lock, 1942, p. 7. For other novels which move rapidly from railway compartment beginnings to conventional Golden Age settings, see John Jefferson Farjeon, *Mystery in White*, London, Collins, 1937 and Leo Bruce, *Death of a Commuter* [1967], Chicago, Academy, 1987. Other justly (if illegally) rubbed-out bad baronets appear in Dick Donovan, 'A railway mystery', in Donovan, *Riddles Read*, London, Chatto & Windus, 1896, pp. 204–39 and John Rhode, *Death on the Boat-Train*, London, Collins, 1940.

2 Bryan Morgan, 'Introduction', to Morgan (ed.), *Crime on the Lines: an Anthology of Mystery Short Stories with a Railway Setting*, London, Routledge & Kegan Paul, 1975, p. x. Morgan's solution was to reprint only those stories where railway content is essential. That might seem over-scrupulous; until one ploughs through the dross cluttering Peter Haining's recent anthology, *Murder on the Railways*, London, Orion, 1996.

3 C. Hamilton Ellis, *Railway Carriages of the British Isles from 1830 to 1914*, London, Allen & Unwin, 1965, p. 13.

4 Morgan (ed.), *Crime on the Lines*, p. xiii. This conjunction can be exploited deviously. The cover design for a paperback edition (London, Grafton, 1961) of Georgette Heyer's *Envious Casca* [1941] flaunts a cigarette card showing a 'Schools' class locomotive in Southern Railway livery, and a British Railways (Southern Region) station sign. Clearly enough, we are about to enjoy dirty deeds in a train. Not so: the only train in this whodunnit conveys a Scotland Yard detective bent on sorting out who stabbed Lexham Manor's squire in his bedroom. Similar disappointment

comes from reading a recent edition of E. and M. A. Radford's *Death of a Frightened Editor*, Leicester, Linford, 1996. This book's cover trumpets a steam hauled express train; but nasty Mortensen met his end on the electric *Brighton Belle*.

5 H. R. F. Keating, *The Bedside Companion to Crime*, New York, Mysterious Press, 1989, p. 76.

6 John Dickson Carr provides one distinguished example, recording several different detectives' triumphs under several different names. More recently, Ruth Rendell and Edith Pargeter (among many others) have used the same device. It may be reversed: Nick Carter's exploits were penned by many hands. Plump and complacent, the crime writer Joseph Newton sits comfortably in his first-class seat on the Cornish Riviera express, heading for a brief holiday in his twenty-seven-bedroomed country cottage. Idly he picks up a newspaper purchased at Paddington's bookstall, and turns to a story under his own name. 'For the moment he cannot remember who wrote it. Poor stuff, he thinks. He must find out which "ghost" was responsible, and sack him:' G. D. H. and Margaret Cole, 'A lesson in crime', in G. K. Chesterton (ed.), *A Century of Detective Stories*, London, Hutchinson, 1935, p. 260.

7 Hugh Windsor, *Lead Him to Death*, London, Thriller Book Club, 1963, p. 7; Cole and Cole, Lesson in crime', p. 264. 'By a curious confusion', Chesterton tells us, 'many modern critics have passed from the proposition that a masterpiece may be unpopular to the the other proposition that unless it is unpopular it cannot be a masterpiece:' G. K. Chesterton, 'On detective novels', in Chesterton, *Generally Speaking: a Book of Essays*, London, Methuen, 1928, p. 2; see also Chesterton, 'A defence of detective stories', in Chesterton, *The Defendant*, London, Dent, 1901, pp. 157–62. For a more recent challenge to schemas distinguishing serious fiction from 'paraliterature' see Ian Ousby, *The Crime and Mystery Book*, London, Thames & Hudson, 1997, pp. 13, 156–60. Not only crime fiction has been slighted by precious critics, of course. We will pay some attention to other despised genres here: a fair bit to spy stories, a little to horror and science fiction, none to Westerns or family sagas. For railways and Westerns see Bill Pronzini and Martin H. Greenberg (eds), *The Railroaders: the Best of the West*, New York, Fawcett, 1986; for the railroad Western driven into thriller territory, see Whit Masterson, *The Gravy Train*, London, Hale, 1972. As these cases suggest, boundaries between genres are policed more lightly than summary accounts imply. When members of the Crime Writers Association were polled to find the top one hundred crime novels of all time, their composite list included at least sixteen books usually classified as thrillers. See Susan Moody (ed.), *Hatchard's Crime Companion*, London, Hatchard's, 1990, pp. 1–52.

8 Oddly, to some eyes. In John Banville's *The Untouchable*, London, Picador, 1997, p. 81, Victor Maskell (read: Anthony Blunt] disparages '*The Orient Express* (read: *Stamboul Train*], the first of Querell's (read: Graham Greene's] overrated Balkan thrillers'.

9 P. G. Wodehouse, 'Honeysuckle Cottage', in Wodehouse, *Meet Mr Mulliner*, London, Jenkins, 1927, pp. 270–1. Adepts will appreciate that Wodehouse wrote before Ronnie Knox laid down his ten rules for Golden Age detective fiction. Rule 5 insists that 'No Chinaman must figure in the story'. See Ronald Knox,

'Introduction', to R. Knox and H. Harrington (ed.), *Best Detective Stories: First Series*, London, Faber & Faber, 1929, p. 14. Mr Mulliner's nephew evidently shared his maker's opinion. 'Who ever first got the idea', Wodehouse enquired querulously, 'that anyone wants a beastly girl messing about and getting in the way when the automatics are popping I am at a loss to imagine:' P. G. Wodehouse, 'Thrillers', in Wodehouse, *Louder and Funnier*, London, Faber & Faber, 1933, p. 54.

10 J. J. Connington, *Truth Comes Limping*, London, Hodder & Stoughton, 1938, p. 96.

11 Following Ian Ousby (*Crime and Mystery Book*) we should distinguish several sub-genres here. Crime fiction's Victorian and Edwardian pioneer years culminated in Holmesian and mock-Holmesian *great detectives*. Flowering principally between the two world wars, rule-bound Golden Age detective fiction was perpetrated predominantly in Great Britain. Dissatisfied with these rules' tight restriction, some writers reacted sharply. In American *hard-boiled* detective stories, still best exemplified by Dashiell Hammett's and Raymond Chandler's work, country house gentility yielded to mean people's lives in mean streets. The Golden Age's gifted amateur detective wilted under a new interest in systematic organisation and method, creating the *police procedural*. Narrowly social concerns – puzzling out who did what from among a small set of nice people, with servants firmly excluded – gave way to *psychological* fiction, pioneered by Patricia Highsmith and often more interested in the criminal than the crime. Julian Symons (*Bloody Murder*, Harmondsworth, Penguin, 1972 and 1985) makes this an evolutionary shift as older and politically conservative Golden Age *detective fiction*, closely focussed on a puzzle to be solved, yielded to a younger and more liberal or radical *crime fiction* more interested in the criminal than in what he or she did. Accepting this broad distinction, Ousby denies teleology. He urges, surely correctly, that older sub-genres continued to live attenuating lives alongside newer forms.

12 Victor L. Whitechurch, 'Peter Crane's cigars', in Whitechurch, *Thrilling Stories of the Railway* [1912], London, Routledge & Kegan Paul, 1975, pp. 16–17. Hazell's moral sense is outraged once he detects tobacco smuggling in Britain, of course. Some things never change: in 1977 Paul Firman tells his readers a neat 'little-Englander' tale about a train loaded with butter which shuffled from one EEC nation to another, collecting millions of pounds in subsidies and rebates at each stop, before the butter was sold (at cost price) in the city where it was loaded: Eric Ambler, *Send No More Roses*, London, Weidenfeld & Nicolson, 1977, p. 28.

13 Christopher Isherwood, *Mr Norris Changes Trains* [1935], Harmondsworth, Penguin, 1942, chapter 1.

14 Anon, 'Introduction', to Anon (ed.), *Best Detective Stories, Second Series*, London, Faber & Faber, 1930, p. 9.

15 Wolfgang Schivelbusch, *The Railway Journey: Trains and Travel in the Nineteenth Century*, New York, Urizen, 1979, p. 66.

16 Jack Simmons, *The Victorian Railway*, London, Thames & Hudson, 1991, pp. 245–9. For yellowbacks see Ousby, *Crime and Mystery Book*, pp. 34–5; Richard D. Altick, *Writers, Readers, and Occasions: Selected Essays on Victorian Literature and*

Life, Columbus, Ohio State University Press, 1989, pp. 147, 162; Raymond Chapman, *The Victorian Debate: English Literature and Society, 1832–1901*, London, Weidenfeld & Nicolson, 1970, p. 60.

17 Oscar Wilde, *The Importance of Being Earnest* [1895], Act 2.

18 Laura Marcus, 'Introduction', to Marcus (ed.), *Twelve Women Detectives*, Oxford, Oxford University Press, 1997, p. viii.

19 Hugh Greene, 'Introduction', to Greene (ed.), *The Rivals of Sherlock Holmes* [1970], Harmondsworth, Penguin, 1971, pp. 13–14; Julian Symons, 'Introduction', to Jack Adrian (ed.), *Detective Stories from the Strand Magazine*, Oxford, Oxford University Press, 1993, p. vi; Michael Cox, 'Introduction', to Cox (ed.), *Victorian Detective Stories*, Oxford, Oxford University Press, 1992, pp. xvii–xxi.

20 'Externally, ffinch Hall was one of those gloomy, sombre country-houses which seem to exist only for the purpose of having horrid crimes committed in them:' P. G. Wodehouse, 'A slice of life', in Wodehouse, *Meet Mr Mulliner*, p. 50. Thinking of somewhere remarkably like Sir Jasper ffinch-ffarowmere's country place, Eric Ambler (*The Mask of Dimitrious*, [1939], London, Fontana, 1966, p. 17) conjured the most hackneyed mystery plot possible: '"The scene of the story … is an English country house belonging to the rich Lord Robinson. There is a party for the English week-end. In the middle of the party, Lord Robinson is discovered in the library sitting at his desk – shot through the temple."' As Michael Gilbert noticed, this archetype inhibited writers addicted to Wimseyish sleuths. 'A purely amateur detective who is also a series character has somehow to account plausibly for the extraordinary sequence of crimes with which he becomes involved. If a corpse is found in the library every time he happens to visit a country house people will soon stop asking him down for the weekend:' Michael Gilbert, 'Patrick Petrella', in Gilbert, *Petrella at Q* [1977], London, Mysterious Press, 1988, p. 14.

21 Hence A. A. Milne's comfortable celebration of weekending railway travel: Milne, 'Saturday to Monday' (which turns out to mean Saturday to Tuesday), in Milne, *Not That It Matters*, London, Methuen, 1919, pp. 38–42.

22 Richard Harding Davis, 'In the fog' [1902], in Alan K. Russell (ed.), *Rivals of Sherlock Holmes*, Secaucus, NJ, Castle, 1978, pp. 361–2 and Graham Greene and Hugh Greene (eds), *Victorian Villainies*, Harmondsworth, Penguin, 1984, p. 398.

23 'As a short-story writer for more than thirty years, I have heard all too often the complaint that, with the disappearance of so many of our traditional short-story magazines, the short-story as an art form is in danger of extinction:' Herbert Harris, 'Introduction', to Harris (ed.), *John Creasey's Crime Collection 1977*, London, Gollancz, 1977, p. 4.

24 Christopher Bush, *The Case of the Missing Men*, London, Macdonald, 1946, p. 130 shows us a conversation between an addicted commuter and a station bookstall clerk adept in crime fiction. Another whodunnit shows us an even deeper conversation of this kind; but here it precedes the discovery of a young woman's corpse *in* the bookstall on Charing Cross station's Dover platform: Henry Holt, *Murder at the Bookstall*, London, Collins, 1934, pp. 7–9.

25 Dorothy L. Sayers, 'Introduction', to Dorothy L. Sayers (ed.), *Great Tales of Detection, Mystery and Horror: Second Series*, London, Gollancz, 1931, p. 19; P. L. Scowcroft, 'Railways and detective fiction, part 1', *Journal of the Railway and Canal Historical Society*, 22/3, 1977, p. 87; Michael Cox, 'Introduction', to Cox (ed.), *Twelve English Detective Stories*, Oxford, Oxford University Press, 1998, pp. vii–viii.

26 Some by newspapers, notably the London *Evening Standard*: see Anon (ed.), *The Evening Standard Detective Book: First Series*, London, Gollancz, 1950; *Second Series*, 1951. General publications which published crime fiction among other material, like *The Strand Magazine*, steadily yielded to specialist crime magazines. Edited from the USA but publishing much British material, the most distinguished among these was *Ellery Queen's Mystery Magazine* (founded in 1941) and the many anthologies and compendia which flowed from it. For an overview see Eleanour Sullivan and Ellery Queen (eds), *The Omnibus of Crime Stories*, London, Robinson, 1991. John Creasy edited irregular *Crime Collection* anthologies for the British Crime Writers Association from 1953. Commercial publishers issued some anthologies, notably Macmillan's long-running *Winter Crimes* series. The most significant current series is Liza Cody and Michael Z. Lewin (eds), *First* (then *Second*, then …) *Culprit*, London, Chatto & Windus, 1992–.

27 G. K. Chesterton, 'Introduction', to Chesterton (ed.), *Century of Detective Stories*, p. 9. In the long story, he explains on the next page, 'it is sometimes possible to realise that a man is alive before we realise that he is dead'. This does help an author to build a convincing setting for murder.

28 Michael Innes, *Stop Press* [1939], Harmondsworth, Penguin, 1958, p. 240.

29 Julian Symons, 'Introduction', to Symons (ed.), *The Penguin Classic Crime Omnibus*, Harmondsworth, Penguin, 1984, pp. 9–10; Adrian, 'Introduction', to Adrian (ed.), *Detective Stories from the Strand Magazine*, p. vi.

30 Agatha Christie, 'The girl in the train', in Christie, *The Listerdale Mystery and Other Stories* [1934], London, Fontana, 1961, p. 60; reprinted in William Pattrick (ed.), *Mysterious Railway Stories*, London, Star, 1984, p. 167.

31 John Dickson Carr, *Scandal at High Chimneys: a Victorian Melodrama*, London, Hamilton, 1959, p. 234. For a developed account of Frith's narrative painting see Jeffrey Richards and John M. Mackenzie, *The Railway Station: a Social History*, Oxford, Oxford University Press, 1986, pp. 318–19. Looking at it, Geoffrey Jaggard (*Blandings the Blest*, London, Macdonald, 1968, p. 157) was surprised to find that that it contained no Wodehouse vignette showing one from so many 'departures of fair young maidens, metaphorically be-gyved, off to do their stretch at Blandings' under Lady Constance's basilisk stare. George Ottley (*A Bibliography of British Railway History: Supplement*, London, HMSO, 1988, p. 362) reports that Carr's novel is built around the characters in Frith's painting. Does this suggestion have a provenance?

32 See J. Alan Rannie, 'The railway journeys of Mr Holmes', *The Railway Magazine*, 1935, pp. 316–21. These errors pale against those lurking in pastiches. Perplexed by London's many termini, American Sherlockians send one married couple to

Edinburgh by the seven o'clock train from Victoria (via Dover?), another to Norfolk by the 11.43 from Paddington (via Bristol?): August Derleth, 'The adventure of the circular room' [1946] and Paul Anderson, 'In the island of Uffa', in Marvin Kaye (ed.), *The Game is Afoot: Parodies, Pastiches and Ponderings of Sherlock Holmes*, New York, St Martin's Press, 1994, pp. 74, 166. In the 1880s, would Holmes' listeners really gasp in admiration when the great detective revealed that Great Western Railway trains ran into Paddington station, not Kings' Cross? (Simon Clark, 'The adventure of the fallen star', in Mike Ashley (ed.), *New Sherlock Holmes Adventures*, London, Robinson, 1997, pp. 176–93). *Bradshaw* in hand, would Holmes really drag Watson on an urgent trip from London to Portland via the Somerset and Dorset Railway? (Basil Copper, 'The adventure of the persecuted painter', in Ashley (ed.), *New Adventures*, p. 308; Copper does have the grace to admit that this itinerary involved 'several changes'!) Doyle made Watson a dense mirror for Holmes' brilliance, but would he really report that his Paddington to Cornwall GWR express thundered '*south-west* through the outskirts of London' [emphasis added], or confuse a milk train with a sleeper? (Stuart Parker, 'The adventure of the marked man' [1944], in Richard Lancelyn Green (ed.), *The Further Adventures of Sherlock Holmes*, Harmondsworth, Penguin, 1985, p. 105; Peter Crowther, 'The adventure of the touch of God', in Ashley (ed.), *New Adventures*, p. 281). After all this nonsense, Barrie Roberts' *Sherlock Holmes and the Railway Maniac* (London, Constable, 1994) provides welcome relief. Impressively blending Edwardian detail with convincing railway material, this novel is an unexpected delight – not least because Holmes' solution turns on a deliciously *recherché* device. A mad German spy smears selected express locomotives' smokebox doors with 'a resinous opiate'. This resin melts as engines run faster. Evaporated by firebox gases blasting through engines' funnels, opiate fumes drift back along locomotives' boilers to drug drivers and firemen as they watch for signals outside their cabsheets. With their footplate crews dozing peacefully, violent crashes now envelop trains drawn by these doctored locomotives. By these ingenious means Roberts explains some smashes which have puzzled railway historians for generations – like the Salisbury curve's ghastly pile up on 1 July 1906. His only false note is the manner in which he executes his villain – crushed by loaded wagons rolling from a siding on to the running line, his foot stuck between blade and stock rail on a hand-operated point. The Board of Trade never would permit that hand lever!

33   Richards and Mackenzie, *Railway Station*, p. 13. 'Perhaps … it was the proximity of all the passengers to the piston-and-cylinder principle', Paul Fussell suggests (*Abroad: British Literary Travelling Between the Wars*, New York, Oxford University Press, 1980, p. 113), 'which, when you get to thinking about it –'.

34   Rev A. W. V. Mace, 'Exposure!', in H. A. Vallance (ed.), *The Railway Enthusiast's Bedside Book*, London, Batsford, 1966, pp. 79–80. Even these titles will impress lay Freudians.

35   Virginia Woolf, *The Years* [1937], Oxford, Oxford University Press, 1992, p. 256. Staying at Rye in August 1907, before her marriage to Leonard Woolf, Virginia Stephen told her diary about one twilit epiphany: 'A great luminous train … with a

body like some phosphorescent caterpillar, & a curled plume of smoke, all opal and white, issuing from the front of it:' Michael A. Leaska (ed.), *A Passionate Apprentice: the Early Journals of Virginia Woolf, 1897–1909*, London, Hogarth Press, 1990, p. 369. Very revealing: no need to ask which Austrian medical mystic's work young Miss Stephen had been reading.

36 H. G. Wells, 'In the modern vein' [1897], in Wells, *The Complete Short Stories of H. G. Wells*, London, Benn, 1922, p. 499.

37 Georges Simenon, *The Man Who Watched the Trains Go By* [1938], translated by Stuart Gilbert, Harmondsworth, Penguin, 1964, p. 30.

38 F. Tennyson Jesse, *A Pin to See the Peepshow* [1934], Harmondsworth, Penguin, 1952, p. 272.

39 Is Rudyard Kipling's '007' the only exception?

40 W. G. Chapman, *Caerphilly Castle* (1924), *Twixt Rail and Sea* (1927), *The 'King' of Railway Locomotives* (1928), *Cheltenham Flyer* (1934), *Track Topics* (1935), *Locos of the Royal Road* (1936), all published by the GWR from Paddington Station. These shilling books enjoyed huge sales – in eight years *The 'King'* sold 60,000 copies. See *Locos*, p. 5.

41 Jo Manton, *Sister Dora: the Life of Dorothy Pattison*, London, Methuen, 1971, p. 224.

42 Jack Simmons, *The Railway in England and Wales, 1830–1914: the System and Its Working*, Leicester, Leicester University Press, 1978, p. 230. Once railway compartments came to seem risky places for women, this opened unexpected criminal possibilities. Sir William Hardman feared that a woman who entered his compartment on a London and South Western Railway train in 1866 was preparing grounds for a false molestation claim. 'These unfounded charges of indecent assault have been very common of late', he tells us; 'and I have determined to object in future to the entry of any unprotected female into a carriage where I may be alone'. Quoted in Jack Simmons, *Railways: an Anthology*, London, Collins, 1991, p. 102. A molestation claim springs the plot in Andrew Garve, *The Cuckoo Line Affair*, London, Collins, 1953.

43 John Gibbons, 'Humour and history of London traffic (part III)', *Railway Magazine*, 75, 1934, p. 159. John Betjeman (*London's Historic Railway Stations*, London, Murray, 1972, p. 88) quotes A. H. Binstead's 1903 quatrain: 'The terminus of Charing Cross / Is haunted when it rains / By Nymphs, who there a shelter seek / And wait for mythic trains'.

44 Alan A. Jackson, *London's Termini*, Newton Abbot, David and Charles, 1969, p. 176. Two things killed this trade. The District Railway's new line from Westminster to Blackfriars gave timid city men quicker service to their offices. Then the South Eastern's new intermediate station at Waterloo ruined the run for gallants attracted by these ladies' services. Seven minutes slaked their appetites; three minutes bred frustration.

45 Martin Page, *The Lost Pleasures of the Great Trains*, London, Weidenfeld and Nicolson, 1975, p. 85.

46 Page, *Lost Pleasures of the Great Trains*, p. 85. Mr Stein smacks his lips: '"The things that go on in these long-distance trains"', he complains in Constantinople. '"Did

she cost you much?"' his interlocutor enquires: Graham Greene, *Stamboul Train* [1932], Harmondsworth, Penguin, 1975, p. 209.

47 D. H. Lawrence, *Lady Chatterley's Lover* [1928], Harmondsworth, Penguin, 1960, p. 285. Lucius Beebe suggests one exception to this rule. From its first run in 1902, *The Twentieth Century Limited* presented passengers with a 'climate of almost unearthly rectitude', he insists. 'There is no record of sleeping space issued for a single passenger being occupied by two. No well heeled salesman sent wine to single women in the diner' (Lucius Beebe, *20th Century: the Greatest Train in the World*, Berkeley, CA, Howell-North, 1962, p. 11). Puritan pleasures on the *Century!* So why, in the 1940s, does aging-but-sprightly radio magnate Ray Soderbjerg whoop it up in his stateroom with a different high-spirited young woman each time he rides the *Empire Builder* from Minneapolis to New York? See Garrison Keillor, *WLT: a Radio Romance*, New York, Viking, 1991.

48 Michel de Certeau, *The Practice of Everyday Life*, Berkeley, University of California Press, 1984, pp. 111–14; Keating, *Bedside Companion*, p. 76.

49 Agatha Christie, *Murder on the Orient Express* [1934], Harmondsworth, Penguin, 1948, p. 26. Leslie Charteris, 'The Rhine maiden', in Charteris, *The Saint in Europe*, London, Hodder & Stoughton, 1954 (reprinted in Tony Wilmot (ed.), *Beware of the Trains*, Hornchurch, Henry, 1981, pp. 37–58 and Haining (ed.), *Murder on the Railways*, pp. 228–44), makes much the same point. Did Erving Goffman read Christie before coining his influential notion of the total institution, where usual divisions between different social spheres – work, sleep and eating – break down? See Erving Goffman, *Asylums: Essays on the Social Situation of Mental Patients and Other Inmates* [1959], Harmondsworth, Penguin, 1961.

50 Cecil Roberts, *Victoria Four-Thirty* [1937], London, Hodder & Stoughton, 1952; Alanna Knight, *A Drink for the Bridge: a Novel of the Tay Bridge Disaster*, London, Macmillan, 1973; David Beaty, *Electric Train*, London, Coronet, 1973; Bill Garnett, *Down-Bound Train*, London, 1973.

51 George Perry, *Forever Ealing*, London, Pavilion, 1981, p. 143; John Huntley, *Railways on the Screen*, Shepperton, Ian Allan, 1993, pp. 186–8. Geoff Ryman copied *Train of Events* in his remarkable Internet novel *253*, London, Flamingo, 1998: see below, pp. 313–15.

52 Keating, *Bedside Companion*, p. 76.

53 For Holmes' principle see Arthur Conan Doyle, 'The sign of four', (1890).

54 Victor L. Whitechurch, 'Sir Gilbert Murrell's picture', in Whitechurch, *Thrilling Stories*, pp. 63–80; Arthur Conan Doyle, 'The story of the lost special' [1898], in Doyle, *Tales of Terror and Mystery* [1922], London, Pan, 1978, pp. 107–24, Charles Irving (ed.), *Sixteen On*, London, Macmillan, 1957, pp. 32–54, and Morgan (ed.), *The Railway-Lover's Companion*, pp. 469–85; Ellery Queen, 'Snowball in July' [1949], in Bill Pronzini (ed.), *Midnight Specials: an Anthology for Railway Enthusiasts and Suspense Addicts*, London, Souvenir Press, 1978, pp. 166–74; Donald E. Westlake, *Kahawa* [1981], New York, Mysterious Press, 1995; Ernest Bramah, 'The Knight's Cross signal problem', in Bramah, *Max Carrados Mysteries*, London, Methuen, 1914, reprinted in Haining (ed.), *Murder on the*

Railways, pp. 181–205. Wilbur Smith's *The Train from Katanga*, New York, Signet, 1965 is another African train caper novel, but disfigured by its sadistic narrative tone. Doyle's story about a lost special invites us to accept that a speeding passenger train could disappear down a vertical mine shaft, leaving not one shred of evidence on the surface. Even the slightest acquaintance with widespread devastation caused when a railway train's enormous kinetic energy met an immovable object would have ruled out this absurd suggestion. See L. T. C. Rolt, *Red for Danger*, fourth edition, edited by Geoffrey Kichenside, London, Pan, 1986; Arthur Trevena, *Trains in Trouble: Railway Accidents in Pictures*, 4 volumes, Redruth, Atlantic, 1980–3.

55 Jonathan Goodman, 'Points of departure', in Goodman (ed.), *The Railway Murders: Classic Stories of True Crime*, London, Sphere, 1986, p. 9. Unlike the vehicle and electronics industries, British Goldan Age crime fiction still enjoys a flourishing export trade to Japan. Turning deftly on timetabled alibis, Seichó Matsumoto's railway mysteries (*Inspector Imanishi Investigates* [1961], translated by Beth Cary, New York, Soho Press, 1989; *Points and Lines* [1970], translated by Makiko Yamamoto and Paul C. Blum, Tokyo, Kodansha International, 1986) could have come from the alibi-breaker's master, Freeman Wills Crofts. Like Crofts in his day, Matsumoto is profitably popular. The English edition of *Points and Lines* claims that this is Japan's best-selling mystery novel, with one and a quarter million copies sold.

56 P. G. Wodehouse, 'Came the dawn', in Wodehouse, *Meet Mr Mulliner*, p. 162. Lest these comparisons appear blasphemous, consider Roedean's Second World War Evacuation. 'Dame Eveline Tanner, the Headmistress, was reputed to have moved the whole school overnight from Brighton to the Lake District', one old girl recalled, 'with a Bradshaw in one hand and a Bible in the other:' Nancy Banks-Smith, 'The dismal diary of Adrienne Mole', in Alan Rushbridger (ed.), *The Guardian Year '94*, London, Fourth Estate, 1994, p. 238.

57 Agatha Christie gives us a particularly neat example in 'The sign in the sky' (in Christie, *The Mysterious Mr Quin* [1930], Harmondsworth, Penguin, 1953, pp. 68–84). For other timetabled alibis see, *inter alia*, Fergus Hume, 'The green-stone god and the stockbroker' [1896], in Cox (ed.), *Twelve English Detective Stories*, pp. 42–57; Max Murray, *The Voice of the Corpse* [1948], Harmondsworth, Penguin, 1956, p. 11; Douglas Newton, 'The railway carriage crime', in Anon (ed.), *Best Mystery Stories*, London, Faber & Faber, 1933, pp. 354–76; John Rhode, *The Murders in Praed Street* [1928], Harmondsworth, Penguin, 1937; Dorothy L. Sayers, *Five Red Herrings*, London, Gollancz, 1931; June Thomson, *Dead Reckoning*, London, Constable, 1960; and Henry Wade, 'The three keys', in Chesterton (ed.), *Century of Detective Stories*, pp. 511–27. Agatha Christie's *The ABC Murders* [1936], London, Pan, 1962 contains little railway material – except that her serial killer challenges Poirot by placing a copy of the *A. B. C. Guide*, open to display train services for the appropriate murder site, by each victim's corpse.

58 J. D. Beresford, 'The artificial mole', in R. Knox and H. Harrington (eds), *Best Detective Stories: First Series*, London, Faber & Faber, 1929, p. 98.

59 Hubert Footner, 'The king of the gigolos' [1937], in Ellery Queen (ed.), *Ladies in Crime*, London, Faber, 1947, p. 166. Emphasis added.

60 Frank King, 'Murder on the 8.45', in Chesterton (ed.), *Century of Detective Stories*, pp. 183–200.

61 Agatha Christie, *The Murder on the Links* [1923], Harmondsworth, Penguin, 1936.

62 Erskine Childers, *The Riddle of the Sands: a Record of Secret Service* [1903], Harmondsworth, Penguin, 1952, pp. 239, 252. This novel had important practical consequences, persuading the British Admiralty to establish the Royal Naval Volunteer Reserve. Here Childers urges England to Awake; but conflicting loyalties soon doomed him. A convinced Irish nationalist, he was executed after the 1916 Easter Rising.

63 Freeman Wills Crofts, 'The case of the solicitor's holiday', in Crofts, *Murderers Make Mistakes*, London, Hodder & Stoughton, 1947, pp. 244–55.

64 Edmund Crispin, 'Black for a funeral', in Crispin, *Beware of the Trains* [1953], Harmondsworth, Penguin, 1987, pp. 95–101. Since this murderer turns out to be the village bobby, Crispin edges round Ronnie Knox's injunction that 'The detective must not himself commit the crime' (Ronald Knox, 'Introduction', to Knox and Harrington (eds), *Best Detective Stories: First Series*, p. 15). Agatha Christie drove a coach and horses through this rule in her interminably-running play *The Mousetrap*.

65 Henry Wade, 'The three keys', in Anon (ed.), *Fifty Famous Detectives of Fiction*, London, Odhams, 1948, pp. 155–68.

66 Agatha Christie, *The Clocks*, London, Collins, 1930, pp. 230–1.

67 John Appleby, *Aphrodite Means Death* [1951], Harmondsworth, Penguin, 1954, pp. 130–1; R. Chetwynd-Hayes, 'Non-paying passengers', in Chetwynd-Hayes (ed.), *The Tenth Fontana Book of Great Ghost Stories*, London, Fontana, 1974; Michael Gilbert, *Fear to Tread*, London, Hodder & Stoughton, 1953; J. J. Marric, *Gideon's Ride*, London, Hodder & Stoughton, 1963; George Sims, *The Sand Dollar*, Harmondsworth, Penguin, 1972; Julian Symons, 'The case of the frightened promoter', in Anon (ed.), *Evening Standard Detective Book: First Series*; Granville Wilson, 'Never call it murder', in Harris (ed.), *John Creasey's Crime Collection 1977*.

68 Arthur Conan Doyle, 'The adventure of the Bruce-Partington plans', in Doyle, *His Last Bow* [1917], London, Pan, 1955, pp. 79–108. Reprinted in L. T. C. Rolt (ed.), *Best Railway Stories*, London, Faber & Faber, 1969, pp. 57–88, and Morgan (ed.), *Crime on the Lines*, pp. 22–46. This device is copied in Walter E. Grogan, *The 10.12 Express*, London, Sisley's, 1920.

69 H. G. Wells, 'The lord of the dynamos', in Wells, *The Complete Short Stories of H. G. Wells*, London, Benn, 1927, pp. 284–93.

70 Margery Allingham, *Dancers in Mourning* (1937), Harmondsworth, Penguin, 1948, p. 187.

71 Freeman Wills Crofts, *Inspector French and the Cheyne Mystery* [1926], Harmondsworth, Penguin, 1953, pp. 152–3 (Euston); Crofts, *Inspector French and*

the Starvel Tragedy [1927], London, Hogarth, 1987, pp. 259–60 (Edinburgh (Waverley)).

72 Ronald A. Knox, *The Viaduct*, London, Methuen, 1925.

73 Basil Mitchell, 'The blue trout', in Dorothy L. Sayers (ed.), *Great Short Stories of Detection, Mystery and Horror: Third Series*, London, Gollancz, 1933, pp. 324–42. Life copies art here, with heavy mortality among train surfers on electric railway services in Brazil: see José Arthur Rios, 'On the waves: a new kind of surf in Rio de Janeiro', *Crime, Law and Social Change*, 1993, 20, pp. 161–75. Like everything else to do with railway enthusiasm, Rio train surfers soon developed their own clubs – but frequent electrocution meant that these clubs suffered unusually high turnover rates among office holders.

74 As in Victor L. Whitechurch, 'The pilot engine', in Whitechurch, *Thrilling Stories*, pp. 131–49. Thorpe Hazell prevents this outrage, of course.

75 G. K. Chesterton, 'The three tools of death', in Chesterton, *The Innocence of Father Brown* [1911], Harmondsworth, Penguin, 1950, pp. 232–48.

76 John Wain, *The Smaller Sky*, London, Macmillan, 1967, pp. 174–84. Some railway station roof deaths have no significant railway connection: a fatal rooftop chase at Waterloo in Reg Gadney's *Somewhere in England* [1971] (Frogmore, Granada, 1974, pp. 155–64); a vagrant falling to his death from North Bridge through Edinburgh (Waverley)'s glass roof in Ian Rankin's *Set in Darkness* (London, Orion, 2000, pp. 64–5).

77 H. C. Bailey, 'The furnished cottage' [1925], in Bailey, *Mr Fortune's Case Book*, London, Methuen, 1936, pp. 471–500; Freeman Wills Crofts, *Death on the Way*, London, Collins, 1932; Freeman Wills Crofts, 'The case of the relief signalman', in Crofts, *Murderers Make Mistakes*, London, Hodder & Stoughton, 1947, pp. 223–32; Freeman Wills Crofts, *French Strikes Oil*, London, Hodder & Stoughton, 1952; Freeman Wills Crofts, 'The level crossing', in Crofts, *The Mystery of the Sleeping Car Express, and Other Stories* [1956], Bath, Chivers, 1982, pp. 95–116 and Pattrick (ed.), *Mysterious Railway Stories*, pp. 207–22; R. Austin Freeman, 'The case of Oscar Brodski' [1910], in Freeman, *The Singing Bone*, London, Hodder & Stoughton, 1912, pp. 9–67, reprinted in Freeman, *The Best Dr Thorndyke Detective Stories*, edited by E. F. Bleicher, New York, Cover, 1973, pp. 1–41 and Morgan (ed.), *Crime on the Lines*, pp. 47–84; Gilbert, *Fear to Tread*; John Rhode, *Tragedy on the Line*, London, Collins, 1931; Matthew Vaughan, *The Discretion of Dominick Ayres*, London, Secker & Warburg, 1976. Freeman Wills Crofts' story 'The raincoat' (in Crofts, *Mystery of the Sleeping Car Express*, pp. 246–60) offers a particularly ingenious variation on this theme, with a murdered corpse damaged by a passing train in a manner contrived to persuade police that this is murder disguised as accident. The killer's purpose is to direct suspicion to a third party. He has not counted on wily Inspector Hubbard. As these latter examples suggest, the 'murder victim as suicide' device soon came to seem so hackneyed that writers could start playing games with it. John Newton, *Last Train to Limbo*, London, Hale, 1972 shows us a man trying to shift points with a crowbar to save a maiden lying across the tracks. When his crowbar slips the locomotive rumbles

past; and the girl's head is severed. As it rolls away, no blood spurts. This head is made from wax. We stand on a film set.

78 Miles Burton, *Death in the Tunnel*, London, Collins, 1934.

79 Douglas Clark, *Doone Walk*, London, Gollancz, 1982.

80 Michael Dibdin, *Blood Rain*, London, Faber & Faber, 1999, pp. 3–9. Once this victim was adequately cooked, his van was collected by a passing pick-up freight. Which cop could locate a crime scene after this train had trundled halfway round Sicily?

81 P. G. Wodehouse, 'The truth about George', in Wodehouse, *Meet Mr Mulliner*, p. 29.

82 Agatha Christie, *The Big Four* (1927), Harmondsworth, Penguin, 1957, p. 54.

83 W. A. Darlington, 'A chain of circumstance', in Irving (ed.), *Sixteen On*, pp. 120–42. George Mulliner escapes such complications by haring off across a neighbouring field, hotly pursued by railway servants, intrigued passengers and sporting yokels: Wodehouse, 'The truth about George', pp. 31–4. Other cases of tugged communication cords appear in Maurice Drake, *The Ocean Sleuth*, London, Methuen, 1915 and David Williams, *Murder for Treasure*, New York, St Martin's Press, 1981.

84 R. Austin Freeman, *The Eye of Osiris* [1911], Oxford, Oxford University Press, 1989, p. 110. The detective is Dr Thorndyke.

85 R. L. Stevenson and Lloyd Osbourne, *The Wrong Box* [1889], London, Blackie, 1961, p. 49. Merely one blackly comic stage in an inept tontine fraud, this body's owner died from natural causes. For a murdered corpse carried in a train's luggage van see Barry Perowne, 'Knowing what I know now', in Sullivan and Queen (eds), *Omnibus of Modern Crime Stories*, pp. 279–93.

86 J. S. Fletcher, 'The contents of the coffin' [1909], in Hugh Greene (ed.), *Further Rivals of Sherlock Holmes* [1973], Harmondsworth, Penguin, 1976, pp. 207–23.

87 Freeman Wills Crofts, *The Cask* [1920], Harmondsworth, Penguin, 1952; Crofts, *The Sea Mystery* [1928], Harmondsworth, Penguin, 1959; John Ferguson, *Stealthy Terror* [1935], Harmondsworth, Penguin, 1939, pp. 76–8.

88 But not if the consignee's steam roller needs a new driving shaft so urgently that he sends a lorry to collect it from a strike-bound goods yard, only to find that the shaft's packing case contains a corpse: Roy Vickers, 'The clue of the red carnations', in Vickers, *The Department of Dead Ends* [1949], Harmondsworth, Penguin, 1955, p. 115.

89 Pamela Branch, *The Wooden Overcoat* [1951], Harmondsworth, Penguin, 1959, p. 46.

90 Pamela Branch, *Murder Every Monday* [1954], Harmondsworth, Penguin, 1956, pp. 140–1 (emphasis added); R. Austin Freeman, *Dr Thorndyke Intervenes*, London, Hodder & Stoughton, 1933; Peter Lovesey, 'The lady in the trunk', in Tim Heald (ed.), *A Classic English Crime*, New York, Mysterious Press, 1991, pp. 77–94; Gerald Kersh, *Prelude to a Certain Midnight* [1947], Harmondsworth, Penguin, 1953, p. 142; Gladys Mitchell, *Come Away, Death* [1937], Harmondsworth, Penguin, 1954, p. 285; Oscar Wilde, *The Importance of Being*

Earnest [1895], Act 1. For the grim realities behind these fancies see J. R. Whitbread, *The Railway Policeman: the Story of the Constable on the Track*, London, Harrap, 1961, pp. 186–98; Jackson, *London's Termini*, pp. 224–5, 260; Frederick Porter Wensley, 'Murder in a trunk' and Jonathan Goodman, 'A coincidence of corpses', in Goodman (ed.), *Railway Murders*, pp. 117–30, 131–60.

91 Nicholas Blake, 'A study in white', in Sullivan and Queen (eds), *Omnibus of Modern Crime Stories*, p. 148. Emphasis added.

92 John Dickson Carr's first rule (from four) states that 'The criminal shall never turn out to be the detective, or any servant, or any character whose thoughts we have been allowed to share:' Carr, 'The grandest game in the world' [1946–63], in Carr, *Door to Doom*, pp. 323–4. For the extension of legal argument from the pivotal 1836 *Priestly* v. *Fowler* butchery case to master-servant relations on British railways see R. W. Kostal, *Law and English Railway Capitalism, 1825–1875*, revised edition, Oxford, Clarendon Press, 1997, pp. 259–79.

93 Arnold Ridley and Bernard Merivale, *The Wrecker*, London, French, 1930, Act 3.

94 Victor L. Whitechurch, 'Saved by a train wrecker' [1899], in Paul Jennings (ed.), *My Favourite Railway Stories*, Guildford, Lutterworth Press, 1982, pp. 79–86.

95 W. B. Maxwell, 'The long-distance train', in Lewis Melville and Reginald Hargreaves (eds), *Great English Short Stories*, London, Harrap, 1931, pp. 837–50.

96 L. A. G. Strong, 'The gates' [1931], in Strong, *Travellers: Thirty-One Selected Stories*, London, Methuen, 1945, pp. 55–64.

97 Michael Innes, 'Murder on the 7.16', in Haining (ed.), *Murder on the Railways*, pp. 246–9. It is a fair bet that ironical Innes wrote this brief tale for the London *Evening Standard*'s long-running short story page.

98 See the photograph in Edward Beal, *Scale Railway Modelling To-Day*, London, Black, 1939, p. 3. Lord Buffery, President of the Royal Society, constructs a similar model – but merely so that Michael Innes might contrast serious Establishment sons with childish Establishment fathers. See Innes, *The Journeying Boy*, London, Gollancz, 1949, p. 111.

99 J. R. L. Anderson, *A Sprig of Sea Lavender*, London, Gollancz, 1978, pp. 11–12.

100 Freeman Wills Crofts, *Death of a Train* [1946], Harmondsworth. Penguin, 1953, pp. 55–6, 141–3. Inept saboteurs manage to derail the wrong train, so this vital cargo reaches the docks – and the war is won. Since 'sound plotting and meticulous technical detail came first' for Crofts (Morgan, 'Introduction', to Morgan (ed.), *Crime on the Lines*, p. xii), it is odd that this novel should contain one thumping incongruity. Facing points controlled entry from the down line to the goods yard at (fictitious) Pullover station on the Southern Railway's main line near Exeter. Nazi sympathisers will use these points in their attempt to derail the radio valves' special train. But many gory Victorian accidents convinced the British state's Railway Inspectorate that facing points were perilous things. If absolutely unavoidable, they must be fitted with special locks controlled from the nearest signal box. Thus Pullover yard's facing point lock must be cleared before the road to the goods yard can be set. In the short period between the previous down train's passage and the special freight's arrival, Crofts' saboteurs must not only mis-set the road but also

disable this point lock. Doing that requires that they creep across the running lines and spend several minutes heaving and tinkering. All this must be done well within Pullover box's signalman's sight. Even wearing camouflaged anoraks, it is not credible that they could manage this task in broad daylight. That's a pity, because Crofts gets everything else so beautifully correct.

101 "'Some man in Whitehall sits and tells the railway just how many slices of bread and scrape it may give us, and how thick to cut the railway slab. It's tyranny'": Innes, *Journeying Boy*, p. 42.

102 The key to one arson case proves to be that highly specialised piece of electrically operated control equipment, a signal reverser: see Freeman Wills Crofts, *Golden Ashes* [1940], Harmondsworth, Penguin, 1959, pp. 132–3. Other books show narrow-gauge railways facilitating brandy-smuggling in Bordeaux and Hull, shifting legitimate cargo in a Watford engineering works and a Welsh quarry (Freeman Wills Crofts, *The Pit-Prop Syndicate,* London, Collins, 1922, pp. 6, 40, 78; *The Loss of the Jane Vosper* [1936], Harmondsworth, Penguin, 1953, pp. 118, 191). Crofts identifies these narrow-gauge lines technically, as 'Decauville' systems.

103 Dorothy L. Sayers, 'Introduction', to Certain Members of the Detection Club, *The Floating Admiral* [1931], London, Macmillan, 1981, p. 1. French soon had imitators. Scotland Yard's Inspector Drury 'had an invariable habit of arranging facts in chronological order, a peculiarity which was so marked that certain of his irreverent subordinates always referred to him as Bradshaw, except when he was present:' W. Stanley Sykes, *The Missing Money-Lender* [1931], London, Penguin, 1937, p. 87.

104 Chapter 19 in Agatha Christie, *Partners in Crime*, London, Collins, 1929; a book written in other crime writers' voices.

105 Agatha Christie, *The Clocks*, London, Collins, 1930, pp. 124–5.

106 In Anon (ed.), *Evening Standard Detective Book: First Series*, pp. 131–9; reprinted in Crofts, *Many a Slip*, London, Hodder & Stoughton, 1955, pp. 69–77.

107 Freeman Wills Crofts, *The Ponson Case*, London, Collins, 1921.

108 Freeman Wills Crofts, *The Groote Park Murders*, London, Collins, 1923.

109 Crofts, *Pit-Prop Syndicate.* On page 237 he provides a map – that Golden Age totem – to help readers appreciate this misdirection. Griffiths, *Rome Express*, p. 303 and Crofts, 'Mystery of the sleeping-car express' print diagrams to show who slept where in railway sleepers. Schematic junction and signal diagrams illustrate several Whitechurch short stories. It would be interesting to discover how many readers can decipher them today.

110 T. J. Binyon, *Murder Will Out: the Detective in Fiction*, Oxford, Oxford University Press, 1989, p. 82.

111 Like some other fictional policemen, for Ian Ousby (*Crime and Mystery Book*, p. 76) French is 'simply dull: not so much plausibly ordinary in the way a realist novelist might make them as colourless in the way a novelist concerned only with the puzzle is bound to make them'.

112 Freeman Wills Crofts, *Sir John Magill's Last Journey* [1930], Harmondsworth, Penguin, 1955, p. 141.

113 In Anon (ed.), *Evening Standard Detective Book: Second Series*, pp. 84–94, and Crofts, *Many a Slip*, pp. 42–50.

114 Crofts, *Sea Mystery*, p. 159. In another book French's method seems to have failed him until railways come to his aid. A torn restaurant bill provides his only clue. Looking for a hotel name with 18–20 letters in a low country coastal town with fewer than seven letters, French is stumped: until he notices that Belgian station destination boards identify place names both in Flemish and French. Back to *Bradshaw*'s continental edition, for towns. Back to *Baedeker*, for hotels. On to the solution, in Anvers (Antwerp). See Freeman Wills Crofts, *Inspector French and the Cheyne Mystery* [1926], Harmondsworth, Penguin, 1953, pp. 191–8.

115 Technical knowledge, note; not pure science. French is sharply (bluntly?) different from speculative scientific investigators, whether amateurs like Arthur Conan Doyle's Sherlock Holmes or professionals like Jacques Futrelle's Professor S.F.X. van Dusen (a.k.a. The Thinking Machine) or R. Austin Freeman's Dr Thorndyke.

116 Victor L. Whitechurch and E. Conway, 'A warning in red', in Cox (ed.), *Victorian Detective Stories*, pp. 518–27. Reporting that Conway's name never appears again in crime fiction, Michael Cox speculates (p. 575) that he provided no more than a plot outline for Whitechurch to write up.

117 The closest competitor is Tom Rolt, first general manager for the Talyllyn Railway Preservation Society. He published a collection of transport spook stories (L. T. C. Rolt, *Sleep No More: Railway, Canal and Other Stories of the Supernatural* [1948], Hassocks, Branch Line, 1974); but only one story, 'The Garside Fell disaster', has much railway content. Often anthologised, this story is a slightly fictionalised account of the ghastly 1910 Hawes Junction (Garsdale] crash: see Peter E. Baughan, *North of Leeds: the Leeds-Settle-Carlisle Line and its Branches*, Hatch End, Roundhouse, 1966, pp. 390–3; C. Hamilton Ellis, *The Midland Railway*, London, Ian Allan, 1953, pp. 140–2; Rolt, *Red for Danger*, pp. 200–4.

118 Hugh Greene, 'Introduction', to Greene (ed.), *Further Rivals of Sherlock Holmes*, p. 12. Hugh Greene found a copy only in the British Museum reading room. Bryan Morgan used the Bodleian Library's copy for his 1975 facsimile edition.

119 Bryan Morgan, 'Foreword', to Whitechurch, *Thrilling Stories*, p. 4. This liberal judgement is supported by the expert way in which Whitechurch takes a foreign spy masquerading as a locomotive fireman through booking-on procedures at a running shed, and his mastery of interlocked track and signalling arrangements (*Thrilling Stories*, pp. 140–1, 184–6, 211–17). In 'The ruse that succeeded' (*Thrilling Stories*, pp. 235–48) he gave a railway-expert British spy master the name 'Colonel Sibthorpe'. This suggests a dry wit; the real Colonel Sibthorpe was a fire-eating early Victorian Tory MP, diehard opponent of railways and all their vil-lainous works. Bearing this in mind, Whitechurch's action in tumbling an unpleasant prelate into a muddy ditch after a railway derailment (*Thrilling Stories*, p. 118) suggests that he both suffered and resented slow preferment in the Anglican church. He should have followed his bent, and worked on the railway.

120 Victor L. Whitechurch, 'Sir Gilbert Murrell's picture' [1912], in Whitechurch, *Stories of the Railway*, pp. 63–80, Dorothy L. Sayers (ed.), *Detection, Mystery and*

Horror: First Series, pp. 492–504, and Morgan (ed.), *Crime on the Lines*, pp. 85–96. For another theft of valuable paintings from a railway truck see Margery Allingham, *Coroner's Pidgin* [1951], Harmondsworth, Penguin, 1959, p. 160.

121 Victor L. Whitechurch, 'Donald Penstone's escape', *Pearson's Magazine*, 3, 1897, pp. 116–20. Headlight codes underpin another ingenious Whitechurch tale: 'Special working instructions', *Strand Magazine*, 18, 1899, pp. 520–5. Travelling secretly for political talks with the British government, the Tsar's life is threatened by bomb-hurling anarchists. A quick-thinking stationmaster saves the situation by running an appropriately lamped-up decoy train past the anarchists' hiding place. Bombs smash this train's carriages to matchwood, but the Tsar speeds safely on his way. With motives focussed on individual murderers' reasons for killing individual passengers, bombs' indiscriminate destruction appears infrequently in British railway crime literature; for other examples see G. D. H. Cole and Margaret Cole, 'A tale of two suitcases', in Cole and Cole, *Wilson, and Some Others*, London, Collins, 1940, and Allingham, *Dancers in Mourning*. Victor Whitechurch's principal detective is Thorpe Hazell, that 'book collector and railway enthusiast, a gentleman of independent means' (Whitechurch, *Stories of the Railway*, p. 11). Correctly enough, Sayers (*Great Tales of Detection, Horror and Mystery: First Series*, p. 6) makes Hazell a specialist railway detective; but it needed Ellery Queen (*Queen's Quorum*, London, Gollancz, 1953, p. 62) to note that Hazell was fiction's first railway detective, a nose before Francis Lynde's *Scientific Sprague* (1912) in the United States. That said, recent excavation has turned up an even earlier Whitechurch railway detective, Godfrey Page, the Railwayac (a contracted form of 'railway maniac'): see Haining, *Murder on the Railways*, pp. 139–40.

122 Michael Gilbert, 'Mr Duckworth's night out' [1959], in Morgan (ed.), *Crime on the Lines*, pp. 151–65. Petrella works with railway policemen here. Himself a practising solicitor, Michael Gilbert's crime fiction displays welcome familiarity with this specialised force. A passing reference in 'The Banting Street fire' recalls Detective Inspector Petrella's involvement, several years earlier, in a case involving organised pilfering from a London goods yard. Crucial evidence in '"To the Editor, Dear Sir"' comes from railway policemen chasing ticket bilkers. See Gilbert, *Petrella at Q*, pp. 80–1. Murders bred from systematic thefts in railway goods yards spring the plot in Gilbert's *Fear to Tread*. Solving these crimes requires close collaboration among detectives from Scotland Yard, divisional forces and the specialised British Transport Police. For a history of this service see Whitbread, *Railway Policeman*.

123 John Creasey, *Murder on the Line*, London, Hodder & Stoughton, 1960.

124 Anderson, *Sprig of Sea Lavender*, p. 46; Appleby, *Aphrodite Means Death*, p. 112; Forbes Bramble, *The Iron Roads*, London, Hamilton, 1980, p. 292; Douglas G. Browne, *The Stolen Boat-Train*, London, Collins, 1935.

125 Ferguson, *Stealthy Terror*, p. 140. Ferguson wrote his novel a dozen years after the year when East and West Coast routes from London each were grouped in the LNER and the LMS. The 1895 race to Aberdeen involved two coalitions of smaller companies. See O. S. Nock, *Railway Races to the North*, London, Ian Allan, 1959.

126 T. S. Strachan, *The Short Weekend* [1953], Harmondsworth, Penguin, 1956, p. 27.

127 Anthony Lambert, *The Yermakov Transfer*, London, Arlington, 1974, p. 56.

128 Ford Madox Ford, *Some Do Not …* [1924], London, Sphere, 1969, pp. 225, 232–3.

129 Edgar Wallace, 'The branch line', in Wallace, *Bones in London*, London, Ward Lock, 1921, pp. 189–207, reprinted in Irving (ed.), *Sixteen On*, pp. 163–80.

130 M. McD Bodkin, 'How he cut his stick' [1901], in Greene (ed.), *Further Rivals of Sherlock Holmes*, pp. 171–182, and Morgan (ed.), *Crime on the Lines*, pp. 13–21; R. Austin Freeman, 'The blue sequin' [1909], in Sayers (ed.), *Detection, Mystery and Horror: First Series*, pp. 396–412, Irving (ed.), *Sixteen On*, pp. 143–62, and Freeman, *Best Dr Thorndyke Detective Stories*, pp. 135–50. Appreciating prevailing loading clearances, Thorpe Hazell shows that an apparent accident, caused by a man leaning too far from a first-class compartment, really was cunningly contrived murder: Victor L. Whitechurch, 'The tragedy on the L.& M.N.', in Whitechurch, *Thrilling Stories*, pp. 29–45, and Pattrick (ed.), *Mysterious Railway Stories*, pp. 85–100.

131 Michael Innes, *The Secret Vanguard* [1940], Harmondsworth, Penguin, 1958, pp. 85–91.

132 Ridley and Alexander, 'The ghost train' [1926], in Pattrick (ed.), *Mysterious Railway Stories*, pp. 147–60. This short story is a prequel to Arnold Ridley's play *The Ghost Train*, later novelised by Ruth Alexander (London, Arrowsmith, 1927). In the play Ted Holmes is long dead when action opens in a station waiting room, the catastrophe he caused a communal memory leading superstitious Cornish folk to keep well away when ghostly trains trundle along the line. Bribed by rascally Germans, railwaymen exploit this popular fear to run machine guns from the local dock to an out-of-the-way clay pit without anybody nosying around: 'Motor-cars would have arouse suspicion in a quiet place like this.' See Arnold Ridley, *The Ghost Train: a Drama in Three Acts*, [1925], London, French, 1931, p. 62. Notable in this play text are the two pages of instructions (based on a vast array of props – from a penny whistle to a garden roller propelled over bevel-edged struts screwed to the stage) required to simulate the arrival and departure, or unhindered passage, of three trains in years before reliable recording and reproduction equipment became available.

133 Branch, *Murder Every Monday*, pp. 17, 120. Slight though it is, Branch handles the railway element in this comic crime novel very sloppily. On page 16 the Krunte Abbas branch is 'disused', and 'weed-hidden'. Turn over the page, and we sit chatting with one character in a train trundling that line.

8

Crime on the train

Tramelled fate

In chapter 7 we reviewed the manner in which British crime novelists exploited the modern railway's machine ensemble. From that discussion we excluded only one element – the train. Writers did not do this. Quite the reverse, in fact: trains merit their own chapter because, in crime fiction, they witness so much mayhem. Set against mundane experience, this is odd. One would not know it from reading whodunnits, but railway travel is safe. Entrust your life to a road vehicle, Jonathan Goodman tells us, and – unless the chauffeuse is an Institute of Advanced Motoring-trained nun commanding a bullet-proof, bomb-resistant, self-catering, oxygen-carrying limousine – you would have been wiser to Let the Train take the Strain. Despite this, he asserts, 'story-tellers have given railways a bad name'.[1] How very true. Consider some striking cases from outside Britain. Despite its title no foul deed in *Strangers on a Train*, Patricia Highsmith's American psychological thriller, is connected organically to the railroad.[2] As with Georges Simenon's *The Venice Train*,[3] Highsmith's Texan highballer merely brings strangers into significant conjunction. Idly talking in their Pullman car, two travellers discover that each would benefit if somebody else existed no longer. The solution is simple, at least for one passenger. Each will murder the other's obstacle. Lacking motive's thread, detectives will be baffled by two perfect crimes. Sebastien Japrisot expanded this idea in *Compartiment Tueurs*.[4] Intending to cover a cheque fraud, three people conspire to murder an actress. One of these three is a police detective, well placed to monitor any blundering investigation. The conspirators decide to murder one passenger, randomly chosen, who shares the actress' six-berth couchette on the night train from Marseilles to Paris. At a later date they will murder another person who travelled in that couchette. Only then will they attack their real target. The detective assures his accomplices that police attention will lock on to the first murder, interpreting the second and third as attempts to eliminate incriminating witnesses. Since the significant murder will have no connection (beyond unlucky propinquity) with the other deaths, there will be no motive for detectives to discover. Their plot unravels for unlikely reasons; but Japrisot gives us a beautiful device, rooted four-square in railway travel's pervasive anonymity. Fears about what strangers on a train might do gives this amoral little tale its powerful frisson.

Miss Liberty, an old maid on the Euston to Heysham express, discusses the Sapper novel on her lap with young Humphrey Paxton, another Sapper fan. "'Things of that sort do happen'", she tells Humphrey. "'Quite ordinary people – people like ourselves in this compartment – become mixed up in them. And that, of course, is why this book makes me a little nervous; one can never be quite sure – and particularly in *trains*".[5] How very perceptive! In Britain as elsewhere, fictions' trains prove to be dangerous things. As we shall see below, crime novels and short stories insinuate that few trains arrive at their destinations carrying the complement of living passengers with which they started out. Beyond this, strikingly large numbers of characters perish in railway accidents. Having outlived their usefulness, some are exterminated by ruthless authors. A. J. Cronin sent one villain to perdition with a ticket for the 5.27 Burntisland to Dundee service on the last Sabbath day in 1879 – the train which fell with Thomas Bouch's Tay Bridge.[6] Relatives or former employers make excellent railway crash victims, sacrificed so that heroes or heroines, pawns or victims can be forced to face the world alone. "When I was demobbed, Major Denham, he took me on as chauffeur'", hapless Briggs explains. "'But he went west in that French railway smash in 1920 and I was down and out'".[7] Ned Balfour was orphaned at five. As a senior railway-wallah under the Raj, his father's business often involved train travel; but does it not stretch credence that both he and his wife should die in that crash at Baroda? Had she been discussing railway accidents, Lady Bracknell's point would have been well taken: "'To lose one parent … may be regarded as a misfortune; to lose both looks like carelessness'".[8] No more than filial duty, statistical probability did not interest Edward Percival Fox-Ingleby, prig and bounder. He enjoyed one wonderful Edwardian day at Eton. First he was elected to Pop. Then, less than an hour later, a telegram told him that 'Father and Mother had been killed in a railway accident while on their way to open a Liberal bazaar and jumble sale at Wolverhampton'.[9] Freed from their meddlesome do-gooding, this vicious young spark could develop fully, like a Death's Head moth emerging from its chrysalis, into a lying, wenching, tenant-exploiting squire and Tory cabinet minister. "'There was a girl once'", Douglas Rutherford's stiff-lipped hero tells a second girl. "'I was very fond of her. Only something happened, one of those little games fate plays. She was killed in a train smash in France only a few months after I first met her. I was in the train, too, but I was at the other end of the coach when it happened and I only got a bad shaking. Danielle died in my arms by the side of the railway lines. She was in great pain. It wasn't very pleasant.'" "'Thank you for telling me that'", his new girl blurts through her tears. Nice technique![10] So pervasive did fictional train crashes become that imaginative villains started conjuring them for nefarious purposes. Molly Merton, that expert English forger, damaged her back in a getaway car chase. Reinventing herself as Mother Croft, a thoroughly unconvincing Australian matron, she insisted that her injury was sustained in an Italian train smash. Elsewhere, we find kidnapped persons' amnesia ascribed to post-traumatic stress from a train crash which never happened.[11]

"'Let's review the menu'", Captain Hastings suggests. "'Robbery? Forgery? No, I think not. Rather too vegetarian. It must be murder – red-blooded murder – with trimmings, of course.'"[12] Murder, or even robbery, on fiction's trains provides plenty of trimmings for readers to savour. So many, in fact, that we must do a little sorting. Later sections in this chapter will explore the setting where most crime tales place – passenger trains. Before that, we need to spend a little time on railway workers as villains or victims, and explore some less conventional trains.

Railway servants

We saw in chapter 7 that British law treated railway workers as servants, and that Golden Age conventions confined servants to peripheral roles in crime fiction. Most novels and short stories observe this rule; but not all. A Kentish passenger guard and a crossing keeper conspire with a wholesale tobacco smuggler, selling their trust for a share in illicit profits. More venially than this, the guard on an 1855 Folkestone boat train conspires to rob a bullion consignment bound for the Crimea.[13] A station ticket clerk murders a wealthy passenger, stowing her corpse in a misdirected trunk for disposal at a more convenient time.[14] Having been chased along a racing Midland Railway express train's roof, another tale's hero sees off his villain (after this bounder has shot the engine driver) by hurling lumps of coal at him and hitting him on the head with the fireman's shovel.[15] Knowing that for security reasons travelling post offices were locked off from other carriages, and hence that old TPO carriages with side corridor connections continued in service long after central connections became standard equipment on passenger stock, Hamilton Ellis explains how an armed mail robber could burst from hiding in a redundant side bellows, threatening post office sorters on a fast running train. Appreciating the powerful momentum with which heavy mail pouches lifted from lineside stanchions smashed into the moving sorting carriage, he then can explain how this robber came to be disabled and disarmed.[16] The killer in Nicholas Blake's tight little teaser (murder in a Glasgow express stuck fast in a snowdrift on Shap summit) turns out to be the train's guard, concerned to disguise his part in an earlier large-scale theft. British Railways' Southern Region electric trains are protected by a dead man's handle, arranged to cut traction motors' power when hand pressure slackens. So why was motorman Goggett's knife-stuck body found three miles short of Clough, after his train had arrived at that station? Father Brown's postman principle solves that problem: rendered socially indistinguishable by uniforms, one railwayman can pass for another before passengers' jaded eyes.[17] Impersonation also figures in a story revealing that its author had read *La Bête Humaine*. A clean-shaven fireman from Holbrook shed covets his bearded driver's wife. As their down express drags up towards Blea Moor summit he drugs the driver, then smashes his skull with a heavy spanner. Pulling on a false beard, he now feigns drunkenness as his train passes a signal box. Once beyond the signalman's sight he burns his false beard in the locomotive's firebox, then pushes the dead driver down a high embankment. With this long fall disguising effects from that spanner blow, our fireman has committed the perfect murder. Except that he failed to notice how, in slumping on his footplate, the driver's leg came to rest against the locomotive's firebox backhead. Invisible under his trousers, a terrible weal burned into his leg – while the signalman thought he saw this driver reeling on his footplate.[18] Novels suggest that British restaurant and buffet cars are staffed largely by homicidal folk. (Perhaps the passengers drive them to it.) On the always unreliable Continent, an Italian restaurant car's waiter poisons a passenger's soup, 'but she was a Scotchwoman and it wasn't strong enough'.[19] Obvious, really: they breed them tough in north Britain.

Goods train

Given their supreme importance for Victorian and Edwardian railway companies' balance sheets, we might expect to find goods and mineral trains figuring largely in railway crime fiction. We would be disappointed. No novels and short stories concerned themselves with humble mineral trains, as they trundled slowly around the country. Even goods trains appeared rarely. Victor

Whitechurch showed us a bullion-laden plutocrat arriving at a country station on the last passenger train from London one night. The stationmaster murdered him in his station office, then bribed the guard on an up goods train to carry the corpse away in his van, turfing it out on the running lines a good distance nearer London. This train's role was limited to disguising where murder took place. In an unpleasant variation on this scheme, a solicitor with a bullet in his brain was dragged several miles along a railway track, attached to a goods wagon by a brewer's hook. Here the goods train served simply to make murder look like accident.[20] Only one story used close knowledge about goods workings to construct a plot capable of enthusing both crime fiction adepts and railway specialists. A rambling East Anglian branch line terminates at Leston St Peter. Living unhappily in this village, a husband learns that his wife is carrying on with Fred, a local railway worker. While Fred attends to wagon labels for the evening pick-up goods, this wronged husband creeps up behind him and crowns him with a hammer. Tumbling Fred's corpse into a water-filled ditch, the husband settles down in a wagon loaded with crated export goods. This wagon will carry him away from his faithless wife, delivering him to some coastal port. There he will sign on in a ship's company and sail away to a new life in some new country. The 'ancient six-coupled locomotive which might once have belonged to the Midland and Great Northern Joint Railway' duly trundles her train down the branch, collecting more wagons at each station. The murderer notices their arrival at a spanking new hump marshalling yard. He has no choice but to notice his wagon's thumping shunt. Marshalled in a new train, this wagon sits ready for the next stage in its journey. The murderer falls asleep. He wakes to see policemen standing around a sodden corpse. Fred died too soon, before he could slip a new piece of paper under the spring in the wagon's label holder. Lacking that new instruction, it was shunted for the destination specified on its previous label: Leston St Peter.[21]

Ghost train

If crime writers paid slight attention to goods trains (and none to mineral trains) then they spent a remarkably large amount of time on trains removed from the natural world. As we saw in Part I of this book, canonical texts – *Rain, Steam and Speed, Dombey and Son, Anna Karenina, La Bête Humaine* – forged varied connections between the modern railway and death. Transmitted by widespread state and public concern over railways' safety standards, this connection appeared in late-Victorian popular culture, as the fairground ghost train. No surprise, then, that that less than fifty years ago we readers should watch as flighty Mrs Fothergill was shot through the left ear while trundling past disorienting mirrors and menacing automata on Seabourne Pier's Ghost Train.[22] Here modern fears about railway smashes collided with echoes from older supernatural terrors, generating nervous laughter. This structure of feeling soon migrated from the fairground to larger railway systems. Binnacle's body was bisected by clanging platform gates at Tottenham Court Road tube station. Fellow passengers watched his top half levitating above a seat while, in the rest of his story, Binnacle searched underground lines for his missing legs.[23] R. Chetwynd-Hayes's extended ghostly family also junketted around London's underground and suburban train services, sailing serenely past terrified ticket collectors.[24] More commonly than these cases suggest, terror trumped laughter on ghostly train journeys. In Amelia B. Edwards and Charles Dickens's story 'The four-fifteen express' a spook travelled in a first-class carriage, then demate-rialised outside a station waiting room. We never learn what ontological state the only other passenger on G. K. Chesterton's 'unnaturally dark train' to Paddington enjoyed – and that makes his story all the more creepy. Reticence about that grubby old man with his Dickensian carpet bag who left a warm train for deserted country in a blizzard when his train stopped at a signal check, and about the figure who seemed to be chasing him, gave Walter de la Mare's ghost story its frisson – and ruined the life of a young woman unfortunate enough to have shared his compartment. In another de la Mare story, a young man met a beautiful young woman's apparition in a London suburban train. She was there in the flesh next night, intimating suicidal tendencies. Then they married, and she was saved.[25] In Fred Benson's cruel little parable about class and English social life, a social climber swelled and shrank physically according to the company he kept. Preparing to travel from London to host a glittering house party at Newmarket, Jacob Conifer was shocked to discover only suffi-cient money in his pocket for a third-class ticket. 'The train was absolutely packed', Benson reports, 'and he was thrust into a corridor choked with the pro-letariat'.[26] Proud, plump and class-conscious in London, a shrivelled and unconscious Conifer was carried from his third-class corridor at the train's first stop. Waking to find himself in a Poor Law hospital, this social traveller evapo-rated, sublimating from shame. Middle-aged Martha's end was no less bizarre. In the mid-1970s her body disintegrated outside Mile End station after she time-travelled the Central Line to join her thirty-five-year-dead blitzed lover. Another short story ends with a railwayman dead from heart failure after being chased by a phantom Inner Circle train to the very tunnel refuge where he stowed his murdered mate's body. John Pudney shows us a depressed middle-aged man dissuaded by the apparition of his boyhood self from killing himself under a train's wheels in a North Downs tunnel. Andrew Caldecott's commuting railway enthusiast found his train swaying on to a never-built railway line. He seemed to kill a man at this line's terminus and to be hanged for that crime: but his broken-necked body was discovered hanging in his own house.[27] Finally, one forgotten short story introduces us to a celebrated character from Europe's cultural history: Faust-on-railway. A mysterious figure gives one punter the next day's evening paper. Using it, he pummels the bookies at Gatwick races. Only when travelling back to Waterloo does he notice that stop-press item: 'Death in race-train'.[28]

In all these cases, horror works by suggestion. Show the ghost train's machinery in all its tawrdry splendour, and effects collapse. Stephen Laws' horror thriller grows ever more fatuous as demonic monsters fight up and down a Kings' Cross-bound InterCity 125 train. Bombs detonate; the body count rises; the whole train explodes. Who cares? 'This Blue Arrow has an evil name', John Dickson Carr reports of the French portion on an overnight London–Paris service:

> Superstitious porters have many tales about this train. Its engine is misshapen, and sometimes there rides in the cab a blind driver named Death. Along the moonlit waste people have been ground under the wheels, with no sound save a faint cry and a hiss of blood on the firebox. On this run, too, there was once a fearful wreck; they say that on some nights, when you pass the place, you can see the dead men peering over the edge of the embankment, with their smashed foreheads and lanterns hanging from their teeth.

Overripe atmosphere tumbles into bathos here. By contrast, the most famous of all railway ghost stories shows how restraint builds tension. The signalman in Charles Dickens' creepy tale broods in his tiny cabin, set close to a yawning tunnel mouth in a deep cutting. No wonder that he starts seeing things; nor that those things kill him in due time.[29]

Night train

Fiction's ghost trains transport premodern fears about ghosts and ghoullies to the railway's modern life world. Atavism throws its glamour over night trains no less fully. 'A certain queer, half-guilty feeling' crept over one character 'whenever he saw a train go by – especially a night-train, with all its blinds down, rife with mystery'.[30] Martin Amis elevates this mystery to existential angst. 'Suicide is the night train, speeding your way to darkness', he tells us. 'You won't get there so quick, not by natural means. You buy your ticket and you climb on board. That ticket costs everything you have. But it's just a one-way. This train takes you into the night, and leaves you there. It's the night train.'[31] Privileging possibility over closure, Martin James inflects mystery differently. 'There I'll be on the speeding Night Train', he insists, 'peering from my window at the dark landscape fleeing by, knowing all the time that everything that's happened to me so far can't hold a candle to all the stuff that's waiting for me further on down the line.'[32] Choices, choices. But Amis gets it right: old Death, not new life, waits down this line.

One set of night trains produces particularly juicy fictional fruits – the long-distance international express. These things are dangerous, novelists tell us. As Eric Ambler's Turkish spymaster warns a British armaments engineer contemplating a trip on the Orient Express,

> Imagine yourself sitting there for hour after hour trying to stay awake lest you should be knifed while you slept; not daring to leave the compartment for fear of being shot down in the corridor; living in terror of everyone – from the man sitting opposite you in the restaurant car to the Customs official. Picture it, Mr Graham, and then reflect that a trans-continental train is the safest place in the world in which to kill a man.[33]

Actuarial statistics deny Colonel Haki's warning. Fiction supports him. Rome to Paris, murder;[34] Paris to Rome, murder;[35] Paris to Milan, murder;[36] Marseille to Paris, murder;[37] Paris to Nice, murder;[38] Calais to Basle, murder;[39] Basle and Milan to Bucharest, murder;[40] Istanbul to Paris, murder;[41] London to Paris, murder;[42] Paris to London, murder.[43] One might hope to avoid danger by avoiding the Continent, that notoriously immoral space. '"This is London, not an international train"' a senior British spy tells his assistant. '"No pushing a dead man into a tunnel and being a hundred miles away in another country before he's missed."'[44] Such complacency! London to Edinburgh and Glasgow, murder;[45] London to Perth, murder.[46] Leeds to London, murder.[47] York to London, murder.[48] Long-distance night trains are dangerous things, even in boring Britain. Their body count is so high that one wonders how any traveller dares to close her eyes on any of them.

Physical danger compounds with sexual excitement elsewhere in railway fiction, but never so blatantly as on international expresses. '"Tell me what you're doing on this train,"' an American journalist demands of an English rose on a Vladivostok-bound Trans-Siberian service. '"I'm an adventuress,"' she replies.[49] Paul Jennings would not be surprised by this, watching from his sidelined stopper as the Harwich boat train scorched past in the night, 'full of spies and international engineers and actresses'.[50] ('Actress' = 'tart' here, of course.)

"'Baroness! What the mischief are you doing in this train?'" Hon Charles d'Arcy Mildenhall (Dragoon Guards major, and British spy) demands of voluptuous Beatrice von Ballinstrode as he wakes on the last peacetime service from Vienna to neutral Zurich. "'And how did you find your way into my *coupé.*'"[51] Travelling to work each morning ("'First-class, non-smoking, *Morning Post*; never in a hurry, nine-thirty seven, isn't he?'"[52]) any commuter might expect not to find exotic sex spurting out in railway carriages. Fiction suggests otherwise. "'Look here, old boy'", the British Museum's director urges a Harvard professor who shares his compartment.

> Do you remember a certain conversation you and I had in a railway carriage over six months ago, when you'd first come to England on your sabbatical? You were complaining of the lack of adventure and rowdyism in your prim, buttoned-up life. And I said, "What do you mean by adventures, anyway? Do you mean in the grand manner?" I said, "Do you mean a slant-eyed adventuress, sable and all, who suddenly slips into this compartment, whispers 'Six of diamonds north tower at midnight' – or some such rubbish?"[53]

Primed by popular fiction (and, later, by Hollywood movies), that is just what readers came to expect. Sitting in the eastbound Calais–Cologne–Constantinople Orient Express, Myatt remembered youthful hours spent reading railway romances – 'stories of king's messengers seduced by beautiful countesses'.[54] Victor Maskell contemplated his Soviet controller: 'He liked trains. I imagined him on the Blue Train with a gun in his hand and a girl in his bunk'.[55] Setting out on the eastbound Trans-Siberian with years spent reading English thrillers and whodunnits behind him, Peter Fleming anticipated standard amenities on long-distance continental trains:

> Complacently you weigh your chances of a foreign countess, the secret emissary of a Certain Power, her corsage stuffed with documents of the first political importance. Will anyone mistake you for No 37, whose real name no one knows, and who is practically always in a train, being 'whirled' somewhere? You have an intoxicating vision of drugged liqueurs, rifled dispatch-cases, lights suddenly extinguished, and door-handles turning slowly under the bright eye of an automatic ...[56]

We could trace this archetype back to real figures like Lola Montez, her corsets bursting with naval treaties or letters calculated to bring down a royal house, as she scorched between European capitals in late 1840s express trains at speeds up to forty miles an hour. As British crime fiction flowered, fake Lolas materialised. Princess Zichy flaunted her wiles on the Nice express, scheming to lift Victoria's costly present to the Czarina from a frisky Queen's Messenger. Exploiting 'the sinuous vitality of the panther' in her movements, vampish

Baroness Vali von Griesbach squiggled up to a King's Messenger on the *Belle Epoque* Orient Express.[57] We catch Lola's scent even in Max Beerbohm's *Zuleika Dobson*. On the opening page exquisite Zuleika, British university fiction's première sexual bacillus, arrives at the Great Western Railway's Oxford station – that antique wooden erection 'which…does still whisper to the tourist the last enchantments of the Middle Ages'. She carries her own library to this book-stuffed town. 'Both books were in covers of dull gold', Max tells us. 'On the back of one cover BRADSHAW, in beryls, was encrusted; on the back of the other, A.B.C. GUIDE, in amethysts, beryls, chryoprases, and garnets'.[58] With Oxford's undergraduate population drowned for love of her, Zuleika consults her library. Unable to find a good connection, she orders a special train – for Cambridge. This Siren is a lively lass, but no major figure in our story. Railway fiction's vamp blooms most fully in the Scottish spy and sensualist Lady Diana Wynham's voluptuous person. In her novel's last pages she takes leave of her loyal secretary and lover, Prince Séliman, as she boards the Orient Express at Paris' Gare de l'Est. '"I have a ticket for Constantinople"', she tells him. '"But I may stop off at Vienna or Budapest. That depends absolutely on the colour of the eyes of my neighbour in the compartment. I have reserved rooms at the Imperial, on the Ring, and at the Hungaria, on the quay at Budapest; but I am just as likely to sleep in some horrible hotel in Josephstadt or in a palace on the hillside at Budapest."'[59] No matter where she lays her head, we know that she will get little sleep. Others soon enrolled in her lascivious train ('"My pedigree's Mitropa out of Wagons-Lit"', one German spy reports[60]), down to SMERSH corporal Tatiana Romanova bonking Bond through the Balkans on the westbound Orient Express.[61] Eastbound on that train, class-treacherous Countess Orlovska copied proletarian Tatiana's methods – offering Moscow gold (and softer inducements) to corrupt an upstanding Free World spy. Eager to divert his attention from her other secrets, Countess Magda Schverzinski rubbed up against a concussed British academic physicist on a transcontinental train outside Bucharest. Svelte Baroness von Ballinstrode used all her considerable wiles on a similar train, vainly seeking to explore Charles Mildenhall's tin document box.[62] As with other clichés, adroit writers soon learned to turn this trick differently: making an English maiden dissemble as a travelling courtesan for disinterested matrimonial reasons;[63] rewarding an adventure-yearning city clerk for faithful service with a fake spy-houri;[64] reversing the usual gender pattern by arranging for a comfortably-circumstanced woman in the Dover boat train to be seduced by a suave gigolo.[65]

The British passenger train

In thrilling fictions set on international trains, exoticism seduced readers. Trundling up and down the BedPan line between Luton and Kings Cross (Thameslink) – surely London's least seductive station? – each weekday, few commuters could expect to be propositioned by a patrician vamp. Lacking this spice, what interest might criminally-inclined writers conjure from the tediously familiar British passenger train? Two things.

Anonymous privacy

First, they could explore railway travel's democratic nature. Sir Julian Sheriffe 'hated train journeys: resented with irritable intolerance the enforced contact with any Tom, Dick or Harry who could afford a railway ticket'.[66] Hence, of course, the Englishman's idea of Heaven – an empty compartment.[67] Only by spending real money could one escape pollution from travelling strangers. Carrying important wartime despatches from Norway, Peter Fleming missed the London train at Inverness. Sustained by Eton and Christ Church, Oxford's aristocratic insouciance, he ordered that a special train be prepared.

> And there it was when the time came: an enormous railway engine, a sleeping-car, and one or perhaps two other coaches to keep it properly trimmed at high speeds. The sleeping-car was a special one, panelled with exotic timbers from different parts of the Empire; I think it had been in some kind of exhibition. It was a lovely train. And how pleasant to be able to say to various old friends that one met in the Station Hotel, 'You don't happen to want a lift to London tonight, do you?' And when the three or four who accepted were on board, with how casual, how proprietary, how smug an air one glanced at one's wrist-watch and, leaning out of the window, said to a kindly railway official, 'I'm ready to start, if your people are'.[68]

Peter Fleming's uniform persuaded LMS staff that the British government would pick up his tab, but private persons seeking private railway travel had to bear the cost themselves. In consequence, 'The man who sports with Specials is presumably not unembarrassed with the goods of this world'.[69] '"Mr Beck!"' a Dorset landed proprietor about to be accused of murder exclaims to the private detective he has called down from London. '"Why, I thought you couldn't have got here before midnight!"' '"Special train"', laconic Paul Beck replies. '"Your wire said 'Expense no object'."'[70] If expense influenced choices rather than determining them, then by purchasing all seats in a compartment one could ensure privacy, particularly on a non-corridor train. 'By 6.15 the next morning, Selby, his wife and I were in a reserved, locked, first-class compartment, speeding rapidly west', Dixon Druce told his readers in 1899. 'The servants and Mrs Selby's own special maid were in a separate carriage.'[71] Having disbursed serious money to avoid pollution from first-class strangers – let alone the hoi polloi – how could this not be the case?

The railway carriage is a public vehicle. With wit and determination one might contrive to shut out other travellers by unofficial means – like that 'companionage' of eight people who, scattering coats and hats on vacant seats, managed for seven months to dine together in one first-class compartment each Friday evening on the down *Brighton Belle*.[72] But under normal circumstances no passenger might choose her or his companions: 'for a train, like the Ritz, is open to everyone, first- and second-class passengers alike'.[73] Who travelled with whom was a matter for the railway company, or for chance, to determine. And chance could play wicked tricks, even in first-class compartments: putting a retiring colonial policeman opposite a garrulous spinster convinced that a serial killer roams her quiet village; forcing a female detective novelist of the decayed golden age school (author of such deathless treasures as *Vengeance at the Vicarage*, *Revenge at the Rectory*, and *Murder in the Cathedral* – '*Her* work of that title; not the late Mr T. S. Eliot's') to watch while a tweedy elderly man inscribed uncomplimentary judgements on her latest masterpiece's flyleaf.[74] Since both these beginnings end badly, we must conclude that these travellers would have done better to stare fixedly at their compartments' ceilings. This would have been the conventional action, of course. 'It is one of the canons of correct conduct', R. Austin Freeman tells us, 'scrupulously adhered to (when convenient) by all well-bred persons, that an acquaintance should be initiated by a proper introduction.'[75] Hence poor Alethia Debchance's discomfort as she sat 'in a corner of an otherwise empty railway carriage, more or less at ease as regarded body, but in some trepidation as to mind'.[76] What, Alethia agonised, should she do if somebody to whom she had not been introduced properly clambered into her compartment? British railway travel's fabled insociability provides the answer: ignore the blighter, and hope that he would go away. Osbert Sitwell commended the technique employed by 'a famous professor, now alas, dead'. A bore insisted on knowing whether snow had fallen where he had come from the previous day. 'He … countered with the enigmatic reply, "I did not come from anywhere yesterday", leaving his interlocutor puzzled and silent'.[77] Fear of some freezing rebuff like this inhibited a young man in the only first-class compartment ('provided for the rich and thriftless') on the Wockley Junction to Ashendon Oakshott branch stopper. 'For some minutes after the train had started, the usual decent silence of the travelling

Englishman prevailed in the compartment. Then the young man, who had been casting covert glances at his companion, cleared his throat and said "Er."[78]

Genteel British railway unsociability rode serenely over time and change. In 1855 Nathaniel Hawthorne warned his American readers that in Britain, 'It is foolish ever to travel in the first-class carriages except with ladies in charge. Nothing is to be seen or learnt there; nobody to be seen except civil and silent gentlemen, sitting on their cushioned dignities'.[79] Almost a century and a half later, Hawthorne's compatriot Bill Bryson still worried about not being able to strike up companionable conversations with people on British trains. It must be his fault, he reasoned, because Paul Theroux's travel books showed him able to draw train travelling Britons into revealing conversation at a hat's drop. The *Times Literary Supplement*'s columnist explained how he does it. In *Sir Vidia's Shadow*, his tasteless book about V. S. Naipaul, 'Theroux was up to his old literary trick of passing off fiction as fact'. Many among Theroux's British railway conversations must be fictions, practice passes from a novelist earning crusts in a different enterprise.[80]

Aided by railway companies' strict class segregation, wooden silence might protect English privacy; but how could a nervous traveller be sure that some bounder might not try to scrape acquaintance?[81] A British intelligence service ran regular wartime honey traps for lonely men on the Edinburgh sleeper, with a plausible Welshman plying with 'strong drink and lavish foodstuffs' governments in exiles' couriers heading for Leith-based fishing boats busily maintaining surreptitious connection with occupied Europe. If the booze did not work then the Welshman's sexual wiles might do the trick; or Kirstie (a.k.a. 'the Venus Fly Trap'), a refined young Morningside woman saving hard for her postwar haberdashery shop, might be girded for action. Once any courier rested in Morpheus' arms (or Kirstie's, or Danny Perkins'), then his locked leather despatch case was abstracted and unstitched by a cobbler who had served his time at Lobb's. (This was *very* high class espionage.) When significant papers had been scanned by a multilingual agent with an excellent memory, each case was restitched and returned to its owner.[82] Dim Captain Hastings would be a sucker for this ploy. Falling into conversation with a vivacious young Englishwoman on the Paris to Calais train, he discovered that she was an actress. ('"No – not the kind you're thinking about"' she insisted: always an important clarification in any English novel set on a train travelling to or from Paris.)[83] Densely smitten, Hastings discussed her charms with Hercules Poirot.

'I don't suppose I shall ever see her again. She was quite amusing to talk to for a railway journey, but she's not the kind of girl I should ever get keen on.'
'Why?'
'Well, it sounds snobbish, perhaps, but she's not a lady, not in any sense of the word.'[84]

Poor Hastings! Forgetting that this woman is damned socially by initiating conversation with a man to whom she had not been introduced properly, by this book's end he quivers on the point of proposing marriage to the adventurous siren. '"I – I just met her casually"', a painter stutters about another woman. '"As a matter of fact – it was on a train. After all", he added defiantly, "why shouldn't one meet people in trains?"'[85] Just asking the question shows that he, too, is not fit for polite society. What else could one expect from an artist?

Of course, gentility would not be compromised if one simply speculated about fellow travellers, rather than actually talking to them. 'There are fewer pleasanter diversions', Aldous Huxley tells us,

> than to sit in cafés or the third class carriages of railway trains, looking at one's neighbours and listening (without attempting to enter into conversation) to such scraps of their talk as are wafted across the intervening space. From their appearance, from what they say, one reconstructs in the imagination the whole character, the complete life history. Given the single fossil bone, one fancifully builds up the whole diplodocus. It is an excellent game.[86]

So thinks Miss Yates. Sitting in her super-first-class Pullman seat on the Newhaven boat train, she 'began unobtrusively to take notes of her fellow-travellers, and built up for herself an imaginary picture of their lives'.[87] She got it all wrong, of course; but who cares? 'For aren't we *always* intrigued by anyone who shares a compartment with us?' William Pattrick enquires. 'However many other things there may be to engage our attention, it is a most unusual mind indeed that does not stop for a moment to wonder just *who* or *what* our companions are, and *where* they might be going.'[88] We might lack Sherlock Holmes' prototype's ability to deduce that the figure sitting silently opposite him in a railway compartment was 'a betting man of methodistical proclivities',[89] but that does not inhibit us from trying. As conversation ebbs and flows on a long journey, we might convert travellers into types: the Deep Chap, the Expansive Man, the Flash Card, the Forward Piece, the Comfortable Body, the Fusspot.[90] Companions might prove less than desirable. Like George Mulliner, some could appear to be homicidal lunatics. George had excellent reasons for hiding under the seat in his first-class compartment on the Ippleton to East Wobsley branch train: to escape a real homicidal maniac's attentions on Ippleton station.

The woman who came to sit in his compartment lacked this special knowledge. Nor, when he tried to explain, did George's awful stammer improve the occasion.[91] Scarcely less deluded than young Mr Mulliner's tormentor at Ippleton – or is this judgement too hasty? – was the man who pressed a small golden apple on Mr Hinchcliff in their shared compartment, insisting that it came from the biblical Tree of Knowledge.[92] Some fellow passengers might prove to be dead, like that corpse of restricted growth which fell on Sergeant Beef from a third class compartment's luggage rack.[93] As George Brewster discovered when he tumbled at the last moment into a first-class compartment on the wrong express at Euston, you might find yourself closely closeted with a man determined to explain how he murdered a woman twenty years earlier.[94] You might find yourself trapped with a man claiming an undetectable method of murdering people – and later events might persuade you that he was not joking.[95] You might find yourself trapped with more concrete fellow travellers than these. Disgusted George Verney, a Cold War-period foreign correspondent for a right-wing London newspaper, found himself sharing space on a Warsaw to Moscow train with eight fatuous British leftists bound for a Moscow-funded peace mission, fronted by the usual muddle-headed and bombastic clergyman.[96]

People in your compartment might dissemble. An 'amiable foreign gentleman' sat opposite a government courier at lunch in a Norfolk-bound express, then doped the courier's coffee before stealing a memorandum outlining a new British secret weapon.[97] (Those were the days, when Britain had secret weapons to steal!) Quitting his train one evening, a London commuter known for his sporting instincts found that his chauffeur already had driven away from his usual station, decoyed by a message from a third party (with whom the murderer, impersonating the commuter, had travelled) reporting that his master had made a bet that his car would beat the train to another station. The commuter started walking home, and was killed in a lane. His house could now be rifled: the purpose behind this complicated enterprise. It failed only because the killer entertained his innocent third party by blowing smoke rings – when all his friends knew that the victim was fanatically opposed to smoking.[98] Travelling with a group of other new girls bound for durance vile in Miss Pope's finishing school at Neuilly, young Winnie Pope slid into a first-class lavatory shortly after her boat train left Amiens. She emerged as Jim Elliot, notorious art smuggler.[99] Another man seemed to be snoozing in the corner of a first-class compartment on the Paris-Calais boat train while two others discussed a business coup: but 'Morrison, glancing across the compartment, happened to notice him open an interested eye, look at the speaker, close it again, and remain motionless as if still asleep'.[100] Like General Sir Richard Hannay, distressed to discover how thirty years' soft living turned a go-getting young East African empire builder into a commuting old fogey who bored his compartment's clique with chatter about alpine plants (or like Rufus Pembery, escaped convict turned retired rentier, distressed to be recognised in a railway compartment by a former warder with an inconveniently sharp memory), you might forget ever having known a fellow passenger.[101] On a regular commute, you might think that you knew all your companions reasonably intimately, like those eight first-class folk on the *Brighton Belle*; but only after one man had been discovered bent rigid in the carriage's toilet, poisoned with strychnine, did each member in this travelling club learn how ruthlessly he had blackmailed all the others.[102] You might find yourself sharing a compartment with a bearded man who smoked a remarkably large number of cigars, and whose finger nails kept changing from well-trimmed to hard-bitten, and back again.[103] You might be puzzled that the nun sitting opposite you was wearing high-heels; and by the hairy masculine wrist revealed by a heavily-veiled woman.[104] Your travelling companions' business might not interest you, but they could show excessive interest in yours – like that nosy child lip-reading your whispered criminal conversation with the man sitting next to you.[105] Two blackguards knew very well who young Horace Carr-Mathers was as he sat composedly in his compartment on a London express. Stringing him up like a parcel, they suspended Horace outside the train from a door handle, waiting for a confederate to remove him when this train crawled past a severe permanent way check.[106] Like old Lady Georgina Fawley sitting in the Dover boat train, you might be drawn into conversation with a plausible French jewel thief claiming acquaintance with your late husband.[107] Like doomed Philip Ploss ('the Cow-and-Gate poet'), villains sharing your compartment might even pretend to *be* you. Trundling through the Home Counties with three strangers, Ploss heard his own poem misquoted by somebody claiming to be its author. This turns out to be espionage, with Ploss' soppy verse used to transmit information among a gang's members. Later in this thriller, the same motive led another gang member to interpolate four spurious lines while quoting Swinburne on a train crossing the Forth Bridge.[108] Some fellow passengers might dissemble common acquaintance. As a cross-country train crept from station to station one dismal Sunday, one compartment filled steadily with long-nosed people studiously ignoring each others' existence – but all, to a trained observer's bemused eye, members in a single family.[109] As in Michael Innes' excellent *The Journeying Boy*, you might find yourself having to sort out *two* gangs on one train, with all members studiously ignoring each others'

existence. Unobtrusively aided by Miss Liberty, that old maid whose name prepares us for the revelation that she is a spy committed to the proper British side,
here Mr Thewless thwarted a filthy foreign gang's attempts to kidnap young
Humphrey Paxton on the Irish Mail.[110] This complicated outrage was patterned
on Ethel Lina White's *The Wheel Spins*, where an intelligence courier passing as
a garrulous English governess is kidnapped by foreign agents somewhere in the
Balkans.[111] More recently, anonymity and conspiracy among travellers have
sired a long string of railway thrillers and horror novels set outside Britain.[112]
One might hope to escape all these perils through prudence, by choosing to
travel in an empty compartment. That would not work because, as Nellie
Collins understood, 'there was always the chance of someone getting in who
was *not* really nice. When she was a little girl she had heard a story about a
lunatic who got into a train with a friend of her Aunt Chrissie's and made her eat
carrots and turnips all the way from Swindon to Bristol.'[113] Poor Nellie! Despite
all her careful precautions, railway death has marked her for his own.

Nellie Collins' and Aunt Chrissie's tales echo Victorian fears about unaccompanied women's risks in railway compartments. No surprise then that sex
should spurt out in writers' compartments. We saw earlier that pheromones
drench fiction's glamorous international trains; but less exotic journeys could
also stimulate hormonal activity. One competent young woman knew how to
excite any young man, keeping his libido just below boiling point.

> Chloe had usually found a fairly long train journey, especially in the first-class
> compartment Lord Arglay [her employer] had naturally assumed she would take –
> in the company of an intelligent and personable young man who rather obviously
> admired her, a very pleasant, and even exciting, method of spending the time.
> There was so happy a mixture of the known and the unknown; there was all the
> possibility of advance and yet all the surety of withdrawal: there was in short such
> admirable country for campaigning that she could not very clearly understand why
> she had thrown out a squadron or so to check Mr Doncaster's early moves, and had
> with small expenditure of effort immobilised him.[114]

Across the Channel, Guy de Maupassant's short story 'An idyll' described no
open flirtation between a labourer and a wet nurse travelling from Genova to
Marseilles, yet still packed a powerful erotic punch. He is faintingly hungry. She
has nursed no child for a day. Exploring mutual coincidence of wants, each
relieves the other.[115] Sardonic 'Saki' parodied this tale in 'The mouse'. Bashful
Theodoric Voler enters a second-class compartment – emblem for British petit
bourgeois respectability[116] – at a country station. The only other occupant, a
woman, slumbers in a corner seat. He discovers a mouse entangled in his

clothing. His companion awakes. As their train speeds towards London, he makes ever more frantic efforts to remove the mouse. Discarding more and more clothes, he remains conscious of 'an icy silence in that corner towards which he dared not look'. Then, at the terminus, the woman asks mouse-relieved but massively embarrassed Theodoric to find her a cab: '"Being blind makes one so helpless at a railway station."'[117]

Ways out

With passengers trapped between a private desire for solitude and companies' enforced insistence on crowded contiguity, railway travel's anonymity appeals strongly to crime writers, we see.[118] A second attraction lurks in this genre's nature. While '"people don't expect to be involved in train robberies"', so – as the Scotch Express's commonsensical guard mutters at St Pancras – "Folks don't disappear out of railway carriages, except in books."'[119] True enough; but in books trains are robbed, and passengers (or their souls) do disappear with clockwork regularity. Leaving aside supernatural congealings and evaporations,[120] a moving train offers intriguing variations on that classic device, the sealed room. 'He was born in this railway age', John Dickson Carr – the man who spent a lifetime trying to write one perfect locked room puzzle – tells us in a late book. 'He had no qualms about being locked up here, shut away beyond escape or communication with another compartment, in a train hurtling along at fifty miles an hour'. Conjuring an escapologist's nightmare, Julian Barnes goes beyond this. 'Once, taking the night train from London to Paris', his character tells us, 'I found myself in the locked sleeping compartment of a locked coach in a locked hold beneath the waterline of a cross-channel ferry'.[121] Passengers' isolation frames the first book-length detective fiction with a railway setting. Five travellers share a second class compartment on the Dover train. When their connecting service reaches Paris' Gare du Nord, one of these five lies dead with a bullet in his brain. One of the remaining four killed him; another is a Scotland Yard detective. The reader's task is to identify the villain, and his motive, before that detective does.[122] This archetype soon was copied (and subverted) by other writers. Lightly disguised as a Board of Agriculture official, one detective must identify German spies bent on harming British fleets snoozing at anchor in Invergordon and Scapa, among the five men sharing his Highland Railway first-class compartment on a journey north from Inverness in the First World War. His task is ticklish socially – these fellow travellers comprise one major general, one Royal Naval Reserve officer, one Guardee subaltern and two Australian Army officers. All five appear to be officers – but which of them really are patriotic gentlemen?[123] A detective on the

Holyhead boat train must sort out which among his first-class compartment's respectable occupants – one Catholic priest, one fur-coated business man, one bespectacled elderly gent, one young accountant – actually is Jim Dawson, a daring bank robber. Much as usual, in fact; except that this is a sting. The detective is a fraud, conspiring with his fellow travellers to abstract a large cheque from that ingenuous accountant.[124]

This is not the only way in which misdirection may arise. Authors may direct our attention to one particular compartment, but this must not stop us thinking outside that oblong. "'There *is* such a thing as walking along the footboards of a train in motion, and getting into another compartment'", an Edwardian railway detective tells us. "'I've done it lots of times.'"[125] True enough. Clambering along outside a District Railway first-class carriage, one among Edgar Wallace's Four Just Men assassinates an informer by opening his compartment's door and smashing a phial of prussic acid gas on the floor.[126] Richard Morley reaches Thomas Raines' compartment in the same way, then smashes Raines' head in with a wooden mallet. This blunt instrument he discards by tossing it on a burning slag-heap conveniently close to the railway line – where, sadly for Morley, it fails to be incinerated completely.[127] Exiled in Kent, a white Russian officer clambers along footboards until he reaches a German spy's compartment. He shoots out the light, steals important documents – which he will return to the British authorities, of course – and escapes a hue and cry by lying between his train's wheels at the next station. A daring woman kills her husband on a coastal express racing south from London Bridge, then uses a folding ironing board – with which she thoughtfully has equipped herself for this journey – to cross to a Crystal Palace-bound express running on a parallel track.[128] A boat train from Calais to Paris sees *two* passengers clambering independently along slippery footboards, intent on robbery and murder.[129] In later years, as railway equipment grew more sophisticated, one or several carriages linked by corridors and gangways could form the crime's scene. Victor Whitechurch's story 'How the bank was saved' shows the Great Western's Paddington to Birmingham (Snow Hill) express made up with non-corridor stock, forcing robbers to clamber along external footboards to attack a bank messenger. Since corridor stock certainly would have been used on this service by 1912 (the year when the book containing this story was published), we may assume that Whitechurch wrote it much earlier.[130] Once gangwayed corridor stock was ubiquitous on main line services, it might seem that only desperate contrivance could limit our attention to one carriage. "'You see, I happen to know that the doors at the ends of the coaches on this train were locked, the key being with the guard"', Thorpe Hazell tells a client. "'So it was impossible that anyone could get through to the next coach.'"[131] Why would any railway company do that on a daytime corridor express when it had just spent one fortune building corridor stock, and another advertising these novel amenities, except to oblige a crime writer? True – except that the Great Western company did rule that connecting doors between carriages should be locked on early corridor trains. That guards now could walk through the train's length examining tickets was no reason, in this patrician company's view, why passengers should be permitted to amble where they chose.[132] Sapper limits the number of suspects in a corridor train ingeniously, by having his bookmaker murdered by a bullet (and a raw egg) in a physically isolated slip coach at the tail of a fast-running express;[133] but by suspecting only the four surviving passengers in this coach he displays woeful ignorance of railway operating procedures. This coach would have been controlled by a slip-guard sitting in his driving compartment, alert to separate the coach from its parent train at the right moment, then brake it to a halt at the station to be served. Some recent thrillers set good and bad gangs fighting through all parts of hurtling hijacked diesel and electric trains.[134] Required to sustain readers' interest after initial bloody assaults have been completed, authors set their teams trundling repetitively up and down their thundering trains as if these were testosterone-drenched rugby fields. As, of course, in one sense, they are.

We can be deceived about where and when Death caught his victim's hand. A passenger died at Charing Cross station on the last east-bound underground train one night not because he had been poisoned there, but because a poison administered earlier finally (one might say) took effect there.[135] Unpopular Squire Cargate's apparent heart attack happened – to unseemly glee from groundlings in the vicinity – just after he climbed into a branch train's first-class compartment; but that was no more than the location where he sniffed up a snootful of potassium cyanide-laced snuff.[136] Sir Hector Bassenthwaite lay dying in his first-class compartment when the Guernsey boat train reached Victoria, but the ricin injection which killed him had been administered in Southampton's customs hall, before he caught his train.[137] Poisoned with a doctored travel-sickness pill, Sandra Telford was beyond medical assistance when she caught her diesel railcar at disgraced post-Beeching Sudbury station.[138] More spectacularly than any of these, Little Mumbo had been dead for several hours when his scheming wife lugged his corpse (disguised as a baby) on to a London train, using a handbag so capacious that it must have rivalled Miss Prism's. Once her train was moving, this faithless wife stripped baby clothes from her husband's corpse, leaving a conventionally clad dead midget rolled up in canvas on the luggage rack to be discovered by some passenger.[139]

We can be fooled into seeing crime where none exists. What a splendid idea to spice up a marriage by staging a cod jewel robbery, hurling fake gems into the Adriatic just as the Simplon-Orient Express rumbled over the causeway linking Venice with the Veneto! How satisfactory that Max Carrados could show that the skeleton packed in an American crook's luggage on the 6.32 Stratford-upon-Avon to Paddington express was not William Shakespeare's! (Failing to lift Will's tomb-slab in St Mary's church, Stratford, this crook substituted fraud for grave-robbing. Since only an ignorant American collector would be gulled when he was sold one skeleton rather than another, this scarcely counts as crime in an English narrative.) How unfortunate that, enjoying the breeze through his first-class compartment's open window, this man's head intercepted a tumbling machine gun bullet as it ricocheted from a steel flagpole on Purfleet ranges![140] How cunning for this gentleman to change into a railwayman's clothes in his first-class carriage on the Paddington to Banbury train, then climb out on the side away from the platform at Reading station and find a seat in a third-class compartment! With a trail of fake suicide notes left scattered around, and with his first-class compartment's door swinging on its hinges, nobody but Sherlock Holmes would penetrate this ingenious attempt to bilk creditors.[141] How unfortunate that the woman found dead in her compartment at Liverpool Street should have visited a Cambridge ethnological exhibition! How doubly unfortunate that while she studied artifacts displayed there, a small boy should purloin a poisoned dart from a glass case and drop it in her cardigan's pocket! How triply unfortunate that she should prick her finger on this dart somewhere near Six Mile Bottom![142]

More commonly than this, passengers are murdered on fiction's trains. Sitting comfortably in her seat on a down Great Western semi-fast approaching Reading, worthy Mrs McGillicuddy sees a man throttle a woman in a train running parallel with her own.[143] Two middle-aged men and a woman enter a compartment at Euston. When their train draws to its first halt at Rugby, only one person remains; and he is a *young* man, shot through the heart.[144] A bad baronet finds a heavily-veiled woman sitting in his first-class compartment when he returns from wetting his whistle at Rugby. He lies fatally wounded in a pool of gore when his train stops at Birmingham – and that veiled woman has disappeared.[145] A different case shows us a millionaire snoozing in his special train. He wakes to discover that this train has crashed into a loaded stone wagon. Remarkable enough, in all conscience – but stranger things follow. Our millionaire seems to have gained a club foot, and finds himself draped in unfamiliar bloodstained clothes. Worst of all, a strange man lies dead outside his carriage's door.[146] An improbably honourable English crook executes moral justice on a welshing American industrialist in a German express.[147] Marooned by peace, two paratroopers devise a plan to rob a heavy payroll from clerks travelling on a midlands passenger train. When one clerk resists, robbery inflates to murder.[148] With a silk scarf twisted tightly round her neck, Mrs Main was strangled in her first-class compartment on the 4 p.m. express from London to Warcaster; 'Being an apoplectic woman of full habit, the assassin had found his wicked task comparatively easy'.[149] This would have proved child's play for 'the pocket Hercules', a man whose small stature disguised enormous strength. He throttles a woman in her compartment, then steals the jewels she carries. To avoid detection he leaves this train when it stops for several minutes at a busy junction and surrenders his ticket at the barrier. Then he buys a second ticket to a station further down the line. Passing back through the barrier, he re-enters the fatal compartment and appears to discover the woman's corpse.[150] This ingenious plan is exploded by Paul Toft (nicknamed *Ifill*, from his standard deductive device, the statement 'I feel …'), perhaps the most noxiously effete amateur detective ever invented. Clifford Flush (a.k.a. 'The Balliol Butcher') is a much more robust bloke than Ifill. Deploying his smooth Oxonian patter, Flush insures three women's lives heavily, then ejects them from fast-running passenger trains. '"My fourth case survived"', he recalls. '"It was her evidence which acquitted me. I was of course obliged to marry her and she later threw herself off the Flying Scotsman, for which event I had an unshakeable alibi"'.[151] In Agatha Christie's *Murder on the Orient Express* (1934) almost all passengers and crew in a train's first-class section conspire to execute a villain: we are surprised that the fireman does not turn up, wielding his shovel. Head-shot victims roll from compartments at one station after another.[152] In an imaginative variation on this theme, one bad baronet (from so many, sounding echoes from Victorian melodrama) is rubbed out by being shot in the back, through his seat-back, by a gunman travelling in the next compartment.[153] A drink-befuddled blackmailer is ejected from a fast-running Southern electric commuter train near a south coast resort, to die beside the line.[154] Another drink-befuddled man is bundled to his death from a District Railway underground train; but here booze had been laced with opiates.[155]

As this last case shows, hoary literary clichés loom through railway murders. Inspector Badger accepts a cigar from the burglar he followed into a London train at Maidstone. Predictably enough, his corpse soon turns up beside the four-foot way in Greenhithe tunnel: that stogey was poisoned.[156] A rascally Edwardian husband slays his wealthy wife with a Borgia poison-ring in a Metropolitan Railway underground carriage.[157] A China merchant travelling on the tube perishes after inhaling a 'subtle Oriental poison' at his murderer's invitation.[158] Oscar Schwatz dies in the Cornish Riviera Limited's dining car, scratched on the neck with '"one of the poison thorns used by a certain tribe of South American Indians"'.[159] Happily, many crime writers show more imagination than these examples suggest. Thinking quickly after a terrible railway crash, a villain picks up one stunned survivor – then hurls him into the inferno which once was a gas-lighted carriage.[160] Several killers are caught only because the detective knows more than he about what happens to railway tickets once they have been collected at the station barrier.[161] Another detective needs just one glance at notes scrawled on a stabbed man's shirt cuff ('242, E3, Great Marlow') in a train on the LSWR's Okehampton line, to know where to find a map documenting Russian fortifications at Port Arthur: behind a sepia photograph of Great Marlow in compartment E of the Great Western Railway's third-class carriage, number 242.[162] An embezzling provincial jeweller murders his partner (who happens to be his brother), then takes a trip from Victoria to France. On the outward journey he travels first-class on a through ticket to Paris, impersonating his brother. He leaves *The Golden Arrow* at Calais, secretes himself in a washroom to remove the slight disguise that rendered his appearance similar to his brother's, then waits calmly for the balancing London-bound train. Returning to London as himself, and travelling on a third-class ticket, he fools passport and customs officers. He does not fool dogged Superintendent French.[163] Nor is that gent stymied by an Ulster industrialist's mysterious disappearance. Travelling on the Stranraer sleeper, Sir John Magill is drugged, then slain by an assassin using a connecting door from the next compartment. Murderer and corpse leave the train through a compartment window – not on the platform side, of course – when the boat train stops at Castle Douglas in the wee small hours. Made up appropriately, Magill's rascally nephew now climbs in through this window and impersonates his uncle on the Larne boat.[164] Only careful reconstruction, and French's close knowledge about the railway's machine ensemble, turns a missing person enquiry in County Down into a murder investigation in Galloway.

Doggedly sewing stitch after stitch, Superintendent French sutures the social fabric's wounds. In Freeman Wills Crofts' many fictions, the railway machine ensemble's oiled efficency stands for a calculable and predictable modern world. Intriguing us through ingenious variations on conventional settings and familiar deductive problems, railway crime fiction assures readers that unreason – robbery, fraud, murder – will not disrupt the modern world's smooth progress. Try though they may, wrongdoers find themselves punished by an inexorable police force and a disinterested judiciary. Law-abiding citizens can climb aboard their commuter trains or holiday trains, reassured that railways' status as the safest available form of transport has been confirmed. Briefly disrupted by mayhem on the line or on the train, social life returns to its usual, boring round. Normal service is resumed, strictly to timetable.

Notes

1 Jonathan Goodman, 'Points of departure', in Goodman (ed.), *The Railway Murders: Classic Stories of True Crime*, London, Sphere, 1986, p. 9. As L. T. C. Rolt and Patrick Whitehouse note (*Lines of Character*, London, Constable, 1952, p. 11), embedded control mechanisms mean that 'the railway [is] the safest form of transport ever evolved'.

2 Patricia Highsmith, *Strangers on a Train* [1950], Harmondsworth, Penguin, 1974.

3 Georges Simenon, *The Venice Train* [1961], translated by Alastair Hamilton, London, Hamilton, 1974. Other Simenon fictions contain stronger railway interest. For examples see *The Man Who Watched the Trains Go By* [1938], translated by Stuart Gilbert, Harmondsworth, Penguin, 1964; 'The madman of Bergerac', in *Maigret Travels South* [1940], translated by Geoffrey Sainsbury, Harmondsworth, Penguin, 1952, pp. 131–254; 'Newhaven-Dieppe' [c1940], in *The Man from Everywhere, and Newhaven-Dieppe*, translated by Stuart Gilbert, Harmondsworth, Penguin, 1952, pp. 127–252; *The Negro* [1957], translated by Helen Sebba, London, Hamish Hamilton, 1959; *The Train* [1961], translated by Robert Baldick, Harmondsworth, Penguin, 1967. When a corpse-stuffed trunk turns up in the Gare du Nord's left luggage office (in *Maigret's Revolver* [1954], translated by Nigel Ryan, Harmondsworth, Penguin, 1959, pp. 35–8) Simenon tells us that Maigret spent two miserable years attached to that station's police-post.

4 Paris, Denoël, 1962. Translated by Francis Price as *The 10.30 from Marseilles*, New York, Doubleday, 1963 and Harpenden, No Exit Press, 1990; and as *The Sleeping-Car Murders*, Harmondsworth, Penguin, 1978.

5 Michael Innes, *The Journeying Boy*, London, Gollancz, 1949, pp. 65–6. Original emphasis.

6 A. J. Cronin, *Hatter's Castle*, London, Gollancz, 1931, pp. 149–56. Travelling from Edinburgh, Denis' doomed train started from Burntisland because this was the Fife harbour for ferry services from Granton, on the Lothian shore. In 1873 workers started building Sir Thomas Bouch's suspension bridge over the Firth of Forth, but public enthusiasm waned rapidly when the first Tay Bridge fell. (Alanna Knight, *A Drink for the Bridge: a Novel of the Tay Bridge Disaster*, London, Macmillan, 1973 treats this fall imaginatively.) Its replacement, and the substitute Forth Bridge, were

built like Clyde dreadnoughts to reassure nervous travellers. A canny Scottish line, the North British Railway salvaged the locomotive which fell with Bouch's Tay Bridge, and restored it to service. Ever after, sardonic local railwaymen called it 'The Diver'.

7   H. C. Bailey, 'The cat burglar', in Bailey, *Mr Fortune, Please* [1927], London, Penguin, 1934, p. 42.

8   George Sims, *The Last Best Friend* [1967], Harmondsworth, Penguin, 1971, p. 43; Oscar Wilde, *The Importance of Being Earnest* [1895], Act 1.

9   A. G. Macdonnell, *Autobiography of a Cad* [1938], London, Macmillan, 1951, p. 34.

10 Douglas Rutherford, *Telling of Murder* [1952], Harmondsworth, Penguin, 1956, p. 154.

11 Agatha Christie, *Peril at End House* [1932], Harmondsworth, Penguin, 1948, pp. 58–9, 186; Max Beerbohm, 'A. V. Laider', in Dorothy L. Sayers (ed.), *Great Stories of Detection, Mystery and Horror: Second Series*, London, Gollancz, 1931, p. 536.

12 Agatha Christie, *The ABC Murders* [1936], London, Pan, 1962, p. 20.

13 Victor L. Whitechurch, 'Peter Crane's cigars,' in Whitechurch, *Thrilling Stories of the Railway* [1912], London, Routledge & Kegan Paul, 1975, pp. 11–28; Michael Crichton, *The Great Train Robbery*, London, Cape, 1975.

14 Peter Lovesey, 'The lady in the trunk', in Tim Heald (ed.), *A Classic English Crime*, New York, Mysterious Press, 1991, pp. 77–94. This is pastiche, written for a collection celebrating Agatha Christie's birth centerary. But Dame Agatha herself never stooped to anything so *hackneyed* as a railway trunk murder…

15 Matthew Vaughan, *The Discretion of Dominick Ayres*, London, Secker & Warburg, 1976, pp. 240–3. Much the same happens at the climax of Robert Parker's *Ticket to Oblivion*, London, Macmillan, 1951; but here American technical terms – 'signal tower', 'head conductor' – add little verisimilitude to a tale about filthy Commie attempts to sabotage French railways as a diversion from their plan to heist gold from a Lens–Arras train.

16 C. Hamilton Ellis, 'T. P. O.', in Charles Irving (ed.), *Sixteen On*, London, Macmillan, 1957, pp. 210–15. Dick Donovan, 'The robbery of the London mail' (in Donovan, *Caught at Last*, London, Chatto & Windus, 1897, pp. 79–101) insists that the defalcation in his story took place 'a good few years ago', so that readers would appreciate that non-corridor stock was involved.

17 Nicholas Blake, 'A study in white', in Eleanour Sullivan and Ellery Queen (eds), *The Omnibus of Crime Stories*, London, Robinson, 1991, pp. 135–49; Edmund Crispin, 'Beware of the trains' [1949], in Anon (ed.), *The Evening Standard Detective Book: First Series*, London, Gollancz, 1950, pp. 104–13, Crispin, *Beware of the Trains*, pp. 9–18, Irving (ed.) *Sixteen On*, pp. 197–209, and Bryan Morgan (ed.), *Crime on the Lines: an Anthology of Mystery Stories with a Railway Setting*, London, Routledge & Kegan Paul, 1975, pp. 137–45. Goggett had to be an electric train's motorman in this story, because (unlike steam footplate staff) the uniform which he wore could be mistaken by the uninitiated for a stationmaster's. The period when Crispin sets his story matters, too. His device would be much less convincing before Big Four com-

panies standardised station staffs' uniforms. Pregrouping railway servants' clothing distinguished occupational grades much more minutely – as in the military, from which Victorian railway companies drew so much organisational inspiration. See David J. Froggatt, *Railway Buttons, Badges and Uniforms*, London, Ian Allan, 1986, pp. 138–95.

18 Freeman Wills Crofts, 'Crime on the footplate' [1950], in Anon (ed.), *Evening Standard Detective Book: First Series*, pp. 114–21, Crofts, *Many a Slip*, London, Hodder & Stoughton, 1955, pp. 9–16, Irving (ed.), *Sixteen On*, pp. 186–96, Morgan, (ed.), *Crime on the Lines*, pp. 130–6, and Peter Haining (ed.), *Murder on the Railways*, London, Orion, 1996, pp. 22–30. It is odd that a locomotive's firebox has been used so rarely in British crime fiction to destroy incriminating evidence. Bill Pronzini (*Bindlestiff* [1983], New York, Paperjacks, 1987, p. 83) uses the firebox in a Californian railway museum's Baldwin locomotive for the most obvious criminal purpose: incinerating a corpse. The closest we come to this in a British novel is the climax to Gerald Sinstadt's *Whisper in a Lonely Place*, London, Long, 1966, pp. 174–80 – as a cornered foreign spy steals a steam locomotive on the fifteen-inch Romney, Hythe and Dymchurch Light Railway. Stoking furiously, he lights out for the horizon; but it all ends in tears when his locomotive firebox's fusible plug melts, depositing burning coals and superheated steam in his lap. Nasty!

19 Margaret Hinxman, *The Corpse Now Arriving*, London, Collins, 1983; John Rowland, *The Cornish Riviera Mystery*, London, Jenkins, 1939; Basil Thomson, 'The vanishing of Mrs Fraser' [1925], in Sayers (ed.), *Detection, Mystery and Horror: Second Series*, p. 422.

20 Victor L. Whitechurch and E. Conway, 'A warning in red' [1899], in Michael Cox (ed.), *Victorian Detective Stories*, Oxford, Oxford University Press, 1992, pp. 518–27; John Rhode, *Dead on the Track*, London, Collins, 1943.

21 Charles Irving, 'The railway wagon', in Anon (ed.), *Evening Standard Detective Book: First Series*, pp. 191–7. Somewhat later, Irving edited *Sixteen On*, the first significant railway crime anthology.

22 Beverley Nichols, *Death to Slow Music*, London, Hutchinson, 1956, p. 17.

23 Gerald Bullett, 'The last days of Binnacle', in Bullett, *The Baker's Cart, and Other Stories*, London, Bodley Head, 1925, pp. 143–72. Bullett's story parses a strong British popular belief that only complete skeletal remains could be resurrected when the Last Trump sounded. This belief inhibited anatomical and physiological research to our century.

24 As a Cockney medium explains, '"In my young days I doubt if you'd have come across a travelling haunter once in a blue moon. Now – stone the crows – British Railways and London Transport attract 'em like flies to gum-paper. I suppose it's because the earth-bounds like to keep moving, and you've got to admit the trains do move sometimes. The rush hours are best, of course. They can get around without giving offence, if you get my meaning".' R. Chetwynd-Hayes, 'Non-paying passengers', in Chetwynd-Hayes (ed.), *The Tenth Fontana Book of Great Ghost Stories*, London, Fontana, 1974, p. 180.

25 Amelia B. Edwards and Charles Dickens, 'The four-fifteen express', in Anon (ed.),
    Mixed Sweets from Routledge's Annual, London, Routledge, 1867, pp. 114–34,
    reprinted in William Pattrick (ed.), *Mysterious Railway Stories*, London, Star, 1984,
    pp. 12–37; G. K. Chesterton, 'The secret of the train', in Chesterton, *Tremendous
    Trifles* [1909], London, Methuen, 1920, pp. 9–15; Walter de la Mare, 'The froward
    child', in de la Mare, *The Wind Blows Over*, London, Faber, 1936, pp. 103–38;
    Walter de la Mare, 'Promise at dusk', in Tony Wilmot (ed.), *Beware of the Trains*,
    Hornchurch, Henry, 1981, pp. 27–37.

26 E. F. Benson, 'The disappearance of Jacob Conifer', in Benson, *Desirable Residences
    and Other Stories*, Oxford, Oxford University Press, 1992, p. 215.

27 John Pudney, 'The tunnel', in Wilmot (ed.), *Beware of the Trains*, pp. 18–26;
    Andrew Caldecott, 'Branch line to Benceston', in Caldecott, *Not Exactly Ghosts*,
    London, Arnold, 1947, pp. 35–54; Celia Fremlin, 'If it's got your number', in
    Ellery Queen (ed.), *Ellery Queen's Murdercade*, London, Pan, 1978, pp. 237–48;
    Roy Vickers, 'The eighth lamp' [1915], in Irving (ed.), *Sixteen On*, pp. 101–19 and
    Morgan (ed.), *Crime on the Lines*, pp. 97–108.

28 Holloway Horn, 'The old man' [1931], in Sayers (ed.), *Detection, Mystery and
    Horror: Second Series*, pp. 802–7.

29 Stephen Laws, *The Ghost Train*, London, Sphere, 1987; John Dickson Carr, 'The
    murder in number four' [1928], in Carr, *The Door to Doom, and Other Stories*,
    London, Hamilton, 1981, p. 95; Charles Dickens, 'Mugby Junction: branch line no.
    1' [1866], in Dickens, *Christmas Stories*, London, Chapman and Hall, n.d., pp.
    542–554 (reprinted in Ronald Holmes (ed.), *Macabre Railway Stories*, London,
    Allen, 1982, pp. 13–28; Irving (ed.), *Sixteen On*, pp. 1–18; Morgan (ed.), *Crime on
    the Lines*, pp. 1–12; Richard Peyton (ed.), *The Ghost Now Standing on Platform One:
    Phantoms of the Railway in Fact and Fiction*, London, Futura, 1991, pp. 237–51;
    L. T. C. Rolt (ed.), *Best Railway Stories*, London, Faber and Faber, 1969, pp. 15–29).

30 Simenon, *Man Who Watched the Trains Go By*, p. 5.

31 Martin Amis, *Night Train*, London, Cape, 1997, p. 67.

32 Martin James, *Night Train*, Sydney, Collins Australia, 1989, p. 124.

33 Eric Ambler, *Journey into Fear* [1940], London, Fontana, 1966, p. 45.

34 Arthur Griffiths, *The Rome Express* [1896], reprinted in Graham Greene and Hugh
    Greene (eds), *Victorian Villainies*, Harmondsworth, Penguin, 1984, pp. 295–392.

35 Ruth Alexander, *Rome Express*, New York, Readers' Library, 1932; Michael Bond,
    Monsieur Pamplemousse Takes the Train, London, Headline, 1993.

36 William Haggard, *The Arena* [1961], Harmondsworth, Penguin, 1963, pp. 81–4.
    Strictly speaking, this is attempted murder – with politico-financial assassination in
    the St Gotthard tunnel averted in time's nick.

37 Japrisot, *Compartiment Tueurs*; Léo Malet, *Mission to Marseilles* [1947], translated
    by Olive Classe, London, Pan, 1991.

38 Agatha Christie, *The Mystery of the Blue Train* [1928], Harmondsworth, Penguin,
    1948; Gavin Holt, *Murder Train*, London, Hodder & Stoughton, 1936; E. Phillips
    Oppenheim, 'The case of Mr. and Mrs. Stetson', in Anon (ed.), *Fifty Famous
    Detectives of Fiction*, London, Odhams, 1948, pp. 510–24.

39 Manning Coles, *The Basle Express*, London, Hodder & Stoughton, 1956.

40 Nick Carter, *The Butcher of Belgrade*, London, Tandem, 1974. In Eric Ambler's *The Dark Frontier*, London, Hodder & Stoughton, 1936, Red Gauntlet thugs assassinated Rovzidski just beyond Bucharest, on an overnight branch train to Zovgorod, Ixania's capital city. Topography places this impoverished micro-state somewhere in deepest Transylvania.

41 Agatha Christie, *Murder on the Orient Express* [1934], Harmondsworth, Penguin, 1948; Ian Fleming, *From Russia With Love* [1957], London, Pan, 1959.

42 H. F. Wood, *The Passenger from Scotland Yard*, London, Chatto &Windus, 1888; John Dickson Carr, 'Murder in number four'; Charles Barry, *The Boat Train Mystery*, London, Hurst and Blackett, 1938; Manning Coles, *Night Train to Paris*, London, Hodder & Stoughton, 1952. (Strictly speaking, the last case concerns no more than attempted murder – by defenestration).

43 Graham Greene, *Travels with my Aunt* [1969], London, Vintage, 1999, p. 89.

44 Haggard, *The Arena*, p. 98.

45 Freeman Wills Crofts, 'The mystery of the sleeping-car express' [1921], in Crofts, *The Mystery of the Sleeping Car Express, and Other Stories* [1956], Bath, Chivers, 1982, pp. 1–39, Morgan (ed.), *Crime on the Lines*, pp. 109–29 and Patricia Craig (ed.), *The Oxford Book of English Detective Stories*, Oxford, Oxford University Press, 1990, pp. 138–58. The impedimenta with which Crofts' assassin escapes from a speeding, sealed, Scotland-bound sleeping coach would disgrace no modern high-tech caper movie: two wooden wedges, sixteen feet of brown silk cord, and sixteen feet of thin silk rope. Who would contemplate travelling without this equipment? Complicated paraphernalia underpins some other crimes. Victor Whitechurch shows us both how Polish patriots assassinate a Tsarist secret police agent on an English train, using only 'an auger, a hammer, a large staple with a screw, and a length of very strong rope', and how a German diplomatic bag (which contains a document certain to provoke war if it reaches Berlin, of course) is abstracted from a racing Dover boat train with 'a few yards of very strong fishing twine, a fair-sized snap-hook, and a light walking-stick with a forked bit of wire stuck in the end of it' (Whitechurch, *Thrilling Stories*, pp. 40, 112–13). John Oxenham ('A murder of the Underground', in Haining (ed.), *Murder on the Railways*, pp. 262–85) shows us random murder every Tuesday on a Victorian London underground train, perpetrated by a disgruntled railway ex-employee equipped with a 'spidery implement, with the curved horse-shoe clutch and the pronged lever' and 'the deadly death-tube' (a collapsible airgun). Murdering a philanderer in a locked compartment on a speeding Brighton express requires little equipment not found in the average gentleman's waistcoat pocket. One element is closely specified: a guard's key. The other is more variable: an Indian canoe, an ironing board, or a ladies' folding cutting board pierced at one end with two inch-wide holes set twelve inches apart: Thomas W. Hanshew, 'The riddle of the 5.28' [1910], in Haining (ed.), *Murder on the Railways*, pp. 388, 390.

46 Josephine Tey, *The Singing Sands* [1952], London, Mandarin, 1992; Philip McCutcheon, *Overnight Express*, London, Hodder & Stoughton, 1988.

47 Harry Carmichael, *Money for Murder* [1955], London, Fontana, 1957, p. 15.

48 Henry Holt, *The Midnight Mail*, London, Harrap, 1931. Strictly speaking this is an incompletely murderous attack, ineptly performed.

49 Anthony Lambert, *The Yermakov Transfer*, London, Arlington, 1974, p. 68.

50 Paul Jennings, 'Very Great Eastern', in Jennings, *Iddly Oddly*, London, Parrish, 1959, p. 93.

51 E. Phillips Oppenheim, *Last Train Out*, London, Hodder & Stoughton, 1941, p. 195.

52 Ernest Bramah, 'The crime in the house at Culver Street', in Bramah, *Max Carrados Mysteries* [1927], Harmondsworth, Penguin, 1964, p. 159.

53 Carter Dickson, *The Red Widow Murders* [1935], Harmondsworth, Penguin, 1951, p. 9.

54 Graham Greene, *Stamboul Train* [1932], Harmondsworth, Penguin, 1975, p. 121.

55 John Banville, *The Untouchable*, London, Picador, 1997, p. 147.

56 Peter Fleming, *One's Company* [1934], Harmondsworth, Penguin, 1956, p. 34. Peter Fleming must have discussed these fantasies with his brother, who created not 37 but 007. '"Old man, the story's got everything"', SMERSH's top operative advises James Bond about the honey trap set to catch him. '"Orient Express. Beautiful Russian spy murdered in Simplon tunnel. Filthy pictures. Secret cipher machine. Handsome British spy with career ruined murders her and commits suicide. Sex, spies, luxury train"': Fleming, *From Russia With Love*, p. 193.

57 Richard Harding Davis, 'In the fog' [1902], in Alan K. Russell (ed.), *Rivals of Sherlock Holmes*, Secaucus, NJ, Castle, 1978, pp. 374–83, and Greene and Greene (eds), *Victorian Villainies*, pp. 414–23; Valentine Williams, *The Three of Clubs*, London, Hodder & Stoughton, 1924, p. 40.

58 Max Beerbohm, *Zuleika Dobson* [1911], London, Heinemann, 1946, p. 6. Max's Middle Ages crack comes from Matthew Arnold's *Culture and Anarchy* [1869], of course – where it adorned Oxford University, not the town's railway station.

59 Maurice Dekobra, *La Madonne des Sleepings* [1927], translated by Neal Wainwright as *The Madonna of the Sleeping Cars*, London, Elek, 1959, p. 221. Selling more than a million copies in French and in translation, this mildly salacious novel made Dekobra's fortune.

60 Innes, *Journeying Boy*, p. 141. Founded in 1916, *Mitropa Gesellschaft* was Imperial Germany's attempt to break Georges Nackelmackers' *Compagnie Internationale des Wagons-Lit et des Grands Express Européens*'s monopoly over long-distance European *train de luxe* travel. This challenge collapsed in 1945, with the Third Reich.

61 Fleming, *From Russia With Love*.

62 Robert Parker, *Passport to Peril*, London, Hodder & Stoughton, 1952; Ambler, *Dark Frontier*, pp. 68–72; Oppenheim, *Last Train Out*. For another example (if we need one) see Dennis Wheatley, 'Espionage', in Wilmot (ed.), *Beware of the Trains*, pp. 94–113.

63 Agatha Christie, 'The girl in the train', in Christie, *The Listerdale Mystery and Other Stories* [1934], London, Fontana, 1961, reprinted in Pattrick (ed.), *Mysterious*

Railway Stories, pp. 161–82. This story offers some stylistic interest. Bertie Wooster read vast quantities of crime fiction, but he never tried to write the stuff. Christie's tale shows what he might have done – with her narrative adorned by Rogers, that sauvely Jeevesian family retainer-cum-father figure.

64 Agatha Christie, 'The case of the city clerk', in Christie, *Parker Pyne Investigates* [1934], Harmondsworth, Penguin, 1953, pp. 70–85. Danger thrills here, but elsewhere a dupe dies on a Leeds to London train to establish another man's alibi. '"He thought he was playing the secret agent for a representative of M. I. 5"', his killer reports: Carmichael *Money for Murder*, p. 186.

65 '"Will you excuse my intrusion?" he asked, in a full caressing voice. "The train is absolutely full." […] A moment later the tall, dark stranger had come over to her side of the carriage and, sitting down opposite her, he had said something which had at once amused, thrilled, and yes, allured her': Marie Belloc Lowndes, 'Her last adventure' [1924], in Dorothy L. Sayers (ed.), *Great Short Stories of Detection, Mystery and Horror: First Series*, London, Gollancz, 1928, p. 584.

66 Christopher Reeve, *Murder Steps Out*, London, Ward Lock, 1942, p. 8. Clearly enough, Sir Julian descends from Lord Mowbray (in Benjamin Disraeli, *Sybil: or The Two Nations* [1845], Oxford, Oxford University Press, 1926, p. 104), scandalised to hear that Lady Vanilla was forced to share her compartment from Birmingham to Mowbray with a manacled prisoner and his guard. '"A countess and a felon! So much for public conveyances," said Lord Mowbray'.

67 Paul Fussell, *Abroad: British Literary Travelling Between the Wars*, New York, Oxford University Press, 1980, p. 76.

68 Peter Fleming, *Listener*, 24 November 1949. Reprinted, in modified form, as 'Night special from Inverness', in Fleming, *With the Guards to Mexico! and Other Excursions*, London, Hart-Davis, 1957, pp. 115–22. A modestly cheaper way to keep oneself to oneself was to hire a 'family saloon' which almost all pre-grouping railways were willing to attach, for a not inconsiderable consideration, to the express train of one's choice. In the United States no late Victorian plutocrat could hold up his head unless he travelled in an extravagantly equipped private car: see Lucius Beebe, *Mansions on Rails: the Folklore of the Private Railway Car*, Berkeley, CA, Howell-North, 1959.

69 Burford Delannoy, *The Midnight Special* [1902], London, Newnes, 1911, p. 21.

70 M. McD Bodkin, 'Murder by proxy' [1898], in Hugh Greene (ed.), *Further Rivals of Sherlock Holmes* [1973], Harmondsworth, Penguin, 1976, p. 136.

71 L. T. Meade and Robert Eustace, 'The sorceress of the Strand' [1902], in Russell (ed.), *Rivals of Sherlock Holmes*, p. 325.

72 E. and M. A. Radford, *Death of a Frightened Editor* [1959], Leicester, Linford, 1996.

73 Goodman, 'Points of departure', p. 9. He wrote after British Rail had converted all third-class passengers to second-class with a wave of the marketeer's wand, of course.

74 Agatha Christie, *Murder is Easy* [1939], Leicester, Ulverscroft, 1992, pp. 8–18; Michael Innes, *Appleby's Answer*, London, Gollancz, 1973, pp. 9–16.

75 R. Austin Freeman, *The Eye of Osiris* [1911], Oxford, Oxford University Press, 1989, p. 6.

76 H. H. Munro ['Saki'], 'Forewarned', in Munro, *The Complete Works of Saki*, London, Bodley Head, 1980, p. 441.

77 Osbert Sitwell, *Penny Foolish: a Book of Tirades and Panegyrics*, London, Macmillan, 1935, p. 234.

78 P. G. Wodehouse, *Uncle Dynamite* [1948] in Wodehouse, *Uncle Fred: an Omnibus*, London, Penguin, 1991, p. 217.

79 Nathaniel Hawthorne, *English Notebooks*, edited by Randall Stewart, New York, Russell and Russell, 1941, p. 119. C. Hamilton Ellis (*Railway Carriages in the British Isles from 1830 to 1914*, London, Allen & Unwin, 1965, pp. 161–2) distinguishes among English speakers. Uptight Englishmen and Scots liked compartments' privacy, he suggests. Americans and Irishmen preferred saloons, 'being sociable people fond of moving about a train to converse with each other and with promising-looking strangers'.

80 Bill Bryson, *Notes from a Small Island*, London, Black Swan, 1995, p. 244; J. C., 'Commentary', *The Times Literary Supplement*, 8 January 1999. At one place Paul Theroux raises a familiar objection to Marco Polo's veracity: that he mentions neither the Great Wall nor Chinese tea-drinking (*Riding the Red Rooster: By Train Through China*, New York, Putnams, 1988, pp. 147–8). Throughout this book Theroux claims to converse with people he meets in somewhat halting Mandarin, and we often catch him reading local newspapers and pamphlets. Yet when train 104 pulls into Lanzhou station he seems unable to read large characters inscribed on banners held by (apparently protesting) young people (pp. 216–17). That's the perennial problem with travellers' tales; deciding when lay ethnography shades into straightforward fiction.

81 For the furore over Abraham Solomon's oil painting *First-class – the Meeting* [1854] see p. 287, note 22.

82 Banville, *Untouchable*, pp. 274–8.

83 Philip Sevilla was an utter bounder, working the London end of a white slaving pipeline transporting innocent fair-haired English girls to Buenos Aires whorehouses. Having captured these maidens' affections in a night club, his next move was always to whisk them (by boat train) to Paris for a fortnight's preliminary corruption. Interwar readers still took this move in their stride; what else were Paris-bound trains *for*? See Anthony Armstrong and Herbert Shaw, *Ten Minute Alibi* [1934], London, Penguin, 1938.

84 Agatha Christie, *Murder on the Links* [1923], Harmondsworth, Penguin, 1936, pp. 9, 96.

85 Agatha Christie, 'The dead Harlequin', in Christie, *The Mysterious Mr Quin* [1930], Harmondsworth, Penguin, 1953, p. 175. As well brought-up persons, Susan and Patrick merely admired each other from a distance on their Brighton to London train. Only a derailment further up the line, forcing passengers into pseudo-Blitz camaraderie on a substitute bus service, cracked their British reserve and set them talking: Anne Morice, 'Young man on a train', in Hilary Hale (ed.), *Winter's Crimes 18*, London, Macmillan, 1986, pp. 141–2.

86 Aldous Huxley, *Along the Road: Notes and Essays of a Tourist*, New York, Harper & Row, 1925, p. 33.

87 E. C. Bentley and H. Warner Allen, *Trent's Own Case* [1936], Harmondsworth, Penguin, 1946, p. 17.

88 William Pattrick, 'Introduction', to Pattrick (ed.), *Mysterious Railway Stories*, p. 7. Original emphases.

89 Arthur Conan Doyle, 'The reminiscences of Captain Wilkie' [first published in 1895, but written considerably earlier], in Marvin Kaye (ed.), *The Game is Afoot: Parodies, Pastiches and Ponderings of Sherlock Holmes*, New York, St Martin's Press, 1994, p. 13.

90 Nicholas Blake, 'A study in white', in Sullivan and Queen (eds), *Omnibus of Modern Crime Stories*, pp. 135–49.

91 P. G. Wodehouse, 'The truth about George', in Wodehouse, *Meet Mr Mulliner*, London, Jenkins, 1927, pp. 23–9.

92 H. G. Wells, 'The apple', in Wells, *The Complete Short Stories of H. G. Wells*, London, Benn, 1927, pp. 394–402.

93 Leo Bruce, 'Murder in miniature', in Anon (ed.), *Evening Standard Detective Book: Second Series*, London, Gollancz, 1951, pp. 40–8.

94 Marguerite Steen, 'In view of the audience' [1934], in Jack Adrian (ed.), *Detective Stories from the Strand Magazine*, Oxford, Oxford University Press, 1993, pp. 253–68. George wants to go to Crewe, but this train will stop first at Coalford – that 'dreadfully primitive' industrial town. Since the line to this place leaves the West Coast main line at Stafford, primitive Coalford must be Stoke-on-Trent. Arnold Bennett would not be amused.

95 Dorothy L. Sayers, 'The man who knew how' [1933], in Michael Stapleton (ed.), *The Best Crime Stories*, London, Hamlyn, 1977, pp. 228–38.

96 Andrew Garve, *Murder in Moscow*, London, Collins, 1951, pp. 6–27.

97 Julian Symons, 'The case of S. W. 2.', in Anon (ed.), *Evening Standard Detective Book, Second Series*, pp. 267–8. Was this weapon the Special Operations Executive's fiendishly ingenious exploding rat, one wonders, designed to blow up boilers when fed to the fire by unwary stokers? Or it might have been the same organisation's coal borer, allowing high explosive to be hidden in lumps of fuel which then were tossed lightly into locomotive tenders. Fed to the firebox, this fuel would explode 'with sufficient violence to damage the boiler or at least to render the profession of locomotive driver highly unpopular': declassified SOE records reported in *The New Zealand Herald*, 28 October 1999.

98 H. M. Richardson, 'The man who made rings', in Anon (eds), *Best Detective Stories: Second Series*, London, Faber & Faber, 1930, pp. 347–64.

99 Agatha Christie, 'The girdle of Hippolyta', in Christie, *The Labours of Hercules* [1947], Harmondsworth, Penguin, 1953, pp. 180–94.

100 Freeman Wills Croft, *Fatal Venture* [1939], Harmondsworth, Penguin, 1959, p. 17.

101 John Buchan, *The Island of Sheep*, London, Nelson, 1936, chapter 1; R. Austin Freeman, 'A case of premeditation', in Freeman, *The Singing Bone*, London, Hodder & Stoughton, 1912, p. 69.

102 Radford and Radford, *Death of a Frightened Editor*. This book well illustrates why many readers lost patience with Golden Age puzzles. To work out who was responsible for this crime one needs to know what keratin is, and the effects of acids, alkalis and alcohol on that substance.

103 Dorothy L. Sayers, 'One too many', in Sayers, *Busman's Holiday*, London, Gollancz, 1933, pp. 189–206.

104 Alfred Hitchcock's movie *The Lady Vanishes*; Edgar Wallace, *The Three Just Men*, London, Hodder & Stoughton, n.d., p. 217.

105 Richard Marsh, 'The man who cut off my hair', in Marsh, *Judith Lee: Some Pages from her Life*, London, Methuen, 1912, reprinted in Greene (ed.), *Further Rivals of Sherlock Holmes*, pp. 243–60.

106 Victor L. Whitechurch, 'The affair of the corridor express', in Whitechurch, *Thrilling Stories*, pp. 46–62. This procedure apes conventional techniques for transferring mail pouches from a travelling post office.

107 Grant Allen, 'The adventure of the cantankerous old lady' [1898], in Marcus (ed.), *Twelve Women Detectives*, pp. 63–80.

108 Michael Innes, *The Secret Vanguard* [1940], Harmondsworth, Penguin, 1958, pp. 27–9, 42–3.

109 Michael Innes, *Appleby's End* [1946], Harmondsworth, Penguin, 1969, pp. 7–24.

110 Innes, *Journeying Boy*. For another example, see John Jefferson Farjeon, *The 5.18 Mystery*, London, Collins, 1929. Here our dense young hero climbs into a first-class compartment on the Cromer express at Liverpool Street, only to find himself enmeshed in complicated skirmishings. One gang intends to kidnap the young woman due to travel in his compartment, not knowing that she was replaced by a ringer before the train left London. This replacement is even more beautiful than the original target – and our hero becomes densely smitten, of course. Assisted only by an elderly vicar (who turns out to be the girl's determined father, riding shotgun both on her security and her virtue) eventually he triumphs. What a surprise.

111 Ethel Lina White, *The Wheel Spins*, London, Collins, 1936. New edition as *The Lady Vanishes* (the title under which Hitchcock filmed this novel in 1938), London, Dent, 1987.

112 For the USA see W. J. Chaput, *The Man on the Train*, Toronto, Worldwide, 1988; Bill Garnett, *Hell Train*, New York, St Martin's Press, 1988; Thomas F. Monteleone, *Night-Train*, London, Arrow, 1987. For the former USSR see Warren Adler, *Trans-Siberian Express*, London, Pan, 1979; Tom Hyman, *Seven Days to Petrograd*, London, Penguin, 1988 (based on Lenin's 1917 journey in a sealed train from exile in Zurich to power in Petrograd); Lambert, *Yermakov Transfer*; William Smethurst, *Bukhara Express*, London, Headline, 1994. For western Europe see James Adams, *Taking the Tunnel*, London, Signet, 1993; Colin Forbes, *Avalanche Express*, London, Collins, 1977; John Howlett, *The Christmas Spy*, London, Hutchinson, 1975; Derek Lambert, *The Golden Express*, London, Sphere, 1984.

113 Patricia Wentworth, *The Traveller Returns* [1948], London, Coronet, 1990, pp. 90–1. Original emphasis. Aunt Chrissie was kin to that terrified small boy sharing a non-corridor compartment with a sinister Indian and his basket. When he opens

this basket, a cobra sticks its head out. The boy shrieks – and changes compartments at the next station: Rhys Davies, 'Fear', in Davies, *The Collected Stories of Rhys Davies*, London, Heinemann, 1955, pp. 46–50, reprinted in Wilmot (ed.), *Beware of the Trains*, pp. 114–19.

114 Charles Williams, *Many Dimensions* [1931], Harmondsworth, Penguin, 1952, p. 185.

115 Guy de Maupassant, *The Complete Short Stories*, London, Cassell, 1970, ii, pp. 60–5.

116 Hence the 'concluding glory' in aspiring small shopkeeper Alfred Polly's doomed marriage to Miriam Larkins: 'they travelled second class'. See H. G. Wells, *The History of Mr Polly* [1910], London, Pan, 1963, p. 121. Like Mr Polly, Theodore Vole's ticket would limit him to travel on the London and South Western or the South Eastern and Chatham. By Edwardian years, only these two British companies offered second-class service on express trains. See Jack Simmons, 'Class distinctions', in Jack Simmons and Gordon Biddle (eds), *The Oxford Companion to British Railway History*, Oxford, Oxford University Press, 1997, pp. 84–7.

117 H. H. Munro, 'The mouse', in Munro, *Complete Works of Saki*, pp. 94–8; reprinted in Irving (ed.), *Sixteen On*, pp. 181–5. Munro's work has been little mined by railway writers. Other material worth their attention includes some passages in his novel *The Unbearable Bassington*, and a string of short stories: 'The unrest-cure', 'The Schartz-Metterklume method', 'The seventh pullet', 'The story-teller', 'The name-day', 'The disappearance of Crispin Umberleigh' and 'Forewarned'.

118 Only in escape narratives does crowded railway travel's anonymity become a virtue for British writers. See Eric Williams, *The Wooden Horse*, London, Collins, 1949 and Patrick R. Reid, *The Colditz Story*, London, Hodder & Stoughton, 1952 for skulking travel on wartime German trains, Anthony Deane-Drummond, *We Die Alone* (*Return Ticket* in later editions), London, Collins, 1955 for Italy.

119 James Barlow, *The Patriots*, London, Hamish Hamilton, 1980, p. 180; Harry Blyth, 'The accusing shadow' [1894], in Michael Cox (ed.), *Victorian Detective Stories*, Oxford, Oxford University Press, 1992, p. 309.

120 Notably, that brief manifestation by Harley Quin [a.k.a. (obviously) Harlequin; a.k.a. (less obviously) Death] in Mr Satterthwaite's London-bound express: Agatha Christie, 'The bird with a broken wing', in Christie, *Mysterious Mr Quin*, pp. 206–7.

121 Carr, *Scandal at High Chimneys*, p. 23; Julian Barnes, *A History of the World in 10½ Chapters*, London, Picador, 1990, p. 178. Chapter 17 of John Dickson Carr's *The Hollow Man* [1935], Harmondsworth, Penguin, 1951 is a bravura lecture, with Dr Gideon Fell laying out the many ways in which locked room puzzles may be contrived. The railway carriage's status as locked room can be trumpeted. Edward D. Hoch's 'The problem of the locked caboose' [1976], in Bill Pronzini (ed.), *Midnight Specials: an Anthology for Railway Enthusiasts and Suspense Addicts*, London, Souvenir Press, 1978, pp. 48–69 shows us a nineteenth-century American conductor murdered in his locked caboose, and jewellery stolen from that caboose's locked safe, while the only set of keys nestled in the victim's pocket.

122 Wood, *Passenger from Scotland Yard*. This novel's compexity springs from the striking circumstance that our detective aside, *every* passenger in that compartment was a crook: one jewel-thief, one assassin, one pickpocket and one fraudster 'in the temperance game'. If this was a fair sample, who would ever dare leave England by train?

123 J. Storer Clouston, 'The envelope', in A. K. Barton (ed.), *Mystery*, London, Dent, 1937, pp. 181–97. The two Germans-as-Aussies are not difficult to spot (that *odd* accent); sorting out the RNR officer was a harder challenge.

124 Garnett Radcliffe, 'On the Irish mail', in Dorothy L. Sayers (ed.), *Great Short Stories of Detection, Mystery, Horror: Third Series*, London, Gollancz, 1933, pp. 389–410.

125 Victor L. Whitechurch, 'The murder on the Okehampton line' [1903], in Haining (ed.), *Murder on the Railways*, p. 142. Original emphasis.

126 Edgar Wallace, *The Four Just Men* [1905], London, Pan, 1950, pp. 155–60.

127 James Hilton, 'The mallet' [1929], in Michael Stapleton (ed.), *Best Crime Stories*, London, Hamlyn, 1984, pp. 278–92.

128 Victor L. Whitechurch, 'How the captain tracked a German spy', in Whitechurch, *The Adventures of Captain Ivan Koravich*, Edinburgh, Blackwood, 1925, pp. 44–68, reprinted in Sayers (ed.), *Detection, Mystery and Horror: Second Series*, pp. 444–55; Hanshew, 'The riddle of the 5.28'. A public-spirited citizen offers Hanshew's solution to explain a murder on a West Coast express, but it will not wash: Arthur Conan Doyle, 'The story of the man with the watches' [1898], in Doyle, *Tales of Terror and Mystery* [1922], London, Pan, 1978, pp. 142–59 and Russell (ed.), *Rivals of Sherlock Holmes*, pp. 175–85.

129 Wood, *Passenger from Scotland Yard*.

130 The first British bellows connection appeared in 1869, linking two saloons in the London and North Western Railway's royal train. The first complete train with side corridor and bellows connections went into service on the Great Western Railway in 1892, ten years after the Great Northern company built the first ordinary carriage with a side corridor. Always progressive in carriage design and equipment, the Midland Railway offered equivalent arrangements from 1874 – but in American-style Pullman cars whose open saloons were largely deprecated by British passengers. See Ellis, *Railway Carriages*, pp. 95, 106, 119, 154.

131 Victor L. Whitechurch, 'The stolen necklace', in Whitechurch, *Thrilling Stories*, p. 160.

132 Ellis, *Railway Carriages*, p. 154.

133 Sapper, 'The mystery of the slip-coach', in Sapper, *Ronald Standish*, London, Hodder & Stoughton, 1933, pp. 163–90. Slip-coaches held unexplored potential for crime writers, but E. G Bartlett (*The Case of the Thirteenth Coach*, London, Collins, 1958) and Lyn Brock (*The Slip-Carriage Mystery*, London, Collins, 1928) squandered fine opportunities. Their slip-coaches' quiddities did no more than separate from moving trains so that – for Brock – passengers could be shunted to a dark and remote siding to await another express's arrival; for Bartlett that the coach might roll, under control from a crooked signalman, into a secluded loop and be robbed of the gold it carried.

134 Examples include McCutcheon, *Overnight Express* (set on the East Coast main line below Durham); John Godey, *The Taking of Pelham One Two Three*, London, Hodder & Stoughton, 1973 (set on the New York subway), and Frances Yarborough, *Murder on the Long Straight*, New York, Leisure, 1979 (set on the Nullarbor straight, in Australia). These could not be steam trains, because steam locomotives require watering and other servicing at inconveniently frequent intervals. Of course, this need not deter the truly ignorant. His prologue to Robert Ludlum's *The Gemini Contenders* [1976], in Ludlum, *The Scarlatti Inheritance etc*, London, Heinemann, 1979, pp. 571–83, shows us a steam-hauled freight train trundling from Salonika to Milan in 1939, just after war has been declared. Turnouts are manipulated by hand to set this train on the road. It travels only at night, hiding in marsahalling yards by day. It is hauled by the same locomotive for five days, apparently without refuelling or taking on water – let alone tedious tasks like grate raking, tube clearing and boiler washing. Having arrived in Italy, instead of taking the direct main line from Trieste to Milan this trains skulks through the northern lakes to Switzerland. Having hidden for one night in the extensive freight yard at Zermatt – all of two sidings, the last time I was there – it crosses a non-existent pass back into Italy and chuffs off to Milan. Setting aside that lofty but fictive pass, among all this nonsense just getting the train to Zermatt takes the machine ensemble biscuit. Would Ludlum like to explain how his standard gauge train navigated the Brig-Visp-Zermatt company's metre-gauge line?

135 J. S. Fletcher, *The Charing Cross Mystery*, London, Jenkins, 1923.

136 Richard Hull, *Excellent Intentions* [1938], Harmondsworth, Penguin, 1949, pp. 11–17.

137 John Rhode, *Death on the Boat-Train*, London, Collins, 1940. For a similar plot centred on bullion robbery rather than murder, see R. Austin Freeman, 'The stolen ingots', in Freeman, *The Famous Cases of Dr Thorndyke*, London, Hodder & Stoughton, 1929, pp. 1023–51.

138 J. R. L. Anderson, *A Sprig of Sea Lavender*, London, Gollancz, 1978, pp. 7–9.

139 Bruce, 'Murder in miniature'.

140 Agatha Christie, 'Have you got everything you want?', in Christie, *Parker Pyne Investigates*, pp. 102–16, reprinted as 'Express to Stamboul', in Haining (ed.), *Murder on the Railways*, pp. 9–21; Ernest Bramah, 'The ingenious mind of Mr Rigby Lacksome', in Bramah, *Max Carrados Mysteries*, pp. 131–57; John Rhode, 'The elusive bullet', in Sayers (ed.), *Detection, Mystery, Horror: Second Series*, pp. 329–43.

141 Ronald A. Knox, 'The adventure of the first-class carriage' [1947], in Roger Lancelyn Green (ed.), *The Further Adventures of Sherlock Holmes*, Harmondsworth, Penguin, 1985, pp. 39–51; Adrian (ed.), *Detective Stories from The Strand Magazine*, pp. 360–71; and Haining (ed.), *Murder on the Railways*, pp. 127–38. Written in homage to Doyle by the man who invented Sherlockiana as a cod-academic enterprise, this little story raises ticklish railway issues. On the one hand, Holmes and Watson travel from Paddington to Banbury in a non-corridor express. That was feasible in Holmes' time; but the guard's practice of locking all first-class

compartment doors is anachronistic. Knox's principal error might seem to be having his villain climb from a halted train at Reading, and make his way along the ground to another compartment. Would waiting passengers not see this action from other platforms at such an important junction? No: Reading was the last survivor among I. K. Brunel's large single-sided GWR stations to be converted to parallel platforms. When at last that was done, in 1897, ten new platforms replaced one long single platform. See Adrian Vaughan, *A Pictorial History of Great Western Architecture*, Oxford, Oxford Publishing Co., 1977, p. 22.

142 V. C. Clinton-Baddeley, *Death's Bright Dart* [1967], New York, Dell, 1982, pp. 95–6.

143 Agatha Christie, *4.50 From Paddington*, London, Collins, 1957, p. 8. Three years earlier, Ngaio Marsh had forced Roderick Alleyn and Agatha Troy to watch a woman being throttled in a lineside Saracen fortress in the Alpes Maritimes, from their first-class Wagons-Lit compartment: Marsh, *Spinsters in Jeopardy*, London, Collins, 1954, p. 18.

144 Doyle, 'The man with the watches'.

145 Dick Donovan, 'A railway mystery', in Donovan, *Riddles Read*, London, Chatto & Windus, 1896, pp. 204–39.

146 Delannoy, *Midnight Special*, pp. 36–55. Books talk to books. A loaded stone wagon is such a peculiar obstacle for any train to meet that we must assume that, consciously or unconsciously, Delannoy recalled Cabuche's wagon in *La Bête Humaine*.

147 Charteris, 'Rhine maiden'.

148 Barlow, *Patriots*.

149 Fergus Hume, *The 4 p.m. Express* [1914], London, Mellifont, 1935, p. 49.

150 Douglas Newton, 'The railway carriage crime', in Anon (ed.), *Best Mystery Stories*, London, Faber & Faber, 1933, pp. 354–76.

151 Pamela Branch, *Murder Every Monday* [1954], Harmondsworth, Penguin, 1956, p. 55. Later in this book (p. 108) Flush asserts that he hurled that wife from a train at Bournemouth. Elsewhere he reports that he was at Aix-les-Bains when his wife died, and that his first three women fell from trains at Bournemouth, Folkestone and on the Southern Railway just outside Bath (Branch, *The Wooden Overcoat* [1951], Harmondsworth, Penguin, 1959, pp. 9–10). Unless she refers to the joint LMS/SR Somerset and Dorset line, Branch's last case makes no sense. Her case is weak even if she does mean that line, for Somerset and Dorset trains never rushed down steep gradients from Combe Down to Bath (Queen Square) (after nationalisation, Bath (Green Park)). Indeed, these trains rarely rushed anywhere. Besotted admirers might make this line 'the Swift and Delightful' (or, after it was swallowed by the old GWR enemy, 'the Sabotaged and Defeated'), but passengers *would* insist on calling it 'the Slow and Dirty'. For its history see Robin Atthill, *The Somerset and Dorset Railway*, London, Pan, 1970.

152 J. J. Connington, *The Two Tickets Puzzle*, London, Gollancz, 1930; George Bellairs, *Death on the Last Train*, London, Collins, 1948; Freeman Wills Crofts, 'East wind', in Anon (ed.), *Fifty Famous Detectives of Fiction*, London, Odhams, 1948.

153 J. C. Lenehan, *The Tunnel Mystery*, London, Jenkins, 1929.

154 Hinxman, *Corpse Now Arriving*.

155 William le Queux, *The Temptress*, London, Ward Lock, 1919, pp. 71–2.

156 R. Austin Freeman, *When Rogues Fall Out*, London, Hodder & Stoughton, 1932, pp. 83, 253–6. A doped cigarette followed by a rug-strap round the neck did for Joseph Newton: G. D. H. and Margaret Cole, 'A lesson in crime', in G. K. Chesterton (ed.), *A Century of Detective Stories*, London, Hutchinson, 1935, p. 265.

157 Baroness Orczy, 'The mysterious death on the underground railway', in Greene (ed.), *Rivals of Sherlock Holmes*, pp. 206–25 and Haining (ed.), *Murder on the Railways*, pp. 306–22.

158 Dennis Wheatley, 'In the Underground' [1932], in Wheatley, *Gunmen, Gallants and Ghosts*, London, Hutchinson, 1943, pp. 45–51.

159 John Rowland, *The Cornish Riviera Mystery*, London, Jenkins, 1939, p. 51.

160 Reeve, *Murder Must Out*, p. 266.

161 Connington, *Two Tickets Puzzle*; Freeman Wills Crofts, 'The 8.12. from Waterloo', in Anon (ed.), *Evening Standard Detective Book: First Series*, pp. 131–9 and Crofts, *Many a Slip*, pp. 69–76. In a nice piece of self-advertisment, here Crofts' murderer decides to model his method on another story by his maker, 'Murder on the footplate'. Detailed knowledge about what happens to used railway and Channel ferry tickets traps a fraudster in Crofts' story 'The landing ticket' (in Crofts, *Mystery of the Sleeping Car Express*, pp. 224–46).

162 Victor L. Whitechurch, 'Murder on the Okehampton line', in Haining (ed.), *Murder on the Railways*, pp. 140–9.

163 Freeman Wills Crofts, 'The brothers Bing', in Crofts, *Many a Slip*, London, Hodder & Stoughton, 1955, pp. 161–70. Inevitably, French breaks this fratricidal alibi. Until Nazis rose to power in Germany, the Jewish Bing family ran a famous model train factory in Nürnberg. A delicate quip for Crofts' railway-adept coterie to appreciate.

164 Freeman Wills Crofts, *Sir John Magill's Last Journey* [1930], Harmondsworth, Penguin, 1955, pp. 214–27.

9

'The lost idea of a train': comic fiction

The wealth of crime fiction reviewed in the previous two chapters reveals how grievously commentators have limited their compass by looking for Britain's railway novel only within the literary canon. 'It has been popular culture rather than serious literature which has most enthusiastically taken up the railways,' Jeffrey Richards and John Mackenzie assert, 'responding to the immediacy of the sensations they provoke, to the bold iconographic power, strength and modernity of the steam engine, to the kaleidoscopic nature of train travel, to the whirl and bustle and breathlessness of transience.'[1] Their key point must be conceded; but Richards and Mackenzie give too much ground by urging that contemporaries approached Victorian and Edwardian railways only through sublimity, so readily evoked in crime fiction. Structures of feeling were more complex than this, as we may see by comparing passages written by two novelists born seven years apart: Arnold Bennett (1867–1931) and G. K. Chesterton (1874–1936). A 'romantic realist,' young Bennett was awed by railways' power. As we saw earlier, his first novel opens with broad generalisations about the 'imperious fascination' which trains to London hold for ambitious youths stifled by Northern provincialism.[2] In precisely the sense identified by John Stilgoe,[3] the railway here is a metropolitan corridor piercing backward districts. In his first Five Towns novel Bennett gave Anna Tellwright a holiday in the Isle of Man. She joined an express at Knype (Stoke-on-Trent). 'In a moment, so it seemed, the train was thundering through the mile of solid rock which ends at Lime Street Station, Liverpool.'[4] Lots of power and sublimity there. Arrived on Man, Anna then took a three-foot-six-inch gauge train. Today's railway enthusiasts sanctify narrow gauge travel. Not Bennett: he disdains 'the diminutive and absurd train which by breathless plunges annihilates the sixteen miles between Douglas and Port Erin in sixty-five minutes.'[5] Contrast this with a late essay by Chesterton, known in his time both as a beer connoisseur and a Catholic apologist. Celebrating London's Marylebone, a station 'as quiet and comfortable as the courtyard of an old inn,' he connects these two reputations. He imagines what this terminus might look like if the looming 1926 General Strike should be prolonged.

> My fancy chiefly rests on the remote generations of the future in this simple community, descended from the original primitive marriages between a few railway porters and a few barmaids. By that time the little commonwealth ought to have a whole tangle of traditions ultimately to be traced back to the lost idea of a train. Perhaps people would still go religiously to the ticket-office at intervals, as to a kind of confessional box; and there recite the names of far-off and by this time fabulous places; the word 'Harrow' sounding like the word 'Heaven' or the word 'Ealing' like the word 'Eden.' For this society would, of course, like every other, produce sceptics; that is men who had lost their social memory. All sorts of quaint ceremonials would survive, and would be scoffed at as irrational, because their rational origin had been obscured. At a date centuries hence, the clock in the refreshment room would still be kept a little fast, as compared with the clock in the station. There would be most complicated controversies about this custom; turning on things behind the times and things in advance of the age. The bookstall would have come to be something like the Bodleian or the great lost library of Alexandria; a storehouse of ancestral documents of primitive antiquity and profound obscurity; and learned men would be found spelling their way through a paragraph in one of our daily papers, deluded with the ever-vanishing hope of finding a sort of human meaning in it.[6]

We need little wit to appreciate that late Chesterton's tone differs from early Bennett's. One applauds progress, the other retrogression. One celebrates the stern, the other the whimsical. Writing about railways evidently can sustain both these styles, but in different voices. What underlies this tension, these differences? Setting out to answer that question, we need to return briefly to notions of pastoral. Investigating literary arcadianism towards the end of the long nineteenth century (when Bennett and Chesterton wrote their best work), John Lucas makes Edward Thomas' *Adlestrop* a 'vision of a lost England,' of 'the deep heart of England in the shires.'[7] He then moves to a close reading of E. M. Forster's *Howards End*. Lucas works with simple dyads: country/city; feudalism/modernity. Showing how literary evaluations of country and city shift over time as material interests bloom and fade, Raymond Williams is a good deal more subtle than this. His notion of neo-pastoralism,[8] with precapitalist literary conventions put to work legitimising agrarian capitalist social relations, provides a scale against which to measure Lucas' argument. Edward Thomas' closing lines certainly can be conjured to celebrate English nature-as-a-garden.

> And for that minute a blackbird sang
> Close by, and round him, mistier,
> Farther and farther, all the birds
> Of Oxfordshire and Gloucestershire.

But this ruralist reading can be sustained only if (with Lucas) one ignores the poem's opening quatrain:

> Yes, I remember Adlestrop –
> The name, because one afternoon
> Of heat the express-train drew up there
> Unwontedly. It was late June.

This is a railway poem. Indeed, it is the most famous railway poem in English,[9] and much parodied. Its striking power comes from Thomas' quiet cunning in filling old bottles with new wine, inserting his machine in Edwardians' cultural garden. This train – an express train, direct descendent from Dombey's ravaging 'monster, Death' – disturbs nobody. It is a trusted friend, as much at home in the English landscape as that loved wych elm in the garden at Howards End.

Unnoticed by almost all commentators, *Howards End* could be a candidate for the British railway novel.[10] The house which give E. M. Forster's book its name lies close to Stevenage ('Hilton'), in Hertfordshire. Characters routinely travel between London and Hilton by train. Forster draws fine distinctions:

> Like many others who have lived long in a great capital, [Margaret Schlegel] had strong feelings about the various railway termini. They are our gates to the glorious and the unknown. Through them we pass out into adventure and sunshine, to them, alas! we return. In Paddington all Cornwall is latent and the remoter west; down [in railway parlance: the physical gradient rises] the inclines of Liverpool Street lie fenlands and the illimitable Broads; Scotland is through the pylons of Euston; Wessex behind the poised chaos of Waterloo. Italians realise this, as is natural; those of them who are so unfortunate as to serve as waiters in Berlin call the Anhalt Bahnhof the Stazione d'Italia, because by it they must return to their homes. And he is a chilly Londoner, who does not endow his stations with some personality, and extend to them, however shyly, the emotions of fear and love.
>
> To Margaret – I hope that it will not set the reader against her – the station of King's Cross had always suggested Infinity. Its very situation – withdrawn a little behind the facile splendours of St Pancras – implied a comment on the materialism of life. Those two arches, colourless, indifferent, shouldering between them an unlovely clock, were fit portals for some eternal adventure, whose issue might be prosperous, but would certainly not be expressed in the ordinary language of prosperity.[11]

In the first paragraph of this passage Forster's railway is ubiquitous but minutely differentiated, taken for granted on the basis of intimate knowledge.[12] Tone shifts in the second paragraph. Here King's Cross and St Pancras, those adjacent but very different termini, stand for something special. They represent the tension at the heart of Forster's masterpiece: that Victorian conundrum, best expressed in Matthew Arnold's *Culture and Anarchy* (1869), about how to conserve liberal culture as a cultivated gentry yields power and privilege to a philistine bourgeoisie.[13] The two Schlegel sisters, standard-bearers for rentier gentility, resolve this problem through marriage. Helen protects the frontier with Arnold's Playful Giant (the proletariat) by tying the knot with Leonard Bast, a pathetic autodidactic clerk. Margaret spikes the haute-bourgeois threat by marrying Henry Wilcox, a rich widowed businessman. Through this union she inherits Howards End, England's soul, under his first wife's will.

Brash Henry Wilcox is defined by a preferred mode of travel. His automobile damns him. For Morgan Forster, that Edwardian conservative liberal, car travel is uncouth. Child of an age which took the train for granted, his railway is culturally neutral: a force for good or for evil.

> [Hilton] station, like the scenery, like Helen's letters, struck an indeterminate note. Into which country will it lead, England or Suburbia? It was new, it had island platforms and a subway, and the superficial comfort exacted by business men. But it also held hints of local life, personal intercourse.[14]

'Only connect,' this novel's motto insists, famously. Railways were the nineteenth century's Great Connector.[15] Sexual connection across class boundaries solves culture's difficulty for E. M. Forster. But, as in so many thrillers, genteel sexual connection works best in a first-class railway carriage.

Comic turn

At Paddington, Margaret Schlegel's wedding party entrains in a first-class private saloon for the journey to Shropshire, enjoying 'the low, rich purr of a Great Western express' as far as Shrewsbury. There they lunch, then transfer to limousines for the last stages of the journey. 'Maids, courier, heavy luggage,' we are told, 'had already gone on by a branch-line to a station nearer Oniton.'[16] Social discrimination distinguishes family members from physical and human luggage. This discrimination was not new. A generation earlier, Arthur Quiller-Couch ('Q') had introduced us to Troy Town (Fowey) in Cornwall, a right, tight little port borough decisively opened to landward influences in 1875, when the town's old gate-houses were demolished to allow railway omnibuses to pass. Those vehicles belonged to the Cornwall Mineral Railway, which the previous year had opened a mixed gauge branch line to Fowey from

'Five Lanes Junction' (Par) on the Cornwall Railway's main line from Plymouth to Falmouth.[17] In *The Astonishing History of Troy Town* (1888), Fenian bombers masquerading as gentry travelled first class by train from London to Troy. Of course, their servants travelled third. Arrived at Five Lanes Junction, these servants trundled to Troy over the steeply graded branch. Their employers disdained that action, avoiding the possibility of a long wait (only five trains each day, according to my 1910 *Bradshaw*) and a hugger-mugger journey by hiring a post-coach. The Wilcoxes' privileged freedom from branch-line travel is not new, we see; novelty lies in private transport powered by internal combustion engines rather than hayburners. Some kind of profound change is in progress. Five years after Forster published *Howards End*, change's cusp was exposed clearly. Disguised as uppers servants, Ashe Marston and Joan Valentine travelled third class in the 4.15 express from Paddington to Market Blandings, avant-garde for that horde which led their creator to declare later that 'Blandings [Castle] had impostors the way other houses have mice.'[18] Arrived at Market Blandings station, interface between the railway's metropolitan corridor and a fiercely premodern market town ('The church is Norman,' we are assured, 'and the intelligence of the majority of the natives palaeozoic'[19]) they watch their employers – who, of course, had travelled first class from Paddington – whisked away in the ninth earl of Emsworth's sole but stately Hispano-Suiza limousine. Ashe and Joan settle down for a long wait with the luggage. Eventually an open horse cart arrives to provide an interminable, jolting, cold ride from Market Blandings through Blandings Parva, the closed estate village at the Castle's gate, to the mansion's extensive servants' quarters.[20] Comic neo-pastoral, this is a dream world carefully specified in time: a world where the wealthy travel short distances by car while other classes walk, cycle or trundle along behind a plodding horse.

No more than twenty years after Ashe and Joan's chilly journey, motor vehicles had penetrated British life sufficiently deeply for wry Roy Vickers to tell his readers that 'Perhaps the most dangerous and troublesome method of disposing of a murdered body is to pack it in one or more travelling trunks for disposal at a railway station: this method is commonly used in poverty areas where the corpse cannot be conveyed unobserved to an automobile'.[21] Further episodes in P. G. Wodehouse's Blandings Castle saga now showed the family's younger son Freddie Threepwood, ageless bane of the ninth earl's ageless life, blithely tooling around rural Shropshire in his natty two-seater. By 1947 the Castle's location was defined not, as of yore, by the time taken to travel thence by train from Paddington, but as precisely forty-five minutes by car from Shrewsbury.[22] In comic fiction as in life, the train had yielded place to the car (and, for less mon-eyed social groups, the bus) for regional travel. Within a generation, wider car ownership and new motorway construction would see railways' dominance challenged even for long-distance passenger transport. Unnoticed by novelists, deeper usurpation came in road competition for goods and mineral traffic: a more significant matter for railway finances.

Here literature limps after the depressing economic history which we reviewed in chapter 1. British railways' golden age was that retrospectively sunlit Edwardian Indian summer bathing Howards End and Blandings Castle. Insidiously, British railways' decline seeped through comic fiction. We can iden-tify two patterns. One, sharing strong continuities with attitudes common in earlier centuries but renewed by Stella Gibbons' influential tract,[23] sustained metropolitan disdain for a rural idiocy rendered yet less desirable by two gener-ations' agricultural depression. Near the end of Evelyn Waugh's *Scoop* (1938) the press magnate Lord Copper despatches Salter, an elevated minion, from London to deepest Somerset. He goes by train.

> That evening, some time after the advertised time, Mr Salter alighted at Boot Magna Halt. An hour earlier, at Taunton, he had left the express, and changed into a train such as he did not know existed outside the imagination of his Balkan corre-spondents; a single tram-like, one-class coach, which had pottered in a desultory fashion through a system of narrow, under-populated valleys. It had stopped eight times, and at every station there had been a bustle of passengers succeeded by a long, silent pause, before it started again; ... there had been very old, unhygienic men and women, such as you never saw in the Underground, who ought long ago to have been put away in some public institution; there had been women carrying a multitude of atrocious little baskets and parcels which they piled on the seats; one of them had put a hamper containing a live turkey under Mr Salter's feet. It had been a horrible journey.[24]

Here the Great Western Railway's express, like London's Underground (those were the days!), represents modernity, the metropolitan corridor. Leaving this safe, orderly, chromium-plated world, Salter disappears – through a black hole disguised as a 'Flying Banana,' a spanking-new GWR diesel railcar (not that Salter seems impressed with this novelty) – into a parallel universe. This parallel England, this Other, is timeless. The branch timetable is a fiction. The branch train is socially polluting. Through the company's scandalous failure to pro-vided a first-class compartment on its creeping stopper, Salter is obliged to con-sort closely with malodorous proletarian persons clutching squalid packages. In Michael Innes' *The Journeying Boy* Mr Thewless suffers social pollution closely modelled on Salter's predicament. His Taunton is Dundrane, his turkey a pig, his branch train even more tram-like than Salter's. Thewless travels a narrow gauge Donegal railway line aboard 'the bug,' a one-class petrol railcar contrived by fitting flanged steel wheels to a bus body. Thewless, too, is forced to accept excessively close contact with socially unassuming and smelly persons – but these persons do not even speak English.[25] Beyond literary England's borders, Otherness is defined here through class compounded with ethnicity: amused English disgust at quaintly filthy Irish peasant life infused Somerville and Ross's *Some Experiences of an Irish R.M.* (1899), Michael Innes' prime resource in this comic thriller's Irish chapters. In another book Innes takes us on a Salter-like journey to Stella Gibbons territory. 'Travelling through an England enfolded in cold, half-light and gloom,' John Appleby's cross-country Sunday train creeps at a snail's pace through a string of comically dismal settlements, their nature defined by their names: King's Cleeve, Wing, Low Swaffham, Pigg, Little Limber, Snug, Cold Findon, Rust, Appleby's End, Snarl, Linger Junction (change for Sneak).[26] This is grotesquely awful country life contrived for the amusement of a nicely urban class of person; a place of fake-crooked (but authentically supercilious) county families lording it over a cowed, inbred and socially invisible rural proletariat.

The second response to railway decline was new, and more interesting. It rested on the movement which Stella Gibbons satirised and John Lucas sought to understand: a high Victorian and Edwardian literary revaluation of country life. Rural England never was simply *there*, a resource lying to hand for any writer to exploit. This was a literary construct, a conceit, that changed over time. It was created at particular periods by particular sets of intellectuals for particular purposes. Building on Raymond Williams' work, Alun Howkins exposes the bricks with which a novel conceit was constructed.[27] The 1851 census revealed that England and Wales had crossed a historical watershed, becoming the first nation(s) in history where more than half the population lived in towns and cities. As further urbanisation made cities – and, above all, made London, the capital – seem ever more dangerous in physical, social and political terms so, from the 1870s through to the First World War, writers, composers, artists and architects laboured to erect a coherent image of rural England as the nation's essence. Connecting 'Englishness' back to a nurturing past beyond industrialism's deformation, they conjured 'real' rural England as counties south of the Thames from Kent to Dorset (Edward Thomas' 'South Country'),[28] with modest home county Chiltern outliers and a western bulge through the Marcher counties to Shropshire. Thomas Hardy, the Powys brothers, Bloomsbury's weekend encampments in Sussex farmhouses,

'Dickensland' around Rochester, Howards End in Hertfordshire, Mary Webb's Shropshire, the Vale of Blandings; all nestle comfortably in this cultivated southern landscape dotted with woodlands and articulated by hedgerows, gently dominated by smoothly rounded hills, with thatched settlements clustered round village greens.

Against Ruskin's and Wordsworth's earlier insistence that railways despoiled and corrupted precious country districts, this ruralist revision (and long public habituation to railway travel) settled the train comfortably in the English landscape.[29] Michael Innes consigns characters 'into the very womb of England'[30] on the train from Oxford to Worcester and Shrewsbury, along the line which leads to Market Blandings. This view of the South Country as an unspoiled retreat, and rural railway facilities as a benison, marks a novel which uses comedy to anatomise Englishness in an unusually thorough manner. Remembered today only for its hilarious account of a village cricket match, A. G. Macdonell's *England, Their England* (1933) offers an Aberdonian's bemused attempts to understand the English. Like characters in Evelyn Waugh's early books, Donald Cameron lives in a picaresque novel. He moves among different sets of people in London and the home counties, slowly refining Englishness's metal from ore mined in many settings. Crooked financiers in bloated golf clubs, smoothly equivocating diplomats, blindingly skilful artisans, industrial slums, idiot gilded youths: he finds them all in England, but they are dross. Daydreaming on St Catherine's Hill above Winchester, at last Donald casts truth's ingot.[31] Ruminating on the becoming modesty (for a democratic Aberdonian) of Winchester College's motto – 'Manners makyth man' – England appears to him as a massive continuity, an arrow-straight Roman road cutting across downland and water meads. Along this road comes a host of men carrying weapons, but with their pockets stuffed with manuscripts. England, Donald understands at last, is poetical. Englishmen – English women find no place in this vision – are peaceable, impractical dreamers who spring effortlessly to arms when danger threatens. This host thins as he watches, distilling to two archetypes. Lean Will Shakespeare and fat John Falstaff stand proud yet modest, boozy and randy, for their nation's many virtues.

Donald Cameron's solves his cultural puzzle in this daydream, but earlier he fumbles towards the solution while visiting the Chilterns. He goes to the Vale of Aylesbury, 'loveliest of English names.' There Donald is entertained by a squire and his family in their manor house, The Golden Hind. Themselves pressed financially by agricultural depression, these gentle people act generously towards their struggling tenants. Vale folk are untouched by urban or industrial pitch, by passing frenzy. '"You see, Cameron"', his host tells him, '"it's an old country. Incredibly old. And there aren't many changes. Families go on and on and on"'. Asking about the house's name, Donald learns that a local centenarian still boasts that his grandfather told him, on the basis of first-hand acquaintance, that 'the Admiral' – Sir Francis Drake – was a great man. In the village pub – unmodernised by any rapacious brewery, although in this decade new roadhouses spread like scabs along new arterial roads – Donald hears unassuming rustics quote Shakespeare. He hears an old man recall his father's tales about seeing the sails of Nelson's ships in the Channel, about downland beacons set to warn that Boney's invasion had come.[32] Preserved in communal aspic, English mouths pass English truths down English centuries. The South Country's rural community is English culture's heart, Macdonell tells us. This is what Donald Cameron will recall, in refined form, on St Catherine's Hill.

And how does Donald reach the Vale of Aylesbury's Arcady? Like Lord Copper's shuddering minion, he goes from London by train. He goes from Chesterton's Marylebone, a terminus which exudes 'a subtle civilised charm.'[33] In this 'quietest and most dignified of stations,' Macdonell tells us that 'the porters go on tiptoe, the barrows are rubber-tyred and the trains sidle mysteriously in and out with only the faintest of toots upon their whistles so as not to disturb the signalmen.' Everything about this journey breathes peace, comfort and understated good manners. Donald has the train to himself: there is no other passenger. Marylebone's newpaper seller slumbers peacefully. The ticket clerk speaks in a whisper, the guard with utmost respect: 'He reminded Donald of the immortal butler, Jeeves.'[34] The engine driver walks 'stealthily' up the platform, followed by his fireman 'walking like a cat.' The entire train crew display beautiful manners. '"I think we might make a start now, Gerald"', the guard murmurs to the driver. '"Just as you wish, Horace"', Gerald whispers back. Their train dawdles quietly north from Marylebone, travelling along the metals of the Great Central Railway, apparently excluded from the grouped LNER in Macdonell's England. 'It is like no other of the north–south lines,' he reports.

> For it runs through lovely, magical rural England. It goes to places that you have never heard of before, but when you have heard of them you want to live in them – Great Missenden and Wendover and High Wycombe and Princes Risborough and Quainton Road, and Akeman Street and Blackthorn. It goes to places that do not need a railway, that never use a railway, that probably do not yet know that they have got a railway. It goes to way-side halts where the only passengers are milk-churns. It visits lonely platforms where the only tickets are bought by geese and

ducks. It stops in the middle of buttercup meadows to pick up eggs and flowers. It glides past the great pile of willow branches that are maturing to make England's cricket-bats. It is a dreamer among railways, a poet, kindly and absurd and lovely.[35]

Following prevailing literary rules, for A. G. Macdonell the Great Central's rural nature (so dispiriting for its long-suffering shareholders before 1923)[36] makes this a classic English line. But by cleaving to these rules he offends earlier literary discourse about railways. In *Something Fresh* P. G. Wodehouse made railways modern things, alien to rural Shropshire's timeless Englishness. A valuable device for transporting characters from London to Market Blandings, he kept them firmly excluded from Blandings Parva's premodern organic community. Watching champaign landscape pass his carriage window, surfing through the home counties, Macdonell inserts the Great Central Railway's London extension *into* rural England, *into* the nation's cultural heart, *into* the massive continuity of her dream history. It is a pregnant moment. It is also an odd moment, for – to repeat – Donald Cameron rides a main line train. The Great Central might have been the last main line railway to reach London from the midlands, but this was no insignificant twig on the nation's railway network. Macdonnell constructs it as a dozing branch line for good marketing reasons. By the interwar years readers had been trained to appreciate small railways embowered in rural community. Consider opening sentences from Aldous Huxley's first novel. Trading mainly in metropolitan cynicism, Huxley well knew what his readers expected when a character entrained for a South Country mansion.

> Along this particular stretch of line no express had ever passed,' he reports. 'All the trains – the few that there were – stopped at all the stations. Denis knew the names of those stations by heart. Bole, Tritton, Spavin, Delawarr, Knipswich for Timperley, West Bowlby and, finally, Camlet-on-the-Water. Camlet was where he always got out, leaving the train to creep indolently onward, goodness knew whither, into the green heart of England.[37]

Sluiced away by sentimentality's gush, brittle metropolitan cynicism collapses on this branch line resembling that which, some years later, appalled Evelyn Waugh's urbane Salter.

Apotheosis

Very curiously, Huxley's sentimentality is to be laid at Arthur Quiller-Couch's door. Edward Thomas stopped his literary South Country at Devon's eastern border; but Q's Cornwall ran neck and neck with Hardy's Wessex in Edwardian publishing stakes.[38] Retiring from New Grub Street to a less strenuous life, in 1912 Q established the English tripos at Cambridge University. Together with Walter Raleigh at Oxford, and spurred by sharpening industrial and military competition with Germany, Professor Quiller-Couch proselytised English literature as English culture's heart.[39] This crusade pre-echoes in his Cornish novels. Exclude those Fenian interlopers, and *The Astonishing History of Troy Town* (1888) is firmly centred in Fowey. Cornwall is its own place with its own people here, with aliens lurking beyond the Tamar. *The Mayor of Troy* (1906), by contrast, treats local comic absurdities centring on 'the King of Troy' (local people's half-resentful nickname for their complacent mayor) within a discourse framed by English, not Cornish, realities. Foreigners now are Frenchmen or Germans, and routinely maligned.

As a popular novelist Q was content to satisfy market demands for conventional ruralist fictions. In 'A golden wedding,'[40] for example, an ancient miller, evicted many years before when a new railway's road-bed destroyed his water-mill, waits to meet his wife on a station platform. Their livelihood destroyed by on-rushing modernity, these old folk were forced to live apart. Savings dwindled to support the invalid wife in their son's Plymouth household. Bereft of choice and funds, her deserving-poor husband entered the workhouse. Now, soft-hearted guardians have allowed him to leave its walls for a final celebration, fifty years after his wedding day. He will meet his wife from the train. They will take tea together at a local cottage. Sitting hand in hand, they will look down the river to where their old home once stood, before an ineluctably timetabled train carries the wife back to Plymouth – and, we recognise, to death. This tale cloys today's palate: we miss the astringent irony with which Thomas Hardy would lace circumstances like these. But Q knew what he was doing. Like so much else that he wrote, 'A Golden Wedding' was precisely (and profitably) calibrated against contemporary British public taste. Then, unexpectedly, Cornish specificities caught up with him. In 1892 Q went to live at Fowey. In his cod new year's letter to the prince of Abyssinia, his old Balliol chum, he offered a comic account of the 'event which has greatly excited us, and redeemed from monotony (though at the eleventh hour) the year:'[41] a false fire alarm in William Freethy's steam-powered wood-yard. This was an odd choice for the most momentous local event in 1892. In May of that year the last section of broad-gauge track owned by the Great Western Railway and client companies – the main line from Paddington to Penzance, with certain west-country branches – had been narrowed, through Herculean effort married to rational planning, in a single weekend. This event was widely mourned in the west, and elsewhere.[42]

Coming as British railways' prosperity and prestige rose towards their peak, the broad gauge's narrowing was decline's harbinger. Later events rang harmonics on the elegiac note first struck in 1892. Many Victorian cultural critics had thundered that railways dragged deplorable rationalisation and standardisation in their train. After 1923 the state-brokered grouping of many separate railway companies into the Big Four was resented as evidence of just those processes getting under way for the first time. Hitherto dazzling besotted enthusiasts at major junctions, the old companies' technicolour locomotive and carriage liveries faded to four drab uniforms.[43] 'The great systems have extended their tentacles on every hand to absorb the lesser roads in their advance,' Fred Talbot told his readers:

> Consolidation and amalgamation are in active progress, and by the absorption of these fragmentary steel-ways, 'zones of influence' are being created. The grouping process is bringing about the extinction of many lines, the names of which were household words; their achievements in settlement and the general up-building of the community are in danger of becoming obscured, if not actually lost to memory. … Haphazard speculative construction is giving way to rigid system: the interests of the whole are being considered rather than the requirements of the few. … This tendency is depriving railway conquest of its picturesqueness.[44]

A generation after that, many enthusiasts and some citizens thought that British railways' 1947 nationalisation took these processes further, reducing residual variety to bland uniformity. Then came the end of steam locomotion, announced in the 1955 Modernisation Plan and completed (much faster than optimists had hoped) in 1968. Mourned in anticipation, British railway enthusiasts took steam's eclipse by diesel and electric traction to be history's greatest betrayal.[45] Collect the astonishingly wide range of railway periodical literature on sale in Britain today, and you will discover how far elegiac evocations of steam days outweigh celebrations of Eurostar's – or rail privatisation's – brave thrust toward the future. In general public attitudes today, railways' historic role as modernity's spear tip is blunted to the point of fatuity.

Q's direct role in establishing a whimsically elegiac mindset about British railways was limited to two brief stories. 'Pipes in Arcady' (1913) recounts a sight seen from a slow train.

> The whole scene, barring the concertina and the navvies' clothes, might have been transformed straight from a Greek vase of the best period. Here, in this green corner of rural England on a workaday afternoon …, in full sunlight, I saw this company of the early gods sitting, naked and unabashed, and piping, while twelve British navvies danced to their music.[46]

We learn later that these naked men comprised a blind musical troupe whose members strode confidently from their compartment into a lineside pond, believing that a station had been reached, when their train stopped at a signal check. They play for the dancing navvies while their clothes dry. Here Q embowers his Cornish railway in a rural England where classical references transport us straight to Arcady. In 'Cuckoo Valley Railway' (1893) he used this pastoral mode again, but more powerfully and more significantly: this brief story casts a very long shadow.

'Cuckoo Valley Railway' is a slightly fictionalised account of the Bodmin and Wadebridge Railway, 'the least known railway byway in Cornwall.'[47] Built to carry granite, parts of this line never offered an official passenger service. In 1845 the Bodmin and Wadebridge was purchased (apparently illegally, but who bothered with such details so far from London's nosy lawyers?) by the London and South Western Railway Company, as a lever to shift the Great Western's Cornish monopoly. For the usual complicated railway political reasons this never happened. The LSWR's Cornish branch sat isolated from its parent system; until 1888 the Bodmin and Wadebridge lacked any connection to the national network. By the 1960s, when British Railways' Dr Beeching deployed his fatal bedside manner, this deeply obscure line was famous among enthusiasts, because only Beattie well-tank locomotives (introduced for London suburban passenger service almost a century earlier, in 1874) could traverse its sharp curves. A small stud of these spavined relics had to be maintained in Harold Wilson's white-hot technological years, to sustain a sketchy rail service. Life copies art. Galvanised by the special circumstances behind the Bodmin and Wadebridge, in 1893 Bodmin-born Q showed his readers a line promoted

> when the names of Watt and Stephenson waxed great in the land, and these slow citizens caught the railway frenzy. They took it, however, in their own fashion. They never dreamed of connecting themselves with other towns and a larger world, but of aggrandizement by means of a railway that should run from Tregarrick [Bodmin] to nowhere in particular, and bring the intervening wealth to their doors. [Opened with a flourish sixty years before by the line's only locomotive hauling the mayor of Tregarrick on an open truck], then Nature settled down to heal her wounds, and the Cuckoo Valley Railway to pay no dividend to its promoters.[48]

We take a journey on this quaint line. It obeys no timetable. We join the railway's sole engine driver and fireman in the pub, as they wait to transport a bashful newly-married couple back to Tregarrick on a train offering few concessions to passengers' comfort: 'There were eight trucks, seven of them laden with granite, and an engine, with a prodigiously long funnel, bearing the name, *The Wonder of the Age*, in brass letters along its boiler.' Offered the honour of a foot-plate ride, we enjoy a remarkable trip.

> Far down, on our right, the river shone between the trees, and these trees, encroaching on the track, almost joined their branches above us. Ahead, the moss that grew upon the sleepers gave the line the appearance of a green glade, and the grasses, starred with golden-rod and mallow, grew tall to the very edge of the rails. It seemed that in a few more years Nature would cover this scar of 1834, and score the return match against man. Rails, engine, officials were already no more than ghosts: youth and progress lay in the pushing trees, the salmon leaping against the dam below, the young man and maid sitting with clasped hands and amatory looks in the hindmost truck.[49]

This locomotive was the wonder of an age which has passed. This railway is collapsing back into a Nature that has usurped railways' progressive function. The Enlightenment project's steam is spent. Railway decline is inevitable in the Cuckoo Valley. Decline is to be celebrated, if in a wistful mode. It is not to be mourned.

In these six pages Q invented a new way of writing about railways in Britain: what Walter Benjamin later would term *nostalgic memory*, a conservative and yearning regret for lost days. As other imaginative writers copied this tone, so accounts of branch line trains supplanted fictions set on main line journeys. Fast trains yielded to slow trains, the present to the past. Quaintness replaced puissance. Whimsy supplanted power. Fifty years after Q wrote 'Cuckoo Valley Railway,' John Appleby (that rising young Scotland Yard detective, rendered engagingly unconventional by his Oxford literary education) struggled to locate the Sneak to Linger Junction branch train. It obeyed no timetable. Driven by Gregory Grope, 'Its engine … had every appearance of being closely related to that *Stourbridge Lion* which delighted the hearts of the Delaware and Hudson Canal Company on 9 August 1829. Behind the engine were two closed trucks, and behind these was a carriage of the stubby or truncated proportions commonly found in nurseries.' Directly evoking Q's *The Wonder of the Age* and her modest train of granite trucks, this artifact straddles the boundary between toy and real train, between romantic myth and mundane reality. Attracting its driver's attention, John Appleby stopped this remarkable collection of antiques; and learned that Gregory Grope's railway enthusiasm dated from childhood days spent reading *The Wonder Book of Trains*. Controlling his clapped-out contraption in this retired district, Gregory yearned for the metropolitan corridor. '"There's talk of a branch line to Slumber"', he told Appleby. '"There's even talk of electrification, from time to time." His eye swept the half-dozen fields and the little valley which separated Sneak from Linger. "Like on the Chicago, Milwaukee and St Paul run.'"[50] Whimsy pinions modern pretension. Technical advance may thunder forward on other countries' high iron, but Gregory Grope's mixed toy train assures readers that railways' threat is safely neutered in England's South Country.

Reportage mirrored fiction, as local railways snuggled to a rural community's warm heart. 'I, too,' wrote the journalist, doggerel poet and railway fanatic Gilbert Thomas in 1926, railing at the 1923 grouping's erosion of local particularity, 'have seen the station brook babbling out of paradise, and, as the sun has come up through the mist, have heard the song of the lark soaring into the smokeless heavens, and the very noise of a railway engine shunting, blended into one glorious symphony of regeneration.'[51] 'No line could be more typically cross-country than the Bletchley–Cambridge branch of the L. M. S.,' another enthusiast asserted three years after nationalisation.

> Travellers on that line know all about the art of making haste slowly – they have to. Its trains meander along in a dreamy way through a long succession of village stations whose names are poems – Gamlingay, Old North Road, Lord's Bridge – and in spring they run through field after field where the buttercups drench the grass, making its green gold. Like most cross-country trains, these have but two speeds, slow and stop. When the buttercups are out (and I know no part of England where they flower more bravely) the sloth of a train should matter to no one, for all can look at the fields and be satisfied.[52]

Quaint village names, poems, wild flowers, humane leisureliness: in this passage Canon Roger Lloyd – one from that vast host of railway-besotted Anglican priests – conjured a hymn of praise for a railway embedded in a community and a landscape. This could be Donald Cameron heading for Arcady in the Vale of Aylesbury. With death's bitter taste spiking whimsy's sweetness, it might be that lament for Beeching-slaughtered steam branch lines, Michael Flanders and Donald Swann's song 'The Slow Train.'[53] But Arthur Quiller-Couch printed all these men's hymn-sheets.

Literary treatments of the railway embowered in rural community culminate with John Hadfield's *Love on a Branch Line*, a novel inspired by Hadfield's discovery of the just-closed Mid-Suffolk Light Railway.[54] Arcady Hall, a Tudor mansion, graces the border between Norfolk and Suffolk. A private station on a branch line serves this hall, but the branch line has been abandoned by British Railways. This does not mean that trains no longer run. Most of Arcady Hall is rented to a government ministry's statistics unit. Bertie, Lord

Flamborough, the hall's wheelchair-bound owner, puts this rent to good use. "'I own the railway'", he tells the junior civil servant despatched to assess the ministry's statisticians. "'I bought the Branch Line, stations and all, when they closed it down four years ago. The railway people made me a present of the locomotive.'"[55] Along with his dreamy wife, Bertie lives in great comfort on his private train: eating well and drinking deeply, playing loud drum accompaniments to classic jazz records, put gently to bed in his sleeping car when he can eat, drink and syncopate no longer. This all recalls Valentine, Stanley Holloway's character in *The Titfield Thunderbolt*, a 1952 Ealing comedy about Cotswold railway preservation.[56] Valentine bankrolls a threatened branch line's rescue by an entire village, simply so that he can drink all day in his buffet car (excluded from 1950s' restrictive licensing laws) as his train trundles up and down his branch. Arcady's locomotive – "'It's an old Great Eastern "Intermediate" – used to run between Cambridge and Mildenhall'" – needs remarkably little maintenance for her daily runs up and down Bertie's branch, driven by one of his daughters, a devoted retainer, or anybody else who fancies a go. Unlike Titfield's inhabitants, Arcady folk remain blissfully ignorant about the Ministry of Transport's restrictions (inherited from stern Gladstonian days) on who may drive a train, and under what conditions. But this is to cavil. As the hall's name warned us, realism offers no guide to action in this place. *Love on a Branch Line* is whimsical railway neo-pastoral, with the modern impulse attenuated to vanishing point. This magical world is constrained by no material shortages or state regulations, a site for innocent, consummated couplings between the dazzled London civil servant and earl Bertie's three gorgeous daughters. (But only one at a time; this *is* 1959.) The sun always shines in this unspoiled country, and romance always is in season. Along a different branch line we have returned to P. G. Wodehouse's timeless world, to Bertie Wooster unlikelily compounded with Clarence Threepwood. The railway station no longer stands marginal to Market Blandings. Domesticated, neutred, brought fully to heel, the train now penetrates Blandings Parva's organic community, with the gentlest stroll taking one from Bertie's station to Arcady Hall. But modernity is repulsed, not defeated. Though Arcady survives with its eccentric inmates, only the strictest quarantine maintains their fiction. Any brush with Beechingite reality will sweep this perfect world away like a cobweb (or, indeed, like the Mid-Suffolk Light Railway). Until that happens, whimsy rules John Hadfield's gentle utopia. 'As everyone from the age of four onwards knows in their heart of hearts,' W. H. reported in 1974, while British Rail's managers drove relentlessly forward in a diesel and electric world, a proper railway remains for all time an affair of hissing steam locomotives, klickety-bong metals, hand-operated level crossings, cattle trucks, semaphore signals, whistle-blowing guards, stately top-hatted traffic managers and the odd curmudgeonly porter alone on a remote country platform lit by a single smoky oil lamp.[57]

Notes

1 Jeffrey Richards and John M. Mackenzie, *The Railway Station: a Social History*, Oxford, Oxford University Press, 1986, p. 343.

2 Arnold Bennett, *A Man From the North* [1898], London, Hamish Hamilton, 1973, p. 1.

3 See above, p. 61.

4 Arnold Bennett, *Anna of the Five Towns* [1902], Harmondsworth, Penguin, 1973, p. 150.

5 Bennett, *Anna of the Five Towns*, p. 153.

6 G. K. Chesterton, 'The lost railway station', in Chesterton, *The Spice of Life, and Other Essays*, edited by Dorothy Collins, Beaconsfield, Darwen Finlayson, 1964, pp. 133–4. The emphasis on ceremonial here reminds us that Chesterton was a leading Roman Catholic apologist. Somewhat earlier, in 'The prehistoric railway station' (in Chesterton, *Tremendous Trifles* [1909], London, Methuen, 1920, pp. 219–24) he started playing jokes with the Goncourt brothers' stern judgement that railway termini were the nineteenth century's cathedrals.

7 John Lucas, 'The sunlight on the garden', in Carola M. Kaplan and Anne B. Simpson (eds), *Seeing Double: Revisioning Edwardian and Modernist Literature*, London, Macmillan, 1996, p. 61.

8 See above, p. 53.

9 Peggy Poole, *Marigolds Grow Wild on Platforms: an Anthology of Railway Poetry*, London, Cassell, 1996, p. 175. Thomas wrote this poem after a railway journey from Oxford to Worcester on 23 June 1914.

10 Not surprisingly, if we accept Nicola Beauman's judgment that 'One of the most remarkable features of *Howards End* is its modernity' (Beauman, *Morgan: a Biography of E. M. Forster*, London, Sceptre, 1993, p. 221. The honourable exception to railway commentators' impercipience is Roger Green (ed.), *The Train*, Oxford, Oxford University Press, 1982, pp. 32–3.

11 E. M. Forster, *Howards End* [1910], London, Arnold, 1947, p. 13.

12 In a novel which springs so directly from the author's recollected delight in a boyhood home, it is striking that the railway should frame Forster's and his mother's recollected first visit to the loved house. 'Last Tuesday I went to Stevenage', Lily Forster reported. 'I was told by the station people that the "Rooksnest" was 2½ miles from the station' (quoted in P. N. Furbank, *E. M. Forster: a Life. Volume One: the Growth of the Novelist*, London, Secker & Warburg, 1977, p. 15). 'I have, or think I have, a clear impression of my arrival at Rooksnest', Morgan Forster recalled many

years later. 'I certainly remember coming in the train and asking the names of the stations we passed, and pronouncing Welwyn as it is spelled instead of calling it "Wellin" in the approved fashion. I think I remember too coming in the fly and seeing the church and the farm as we passed and also seeing Rooksnest itself but I do not remember entering the house and my next impression is playing with bricks on the drawing-room floor'. See E. M. Forster, 'Rooksnest', in Forster, *Howards End*, edited by Oliver Stallybrass, London, Arnold, 1973, p. 341.

13 Peter Widdowson, *E. M. Forster's Howards End: Fiction as History*, Falmer, Sussex University Press, 1977, p. 71. Numbered among the celebrated *Queens of Kings*, Forster well understood the social meanings carried by different London termini for academic Cambridge in Edwardian days. Trains ran to that town from Liverpool Street, Kings Cross and St Pancras, but the long drag through working-class north-east London made Liverool street socially impossible. Despite its phys-ical magnificence, even trains to Barlow's and Scott's station were disparaged. 'No one ever went to St Pancras by the Great Eastern Railway if they could help it', Gwen Raverat recalled (*Period Piece*, London, Faber, 1952, p. 98); 'and Liverpool Street was unknown to the genteel'. Against this background, how delicious that the Merchant-Ivory sentiment machine should dispatch everybody to Hilton by train from *St Pancras*, not Kings Cross, in their film of *Howards End* (1992). For more on Forster movie adaptations see Peter J. Hutchings, 'A disconnected view: Foster [*sic*], modernity and film', in Jeremy Tambling (ed.), *E. M. Forster*, London, Macmillan, 1995, pp. 213–28.

14 Forster, *Howards End*, p. 13.

15 Harold Perkin, *The Age of the Railway*, London, Panther, 1970, pp. 96–121.

16 Forster, *Howards End*, p. 222.

17 Q, 'The great fire on Freethy's Quay', in Q, *The Delectable Duchy* [1893], London, Dent, n.d., p. 267. E. T. MacDermott suggests that the Cornwall Minerals Railway's introduction of passenger services in late June 1876 over its line from Fowey to Newquay was 'a despairing attempt to make money' when cyclical decline in local industries decimated freight revenues. Q's account of Troy's gate-houses' 1875 demolition implies that this action might have been rather longer-considered than MacDermott suggests. The Cornwall Minerals Railway's plunge into pas-senger traffic made little difference to its fortunes: the line was leased by the GWR in 1877, the company purchased in 1896. In 1862 a second mineral line to Fowey had been started from a junction with the Cornwall Railway at Lostwithiel, but construction was abandoned after seven years at Carne Point, half a mile from Fowey. This branch closed in 1879. With its own line currently operated by the GWR, the Cornwall Minerals Railway company bought out the Lostwithiel and Fowey enterprise eighteen years later, and completed a standard-gauge line to Fowey. This, too, came to be worked by the Great Western. See E. T. MacDermott, *A History of the Great Western Railway*, vol. 2, Paddington, Great Western Railway, 1931, pp. 288, 333–7.

18 P. G. Wodehouse, 'Preface' [1975] to Wodehouse, *Something Fresh* [1915], Harmondsworth, Penguin, 1979, p. 6.

19   Wodehouse, *Something Fresh*, p. 148. 'To alight at Blandings Station', we learn (p. 91) is to be smitten with the felling that one is at the edge of the world with no friends near.'

20   Wodehouse, *Something Fresh*, pp. 91, 95–6.

21   Roy Vickers, 'The clue of the red carnations', in Vickers, *The Department of Dead Ends*, Harmondsworth, Penguin, 1955, p. 115.

22   P. G Wodehouse, *Full Moon* [1947], Harmondsworth, Penguin, 1961, p. 167. For a preliminary discussion about how other writers handled untramelled private motoring's intoxicating novelty see Nicholas Zurbrugg, 'Oh what a feeling! – the literatures of the car', in David Thoms, Len Holden and Tim Claydon (eds), *The Motor Car and Popular Culture in the Twentieth Century*, Aldershot, Ashgate, 1998, pp. 9–27.

23   Stella Gibbons, *Cold Comfort Farm*, London, Longmans, 1932.

24   Evelyn Waugh, *Scoop* [1938], in Waugh, *Decline and Fall etc*, London, Heinemann, 1977, p. 517. In one of history's more unlikely conjunctures, the undergraduate Evelyn Waugh enrolled as a founder member of the Oxford University Railway Club (motto: 'There is no smoke without fire') in 1923. This club's activities were limited to travelling from Oxford to Leicester and back once each term, eating together on the outward journey in the restaurant car on the Penzance-Aberdeen express, Britain's longest scheduled run. In 1924 members held a joint meeting with the parallel Cambridge club at Bletchley, where the meanderingly direct line between the two university towns crossed the old London and Birmingham Railway. It was not a success. 'The Cambridge contingent turned out to be serious students of railway engineering', Humphrey Carpenter reports, 'who were greatly puzzled by the Oxford frivolities:' Carpenter, *The Brideshead Generation: Evelyn Waugh and his Friends*, Boston, Houghton Mifflin, 1990, p. 123.

25   Michael Innes, *The Journeying Boy*, London, Gollancz, 1949.

26   Michael Innes, *Appleby's End*, London, Gollancz, 1946, pp. 45–6. Or, in an earlier manifestation, Warter, King's Cleeve, Wing, Low Swaffham, Pigg, Little Limber, Snug, Cold Findon and Rust: Michael Innes, *Stop Press* [1939], Harmondsworth, Penguin, 1958, pp. 44–5.

27   Alun Howkins, 'The discovery of rural England', in Robert Colls and Philip Dodd (eds), *Englishness: Politics and Culture, 1880–1920*, London, Croom Helm, 1986, pp. 62–88.

28   Edward Thomas, *The South Country* [1909], London, Dent, 1984, pp. 1–4.

29   'The Nadder Valley was the most beautiful place in his known world, more beautiful than the sea at Studland by Old Harry, more beautiful than the woods at home in Surrey, even in bluebell time, and the trains of the South Western Railway were a part of that beautiful whole, with the Downs and the river, the wooded ridge of Black Furlong and the brown, thatched village. He had discovered the *Train in the Landscape*.'C. Hamilton Ellis, *The Beauty of Old Trains*, London, Allen and Unwin, 1952, pp. 13–14. Original emphasis.

30   Michael Innes, *Stop Press!* [1938], Harmondsworth, Penguin, 1958, p. 29.

31   A. G. Macdonell, *England, Their England* [1933], London, Macmillan, 1941, pp. 293–9.

32   Macdonell, *England, Their England*, pp. 222–37.

33 Alan A. Jackson, *London's Termini*, second edition, Newton Abbott, David and Charles, 1985, pp. 29–30.

34 In only one Wodehouse story does Jeeves, that beau ideal of the gentleman's personal gentleman, appear as a butler; but why pick nits in such a well-turned genuflection to Macdonell's master? For the master's own thoughts see P. G. Wodehouse, 'Butlers and the buttled', in Wodehouse, *Louder and Funnier*, London, Faber & Faber, 1933, pp. 209–24.

35 Macdonell, *England, Their England*, pp. 220–2.

36 George Dow, *Great Central*, Shepperton, Ian Allan, 1959–65.

37 Aldous Huxley, *Crome Yellow*, London, Chatto & Windus, 1921, p. 1.

38 As late as 1928, the Great Western Railway's Cornish guide book had to explain that port expansion rendered Q's Troy invisible in modern Fowey: S. P. B. Mais, *The Cornish Riviera*, London, Great Western Railway, 1928, pp. 36–7.

39 Chris Baldick, *The Social Mission of English Criticism, 1848–1932*, Oxford, Clarendon Press, 1983.

40 Arthur Quiller-Couch, 'A golden wedding,' in Quiller-Couch, *Delectable Duchy*, pp. 188–95.

41 Quiller-Couch, 'The great fire on Freethy's Quay', p. 265.

42 'The broad gauge was essentially a West Country institution', David St John Thomas reminds us. 'Past lethargy forgotten, on its last day the local population turned out in force with demonstrations of affection and loyalty:' Thomas, *A Regional History of the Railways of Great Britain. Vol 1: The West Country*, fourth edition, Newton Abbot, David & Charles, 1974, p. 224. He notes some striking manifestations of grief: the gentleman who held up the last down broad-gauge service at Exeter while he expatiated on dying glories from the platform beside *Iron Duke*; farewell messages chalked on carriages in the last up and down trains; the spontaneous demonstration at Dawlish when these trains crossed, with passengers holding hands across the six-foot way, all singing *Auld Lang Syne*; the Ashburton branch engine creeping, crêpe-bedecked, towards Swindon's scrapyard. See also W. M. Acworth, *The Railways of England*, fifth edition, London, Murray, 1900, p. 264; Christopher Awdry, *Brunel's Broad Gauge Railway*, Sparkford, O. P. C., 1992, p. 6; A. H. Malan, 'Broad gauge engines', *English Illustrated Magazine*, 1892, reprinted in David St J. Thomas and Patrick Whitehouse, *The Great Days of the GWR*, Nairn, Thomas, 1991, pp. 27–31; Malan, *Broad Gauge Finale*, Didcot, Wild Swan, 1985. Narrowing also generated perhaps the worst railway poem in English, Horatio Brown's 'To a Great-Western broadgauge engine and its stoker' (reprinted in Kenneth Hopkins (ed.), *The Poetry of Railways*, London, Frewin, 1966, pp. 35–6.) The GWR absorbed the Cornwall Railway – always its creature in fact, if not in name – in 1889.

43 C. Hamilton Ellis, *The Trains We Loved*, London, Allen & Unwin, 1947, pp. 21–4; Ellis, *Beauty of Old Trains*, p. 93; R. K. Kirkland, 'Three faces of independence', in H. A. Vallance (ed.), *The Railway Enthusiast's Bedside Book*, London, Batsford, 1966, pp. 103–17.

44 Fred A. Talbot, *Railways of the World*, London, Waverley, 1924, vol. 1, pp. 1–2.

45 Roger Lloyd, *Farewell to Steam*, London, Allen a & Unwin, 1956.

46   Arthur Quiller-Couch, 'Pipes in Arcady' [1913], in Quiller-Couch, *Shorter Stories*, London, Dent, 1944, p. 24, and Charles Irving (ed.), *Sixteen On*, London, Macmillan, 1957, p. 84.

47   David St J. Thomas, 'A Cornish byway', in Gilbert Thomas and David St. J. Thomas, *Double Headed: Two Generations of Railway Enthusiasm* Dawlish, David and Charles, 1963, pp. 106–115. Actually called 'Cuckoo Valley', the introduction to C. F. D. Whatmath's history of the line takes Q's story to be a 'thinly veiled account of the coming of the B. & W. R. and its effects on the Camel Valley:' Whatmath, *The Bodmin and Wadebridge Railway*, fourth edition, Wokingham, Forge, 1994, pp. 3–4.

48   Arthur Quiller-Couch, 'Cuckoo Valley Railway', in Quiller-Couch, *Delectable Duchy*, p. 57.

49   Quiller-Couch, 'Cuckoo Valley Railway', pp. 61–2.

50   Innes, *Appleby's End*, pp. 101–3. Built by Foster and Rastrick in Stourbridge, Worcestershire, *Stourbridge Lion* was the first steam locomotive to run on an American public railway. Her three sister locomotives (graced with much less imaginative names – *America*, *Delaware* and *Hudson*) – were built by Robert Stephenson in Newcastle. Sadly, none of these three ever turned a wheel in service on the Delaware and Hudson, and *Stourbridge Lion* soon trundled off to terminal storage: G. Freeman Allen, *Railways: Past, Present and Future*, London, Macdonald, 1982, p. 16.

51   Gilbert Thomas, 'Cross-country journeys', in Thomas, *Calm Weather*, London, Chapman & Hall, 1930, p. 42, reprinted in Thomas and Thomas, *Double Headed*, p. 50.

52   Roger Lloyd, *The Fascination of Railways*, London, Allen & Unwin, 1951, p. 120.

53   A song composed for Flanders and Swann's revue 'At the Drop of Another Hat' (Parlophone CDP 7974662).

54   Closed on 28 July 1952, this line connected Haughley with Laxfield *via* not very much in between. For its brief and thin history see D. I. Gordon, *A Regional History of the Railways of Great Britain, Volume V: the Eastern Counties*, Newton Abbot, David & Charles, 1977, pp. 99–100, and N. A. Comfort, *The Mid-Suffolk Light Railway*, Lingfield, Oakwood, 1963.

55   John Hadfield, *Love on a Branch Line* [1959], London, Black Swan, 1989, p. 86.

56   John Huntley, *Railways on the Screen*, Shepperton, Ian Allan, 1993, pp. 180–2. From this remarkable work of amateur scholarship one could construct an account about narrative tone shifting in railway movies which runs parallel to the literary argument presented here: as *The Arrival of a Train at La Ciotat Station* (1895) and *Brief Encounter* (1946) yielded to *The Ladykillers* (1955) and *The Great St Trinians Train Robbery* (1966).

57   W. H., unpaginated 'Preface', to reprint of Wiiiam Heath Robinson, *Railway Ribaldry* [1935], London, Duckworth, 1974. Heath Robinson's cartoon collection was first published by the Great Western Railway to mark its centenary. Did any railway company ever celebrate surviving one hundred years in a more imaginative fashion?

10

Train Landscape: Eric Ravilious, William Heath Robinson and Rowland Emett

Eric Ravilious

We sit in a railway compartment's left-hand corner seat, looking forward and across to views through three windows on the compartment's right-hand side. Each window is framed by delicately conjured detail. Each has its blind, complete with spring-loaded roller and pull tab. Black slots in the sides of each window frame show where blinds lodge. Sealed with yellow and black diagonally striped draught strips, the compartment's door carries a huge number 3 in yellow, shaded black. Evidently enough, we sit in a third-class carriage. The other figures on this door – 990 – will interest only the railway company, or unusually persistent train spotters: this is the carriage's fleet number. Our carriage's door is equipped with a sliding ventilator, a droplight with a battered leather strap, and a lock whose blueish-silver colour recalls dominant tones in the patterned moquette upholstery. Marked ribbing, and sundry humps and hollows, tell us that these seats have supported many passengers. All exposed woodwork is varnished; some might be grained. Shadowed match boarding at the picture's top left insinuates hazy sunshine. Our view of the landscape is obscured neither by telegraph wires nor by drifting smoke from a steam locomotive (which this carriage's antiquity insists must haul our train). Whether we sit facing the engine is impossible to say; the view outside is rendered so sharply that our train could stand at rest, checked between stations by a signal. Visible scenery is rustic. Harvested cornfields shimmer in each window's foreground. A black fence in the lower left window carries the eye to the right and upwards, directing our gaze to middle grounded ploughland at centre and right. Willow-green downs swell above cultivated fields in all three apertures. Window blinds' curved bottom edges counterpoint the downs' rounded ridge line. Stark and white, the figure of a horse stands, 'almost like a lapel badge',[1] beneath the ridge line in the left window. This chalk horse might be plodding along a shadowed hollow way below its hooves.

When an artist who died fifty years ago finds himself declared 'unjustly neg-lected',[2] we may be sure that his stock is rising. That is true for Eric Ravilious, the man who painted this picture: *Train Landscape*. A generation ago, both John Rothenstein's survey of twentieth-century British art and the Oxford History of English Art ignored his work.[3] So did railway art's standard survey.[4] Geoffrey Grigson's conspectus of British landscape painting reproduced one Ravilious image, but only to assert that he could not reconcile representation with abstraction.[5] Other critics found other limitations. For Bernard Brett, Ravilious' war pictures exhibited 'more concern in exercising a pleasing water-colour technique than in capturing the harsh realities of war'.[6] Ian Jeffrey pre-ferred Ravilious' black-and-white book illustrations to his plain watercolour style, 'for books implied seclusion and reverie, as opposed to the public circum-stances associated with painting'.[7] But Edward Hodnett judged these woodcuts no more than decorations, unable to enhance a written text 'because he was

10.1   Eric Ravilious, *Train Landscape*, 1939

trained as and practised as an industrial designer'.[8] Other judgments damn
these engravings as 'charming', displaying no more than a 'delight for scenes of
rural whimsy'.[9] The years turn, and critical fashion with them. Today, Eric
Ravilious looms more significantly in twentieth-century English art. Richard
Ingleby judges his woodcuts second only to Thomas Bewick's. Paintings set him
in yet more exalted company: 'His place in the history of English art is alongside
Turner, Cotman, Girtin and Towne in the great tradition of English watercolour painters'.[10] Ravilious' two main reputations – as a woodcut engraver and
as a watercolour painter – blend in *Train Landscape*. That sharply etched field
fence, those precisely conjured fabric textures and grained timbers, pun
engraving techniques in a watercolour painting. Ravilious' last civilian watercolours depicted four chalk figures. Two were immemorially old – the
Wilmington Giant and Uffington's white horse. The other two – an equestrian
figure of George III near Weymouth, and (in *Train Landscape* and at least one
other picture) the Westbury horse – date from recent centuries. Proud areas
wiped clean of ink on an engraved print block, these chalk figures' stark white-
ness impresses through absence.

Until recent years *Train Landscape* was exhibited on Aberdeen City Art
Gallery's walls, but rarely seen elsewhere. Now one finds it in all sorts of places,
used to illustrate arguments about landscape, about railway history, about social
history.[11] Worthily seeking to humanise concrete jungles, Messrs Sainsbury dis-
tribute block-mounted prints of this image to schools in their supermarkets'
catchment districts.[12] Today, like so much else that Ravilious produced – ceramic
designs, other watercolours, a few murals, many black and white illustrations[13] –
Train Landscape usually is understood through uninterrogated notions about
Englishness. Thus for Nicholas Faith this picture presents 'the Englishman's ideal
view from a railway carriage – a white horse on the Wiltshire Downs'.[14] Alan
Bennett makes it 'redolent of all the journeys by train I remember, particularly in
my teens and during my National Service, when it was still possible to explore the
English countryside by rail, a period that the foolishness of Dr Beeching put an
end to'.[15] Clearly enough, this painting speaks strongly to many English people of
a certain age. How does *Train Landscape* do this?

Conventions

English railway painting obeys its own conventions. In chapter 2 we saw that
the icon for railways' first tumultuous public impact, J. M. W. Turner's *Rain,
Steam and Speed* (1844), used Burkeian sublimity to express how modernity's

master symbol disturbed culturally embedded English elite conceptions about time, space and social hierarchy. As they roared through the nineteenth and twentieth centuries, railways blended celebration with alarm in many paintings and topographical etchings; but once scars from railway construction had been softened by meadow flowers, and railway travel had come to be taken for granted, trains settled comfortably in painted landscapes no less than in literary narratives. Almost fully domesticated, the railway dragon nestled in English countryside, its appearance modified through plastic surgery. Hamilton Ellis assures us that *Brougham* and *Lowther*, two locomotives built by Robert Stephenson for the Stockton and Darlington Railway in 1860, display 'in the shape of the dome casing, and the sweep from the top of the smokebox to the cylinders, that *Line of Beauty and Grace* which Hogarth drew on the palette of his self-portrait in 1745'.[16] Stephenson's new engines set an imperative standard, Ellis argues. Locomotive design on other British railways rapidly adopted Hogarth's S-curve – entraining them all, we might say, in *The Rake's Progress.*

Eric Ravilious produced railway images other than *Train Landscape*. Three railway scenes appear on items in Wedgwood's 'Travel' dinner service. All display modest trains nestled in landscape settings. All were adapted from designs cut to illustrate L. A. G. Strong's *The Hansom Cab and the Pigeons* (1935).[17] Ravilious' enthusiasm for engraving was fired first at the Royal College of Art, the new Society of Wood Engravers' stronghold. But this society sought to revive – as 'art' – techniques which technical change had rendered obsolete in commercial worlds. Ravilious did produce some commercial engravings (*Wisden*'s title page illustration remains his best-remembered example), but most was undertaken for private presses servicing well-heeled clients. This orientation towards the socially comfortable matched his decisions about where to paint. Apart from a student travelling scholarship to Italy in 1924, brief mural commissions (with his wife Tirzah) at Morecambe in 1933[18] and (with Mary Adshead) at Colwyn Bay the next year, and fleeting painting trips to Bristol, the Brecon Beacons and Normandy in 1938–9, until war service took him further afield he never worked outside London, Essex and deep southern counties from Kent to Wiltshire. Watercolour painting is coded as a peculiarly English practice.[19] Ravilious's peacetime watercolours depict and celebrate Edward Thomas' Channel-hugging 'South Country'.

Viewed through this cosy world's assumptions, *Train Landscape* can seem a cosy painting as it reinforces messages from Ravilious' other railway watercolours. A tiny quarry locomotive chugs cheerfully up a steep gradient in *The Dolly Engine* (1934). *Alpha Cement Works* (1934) shows us the same locomotive snoozing away a summer lunch break. In *Train Going Over a Bridge at Night c.* 1938, a self-important tank engine chuffs pompously straight across the picture space from left to right, hauling two short carriages. In *The Westbury Horse* (*c.* 1939) a tiny train on the distant plain seems set to crash into the downland horse's snout – as if this were a Hornby clockwork tinplate toy, set careering across a bourgeois family's dining room carpet among English versions of Biedermeier furniture.[20]

As Nicholas Faith notes, in *Train Going Over a Bridge at Night,* 'Eric Ravilious enshrines the essentially English notion of even *real* trains as picturesque toys'.[21] Celebrating South Country downland landscape, *Train Landscape* distantly evokes this genteel playfulness. But only distantly: sitting in our strongly realised railway carriage, we no longer look at a puny train from the outside. For the first time in Ravilious' work railways frame landscape, not the reverse. Railways' nineteenth-century sublimity is subdued, but in a manner different from his watercolour images of toy trains. The train in the landscape gives way to the passengers in the compartment.

But we see no passengers in this compartment: merely sagging upholstery on which many human bottoms have rested. Other Ravilious watercolours show

Eric Ravilious, *Train Going Over a Bridge at Night, c.* 1938   **10.2**

us an unsettlingly dispeopled world, but here our discomfort comes from a more proximate cause. Earlier English images invited the viewer to look across a railway carriage in order to enjoy cultivated social comedy as English travellers suffered, more or less complacently, their constrained proximity to persons to whom they had not been introduced.[22]

Robert Musgrave Joy's *Tickets, Please!* showed a railway guard collecting tickets from first-class passengers through a compartment's window. Most passengers stolidly ignore each others' presence. Refracted through more recent *Punch* cartoons, this image was guyed in one of John Tenniel's illustrations for Lewis Carroll's *Through the Looking Glass* (1872). Playing as a pawn in the Red Queen's chess game, Alice's first move rushes her forward two spaces. Quite naturally, she goes by the fastest available transport: railway train. In a 'satirical seminar on space, time and identity in the railway age',[23] she finds herself accompanying strange passengers: an oddly clothed old man, a goat, a beetle, a horse, a gnat. Tenniel shows us the moment when, trying to inspect Alice's ticket, the Guard abandons his telescope and his microscope for a pair of opera glasses.

The genial old man sitting opposite Alice is Benjamin Disraeli,[24] that self-made man who acted as standard-bearer for progress and reason in an otherwise

10.3   Robert Musgrave Joy, *Tickets, Please!* 1851

John Tenniel, *Looking-Glass Insects*, 1872   **10.4**

benighted late-Victorian Tory Party. Appropriately, Tenniel makes him a thoroughly political figure – clothed in *White Paper*, his pyramid-shaped hat hinting at Dizzy's contemporary Egyptian machinations. Who better to accompany Alice in modernity's exemplar: a Victorian railway train ruthlessly cutting through crusted custom? Except that Iain Sinclair's bravura analysis of this 'cartoon surrogate for *Las Meninas*' ruptures simple readings, showing how faithfully Tenniel illustrated Carroll's frantic, half-sublimated sexual fantasies about pre-pubertal Alice's experience in the train's male domain. He shows us Disraeli's goatish beard; his significantly crossed legs; his voyeur's gaze above a blank newspaper. He shows us that thing, 'peculiar and repellant, artichoke-leaved', which pokes from Dizzy's waistcoat pocket. Goats symbolised relentless sexual appetite. Sinclair asks us to note that a Goat sits in this compartment; that this animal's hands rest, steepled, across his stomach (or, perhaps, over his crotch); that Disraeli's raised leg seems to give the Goat 'a mythically engorged member'.[25] We should question only two issues in this analysis. First, Sinclair assumes that since the guard stands at a compartment's window, his train stands at a station. It does not – as so often before corridor coaches were introduced, this guard examines tickets while walking along perilous external footsteps.

That is why he hunkers down with his right elbow hooked over the droplight's frame, braced against his train's movement from right to left across the picture space. Second, Sinclair thinks that the feather in Alice's pork-pie hat connects her to 'the order of birds'. But as Michael Hancher notes, Tenniel nods here to a famous earlier image of female travel in a railway train;[26] an image no less complicated than *Looking-Glass Insects*. Hats of precisely this form rest on both sisters' laps in Leopold Augustus Egg's *The Travelling Companions*, painted ten years before Tenniel put ink to paper. Sitting comfortably in an Italian train, ignoring Mentone's delectable coastal scenery visible through their three first-class carriage windows, these two young women are English. As in *Train Landscape*, their (and our) view of the Italian Riviera is obscured neither by telegraph wires nor the engine's smoke. As with Ravilious' watercolour, Augustus Egg's oil painting suggests calm repose, not rushing progress. Only one gently joggling tassel hints at movement.

Christopher Wood makes *The Travelling Companions* 'perhaps the most delightful of all railway pictures, and the simplest'.[27] That complacent

10.5   Leopold Augustus Egg, *The Travelling Companions*, 1862

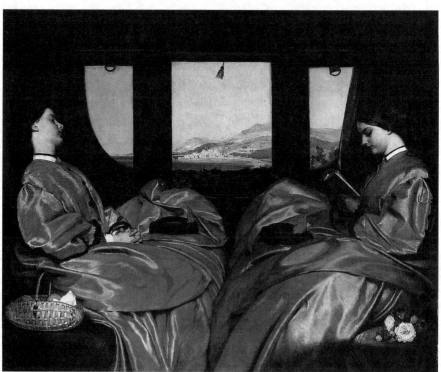

judgement cannot survive Tim Dolin's recent investigation of the double female portrait in Victorian art and literature. He argues that such portraits 'presupposes a particular relationship between the two female figures, and between them and the spectator'.[28] Working out from Daniel Maclise's triple profile sketch of Charles Dickens with his wife Catherine and her sister Georgina, Dolin explores subtly eroticised real and fictive sisterhood in Dickens' 'dark' novels, with *Dombey and Son* not the least of them. This discussion takes him to Egg's painting, which he turns into a Victorian problem picture. As these two English women sit at ease in their subdued but gorgeous dresses, we are invited to explore difference in similarity. The right-hand sister sits demurely, improving her mind with a good book. With her head thrown back against the compartment's partition, her companion in the left-hand seat might be asleep. Or she might be lost in some lascivious daydream: attuned to this painting's code, Victorian observers would have noticed that her dress is not fully buttoned. (And *why* is her leg raised slightly; and *what* is her hand doing?) Dolin suggests that Egg plays subtle variations on male painters' bifurcation of woman as virgins or whores. Recognise this argument, and Christopher Wood's judgement collapses. This is no simple, charming painting. It should disturb us as it disturbed earlier viewers, because '*The Travelling Companions* … strains towards a narrative about both identical and antithetical protagonists, but signifies neither'.[29] A similarly unsettled feeling suffuses *Train Landscape*, but here tension centres on social aspects of modernity, not on gender. Ravilious' empty compartment carries a democratic cargo – notice that huge figure '3' on the door.

In *The Travelling Companions* both sisters ignore celebrated coastal scenery passing their railway carriage's windows. In *Train Landscape* no passenger (other than the painter/spectator) can enjoy downland scenery. That difference apart, here Ravilious nods to Egg: both painters set their easels not quite square to the compartment's side, so that we look forward and to the left. But Ravilious' dispeopled world also nods towards Chirico's dispeopled squares. Turn the page from *Train Landscape* in Constable and Simon's monograph on Ravilious' watercolours and we plunge straight into paintings from the second world war, to events treated as surreal experiences. Planes and ships are conjured as monstrous, alien objects posed against more-or-less natural landscapes, as Ravilious' surrealism modulates through irony, that thoroughly English trope.

Ravilious once yearned to paint a Portsmouth admiral's bicycle, but military authorities decided that an official war artist should paint more offensive subjects.[30] *R. N. A. S. Sick Bay, Dundee* shows us singularly unwarlike – ducklike –

10.6   Eric Ravilious, *R. N.A. S. Sick Bay, Dundee, c.* 1941

mid-grey flying boats wallowing on light grey water, viewed through the windows of a precisely realised and dun-coloured wooden hospital ward. Scarlet stripes on a tiny white ensign provide just one splash of strong colour. Distanced by glazed windows, ironic quirkiness deflates modern war's sublimity. Bombast deflates. Ravilious pulls off just that trick in *Train Landscape*, among his last civilian paintings. This railway carriage could be a triptych's frame, surrounding three sacralised South Country vistas. But skewing his viewpoint shifts the painting's location from church to theatre. This carriage now looks like a triple proscenium, framing sections from a painted backcloth. Could we move around this carriage, shifting relations between foreground and background would destroy Ravilious' careful illusion. He recognises the illusion, and expects that we will share his recognition. Very gently, *Train Landscape* satirises modernity in an old country. Two elements collide in this painting's structure of feeling. Technological sublimity, strongly rooted in conventions governing railway painting, is undercut by irony, by whimsy. It is tempting to make this a reactionary move, celebrating Old England's bones poking through transient modern flesh. This is much too simple. To show why that is, we must consider some work by two twentieth-century English artists who produced celebrated railway drawings: William Heath Robinson and Rowland Emett.

Heath Robinson

Ravilious's use of the technological sublime[31] strongly evokes Heath Robinson: English industrialism's gentle anarchist, 'the greatest comic artist of his time'.[32] Eric Ravilious made himself into a major English black-and-white illustrator. William Heath Robinson (1872–1944) carried that fate in his genes. His grandfather, Thomas Robinson, bound books in Newcastle for Thomas Bewick (and for George Stephenson, apostrophised as The Father of Railways) before moving to London and turning his hand to wood engraving. His son Thomas was apprenticed to a watchmaker, but followed his father into wood engraving before branching out as a newspaper illustrator.[33] By the time Tom, Charles and Heath Robinson had to decide how to earn their livings, there was no decision to take. All three followed their father, becoming illustrators. None contemplated adopting antique activities like cutting a design directly on a wooden block – that skill which Eric Ravilious would be trained to revive. From the 1880s, zinc line blocks transformed commercial art, generating strongly increased demand for drawings in newspapers, magazines and mass market illustrated books.[34] Working in ink on paper, all three Robinson brothers grasped this market opportunity. Heath Robinson absorbed influences from all those prominent (and prosperous) established and rising illustrators whom he met through family connections, through study at Islington School of Art and (briefly) at the Royal Academy Schools, and through many years' membership in the London Sketch Club. Very rapidly, he taught himself to turn out drawings in a wide range of styles to satisfy different commercial clients' demands. His Memorial Exhibition in 1945 proclaimed Robinson 'one of the greatest black-and-white illustrators in the history of art'.[35]

Heath Robinson's range would astonish many people today. Working for book publishers, as a young man he produced creditable pastiches of many leading illustrators' styles. When illustrated books fell from fashion after the First World War, he turned almost wholly to comic drawing. Largely produced for newspapers and magazines, much of this work treated postwar English middle-class people's quiddities. Reduced living space and evaporating domestic servant

cohorts introduced unpleasant novelties for such people. Punning H. G. Wells'
technological utopias, Robinson showed how one might manage in cramped
flats, maisonettes and bungalows. Living space could be increased through ingenious domestic devices derived directly from nineteenth-century patent furniture.[36] Servant labour could be replaced by 'labour-saving' machines.[37]

In these flights of domestic fancy Robinson exploited something which had
grown steadily on him since, many years before, he illustrated Uncle Lubin's
balloon flight in his own book for children:[38] a fascination with bizarre

10.7   William Heath Robinson, *The Bungalow Bedroom*, n.d.

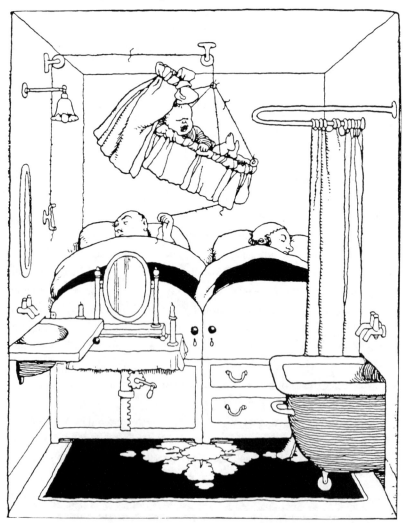

machinery. Today, most people think that Heath Robinson drew nothing but crazy machines constructed largely from second-hand timber and knotted string. That perception is mistaken, but he did produce many images of this kind. Some were produced for magazines. Others were offbeat satires commissioned by commercial companies astute enough to advertise their products through humour. 'Steel girders, Swiss rolls, welding, toffee, paper making, marmalade, asbestos cement, beef essence, motor spirit and lager beer were among the many and diverse subjects to be treated', Robinson recalled. 'As the principles of mechanics are always the same, this variety did not matter very much.'[39] With a bloodline by Frederick Taylor out of Siegfried Giedion,[40] stills from *Metropolis* directed by a man blessed with an anarchic sense of humour, these images satirise conventional manufacturing processes. Intricate divisions of human labour combine with elaborately ingenious and rickety (but always, it seems, *just* technically feasible) machinery. The joke often rests in huge means directed to preposterously tiny ends, as in his *Machine for Testing Artificial Teeth in a Modern Tooth Works*, with its vast rickety crane raising each false tooth before crashing it down on a roast chicken. 'If some lunatic actually built the thing', Furneaux Jordan mused about this drawing, 'it would, one feels, actually function'.[41] Some years ago somebody did build a model of this tooth-testing machine, to accompany an exhibition of Robinson's drawings. That the model captured nothing of the drawing's inspired madness[42] shows that the artist's vision rested in his pen. His drawings drip with understated humour, expressed through understated skill. As critics note, in many mature comic drawings Robinson massed black against white in ways which recall Aubrey Beardsley, his exact contemporary, at the top of his consumptive form in the 1890s.[43]

Heath Robinson's most significant industrial commission came in 1935, when the Great Western Railway Company celebrated its centenary. Most centenary material pouring from the company's pioneer publicity department – a film, *The Romance of a Railway*, radio broadcasts and posters; an essay competition for boys (which such unaccountably large numbers of girls chose to enter) – need not concern us here.[44] But with inspired judgement the GWR also commissioned Heath Robinson to illustrate the railway's history in a shilling paper-covered book. Widely recognised as his most successful single work,[45] *Railway Ribaldry* took the reader through every stage in the GWR's history, from prospecting for a London terminus in the 1830s to the advent of hikers' mystery specials a century later.[46]

As we move from cutting-edge steam age technological innovation in *Building the First Locomotive* (notice the bespectacled and black-coated supervisor in the

right foreground, consulting his blueprint) to integrated transport systems combining steam and internal combustion engines in *The G. W. R. Takes to the Air*,
epic episodes in the railway's history – Brunel's failed atmospheric system, narrowing the broad gauge, the first train (allegedly) to travel at 100 miles per hour,
building Saltash Bridge and the Severn Tunnel – alternate with ingenuities
derived from Robinson's domestic drawings: compartment oil lamps used as feet

10.8   William Heath Robinson, *Building the First Locomotive*, 1935

warmers, deliciously inane suggestions for sleeping, smoking and bathing coaches. Most Heath Robinson industrial drawings treated processes familiar to workers in sponsoring companies, but Greek to the general public: how many lay people knew how asbestos cement was made? *Railway Ribaldry* was different. Blending exasperation with affection, by 1935 British public knowledge about railways' technology was sufficiently developed for a drawing like *Mr. W. Heath*

William Heath Robinson, *The G.W.R. Takes to the Air*, 1935   **10.9**

Robinson's Own Private Railway Engine, not Often Allowed on the G. W. R. to parody small engineering details, not broad processes. Sharing broad common understandings, artist and viewer could join in chuckling at delicate inanities.

As with his other comic mechanical work, to vivify lunatic railway technology Heath Robinson selected a spare style from the wide range which he could command: 'Whatever success these drawings may have had', he insisted,

10.10   William Heath Robinson, *Mr. W. Heath Robinson's Own Private Railway Engine, Not Often Allowed on the G. W. R.*, 1935

was not only due to the fantastic machinery and devices, and to the absurd situations, but to the style in which they were drawn. This was designed to imply that the artist had complete belief in what he was drawing. He was seeing no joke in the matter, in fact he was part of the joke. For this purpose, a rather severe style was used, in which everything was laboriously and clearly defined. There could be no doubt, mystery, or mere suggestion about something in which you implicitly believed, and of this belief it was necessary to persuade the spectator. At the slightest hint that the artist was amused, the delicate fabric of humour would fade away.[47]

This severe style recalled engineering drawing practice. Awed by technical specialists in companies whose products he was hired to advertise, Robinson was heartened to see the delight with which those experts examined drawings remarkably little removed from the blueprints with which they were so familiar. 'Nothing pleased them more', he recalled, 'than to see that which had held them so tyrannically treated with levity'.[48] But Robinson trammels his levity. Colin Voake makes him 'the Wodehouse of art, effortless and urbane'.[49] The comparison is apt, but not in the way Voake intends. P. G. Wodehouse was another exquisite comic craftsman. Slaving long and hard to construct massively intricate plots, he planned precisely the right moment to nudge a plot's cog into mesh. Plum's fiction then lurched forward like any Heath Robinson machine, with mayhem spreading as articulating sprockets activated one crosscutting subplot after another. Glorious confusion rolled onward, beyond human control. (Always prepared to restore order for a trousered fiver, Jeeves is ein Übermensch – as Bertie Wooster well realised.) Building his finely engineered plots and expressing them through twentieth-century English's finest prose style, Wodehouse despised whimsy. Astute businessman though he (or, actually, his wife Ethel) was,[50] he refused to write for *Punch* while the egregiously whimsical Owen Seaman influenced editorial policy.[51] Heath Robinson deprecated whimsy just as firmly. His comic accounts of manufacturing processes address a central modernist conundrum: how can humane values survive in a mechanical age? His big machines may strike us as wildly hilarious but, like those Wodehouse characters unwisely caught singing 'Sonny Boy' for the fourth or fifth time at a tough east end Lads Club concert,[52] Robinson's machine operators do not smile. We readers and viewers roll about with laughter; but we are not being pelted with fruit and vegetables, nor working furiously to match some worm-eaten industrial treadmill's pace. Furneaux Jordan noticed that 'As Heath Robinson's machines and gadgets became more and more absurd and elaborate, … the more solemn and recognisable become the machine-minders'.[53] Those minders had to concentrate completely on their absurd jobs, or (like Chaplin in *Modern Times*) the machines they served would devour them.

Rowland Emett

In *Train Landscape*, Eric Ravilious' theatrical railway carriage nods to Heath Robinson's talent in pointing up technological sublimity's absurd side. With conflict looming clearly, we are invited to contemplate how humane values might survive mechanised warfare. But the charm in *Train Landscape* takes us away from Robinson. As we saw, he despised whimsy. In interwar Britain one turned automatically to *Punch* for whimsy.[54] Although *Nellie*, his most famous creation, first steamed across its pages on 8 March 1944, eighteen months after the aircraft carrying Eric Ravilious disappeared off Iceland, Rowland Emett (1906–90) drew his first *Punch* cartoon in 1939. Painted in the same year, *Train Landscape* anticipates Emett's determined attempt to tame railways' sublimity through whimsy.

In many drawings from the 1940s and 1950s (only a fraction of them treating railway subjects), Rowland Emett nurtured *Punch*'s smug prejudices. That English generalised Other, Foreigners, generated an automatic snigger. Big Four private railway companies might have their faults, but Emett insists that wartime control by government committees – let alone postwar nationalisation – must be worse.[55] Many images flatter London commuters, conventionally clad in bowler hats, black jackets and striped trousers. These, he suggests, were England's most abused citizens in wartime, and in austere subsequent years. Beyond noting that they offer strong evidence of social closure among *Punch*-reading classes, none of these drawings need concern us here. That abnegation ceases when *Nellie* chuffs into view. Consider a somewhat later drawing, *Locomotive No 3 (Hector) at Mrs Bristow's Folly, now used as a Water-Tower*.

This is mock-heroic (note the engine's name) mock-Gothic. Tortured trees frame indolent action. Spindly enclosures house forbidding statuary. An owl roosts in the water tower's topmost turret. A broken masonry arch extends from the tower over the railway track, bearing a water pipe. The mechanism for delivering water to *Hector*'s tanks nods to Heath Robinson; but every other element in this drawing screams *The Castle of Otranto*. Like all other chunks in this ramshackle railway's equipment, *Hector* matches Mrs Bristow's mock-Gothic folly. As in so many other Emett railway drawings, as in John Appleby's interminable Sunday cross-country train journey (characterised by a fellow passenger, that advanced and forward sculptress Judith Raven, as 'an Emett train lurking in the

Rowland Emett, *Locomotive No 3 (Hector) at Mrs. Bristow's Folly, Now Used as a Water-Tower*, 1949

10.11

pages of *Punch*[56]) the modern and the dangerous have been tamed here, turned ancient and fantastical.

Bevis Hillier once asked Rowland Emett

how he saw himself in relation to Heath Robinson. He pondered a moment and then said, 'some years ago *The Sunday Times* did an article to explain me and wrote: "He is, of course, the Heath Robinson of today."' Not long ago, in an article on the work of Heath Robinson, they neatly tucked in any loose ends by remarking: "He was, of course, the Emett of his day."[57]

Neat, but much too simple. Like Robinson, Emett had family connections with black-and-white illustration: his paternal grandfather was court engraver to Queen Victoria. He, too, had brief art school training, this time in Birmingham. There the parallels cease. With his hard, clear line, his sharp alternation of black and white, his formal preference for straightforward (if battered) squares and circles, his robust delight in hand-knitted mechanical contrivances, Heath Robinson's industrial cartoons look back to technical illustrators: many of his drawings would not look out of place in a deluded nineteenth century volume of *The Engineer*. Despite some years spent working in an engineering company and wartime work as an aeronautical draughtsman, with his 'spidery, filigree style'[58] and wash shading Rowland Emett casts a wistful glance back to Victorian illustrators working in artistic and literary, not engineering, domains. Some drawings yearn after George Cruikshank.[59] In *Mr William Funnell's Final Gesture of Defiance in the Face of Nationalisation*, he parodies Gustav Doré's vision of Arthur's last voyage, from the 1868 edition of Tennyson's *Idylls of the King*. *Hero*, a *Nellie*-class engine, lies in state on a sombre barque, with her funnel adapted as the boat's mast. Purloined from a passing fish truck, tarpaulin sails hang limply in the evening calm. Using a railway signal as an oar, William Funnell charts a tearful course for the sunset as three grieving railwaymen wave farewell from the shore.

Like Q's *The Wonder of the Age*, Emett's *Nellie*, *Hector*, *Hero* and their friends[60] are tiny brass-bound steam engines with enormously long chimneys. They work the Far Twittering and Oyster Creek Railway in Cloud Cuckoo Valley, trundling rotting and weedy tracks from Far Twittering through Wisteria Halt, Paddlecombe, Prawnmouth, Friars Ambling, King's Bedpost, St. Torpid's Creek and Little Figment to Oyster Creek. So remote is this line, and so antiquated its equipment, that it escapes nationalisation in 1947. Just like the ramshackle light railway empire operated by Colonel Holman Stephens ('a spiv who ran a number of decrepit, unremunerative country railways using a collection of totally unsuitable secondhand equipment'),[61] which escaped the Grouping of many different British railway companies into the Big Four one generation earlier. Which thrusting modern industrial concern could covet this disarticulated collection of twisted ruins? Discovering one of the colonel's rotting South Country branch lines (the delightfully-named Hundred of Manhood and Selsey Tramway) gave Rowland Emett the starting point for his Far Twittering branch;[62] though he underlined his point by turning a standard

Rowland Emett, *Mr. William Funnell's Final Gesture of Defiance in the Face of*   **10.12**
Nationalisation, 1949

gauge railway into a narrow gauge railway (in contemporary journalists' parlance, a 'toy' line). Whimsy rules every action on this line, with sublimity
reduced to vanishing point. Like Heath Robinson's drivers, firemen and guards
in *Railway Ribaldry*, William Funnell and his workmates do not smile. But
Robinson's rubicund workers are busy, their attention concentrated on performing minutely specified (if frequently imbecile) tasks. Long-jawed and

big-eyed, Emett's spindly railway workers remain conspicuously idle. They stare mournfully at the viewer. They know that their labour is futile, their railway doomed. Modernity is no more than an ancient rumour on the Far Twittering and Oyster Creek Railway. Only once does *Nellie* rise from depressed torpor. Tired of Cuckoo Valley inhabitants' indifference to their railway, in *Nellie Come Home!* (1952), a book written for children, she sets sail westward with her footplate crew. They all land safely in the USA. There, technological sublimity still rules – with railways retaining their nineteenth century reputation for power and terror. Poor little *Nellie* finds herself spreadeagled across a huge American steam locomotive's pilot, like the wistfully passive heroine in a silent movie. But a little terror goes a long way in the South Country. Emett's engine and crew soon are sated by exhilarating novelty. Yearning for the quotidian, they return to heroes' welcomes in boring little England. To their delight, Cuckoo Valley folk missed them sorely while they were away. The Far Twittering branch poddles on towards a timeless future, powered by ancient steam locomotives. *Such* a comforting message for *Punch* subscribers.

Unlike Heath Robinson's comic work, Rowland Emett's drawings translated smoothly into three dimensions. From the early 1950s he enjoyed a new career constructing 'Gothick-Kinetic Things' for corporate clients and film companies.[63] His introduction to this work, and his railway apotheosis, came with the 1951 Festival of Britain. There, in a corner of a resolutely modernist exhibition build on a South bank bomb site, the Attlee government's attempt to call a new Britain, Phoenix-like, from war's flames, he was invited to contrive a refuge for visitors suffering from modernism overload.[64] Making his *Punch* drawings flesh in the Far Tottering and Oyster Creek Railway made Emett world-famous. One visitor fondly remembered 'that extraordinarily whimsical railway system of which the locomotives, *Nellie, Neptune* and *Wildgoose*, were compounded of rum barrels, divers' helmets, Cranford tea kettles and other objects of inspired improvisation. On the wittily designed stations were forbidding notices: "Do NOT tease the engines"; "WARNING: when Red Lobster is hoisted, Tide is OUT"; (at the entrance to a tunnel) "Do NOT feed the Bats'" and that petulant one – "Trains cross here, so THERE."'[65] Privately promoted, this little railway was a huge financial success, recouping its capital cost within three weeks.[66] As the three engines trundled their trains along a one-third mile track, offering passengers startling prospects of a Wellsian future in the middle distance (the Skylon, the Dome of Discovery),[67] so arcadian attitudes to railways congealed. The British railway heritage industry was born on the Far Tottering line, threading its fake-antique course among temples to modern teleology.

Conceptual paradoxes matched physical incongruities. Those steam outline locomotives were powered by the last enemy, internal combustion engines. Whimsical interpretations of early steam-age superstructures were entirely cosmetic, held together with the latest epoxy glues.[68] Fake called to fake. Nineteenth-century railway sublimity irrupted only once. 'The tragedy which took place on Wednesday 11 July [1952] had nothing to do with the railway's design', we learn, 'but with human error, where two of the engines were accidentally driven on to the same track and came into a head-on collision. Fire broke out, a number of children were injured and one woman died in the wreckage'.[69] Death obtrudes through whimsy.

Ravilious revisited

Eric Ravilious had been dead for eleven years when Rowland Emett's festival railway turned its first wheel. *Train Landscape* compounds power with whimsy; but not in any stable manner. In 1939, charm softened an image speaking principally to humanists' concerns about how to preserve human integrity in a manufactured world. This was Heath Robinson's great comic theme. But one modern judgement makes Ravilious' glimpse of the Westbury Horse and sweeping downland seen through the window of an empty railway carriage demean the past, reducing historical experience 'to a decorative place in modern life'.[70] With railways' technological sublime all but evaporated, today we must be tempted to read *Train Landscape* through the remarkably well developed British railway heritage industry's sentimental celebration of glorious dead days. A host of later interventions modified this image more or less profoundly, but the basic pattern was laid down by Rowland Emett. *Train Landscape* showed Eric Ravilious meditating on relations between humankind and a man-made but inhuman technology. His rising public and critical reputation in our time exposes him to recruitment for a politics concerned to reassure us that – with eyes firmly averted from Britain's third-rank international status, and from technical challenges inflecting old difficulties in new ways – there always was an England.[71]

There is little doubt that Ravilious would not have chosen to march in this company. Our current image of this artist was formed by two books: Freda Constable's and Sue Simon's monograph on his watercolours (with its significant title, *The England of Eric Ravilious*), and Helen Binyon's loving, reticent and subtly disingenuous memoir of her friend.[72] Binyon tells a simple story. Born in 1903, the son of a failed Acton draper turned scarcely more successful

Eastbourne antique dealer, Eric Ravilious won scholarships to Eastbourne School of Art and then, in 1922, to the Royal College of Art in London. Here he took an important part in that college's contemporary 'outbreak of talent'. Fellow students included Henry Moore, Raymond Coxon, Barbara Hepworth and Enid Marx; but Ravilious linked up most strongly with Edward Bawden and Douglas Bliss.[73] All three had been mightily impressed by watercolours recently exhibited by Paul and John Nash. Both older men became Ravilious' friends; Paul Nash taught him. After finishing his studies, Ravilious worked mostly as an illustrator while teaching part time – first in Eastbourne, then at the RCA and Oxford. He beguiled Tirzah Garwood, his brightest and most beautiful Eastbourne student. Her retired lieutenant-colonel father and the memsahib eventually were charmed into consenting that this arriviste dauber might wed their daughter, in 1930. Three children arrived over the next decade. Eric and Tirzah scraped a modest living from art (and, in her case, also from craftwork).[74] In the mid-1930s a former RCA fellow-student who now headed Wedgwood's design team, Victor Skellern, persuaded his directors to commission designs from Eric Ravilious. As should any proper 1930s artist, Ravilious complained that Wedgwood chose to produce his least interesting and adventurous patterns; but what little earthenware and china did reach the shops is highly appreciated by today's collectors, and commands high prices.[75] Together with Eric Bawden and his wife, the Raviliouses divided their time between London flats and a country cottage in Great Bardfield, Essex.[76] Later, Eric and Tirzah found their own rural Essex pied à terre at Castle Hedingham. In 1941 they rented Ironbridge Farm at Shalton, near Braintree, paying half the rent to their landlord (the Labour politician John Strachey) in Eric's pictures.[77] From 1934 frequent visits took Eric, at least, to Peggy Angus' Sussex cottage, Furlongs. Ravilious rooted out two abandoned horse-drawn Crimean War fever wagons from local ditches, then arranged for them to be secreted in undergrowth near Furlongs. One was fitted up as a bedroom, the other as a studio.[78] He recorded all these places' quiddities as watercolour painting overtook engraving in his work. Helen Binyon makes Eric Ravilious jog along in Bohemian comfort until war arrived in 1939. He then became an official war artist, producing highly distinguished watercolour images until his plane vanished off Iceland in September 1942. That mysterious disappearance, with his maturing skill rudely abrupted, completes Binyon's disarmingly plain story.

Richard Ingleby called his recent celebration of Ravilious' work 'Doomed youth'. That was perceptive. Thirty nine might seem rather old still to be a doomed youth, but Helen Binyon constructs an art school version of the gilded

Oxbridge undergraduate: an extravagantly talented overgrown adolescent. Ingleby's title comes from a poem by Wilfred Owen, whose own death in early November 1918 underscored his poems' attack on war's futility. Soon enough those poems were recruited to a wider claim: that interwar Britain's economic and political performance was so dismal because all those public school boys and Oxbridge undergraduates turned infantry subalterns, one entire generation's natural leaders, died in Flanders' fields. Fought through movement rather than trench warfare's static slaughter (on western fronts, at least), the Second World War did not conduce to this 'lost generation' social myth. In English visual arts, Eric Ravilious' mysterious disappearance alone refreshed the archetype. No surprise, then, that Helen Binyon should conjure Ravilious ('the Boy' to fellow students) as a very English jeune doré – spending much more time in the students' common room than the studio, entrancing every pretty girl with his 'almost Pan-like charm', turning out fine work in widely different media with little apparent effort,[79] so wrapped in being an English artist that he had no time to chatter about theory or politics, those continental distractions.

Helen Binyon claimed that interwar art theory washed over Eric Ravilious without effect. As a good commonsensical English artist, he proved immune to surrealism's and abstraction's siren songs. But Paul Nash, his mentor and friend, took a close interest in surrealism. Ravilious' own watercolours depict eerie, surreally dispeopled landscapes. Binyon asserts that Ravilious was utterly unpolitical – then notes that he contributed pictures to 'Artists against Fascism' exhibitions in 1937 and 1938. She quotes him muttering that each week's *Statesman* got more depressing. Sixty years ago, reading each week's issue of *The New Statesman* signified a firm political position, of a decided colour. Viewed through these spectacles, *Train Landscape* looks a rather different painting. Always fascinated by interaction between humanity and landscape, no passengers ride in Ravilious' compartment; but everything which we observe – white horse, cropped downs, harvested fields, carpentered fence, coach-built railway carriage – was created by human labour. We do not know the names of the people who made all these things, but that matters not a jot. In Augustus Egg's *The Travelling Companions* or Robert Musgrave Joy's *Tickets, Please!* we see precisely depicted individual passengers. These are first-class compartments, refuges for people who expect to appear in written history. By picturing an empty but well-used third-class carriage Ravilious celebrates many generations of English common people's work. Hidden from history, these people made the world which we see, and in which Ravilious lives: 'inside the carriage he glories in the ingenuity of modern man'.[80] Like that stark white horse these people's anonymous ubiquity informs this image through absence: how could any painter crowd into one compartment everybody whose fruitful labour went to make this scene?[81] English nationalist readings of *Train Landscape* emphasise cultural continuities between Wiltshire downland – among the earliest sites for human settlement in the country – and a railway system sliding into historical irrelevance. Viewed from different assumptions, this painting shows us a world made by millenia of English labour, but now (in 1939) threatened by German fascism. Ravilious uses resources provided by two previous generations' celebration of the South Country to celebrate an inclusive common culture which must be defended in the coming war. This celebration has its national element, of course; but it directs our attention to class as much as nation. Why else should Ravilious give that huge figure '3' such prominence in his design? *Train Landscape* anticipates the vision which certain Left historians and critics – Edward Thompson; Richard Hoggart; above all, perhaps, Raymond Williams – tried to conjure after the war which killed Eric Ravilious: an English (or, for Williams, an Anglo-Welsh) world nourished by most people's lived experience, a world celebrating a common culture inherited from the past but informing both present and future.[82] Ravilious did not live to see those people write out their vision. Perhaps the most disquieting thing about looking at *Train Landscape* today is our suspicion that this noble vision has followed the Great Western Railway's matchboarded carriage into history's dustbin.

Notes

1   Ian Jeffrey, *The British Landscape, 1920–1950,* London, Thames & Hudson, 1984, p. 14.

2   Nicholas Faith, *Classic Trains,* London, Boxtree, 1997, p. 21.

3   John Rothenstein, *British Art Since 1900,* London, Phaidon, 1962; Dennis Farr, *English Art: 1870–1940,* Oxford, Oxford University Press, 1978.

4   C. Hamilton Ellis, *Railway Art,* Boston, New York Graphic Society, 1977.

5   Geoffrey Grigson, *Britain Observed: the Landscape through Artists' Eyes,* London, Phaidon 1975, p. 168.

6   Bernard Brett, *A History of Watercolour,* London, Optimum, 1984, pp. 207, 209.

7   Jeffrey, *British Landscape,* p. 15.

8   Edward Hodnett, *Five Centuries of English Book Illustration,* Aldershot, Scolar Press, 1988, p. 277. For full details on Ravilious' work as an engraver, see J. M. Richards, *The Wood Engravings of Eric Ravilious,* London, Lion and Unicorn Press, 1972.

9   Hodnett, *Five Centuries,* pp. 277–8; Richard T. Godfrey, *Printmaking in Britain: a General History from its Beginnings to the Present Day,* Oxford, Phaidon, 1978, p. 122.

10 Richard Ingleby, 'Doomed youth', *Art Review*, no. 48, April 1996, pp. 23, 26. See also Patricia Andrew, *Eric Ravilious, 1903–42: a Re-Assessment of his Life and Work*, Eastbourne, Towner Art Gallery, 1986.

11 Denis Cosgrove, *Social Formation and Symbolic Landcape*, second edition, Madison, University of Wisconsin Press, 1998, p. 265; Nicholas Faith, *Locomotion: the Railway Revolution,* London, BBC, 1993, p. 191. Jack Simmons (ed.), *Railways: an Anthology*, London, Collins, 1991 carries a photograph of a gleaming Patrick Stirling single on its front cover – and *Train Landscape* on its back cover.

12 Alan Bennett, 'Four paintings', *London Review of Books*, 2 April 1998, pp. 7–10.

13 Caroline Palmer, 'Small pieces of England', *Design*, no 455, November 1986, p. 44; Anon, 'Eric Ravilious', *Ceramic Review*, no 103, 1987, p. 9; Alan Powers, 'Country life', *Crafts*, no. 143, November/December 1996, p. 36.

14 Faith, *Locomotion*, p. 191.

15 Bennett, 'Four paintings', pp. 9–10.

16 C. Hamilton Ellis, *The Beauty of Old Trains*, London, Allen & Unwin, 1952, p. 51.

17 Richard Dennis, *Ravilious and Wedgwood: the Complete Wedgwood Designs of Eric Ravilious,* Shepton Beauchamp, Dennis, 1995, p. 48.

18 Decorating public rooms in the LMS's celebrated (but now-disgraced) moderne Midland Hotel.

19 As in all those Golden Age country house whodunnits. To take one example from many, Joanna Cannan, *Murder Included* [1950], Harmondsworth, Penguin, 1958, p. 145 shows us an East Sussex Palladian mansion's bedrooms defiled with 'water-colour landscapes by a Victorian Lady d'Estray'.

20 Freda Constable and Sue Simon, *The England of Eric Ravilious*, London, Scolar Press, 1982, plates 6, 27, 37.

21 Faith, *Classic Trains*, p. 21. Original emphasis.

22 Hence the furore caused by the first version of Abraham Solomon's *First Class – the Meeting* (1854), where a young woman talks to a young man while her father slumbers. Solomon was forced to paint a second version, with the two men talking while the maiden gazes adoringly from a distant corner. See Jack Simmons, *The Victorian Railway*, London, Thames & Hudson, 1991, p. 128.

23 Ian Christie, *The Last Machine: Early Cinema and the Birth of the Modern World*, London, British Film Institute, 1994, p. 17. And, of course, on conventional Victorian parallels between a railway journey and a life's journey,

24 Martin Gardner (ed.), *The Annotated Alice* [1960], Harmondsworth, Penguin, 1965, p. 218. Hamilton Ellis (*Railway Art*, 79) restores the political balance, reproducing a delicious cartoon parody of W. P. Frith's *The Railway Station* (1863) which shows shifty Gladstone arrested while Queen Victoria sweeps along Paddington's platform 4.

25 Iain Sinclair, *Downriver*, London, Pimlico, 1991, pp. 178–83.

26 Michael Hancher, *The Tenniel Illustrations to the "Alice" Books*, Ames, Ohio State University Press, 1985, p. 86.

27 Christopher Wood, *Victorian Panorama: Paintings of Victorian Life*, London, Faber & Faber, 1976, p. 212.

28 Tim Dolin, 'Companion pieces: Dickens' sister-travellers', *Word & Image*, 10, 1994, p. 107.

29 *Ibid.*, p. 113.

30 Ingleby, 'Doomed youth', pp. 24–6.

31 A term elaborated in David Nye, *American Technological Sublime*, Cambridge, Mass., MIT Press, 1994.

32 R. Furneaux Jordan, 'Introduction', to W. Heath Robinson, *The Penguin Heath Robinson*, Harmondsworth, Penguin, 1966, unpaginated.

33 W. Heath Robinson, *My Line of Life* [1938], Wakefield, E. P. Publishing, 1974, pp. 3–5, 8–9.

34 John Lewis, *Heath Robinson: Artist and Comic Genius*, London, Constable, 1973, pp. 43–4.

35 Jordan, 'Introduction' to *Penguin Heath Robinson*.

36 Siegfried Giedion, *Mechanisation Takes Command: a Contribution to Anonymous History*, New York, Oxford University Press, 1948, pp. 389–481.

37 Hence the proposed 800-square-metre 'World of Heath Robinson' exhibition, 'with a full-scale walk-through house full of labour-saving devices, and a 1930s street with shops, a cinema, a sports centre and a driving school'. See P. Antonelli, 'The absurd world of Heath Robinson', *Arbitare*, no. 307, 1997, p. 182.

38 W. Heath Robinson, *The Adventures of Uncle Lubin*, London, Grant Richards, 1902.

39 Robinson, *Line of Life*, p. 176.

40 Frederick W. Taylor, *The Principles of Scientific Management*, New York, Harper, 1915; Giedion, *Mechanisation Takes Command*.

41 Jordan, 'Introduction' to *Penguin Heath Robinson*.

42 Colin Voake, review of W. Heath Robinson exhibition at Prescot Museum, Merseyside, *Crafts*, no. 76, September-October 1985, pp. 50–1.

43 See, for example, Lewis, *Heath Robinson*, pp. 50–1, 133.

44 See Roger Burdett Wilson, *Go Great Western: a History of GWR Publicity*, Newton Abbott, David and Charles, 1970.

45 Jordan, 'Introduction' to *Penguin Heath Robinson*; Lewis, *Heath Robinson*, p. 176.

46 W. Heath Robinson, *Railway Ribaldry*, Paddington, Great Western Railway, 1935. A facsimile edition was published in London by Duckworth in 1974.

47 Robinson, *Line of Life*, pp. 106–7.

48 *Ibid.*, p. 176.

49 Voake, review, p. 51.

50 Frances Donaldson, *P. G. Wodehouse: a Biography*, London, Weidenfeld and Nicolson, 1982, p. 97.

51 R. B. D. French, *P. G. Wodehouse*, Edinburgh, Oliver & Boyd, 1966, p. 112.

52 P. G. Wodehouse, 'Jeeves and the song of songs', in Wodehouse, *Very Good Jeeves!* [1930], reprinted in Wodehouse, *Life With Jeeves*, Harmondsworth, Penguin, 1981, pp. 418–34.

53 Jordan, 'Introduction' to *Penguin Heath Robinson*. Ian Hunt's sour essay ('Cranes, chains and automobiles', *New Stateman and Society*, 16 September 1994) berates

Robinson's industrial drawings. They put great effort into illustrating 'some disappointing cause such as manufacturing fish paste', he claims. All those blank-faced workers 'test whether the results are up to standard, rather than … show any excitement that the patent might be taken up'. Ah, New Labour's thrusting entrepreurial delights! Has everybody on the *Statesman* outgrown whiskery ideas like alienation?

54 E. V. Knox succeeded Seaman in 1932, but not until Malcolm Muggeridge took the editor's chair in 1953 was Seaman's stifling whimsical taste challenged. See R. G. G. Price, *A History of Punch*, London, Collins, 1957. Rowland Emett's last piece for *Punch* appeared in the June 1953 Coronation issue.

55 See his introduction (written in a spidery hand from The Flanges, Gently-Round-the-Bend at 4 o'clock 1949) to Rowland Emett, *Buffer's End*, London, Faber & Faber, 1949: 'The ruthless Nationalisation of our Prime Movers inevitably leads one to ponder forms of Private Transport not so easily tampered with'.

56 Michael Innes, *Appleby's End*, London, Gollancz, 1946, p. 14.

57 Bevis Hillier, 'Foreword', to Rowland Emett, *The Early Morning Milk Train: the Cream of Emett Railway Drawings*, London, Murray, 1976.

58 Anon, 'Rowland Emett', in Deborah Andrews (ed.), *The Annual Obituary 1990*, Chicago and London, St. James Press, 1991, p. 680.

59 Notably one drawing from *Buffer's End* [1949], in which two Fitzrovian poets lounge in a flower-decked countryside, composing odes. 'I suppose it's psychoneurosis', one tells the other, 'but I've got an awful feeling of something nasty creeping up on me'. Unseen behind them, a monstrous train sheds a hard line of prefabs across the South Country. Here Emett looks back very directly to Cruikshank's anathema on urban sprawl, *London Going Out of Town* [1818], and his attack on the Railway Mania, *The Railway Dragon* [c1845].

60 *Wanderer, Plato, Lotus* (working the Lazybeach Special); *Tawny Pipit* (working a bird-watcher's special); *Dormouse* (a tiny engine fast asleep, but not in a teapot); *Pablo* (filling an export order for Mexico); *Sun God* (a solar-powered steam locomotive used only in summer months when postwar fuel economy regulations bear particularly heavily); *Dr Syn* (her name filched from a Pacific on the 15-inch gauge Romney, Hythe and Dymchurch Railway); *Bard of Avon, Robert the Bruce* and *Owen Glendower* (in a drawing vilifying railway nationalisation).

61 Paul Waters, 'Introduction', to John Scott-Morgan, *Railways of Arcadia: a Photographic Survey of the Colonel Stephens Railways*, Bromley, Waters, 1989, p. 5. A challenging assignment for any student art historian would be to link Holman Stephens' shambling railway imperialism to his pre-Raphaelite father's art work. But F. G. Stephens did manage to offend the Brotherhood by suggesting (in an article in *Germ*) that they should take modern machinery seriously. See Ellis, *Railway Art*, p. 76.

62 Complete with mechanical lunacies like *Ringing Rock*, the line's one operational locomotive (two others lay beyond resuscitation), having to be helped on her limping way with the fireman's crowbar for three weeks after one of her two cylinders failed: see Vic Michell and Keith Smith, *Branch Line to Selsey*, Midhurst, Middleton, 1983; David Bathurst, *The Selsey Tram*, Chichester, Phillimore, 1992.

For a lightly fictionalised account of this railway see James Kenward, *The Manewood Line*, London, Paul 1939.

63   Eric Keown, 'Emett', *Graphis*, 42, 1952, pp. 292–301.

64   Denying Robert Hewison's determination (in her view) to shoehorn fake 'heritage' into everything, the 1951 Festival's most recent history conjures it as a smoothly uniform modernist and social democratic celebration: Becky Conekin, '"Here is the modern world itself: the Festival of Britain's representation of the future', in Becky Conekin, Frank Mort and Chris Waters (eds), *Moments of Modernity: Reconstructing Britain, 1945–1964*, London, Rivers Oram, 1999, pp. 228–46. Oddly enough, but surely fortunately, this account entirely overlooks Rowland Emett's little railway.

65   Hillier, 'Foreword' to Emett, *Early Morning Milk Train*. Far Twittering had to become Far Tottering because the comedian Gillie Potter held an unexpected lien on the earlier name. Not everybody was entranced by Emett's fancy. William Feaver ('Festival star', in Mary Banham and Bevis Hillier (eds), *A Tonic to the Nation: the Festival of Britain 1951*, London, Thames & Hudson, 1976, p. 53) thought it 'so deliberately whimsical as to be almost beyond a joke'.

66   Harry Barlow from Southport held the concession; and his workshops built the three locomotives and their rolling stock. See Jacqui Grossart, *Rowland Emett: from 'Punch' to 'Chitty-Chitty-Bang-Bang and Beyond*, London, Chris Beetles, 1988, pp. 9–10. In an interview published posthumously in *Railway World* (April 1991, p. 219) Rowland Emett claimed that his festival railway's revenues were exceeded only by the neighbouring funfair's Big Dipper.

67   With benefit of hindsight, Reyner Banham thought this incongruity less marked than it seemed at the time. 'What now seems so striking about [the Emett train] is that while it … makes visual reference to beloved English topics – in this case George Stephenson, dead seagulls, Heath Robinson and faked-up period detailing – it does so within a general idiom of skinny and tapering space-enclosing frame-works and curved roofs that is far closer than any of us could see at the time to the "international" style of the more serious structures on the South Bank:' Banham, 'The style: flimsy … effeminate?' (in Banham and Hillier (eds), *Tonic to the Nation*, p. 191).

68   Anon, 'Araldite in Emett models', *CIBA Technical Notes*, February 1969.

69   Frank Taylor, 'The temple of mystery, Battersea', in Banham and Hillier (eds), *Tonic to the Nation*, p. 175. See also Don Rowlands, 'The Emett festival railway', *Narrow Gauge*, no. 102, 1988, p. 8.

70   Constable and Simon, *England of Eric Ravilious*, p. 30.

71   Cosgrove (*Social Formation and Symbolic Landscape*, pp. 264–5) makes *Train Landscape* a heritage icon, a deeply conservative painting celebrating private owner-ship disguised through common values. *Post hoc ergo propter hoc* is not good logic. I show below why I think Cosgrove's interpretation mistaken.

72   Helen Binyon, *Eric Ravilious: Memoir of an Artist*, Guildford, Lutterworth Press, 1983. Disingenuous because, to take the most important matter, Binyon always presents Eric, his wife Tirzah and their three children as a carefree bohemian family.

Alan Bennett ('Four paintings', p. 8) reports how much he likes Eric's watercolour *Tea at Furlongs*, 'which was the Raviliouses' Sussex home'. Far from it. Furlongs was an isolated farm cottage rented by Peggy Angus. Ravilious and Helen Binyon had been students together at the RCA, but lost touch. Peggy Angus brought them back together. Tirzah certainly visited Furlongs in 1934, but Eric's many later visits were made to meet Binyon, with whom he conducted a flaming affair for five years. In 1938 Binyon's concern for Tirzah forced an end to this relationship. See Richard Morphet, 'Eric Ravilious and Helen Binyon', in Binyon, *Eric Ravilious*, pp. 14–15. Had Helen Binyon not died before her book saw the press, we would know none of this.

73 Constable and Simon, *England of Eric Ravilious*, p. 14. 'Outbreak of talent' was Paul Nash's phrase. Appropriately enough, Ravilious' rare excursion into oil painting ('Edward Bawden Working in his Studio' [c1930]) is reproduced as the frontispiece to Paul Huxley (ed.), *Exhibition Road: Painters at the Royal College of Art*, London, Christie's and the Royal College of Art, 1988.

74 Despite his status as a coming man in the British art world, Eric Ravilous never brought home more than £300 a year: H. S., *Tirzah Garwood, 1908–1951*, Eastbourne, Towner Art Gallery, 1987, unpaginated.

75 Dennis, *Ravilious and Wedgwood*; Peter Williams, *Wedgwood: a Collector's Guide*, London, Quantum Books, 1992.

76 Powers, 'Country life' discusses the artistic colony which Eric Bawden formed at Great Bardfield. In sharp contrast to Helen Binyon's fine art-focussed account, Powers links Bawden – and, through him, Eric and Tirzah Ravilious – back to the Arts and Crafts movement.

77 Binyon, *Eric Ravilious*, p. 129; *Who Was Who, 1941–1950*, p. 956.

78 Peggy Angus, 'Furlong and friends', in Anon (ed.), *Furlongs: Peggy Angus and Friends*, Eastbourne, Towner Art Gallery, 1987, unpaginated.

79 The reality was different. His wife remembered that he tore up three or four watercolours for each one which satisfied his fastidious taste: Andrew, *Eric Ravilious*, p. 21.

80 Constable and Simon, *England of Eric Ravilious*, p. 30.

81 This suggests that it might be fruitful to read *Train Landscape* through Ford Madox Ford's *Work* (1852–63): a painting which seeks to encompass English social life through inclusion.

82 Richard Hoggart, *The Uses of Literacy*, London, Chatto & Windus, 1957; Raymond Williams, *Culture and Society*, London, Chatto & Windus, 1958; E. P. Thompson, *The Making of the English Working Class*, London, Gollancz, 1963.

11

Return ticket
to postmodernism?

Like wagons sitting on a marshalling yards' sidings, it is time to bring together themes from preceding chapters. Although we have glanced at other nation states in passing, our interest in this book has centred on relationships between railways and culture in Britain, the country which gave the modern railway its birth. The Introduction set out a case for railways as nineteenth-century modernity's epitome. Chapters 2 and 3 suggested that influential early texts – J. M. W. Turner's *Rain, Steam and Speed*, Charles Dickens' *Dombey and Son* – constructed cultural profit-and-loss accounts for Britain's new railways. Here – and in other canonical texts (Leo Tolstoy's *Anna Karenina*, Émile Zola's *La Bête Humaine*, Arnold Bennett's *Accident*) – older cultural tensions counterposing love and death with duty resonated in the railway's new life world. This was a metropolitan and disciplined life world, to be apprehended exclusively through notions of the sublime. Women entered this male world, we saw, only on sufffrance. Moving from canonical to popular texts, chapter 7 showed that crime fiction echoed themes from railways' 'literary' representations; but that despised crime writers explored the railway's machine ensemble far more fully and imaginatively than more celebrated writers managed. Chapters 9 and 10, on comic fiction and on Eric Ravilious' watercolour painting *Train Landscape*, explored how artistic structures of feeling shifted as railways yielded to more private methods of transporting people and things. Modernity always implied some superseded pre-modern Otherness.

We can use one last issue to draw these separate interests from their sidings and link them in a single train. If railways served as modernity's epitome in the long nineteenth century, then what are we to make of them at the turn of the twenty-first? Has the sun set on railways' significance in cultural representation, no less than in freight haulage and long-distance passenger transport? Like 'stuffed steam' artifacts gleaming in York's National Railway Museum, has railways' cultural significance declined to antiquarian pedantry? We will set off to answer these questions along an odd route: by considering three fictional accounts of refreshment facilities in three different British railway stations. The first description sets us down late one evening in Stradhoughton, a Yorkshire industrial town. Not a pretty sight.

> Below the ticket office was the buffet and main waiting-room. The buffet end was closed, its counter still lined with thick cups and the floor littered with crusts of bread, but there were about a dozen people still in the waiting-room, most of them asleep with their feet up on the scratched tubular chairs or their heads down on the rockety tables, among the flattened straws and empty lemon-squash cartons. I went in and stood by the door, under one of the large, empty-looking pictures of fields and hills that lined the walls. A few people were awake: half a dozen soldiers, all in civvies, going home on leave, three old prostitutes, a man in a large black coat.[1]

A familiar picture greets Billy Fisher here, in the late 1950s. Those thick cups and bread crusts make Stradhoughton heir to a proud tradition of British railway food: undrinkable coffee, gristly pork pies, curly-edged and fly-specked 'railway sandwiches'.[2] Fifteen years later, Jack Carter (a Cockney hard man) walked into the bar on London's Waterloo station. Moonlighting from day jobs helping breweries eviscerate Victorian public bars for an Elizabethan saloon bar trade, British Rail's interior designers have struggled to drive this place upmarket. 'It's all carpets and ice if you want it', Carter reports, 'and soft lighting and smart colours.' Doomed labour. Waterloo's bar 'still hasn't lost any of the British Rail tradition', we learn. 'It still manages to give the impression of dirt and un-emptied ash-trays and tat. It always will, whatever they do.'[3] Twenty years after that, Martin Amis set Richard Tull walking through another London terminus, Liverpool Street. 'The railway station had changed since he had last had call to use it', Amis reports.

> In the meantime its soot-coated rentboy-haunted vault of tarry girders and toilet glass had become a flowing atrium of boutiques and croissant stalls and limitless capuccino. Trains no longer dominated it with their train culture of industrial burdens dumbly and filthily borne. Trains now crept in round the back, sorry they were so late, hoping they could still be of use to the proud, strolling, capuccino-quaffing shopkeepers.[4]

Iain Sinclair, another London dystopian, lays economic foundations for the change which impressed Martin Amis' character. Vultures tearing at the nationalised railway's expiring body, Thatcherite financiers (Stagg's Gardens' true inheritors), 'didn't care where the trains went', he reports – 'the attraction lay in tying up the station concourse. The slower and more complicated the service, the better for business; a captive scatter of sullen commuters bored into stock-piling reserve sets of dollar-signed boxer shorts, croissants, paperbacks, gas-masks, ties to hang themselves...the potential yield had them drooling. Soon there were more stations than railways.'[5]

These delicately jaundiced accounts of metropolitan termini's retrofitted delights direct our attention to two matters. The first concerns evanescent permanence, the second what evanescence might portend.

Sic transit gloria mundi

Writing sixty-five years ago, for Osbert Sitwell 'Trains sum up, to my mind, all the fogs and muddled misery of the nineteenth century. They constitute, in fact, so many slums on wheels'.[6] One generation later, Billy Fisher's Strad-houghton buffet still inhabited Victoria's steam age. Jack Carter strode through Waterloo some years after the last steam locomotive chuffed from that terminus; but winds scouring encrusted grime from the station roof still wafted evocative perfumes – *Bulleid No 5*, *Evening in Nine Elms Loco Shed* – around platforms below. Carter thought these scents ineradicable. He was in good company. At the turn of the twentieth century the steam railway's *Gestalt* seemed solid as Victorian furniture. Like European *anciens régimes*, and hitherto existing socialism in its turn, this security melted into air. As the dismal decline which we reviewed in chapter 1 set in after 1918, enthusiasts mourned ever-dingier locomotive and rolling stock liveries when many private companies dwindled to the Big Four in 1923, and again when those four were nationalised as British Railways in 1947. The railway machine ensemble's glamour survived all this. It could not survive British Railways' 1955 modernisation plan. Dooming steam traction, this plan underpinned the transformation which impressed Richard Tull at Liverpool Street. He ambled through a terminus served exclusively by diesel and electric trains; a place different in kind from Billy Fisher's Stradhoughton.

Passing through Paddington station one day in the late 1960s, a commuter looked at main line passenger trains standing obediently at platforms: 'Their locomotives were huge, coffin-shaped, smelling of hot oil'.[7] We know that these non-standard diesel-hydraulic Western Region express locomotives themselves soon would die, but already the steam railway's machine ensemble rested within their coffined shapes. After steam traction ended on British Rail in 1968,[8] steam locomotives hauled fiction's writers only on journeys to the past, to lost worlds.

Riding the Taurus Express, Sir Hubert Bligh (Tory MP and British spy) realised 'that he was here in this vast Victorian anachronism of a train, behind a monstrous ancient engine as hot and noisy and steaming as a dragon from the pits of hell'.[9] Pathetic fallacy ambushed an ageing American spook in his nation's London embassy: 'His office windows were flanked by prints of old locomotives of the Atchison, Topeka and Santa Fe Railroad. He stared absently at the great iron machines thinking that he belonged to a much older America.'[10] In 1986 Paul Theroux found no charm in Datong's scarred physical presence, but he adored hand-built artifacts from that Chinese city's famous factory: 'steam locomotives – those brand-new antiques that they turned out year after year'.[11] Insistently washed by history's imperial tides, from ancient Greeks to modern British, French and Russians, Hav is a fuzzily-located but decisively-isolated east Mediteranean coastal city state. When yet another nation's battle fleet appears off this city's port in our time, refugees stream along its solitary escape route – the steam railway. A century ago, engineers opened this peninsula to landward influence by tunnelling under a formidable escarpment. Absorbed by the city which it serves, Hav's steam railway is a palimpsest, a surface scraped and overwritten, with vanished supremacies looming through half-erased inscriptions. On one locomotive, 'Beneath the numerals on its cab I could just make out, not quite obliterated even now, the old Cyrillic characters of the Imperial Russian Railways.'[12]

Her skill in walking cultural margins – as a Welsh woman writing in English; as a Welsh woman living in Wales but appreciated in English literary coteries; as a Welsh woman who lived and wrote for some decades as a man – informs every page in Jan Morris' *Last Letters From Hav*. Raymond Williams was no transsexual, but his interest in social edges was no less serious. His father spent a working life pulling levers as a signalman at Pandy, near Abergavenny on the Great Western's secondary main line from Newport to Shrewsbury. Gauzily disguised as Harry Price, his son's first novel shows the father arriving with his new wife at Glynmawr, a settlement remarkably like Pandy in location and detail, in 1920. Deftly, Williams conjures two intersecting life worlds. One is the Abergavenny (Gwenton) district's farm-centred social network. The second is the Great Western Railway's steam-powered occupational community. Both spring vividly to life under Raymond Williams' hand.[13] Like Thomas Hardy, spinning imagined Wessex from his mother's stories, Glynmawr in 1920 is Raymond Williams' starting place. This is a child's flat world, taken for granted. His last fictions, the abrupted *People of the Black Mountains* trilogy, formed Williams' monumental attempt to give historical shape to that world by probing human experience in his natal district from first settlement to present times.[14] Less ambitious in scale than this, his Border trilogy charts social and economic changes eroding his father's world. Early chapters root *Border Country* in Glynmawr, Gwenton and the railway. When the novel closes two decades later, these roots have loosened. In 1926 Glynmawr's valley still lies 'sheltered, and almost isolated under its dark mountains'; but in that year's general strike 'a different history exerted its pressures, and reached, with the railway line, even this far'.[15] Modernity's true child, class struggle travels the metropolitan corridor to deep Gwent. Inflected and refracted through local circumstances and particular personalities, social relations shift on the railway. Increasing motor traffic reduces passenger and goods revenue. Childish certainties dissolve. By 1938, when Harry and Ellen's bright son Matthew takes up his scholarship at Cambridge, this world has become all edges. Earning marginal and declining profits, the Great Western Railway Company will be nationalised after the looming Second World War. As Matthew Price, Raymond Williams sets out to explore those social boundaries – of class, between Pandy and Cambridge; of ethnicity, between English and Welsh; of language, between English and Welsh speakers within Wales – which he would patrol for the rest of his life.[16]

'There is something at once startling and dreamy in the railway modernisation scheme just announced', Paul Jennings told the *Observer*'s readers in 1955.

> In one sense it is as revolutionary, in its resolve to do away with steam in Britain, as was Kemal Ataturk's abolition of the fez and the veil in Turkey. For let no one imagine that the change will affect the railways only. Once those gaunt strong engines, named after people and places one has never quite heard of – Sir Henry Thompkins, Stindon Hall – are replaced by secretive diesels; once continuous brakes in goods trains have silenced for ever the night-long mysterious bing-bong-bang from misty, moonlit yards that for generations has told millions, in their warm beds, of our ancient, endless commerce; once the fretwork stations are replaced by pin-bright foyers, it is idle to suppose that the station hotels, the houses, and the blue brick churches and the people in them will remain the same. A certain openness, a certain ancestral, earthy communion with fire and water and the lonely native hills, will have gone for ever.[17]

Paul Jennings feared larger changes looming behind steam traction's eclipse; but his elegy spoke to a tragedy written in classical physics' vocabulary. Steam locomotives were scandalously wasteful creatures, turning into useful work only 5 per cent of the energy which they consumed.[18] This profligacy was accepted in Victorian days for two reasons. First, no competing prime mover bettered that rate. Second, one physical advantage moderated spectacular thermal inefficiency. Hauling their trains around, locomotives exploited an iron (later steel) wheel's exceptionally low friction on an iron (later steel) rail. This advantage brought costs. Low frictional resistance (and, initially, puny locomotive power) dictated gentle gradients. In their turn, these dictated expensive civil engineering works. Steam railways' vast hunger for construction capital was firmly rooted in the physics of friction. Labour-intensive businesses, and always subject to close state scrutiny, modern railways also proved expensive enterprises to run. Like any other capitalist enterprise, British railway companies sought economies when revenue failed to exceed costs by a satisfactory margin. Strict constraints limited what could be done: this industry commodifed service on capital sunk in extensive infrastructure, not intensive factories. Companies might wish to decline unprofitable freight traffic, but lawyers ruled that out until the 1962 Transport Act removed railways' common carrier status. Unprofitable route mileage could be reduced. We think that Dr Beeching invented this idea as he sought to prune an uneconomically sprawling nationalised network back to a sustainably profitable core; but line closures date almost from the modern railway's birth. 'During the past few years a great number of little railways have become derelict and are like country lanes', one novel tells us. 'Petrol has conquered them, and perhaps in the end they will become roads of garages, and mock-Tudor tea-rooms and bungalows.' Another post-Beeching bleat, surely? Not so: this dates from prewar days.[19] Companies might contemplate labour economies by leaving stations unmanned. Concerned about good public relations and legally obliged to accept any traffic which might be offered, competing Big Four private companies kept stations well staffed, except for minute passenger halts. Not until Beeching's years did this alter.

Like Paul Jennings, many people knew that some things would change as railway traction shifted from steam to diesel engines, and to electric motors. Few anticipated how dramatic these differences would prove to be. In the early 1940s, Groombridge Junction, with its twelve through running lines, was a place where 'the suburb and the people in it belong to the Railway'.

> The dark, flat houses cling under the railway-bridges like ticks on the belly of a rhinocerous. The Railway owns them: railwaymen inhabit them. The mainstay of Groombridge Junction is the steady job-holder on the Railway – mechanic, porter, guard, or clerk. …Young men conspire to punch tickets in the Station. Expectant mothers, feeling the kick of unborn generations, think: *Please God, if it is a boy, his father will get him on the Railway, and so his future will be assured.*[20]

Taking this solidity for granted, in 1956 one astute observer expected British railwaymen's occupational traditions to bend and yield under Modernisation's goad, absorbing and cushioning change.[21] A passage in John Wain's short story echoes this sanguine hope, as a bank employee travelling on a newly electrified Manchester suburban service envies the motorman his stable existence: 'The man had his roots. He had his mates to chat to all down the line.'[22] John Trench's whodunnit shows us some of these mates in deepest Dorset, as a country junction's porters and ticket collector observe a hovering passenger 'with the fathomless absence of expression reserved for a toff in difficulties'. Once he has taken himself off by taxi they all return to matitudinal pursuits: 'The porter who had spoken first scratched his head and kicked at a barrow'.[23] Nothing much has happened here since young Thomas Hardy's days. Nothing much will happen in future years. 'The railway, especially the archetypal, world-changing British railway, must smile to itself', Paul Jennings judged, 'when people talk in this counting-house fashion about modernisation, dieselisation, nationalisation and the rest of it, as though it were a dead lump of machinery entirely controlled by us. For the railway has a secret, withdrawn life of its own, like the land.'[24] Alas for mystic complacency! All too soon this secret life began to falter, these regiments of mates to thin, those roots tapping local sentiment to wither.[25] 'Like most people at the present time, the Beresfords travelled mainly by car', Agatha Christie told her readers in 1968. 'The railway journeys they took were few and far between.'[26] Fiction's travellers began to forget that railways existed. '"How did you get through the police cordon?"' one murder suspect asks his accomplice. '"It was Matt",' she explains. '"He took me to the station and we came to London on a train."' He draws the moral: '"As simple as that. And I never thought of it…"'[27] Nor, evidently, did all those policemen. Despised and forgotten, entropy attacked the railway's machine ensemble: 'The train out of Fenchurch Street has been salvaged from some condemned fairground. It shakes the boardwalk at Limehouse so fiercely that the station threatens to collapse into a heap of rotten timber'.[28] Declining passenger traffic, and goods yard closures, doomed many railway stations, large and small. Insignificant places could be demolished with little difficulty. 'It was the time when things were beginning to happen to railways', Tuppence Beresford recalled: 'small stations were closed, even pulled down, grass sprouted on the decayed platforms.'[29] Large city centre stations, cathedrals for an industrial age, proved a little more difficult to flatten. Some died: Glasgow (St Enoch); Glasgow (Buchanan Street); Edinburgh (Princes Street); Leeds (Central); Liverpool (Central); Liverpool (Exchange); Nottingham (Victoria); Swansea

(Victoria). Unloved Birmingham (New Street) was rebuilt – and the new edifice soon won Guinness' plaudits as 'the ugliest, most depressing and inhuman station in Britain'.[30] Facing down protesters fighting to save Philip Hardwick's Doric Propylœum and Great Hall, in 1962 British Rail managed to demolish London's Euston station, rebuilding it in lavatory tile.[31] BR met their Waterloo four years later, when their intention to butcher William Barlow's vast train shed at St Pancras, together with George Gilbert Scott's spiky Gothic Midland Grand Hotel front building, provoked outrage.[32] New strategies had to be evolved. Benign (some said malign) neglect was one. Retracing J. B. Priestley's *English Journey* fifty years later, Beryl Bainbridge adored the 1854 Royal Station Hotel, incorporated in the frontage to Newcastle-upon-Tyne's Central Station: 'a huge, rambling mausoleum of a building, with a grand central staircase and old chandeliers'. She was puzzled why one long wall in a basement snack-bar was hidden by curtains patterned with charging elephants. Then she looked behind the curtains, discovering windows offering splendid vistas over the 'closed and deserted' platform 9 in John Dobson's magnificent curved train-shed. When train services ended, Tilbury (Riverside) became 'a mausoleum built to house the absence of Empire … A cantilevered shed, epic in scale, runs away to piers. Customs Houses, platforms that once connected with the city. But now you will have to conjure from your grandfather's memory the oak-panelled saloons, upholstered in tapestry, the floors covered with Turkey felt.'[33] If politico-architectural historical reasons prevented owners from disgracing great stations through demolition or neglect,[34] then profitable new uses had to be found. By removing rail access a protected station could enjoy a second life as an exhibition hall at Manchester (Central), a supermarket at Bath (Green Park).[35] If trains could not be excluded completely from Victorian termini then one might reduce their significance by turning the place from a setting for trains to arrive and depart amid the odd shack selling tea and newspapers into merchandising malls with the odd diesel or electric train sidling around in an embarrassed fashion: what Richard Tull saw at Liverpool Street.[36]

We saw in chapter 7 that, infused with literary coteries' complacently ignorant contempt for science and engineering, some British authors got things wrong when they tried to conjure the steam railway's machine ensemble. *Border Country*'s lightly-worn expertise shows that knowledgeable writers could use railways' social and mechanical organisation adroitly: but errors inflated in number and scale as railway travel became less familiar. Preparing to write *The Great Train Robbery*, his caper novel inspired by Ronnie Biggs and chums' efforts at Linslade in 1963,[37] Michael Crichton laboured to understand

Victorian London's criminal underlife. Since his plot concerns a bullion robbery on a boat train, his railway detail must convince. Mostly he succeeds; but then he dresses the SER's locomotives and carriages in startlingly bizarre liveries. Crichton's transatlantic origins led him astray at a couple of other places, too. Victorian express trains carried a senior passenger guard, not a 'conductor'; and no British railway official was described, American-style, as a 'train despatcher'.[38]

Writing a century after the events he describes, Basil Copper consigned a full-corridor train on a short suburban journey from Waterloo to Brookwood Cemetery in 1880, twelve years before the GWR trumpeted Britain's first corridor express service on its main line from Paddington to Birkenhead.[39] *Bradshaw* in hand, Matthew Vaughan's solitary hero sits all day watching trains on Clapham Junction station in 1896, imagining where they all are bound. He compares the elegance of Duguld Drummond's locomotives for the LSWR with G. J. Churchward's 'finely-wrought demons' working the GWR's main line from Paddington – six years before Churchward succeeded William Dean as the Great Western's chief mechanical engineer.[40] Boat train passengers to Southampton in 1921 catch 'the first whiff of salt air mixed with the coaldust of the Southern Railway',[41] two years before that company was born in the 1923 grouping. In Hugh Rae's *Privileged Strangers*, events turn on struggles between Edwardian railway companies and trades unions. Given this setting, we must be shocked when an express train thunders unaided up 'the 1 in 12 section on to the tops of the Brewsters'.[42] As every British schoolboy used to know, almost all trains had to be banked up the steepest main line gradient in England, Worcestershire's Lickey Bank. The Lickey's ruling gradient was (and is) 1 in 37¾: chicken feed for Rae's locomotive, but a long nightmare for the Midland Railway's operating department.[43]

Not all British railway nonsense happens in Britain. In Nicholas Meyer's Sherlockian spoof Holmes, Watson and Sigmund Freud order up a special train to pursue wicked Baron von Leinsdorf's special from Vienna to Bavaria.[44] Running short of fuel (but not, miraculously, of water), Holmes and his companions break up their special's single coach – just like Union saboteurs pursued by Old Stone Face in Buster Keaton's *The General*. Again copying that masterpiece, Holmes sets the road for his train by hopping off the footplate at suitable junctions and setting switches *by hand*. On signalled and interlocked European main lines at the turn of the twentieth century this is simply ridiculous.[45] Escaped with his chum from a Boer prisoner of war camp, Raffles recognises the engine hauling a short goods train on the Umtali-Beira line. "'This is an old

London and South-Western Railway locomotive – 'Brockenhurst' class'", he tells Bunny Manders. "'I recognised it as soon as I saw it.'" Curious, that. The LSWR ran on standard gauge track. Originally constructed to two-foot gauge, the Umtali-Beira line was widened in 1900 – but only to 3 foot 6 inches.[46] Sebastian Faulks's hero heard guns rumble on the Western Front 'like a train going *through* an embankment'.[47] Mancunian Stanley Wagstaff saved his pennies for twenty years to fund one trip on the Trans-Siberian Railway. When he climbed aboard Rossiya No. 2 that day in 1973 he knew everything about this railway's history, its route, its stations; yet he still believed that the Russian five foot gauge was the world's widest.[48] Heading for Xining, train no. 275 halted at Lanzhou 'while the locomotive's boilers were filled with fresh water'.[49] Presumably all the passengers then spent happy hours playing mah jongh while fresh water boiled in these oddly multiple boilers.

The crassest error arrives in a recent Australian heritage chic whodunnit. In the late 1920s a murderer pumps chloroform through a stationary first-class carriage's air conditioning system (which, of course, it would not possess). Once all passengers are snoring happily, she murders one traveller by stringing her up from a lineside water crane while the locomotive's tender is replenished.[50] Nobody sees her do this, including the footplate crew who spent several minutes swinging the bag from the water crane to their tender's filler. One scarcely knows what to admire more here – the author's ignorant effrontery, or her publisher's contempt for his public's acquaintance with the steam railway's machine ensemble.

Richard Tull noticed that when trains no longer dominated Liverpool Street, their 'culture of industrial burdens dumbly and filthily borne' simply evaporated. As so often since 1830, fiction's trains carry more than freight or passengers. Puffing along modern life's warp and weft – weaving life with death, commerce with personal intercourse – other things evaporated when steam railways withdrew to the social margin. An American adult literacy class' meeting room reveals deep roots anchoring Martin Amis' train culture in modern political and social life.

> The bookcases were oak and went most of the way up the walls; there was a mural above, a Bentonian, popular-front vision of biplanes buzzing the statue of Liberty, locomotives rushing through wheat fields, glorious, muscular laborers going to work – a Howard Ferguson dreamscape. (They didn't need hortatory READ BOOKS propaganda back then; there were other struggles). The class was seated around a large, round oak table. They were what the WPA muralist had in mind: a saintly proletariat.[51]

This comes from *Primary Colors*, that slightly fictionalised account of how Slick Willy slithered into the White House; a novel *à clef* written by one political insider for others to decode. They would find little challenge in connecting this room's decoration, and its clarioned political subtext, to Thomas Hart Benton's monumental murals in New York's New School for Social Research – works 'filled with images of a corrupt materialistic society, teeming crowds of grotesque figures and relentless thrusting machines'.[52] Grist for Left political melancholy, Anonymous' New Deal shrine evoked the great future that we all have left behind, a time when one still might dream about progressive steam trains rushing through fecund wheatfields. We know, as the painter did not, that the American old Left soon would be decimated in anti-communist crusades. We know, as the painter did not, that by the later 1930s American steam locomotives rushed to their last roundup.[53] We know, as the painter did not, that the great transcontinental passenger trains followed not far behind them. In the nineteenth century, building and operating American railroads generated a vast, rich vein of folk song. Their echoes infuse Steve Goodman's wistful *The City of New Orleans*, a song warbled to such effect by Arlo Guthrie – native son to Woody Guthrie, icon for ageing American leftists.

> Good morning America! How are you?
> Say, don't you know me? I'm your native son.
> I'm the train they call the City of New Orleans
> I'll be gone 500 miles when day is done.[54]

Valediction to the proud highballer, Goodman's elegy mourns the American long-distance passenger train's passing, and the world for which it stood. A century and a half's contested cultural meanings on and around the notion of modernity slipped into oblivion. Rushing along the high iron, these meanings were not limited to it. The metropolitan corridor's wash effects spread broadly on each side. Once, the steam train symbolised and embodied hopes for a larger, better, fairer, more humane society maturing in the modern world's womb.

Railway folk song may have expired, but the train's status as modernity's epitome lingers in some other places. Broad surveys of railway history and operation live within a literary genre governed by strict rules. Typically, we notice these rules only when they are broken. 'The train makes us think of our mortality', Roger Green insists; 'but its own days are numbered too. Steam trains have gone. The others will follow. Giving them names like "High Speed" and "Advanced" will not save them.'[55] Green is a rare pessimist in an optimistic chorus. Again and again we read similar narratives in railway historians' broad surveys: stories of progress, of improvement over time as rudimentary pioneer days yield to steady technical advance in locomotives and rolling stock, in permanent way and signalling systems. Administrative arrangements grow steadily more rational, more business-like. Gritted fingers wring descriptions of railway decline from sobbing word-processors, but these books almost always end with a rousing, future-oriented peroration. British – and, *sotto voce*, other countries' – railways have a great future behind them, they tell us; but days ahead promise some new delights.[56]

That structure of feeling also influences other cultural representations. Lynne Kirby urges strong elective affinities between railways and early movies. As they sat isolated behind their plate glass windows, landscape vistas unrolling before their eyes prepared late-Victorian train passengers for the novel experience of watching silent movies.[57] Today's male adolescent-oriented action movies revive tropes from those days. As his driverless diesel express barrelled into Chicago's Union Station, Arthur Hiller's *The Silver Streak* (1976) reawakened Hollywood studio chiefs' interest in messy collisions between trammelled subjects and immovable objects. Andrei Konchalovsky's *Runaway Train* (1985) recycled Hiller's plot (astonishingly for such a lousy movie, on a Kurosawa screenplay), this time on a brakeless and driverless Alaskan freight train. Other movies exploited *underground* train crashes' special frisson – on the New York subway in Jan de Bont's *Speed* (1994), Roger Donaldson's *Die Hard: With a Vengeance* (1995) and Joseph Ruben's *Money Train* (1995); in the Channel Tunnel (with a helicopter in tow) in Brian de Palma's *Mission Impossible* (1996). Seventy years ago, the 'cornfield meet' between two driverless steam locomotives rushing together with exhausts barking and throttles wedged wide open enjoyed happy popularity as a silent movie cliché. Geoff Murphy's *Under Siege 2* (1995) updated this to the diesel age, as an American transcontinental passenger train smashed headlong into a gasoline train on a high trestle. This climax was pinched directly from Buster Keaton's *The General* (1927), but with a powerfully pumped-up octane rating to satisfy blood-lust among all those young men (and some young and not-so-young women) in the audience. This big crash was choreographed by another favourite movie cliché: the mad scientist, here updated as a computer nerd. For a mere one billion dollars from skulking Middle Eastern financiers he will direct a secret American orbiting weapons system to activate a geological fault running below Washington DC, fracturing the hardened vessel containing the Pentagon's equally secret nuclear reactor. This will wipe out the USA's military command and control structure, killing eight million people on the eastern seaboard in the process. This is rail-borne nuclear terrorism, distanced by gee-whiz technophilia. Since Alastair Maclean's 1977 treatment for *Death Train*,[58] most connections between nuclear bombs and trains have been much more direct than this, with the former stowed away on the latter. Narrative flow in John Woo's *Broken Arrow* (1996) wafts us from a hijacked stealth bomber to a freight train running out of control. This freight train carries a nuclear device removed from the bomber and primed to obliterate Denver, Colorado. As here, most action movies prove longer on thuggery than thought. John Badham's *Blue Thunder* (1983) is an exception. The train is an active political agent in this movie, saving America from oppressive panoptical state surveillance when a humble yard switcher trundles sedately through a whisper-quiet helicopter, mashing state-of-the-art remote sensing devices to silicon chips. This action inspired other directors. In John Ralnius' *The Fugitive* (1993), Harrison Ford's unjustly jailed convict gets a break when his prison-bound bus is minced by a train. Arnold Kopelson's *Eraser* (1996) ends with a yard switcher crushing the limo in which Big Arnie has trapped a corrupt federal defense under-secretary and his crooked FBI sidekick. Pullulating with equivocating lawyers, the justice system cannot punish these villains. Aided by that relentless switcher, Schwarzenegger executes vigilante law. In fiction, some authors still find plot possibilities in cutting-edge technology. A high-speed inter-city *pendolino* may be the Italian state railway system's ultra-modern pride, but a passenger can be murdered no less simply here than on a humble *rapido*. High-tech control devices also can facilitate murder in novels. Seeking vengeance against callous railway authorities responsible (as he thought) for asphyxiating his sheep in a summit tunnel on the North Island's main trunk line, an unhinged New Zealand grazier plants a bomb on an overnight Auckland to Wellington passenger train. Controlled by a sensitive altimeter, it will explode just where his sheep died. Another bomb, this time attached to a Japanese *Shinkansen*'s odometer, will be triggered if the train travels too slowly.[59] While the tunnel still was building, J. A. Adams' sloppy thriller proposed that a terrorist group opposed to British withdrawal from Hong Kong might hijack a Channel Tunnel train.[60] He quite failed to appreciate thriller-plot potential in a flaming train stuck somewhere between Kent and the Pas de Calais. History defeats even pulp novelists.

Postmodern turnout?

Pondering how to evade capture and execution as British spies in First World War Bavaria, Peter Pienaar explained to Richard Hannay that Germans "'are like steam engines which keep to prepared tracks. There they will hunt any man down, but let him trek for open country and they will be at a loss."'[61] Like Pienaar's and Hannay's hunters, inflexibility was the modern railway's Achilles' heel. With their internal combustion engines' moderately increased thermal efficiency outweighing their rubber tyres' substantially increased frictional resistance on macadamised and tarsealed surfaces, road vehicles captured more and more medium and short-distance passenger and goods traffic from trains. As cars, buses and trucks trekked for open country, predictability yielded to flexibility. For Wolfgang Shivelbusch, that stern neo-Frankfurter, this signified social decline:

> Here is a movement that follows all the typical stages in the history of innovations: some novelty fulfils its historical role – namely, to reshape reality in the sphere of collective consumption – and only later finds its way into the realms of private, domestic consumption. The public phase of an innovation can be termed *heroic*, in that it changes reality. The subsequent private phase must be termed *conformist*, in that, on its own, it demonstrates no change of dynamic, but functions rather to affirm and stabilise. Thus, for example, the transportation revolution in the nineteenth century began publicly, with the railroad as a means of mass transportation; in the twentieth century it took a private and domestic form with the family automobile. ... What comes after is a *reduction*. It is not merely in scale or dimension that the machines in question are reduced when they move from the public sphere into domestic use – cars are smaller than locomotives, television sets smaller than movie screens – but the essential character of things is also diminished; the heroic aspect is lost, so to speak. In comparison with their tiny successors the railroad and cinema are powerful instruments that excite the imagination, inviting near mythic associations.[62]

How refreshing to read this trumpet blast calling us back to the modern world's virtues! Over recent decades, floods of social theory have swept us in the opposite direction. We have been invited to praise the private over the public, surface over depth, play over analysis, decentred selves over unified identities. Like Arcady Hall's inmates in John Hadfield's *Love on a Branch Line*, we have been invited to accept that, some years ago, the modern world simply evaporated – and was replaced by whimsical *pomo*, by postmodernity. If we did not notice this happening at the time, then we simply were not paying attention.

How seriously should we take this argument? Perry Anderson's archaeology reveals the shifty footwork lying behind one scholarly generation's work on postmodernism and postmodernity. All things to far too many scribbling people at any one time, for some scholars – one thinks immediately of Jean-François Lyotard, author of that powerfully influential polemic, *The Postmodern Condition* (1984) – pomo also has been several different things to one person at different times.[63] If, as we are informed so often, we now live in a postmodern world, then when did modernity die? Opinions differ. For Christopher Jencks, prophet for postmodern architecture, it came on 15 July 1972 – when the Pruitt–Igoe public housing complex was demolished in St Louis. Writing a report on the state of contemporary knowledge for the Quebec government's university council, Lyotard located the break precisely in space but less precisely in time: around 1942, in those God-awful Nazi death camps.[64] No more modernity after Auschwitz, it seems. But the death camps turned *echt*-modern techniques to inhuman purposes. We saw in chapter 1 that the final solution's machine ensemble blended a range of mundane modern social and mechanical technologies. One essential element in this ensemble was Europe's modern railway network, along which those dreadful transports chuffed slowly towards Birkenau, Sobibor, Treblinka and Majdanek. The ghastliest moment in Europe's grisly short twentieth century, death camps industrialised human slaughter in a manner no less modern than that in which nineteenth-century Chicago's meat packing plants transformed hogs into pork and bacon. Why, then, should the death camps signify modernity's supercession? And if modernity died in 1942, then what succeeded it in 1943?[65] Answer comes there none. Treated critically, Enlightenment ideas still offer the best realist toolkit for understanding social life.[66] Performing footling arabesques on idealist pinheads, pomo theorists' anti-realist conceptual vocabularies offer little purchase on events at the twenty-first century's threshhold. Theirs is another tale told by Macbeth's idiot, signifying not a lot about the world in which we live and breathe.

Let us creep away from this idiot mumbling in his stocks. Perry Anderson tells us that one major problem with pomo is its epigones' tendency to bind many different issues in one elastic bandage. A decade ago, John Frow urged that three topics must be kept separate if analytical light were to shine through this bandage: *modernism* as a set of cultural practices, *modernisation* as an economic process with social and cultural implications, and *modernity* as a post-traditional historical period.[67] Our interest rests with the last category. Like modernism, postmodernism can be a useful term only when applied to artistic and literary practices. Taking it beyond that range brings confusion and disrepute.[68] Now let us see what happens if we bring modernity's epitome to this party. The postmodern turn, we are told all too often, celebrates a decisive shift from serious depth to frivolous surface. That happens to discourse about railways in British comic fiction. Take this line and 'the postmodern turnout' was invented by Q in 'Cuckoo Valley Railway'. Since that short story was first published in 1893, postmodernism approaches its one hundred and tenth birthday today. No wonder, perhaps, that the creature staggers around on its last legs. If 1893 seems excessively remote then we could set the postmodern turnout around 1915, as Ashe Marston and Joan Valentine freeze on an open horse cart while the quality putter along in their Hispano-Suiza. Nice timing, with modernity superceded at British railways' apogee. Richard Davenport-Hines suggests that postmodernism is Gothic in new clothes: a familiar reaction against Enlightenment rationalism's cultural child, literary realism. Take this argument seriously and we could locate the post-modern turnout in the middle forties, with Rowland Emett's wistfully Gothic *Locomotive No 3 (Hector) at Mrs Bristow's Folly, Now Used as a Water-Tower.*[69] Whichever date we choose, the notion of a postmodern turnout insists that the train belongs to a past slipping away behind us. Modernity's archetypal object – with vast kinetic energy guided by inch-high wheel flanges, with History's direction controlled by fixed rails and complex control systems, with trains owned and operated by huge centralised capitalist joint stock companies employing the latest management techniques under close state surveillance – yields to a privately owned motor car that can be steered wheresoever the driver chooses. Power (the train as a site for collective consumption, a symbol of progress intimately compounded with death) yields to whimsy (the car as a site for lively individual consumption; a leisure vehicle, its back seat a site – as parents feared and fear – for priapic fumblings). Mr Dombey's death-haunted ride on the London to Birmingham main line yields to Lord Flamborough's Arcadian frolic in *Love on a Branch Line.* Our train arrives at a strange terminus. As that arch modernist T. S. Eliot predicted, 'This is the way the world ends/Not with a bang but a whimper'.

In its turn, railway whimsy has died: steam locomotion's eclipse killed it. *Oh, Dr Beeching!,* that vile television sitcom, debases *Carry On* movies, not *The Titfield Thunderbolt.* Rowland Emett's last railway whimsy adorned *Punch*'s Coronation issue in 1953. The few fictions about steam railway preservation trail dourly after an exhausted social realism, not *Love on a Branch Line.*[70] Since 1968, whimsical railway material has been produced only for children: Oliver Postgate's charming *Ivor the Engine* books and television programmes; Wilbert and Christopher Awdry's moralising *Thomas the Tank Engine* books and Britt Allcroft's video versions of these (and other) *Thomas* stories; BB's limp gnome sagas; Ray Pope's novels about 'model railway men'.[71] Nick Park's terrific Hornby railway chase scene in *The Wrong Trousers* (1994) nods to silent movies' train chases – but this Plasticine epic was produced to delight young children, not adults.[72] Railway whimsy's descent from adult to juvenile audiences is instructive. Wolfgang Schivelbusch documents social meanings conjured by chocolate and coffee in eighteenth-century Europe. Coffee was a sober, dark-clothed,

protestant, commercial and democratic drink. Enjoying their morning chocolate, genteel folk in absolutist regimes swallowed aristocratic values, gaudy dress,
conspicuous material extravagance, and unbridled sexual license. Absolutism's
collapse brought down chocolate. Dressed in dark jackets and trousers, sober
men of affairs in France or Austria now drank coffee. Chocolate morphed into a
drink, then a food, for marginal women and children, not for influential men.[73]
The cultural injunction that boys should play with trains and girls with dolls con-
strains a full comparison (though *Thomas the Tank Engine*'s strong appeal across
gender lines dissolves this difference for today's tots); but railway whimsy's limita-
tion to children's books and television programmes suggests a parallel career.
Whimsical railway stories written for an adult audience – Q's unexpectedly influential invention, shaping British cultural reponses to railway travel for three generations – no longer find a publisher.[74]

Writing the text

Postmodernity is an increasingly weedy siding in social theory, but postmodernism retains value as a literary term. In *S/Z* (1970) Roland Barthes chopped
up a Balzac novella, *Sarrasine*, into 561 numbered fragments, then offered a
playful take on each of them.[75] Serious purposes lurked behind this play.
Barthes wanted to liberate readers oppressed by authors, to put readers in charge
of deciding what particular texts meant. He sought to encourage *writerly* texts,
where readers could intervene positively, engaging their own wit and imagination. Readings must be plural, he insists. This injunction is met more easily
when a text's form is open, not closed. With readings illimitable (in principle, at
least), an author who wants to encourage the reader stuffs her text with nods
and winks, paradoxes and allusions, jokes and mystifications. Then she sits back
to watch readers enjoy themselves by spinning meaning from materials assem-
bled with such understated sweat. No reading is privileged here: Jacq's interpretation is as good as her master's.

How does this bear on railways' cultural representation? At first sight, this
machine ensemble seem unfitted for writerly texts. A train's direction is controlled by wheel flanges and point blades. Passengers and railway staff suffer
tight discipline. Railway companies suffer close surveillance from state agencies.
Surely, only closed literary forms can treat this closed world? As we saw in
chapter 7, the Golden Age whodunnit is just as much at home in a railway
carriage or compartment as in an isolated country mansion. Formal closure
reassures comfortably-circumstanced social groups in these fictions. More or

less troubled by the plot's events, Bennett's *Accident* and Tolstoy's *Anna Karenina* end with quotidian social worlds crusting over disruption's wounds. Like railway-based whodunits, these are closed texts. So is Michael Nyman's *Musique à Grande Vitesse* (1993).[76] Commissioned for the ceremony to inaugurate the Paris–Lille TGV line, here 9, 11 and 13 beat rhythmic cycles complicate, but do not disrupt, earlier four-square fish-plated train music's certainties as Nyman's new high-speed train wafts business-class passengers along welded steel rails.[77] Even Steve Reich's *Different Trains* (1988)[78] has a form less open than appearances might suggest. Composed for tape and string quartet, this piece falls in three sections. In the first, Reich recalls childhood journeys on luxury passenger trains crossing the USA. Snatches from taped interviews with retired train staff set the musical frame. Evoking echoes from Dickens' train-rhythm prose in Dombey's death-haunted ride, each interview fragment's speech rhythm establishes a groundwork for minimalist musical manipulation, counterpointed by ringing crossing bells and American steam locomotives' chime whistles. This is modernist train music, celebrating American passenger railways' glory in the late 1930s and 1940s, before competition from cars, trucks and aircraft brought ruin. The second section takes us to Europe. Realising several decades after the event that other Jewish children made different train journeys while he rode *The Twentieth Century Limited* and *The Super Chief*, Reich listened to Holocaust survivors' archived testimony about cattle-waggoned rail transport to the camps. Again, speech fragments establish musical rhythms; but these are set against European steam locomotives' shrill whistles and, increasingly, against wailing air-raid sirens. Whistles' pitch sharpens subtly as this section approaches its climax, increasing musical tension as witnesses report ever more dreadful events in deadened prose. The third section returns us to north America. Their speech rhythms transmuted to the Kronos Quartet's precise musical phrasing, retired railroad staff contemplate their great trains' passing. Our understanding of modern railways is stained by the death camps, but we find troubled peace in the good old, safe old US of A. As his spare little masterpiece ends, Reich leaves us less complacent than when we began this journey; but he allows us no space to decide what his text means. Despite the nod to Jacques Derrida in his title, this composer remains firmly in control throughout his tightly specified score. Imaginative and powerful, intriguing and wrenching: *Different Trains* is all these, but it is no open text.

The journey to that form started long ago. Nineteenth-century expansion sent rails spinning through all the world. Climb aboard one train in Portugal, and you can step off another in Vladivostok. Climb aboard one train in Nova

Scotia, and you can step off another in southern Patagonia. Like thrillers, railway travel literature emphasises potential, as open horizons tempt travellers across yet another mountain range rearing, blue and mysterious, in the far distance. Over a century ago, Fanny Frances Palmer's *Westward the Course of Empire Takes Its Way* captured this sense of intoxicating liberty.

Using a similar high viewpoint and division of the picture space, Palmer punned J. M. W. Turner's *Rain, Speed and Steam* here; but she also simplified his message. Her emigrant train bears civilisation across America's high plains towards an empty western horizon, a better future.[79] By contrast, Turner is wracked by competing impulses: admiration for the thrusting new railway, regret for the old world which it desecrates and destroys. In chapter 2 I suggested that *Rain Steam and Speed* is a painting about rape, as a beautiful classics-based patrician and metropolitan culture (exemplified by rounded Thames-side landscape features) is overwhelmed by the on-rushing train's sublime male modernity. I suggested that, at the last, Turner tips his image's balance towards regret and away from celebration. Other people looking at this picture will judge that this balance tips the other way: that is an open text's virtue. Turner's image is radically unstable, suggesting first one attitude to a viewer, then its opposite. In Charles Dickens' *Dombey and Son*, Mr Dombey's miserable ride to

11.1   Fanny Frances Palmer, *Across the Continent: 'Westward the Course of Empire Takes its Way'*, 1868

Birmingham, and Carker's death, are closed texts. No critic has been able to discover much ambiguity in the messages which Dickens rams down our throats here. Episodes set in Staggs Gardens are different. As with Turner's image, regret balances celebration. Many commentaries take Dickens' balance to come down on regret's side. In company with some others, I disagree. Does not he suggest that losing the old Gardens' humane messy and higgledy-piggedly nature (physical arrangements epitomising Gardeners' mundane economic insecurity) was a small price to pay for benefits flowing from the modern railroad? Straining hard, some critics make this look like rape; to me it looks more like consensual fertilisation. Hitherto struggling to make a living, Staggs Gardens' residents now enjoy solid prosperity in their new railway-centred settlement. Workers directly employed on the railway are no less blessed. The worthy Toodles' flourishing condition shows that, for Dickens, the real issue is to ensure that modern railways' benefits are spread among Victorian social classes, not monopolised by slimy financial moguls like *Little Dorrit*'s Merdle.

Today, Dickens' and Turner's open texts are more than one hundred and fifty years old. With its springtime of freedom long past, is the railway now doomed to closed representations? Not quite. The Danish director Lars von Trier's *Zentropa* (1991) is the most writerly railway movie ever made. Critics divide sharply over what it means.[80] Von Trier's text is insistently intertextual; but do all those knowing allusions genuflect to American *film noir* or Tarkovsky, to Bergman or Fassbinder, to *The Third Man*, *Citizen Kane* or *Twin Peaks*? Here, for what it is worth, is my reading of this movie. One character, Hartmann, ran Germany's Zentropa railway company under the Nazis. With the Third Reich fallen, he is reduced to playing with a huge model railway in the family mansion's attic. This layout offers a familiar metaphor for railways as a disciplined and constrained closed system, and for a railway movie as a closed text. At a personal level, as the camera tracks down from Hartmann's daughter Katharina bonking the movie's central character to her father's slashed wrists in his bathtub, we understand that this old man's day has passed. At a structural level Hartmann's model railway signifies the Reich's deadly skill in appropriating modernity's machine ensembles, putting them to work not only against external enemies but also against significant sections of its own population. The movie circles around Leopold Kessler, a young American of German extraction, a classic innocent abroad. Taken to Germany in 1945 to assist Zentropa's reconstruction, Kessler travels trains as a sleeping car attendant. (*Zentropa*, son of *Mitropa*: an understated railway joke.) Travelling these trains takes Kessler, and us, through a bewildering kaleidoscope. Some journeys force us to acknowledge modern railways' complicity in atrocity, notably when the camera settles on striped pyjama-clad scarecrow figures packed together on wooden shelves in a train's carriages. Stacked with cinematic in-jokes (shifting back projection, quirky dissolves, multiple projection, an *auteur*-hand insistently pulling down the window blind when Kessler tries to find out where he is), this might all seem no more than pomo playfullness. But like the movie's lighting, this humour is bleak. As in many Gothic novels, we see a world in ruins. Which world? Take *The Third Man* for *Zentropa*'s model, and this becomes *Mitteleuropa* after Nazism collapsed. But von Trier called his movie *Europa*: only later did it take its more familiar title. Among much else, he offers us high class journalism; a contemporary meditation on Europe's possibilities, written while the Soviet empire lay in smoking ruins. Certainties dissolve, like Hartmann's control over his railway system. Kessler may be naive, but he could choose to learn. He could decide what to do, which line to travel, whom to join. Should he throw in his hand with Katharina and help the Werewolves, a bunch of unregenerate Nazis keeping the faith for a reborn Reich? Or should he help that almost equally sinister American, Colonel Harris, ruthlessly building his branch line for consumer democracy across rubble-strewn Europe? Both offer Kessler a guiding myth. Which should he accept? Should he accept neither? If he takes that third course, then how should he act? Olympian aloofness is no viable stance in Europe's political flux after 1989. 'Go deeper', characters keep telling him. Analyse and critique; understand; then act on that understanding. Final scenes force him to act. Partisans hold Katharina hostage, pressuring Kessler to set a time bomb on a Bremen train. He primes this bomb, then defuses it, then primes it again. In the hoariest railway cliché (remembering *The General*, anticipating *Under Siege 2*) it explodes just as his train crosses a bridge over a major river. Kessler drowns. He ends up going deeper (in the water) because he could not go deeper (in analysing chaotic political circumstances). He tried to stay aloof, but the fence was no place to sit out a political and social crisis. Failing to exercise informed choice, Kessler found himself pushed around by events. Symbolised by Zentropa's rail network, von Trier tells us that Europe faced big choices as the 1990s dawned. Historians will judge the wisdom of politicians's decisions, and whether citizens acted properly in their efforts to influence those decisions. Historical experience constrained what could be done, but it did not limit all action. *Zentropa*'s metaphorical railway might not run towards an empty horizon like Fanny Frances Palmer's prairie train, but nor did it curve back in a closed oval like Hartmann's model railway layout. Building out from the thriller, here railways stand at the centre of an obdurately open text. My account is not the only set of meanings which may be dug from this richly complicated movie: readings are illimitable. We should celebrate that openness, not deny it. Lars von Trier tells us this by piling jokes and quirks into his text, multiplying all those nods, winks, assonances, dissonances and non sequiturs which readers can use as building blocks in constructing different accounts. This is not self-indulgent pomo play-fulness. It is a way of clearing free spaces in our heads. It is democratic practice.

So it is in the novel which parallels von Trier's exhilarating movie: *253*.[81] Insistently, Geoff Ryman stacks the odds against an open text. On 11 January 1995 we take a seven-and-a-half-minute trip on a Bakerloo line tube train from Embankment station to the terminus at Elephant and Castle. This train con-tains 253 seats, so the novel introduces us to 253 characters. Some travel all the way; others enter or leave the train at intermediate stations – Waterloo and Lambeth North. Each character is conjured in a feuilleton occupying precisely 253 words. With and against these fierce constraints, Ryman piles up his vast, serious, playful soap opera. 253 people spend a few minutes on one from many trains on one from many lines in London's Underground system.[82] Watching these passengers pass as we stand on a station platform, we might think them atomised. We would be wrong. Webs of acquaintance and common experience snake out to connect passengers in different carriages, or in the same carriage. An elaborate index guides the reader through this rail-borne social network, facilitating the infinite number of different narratives which might be con-structed. Not everybody is linked in this web, of course; some passengers sit alone and lonely, excluded from Ryman's fine-spun network. The first character we meet, passenger 1, is the train's driver. Against all regulations, as the train leaves Lambeth North station he hangs his jacket on his cab's dead man's handle. Then, exhausted, he falls asleep. As with *Train of Events*, everything which we read from this point forward is coloured by our knowledge that our train's journey will end in a hideous crash.[83] As we meet each new character, we ponder whether he, she or it will survive the looming disaster.

Only four passengers still sitting on the train when it reaches the terminus do survive: Tahsin Cilekbileckli, the gravely injured driver, passenger 1; Tom McHugh, a drunken dosser; Who?, a freeloading London pigeon; and Anne Frank, passenger 253. Fifty years earlier, Anne survived an Auschwitz transport's long, nightmare journey. Shivering on Auschwitz-Birkenau's single platform, she was selected for lingering death as a slave labourer, not for sudden death in a gas chamber. Then she lost her memory. Now, after a seven-and-a-half minute journey through dark tunnels, chance – not the SA – selects her for life. She regains her memory. Amid mangled wreckage at the Elephant and Castle, a bloodied hand passes her a list 'of useful people who will survive':

> the unemployed
> the sick
> the retired and elderly
> the mentally subnormal
> prisoners
> pre-school infants
> children driven to school
> people with cars
> housewives
> nuns …

Echoes collide. This list recalls Christian chiliastic enthusiasm for an afterworld turned upside down. It evokes Borges' cod Chinese bestiary, among literary post-structuralism's most precious icons. Other echoes sound, fifty years deep. 'Anne is murmuring the Kaddish now, for the dead. She wanders and bears witness. She cannot forget them, nor can she die.'[84] Geoff Ryman explores many issues in this striking novel. Among these, he forces only one on our attention. No less haunted than Anne Frank with her recovered memory, Ryman speaks for the socially excluded, for those who have been done-down. Beyond this, he is content for readers to construct their own versions of what his book means. Against railway fiction's steady pressure to formal closure, he gives us an open text. Among all those little prose poems encapsulating passengers' life histories he interlards other material: quirky personal ads, suggestions for things to do on the tube, cod-New Age teases ('the Secrets of the Ancient Canadians': Ryman was born in Canada), an advert selling advertising space, a reader satisfaction survey. Pomo playfulness again? No. Other interleaved advertising material urges readers to buckle down and write their own stuff, to learn how to use words carefully, to learn how to describe characters, to buy a computer and install Internet software. *253* carries an unusual subtitle: *the Print Remix*. This work first appeared as an Internet novel. Folk who logged on had only to observe basic parameters (253 characters, each conjured in 253 words) and they were free to modify Ryman's text, make some parts of it their own. The ultimate open railway novel, *253*'s print remix is a remarkable piece of writing, by turns ironic and melancholy, farcical and angry, scandalised and enchanted. By putting his railway novel on the Net, Ryman opened new ways to explore relationships between railways and culture. But the Net is merely the latest stage in the long process of accelerating transportation for people, things and information from one place to another. Acceleration remains rooted firmly in the device which, for the first time in human history, allowed humankind to transcend organic limitations: the modern railway. *253* marks an

important new step in railway fiction, but (like many train journeys) it also leads
us back to the place from whence we started. If that place now seems a little different, then this book will have had some effect.

Notes

1 Keith Waterhouse, *Billy Liar*, London, Joseph, 1959, pp. 180–1.
2 'I assure you Mr Player was wrong in supposing that I thought you purchased infe-
rior coffee', I. K. Brunel wrote to the Great Western Railway's concessionaire at
Swindon station's new refreshment room. 'I thought I said to him that I was surprised that you should buy such bad roasted corn. I did not believe you had such a
thing as coffee in the place: I am certain that I never tasted any' (Stuart Legg (ed.),
The Railway Book, London, Hart-Davis, 1952, p. 234). Charles Dickens's sadistic
Boy ('Main line: the Boy from Mugby', in Dickens, *Christmas Stories*, London,
Chapman & Hall, n.d., pp. 533–42) lauds Rugby station's 'barrier of stale sponge-
cakes', its 'stale pastry', its sawdust 'British Refreshment sangwich'. In *He Knew he
was Right* (1869) Anthony Trollope excoriated this last object: 'that whited sepul-
chre, fair enough outside, but so meagre, poor and spiritless within, such a thing of
shreds and parings, with a dab of food'. Filson Young (*Letters from Solitude, and
Other Essays*, London, Chapman & Hall, 1912, pp. 223–4) denounced the muddy
claret with which Liverpool Street's refreshment room regaled the thirsty traveller,
and the 'portion of the limbs of a dead fowl with a quantity of damp ham piled
upon a plate' which passed for food in that place.
3 Ted Lewis, *Jack Carter's Law* [1974], London, Allison & Busby, 1993, p. 180.
4 Martin Amis, *The Information*, London, Flamingo, 1995, p. 261. Part of the surprise here is that *Liverpool Street* has been yuppified. Rail terminal for London's
north-eastern working-class suburbs, those inexorable generators for what once was
the world's most intensively-worked passenger traffic, this station's proletarian
nature suffuses hostile fictional descriptions. See, for example, Young', *Letters From
Solitude*, pp. 219–26 and John Jefferson Farjeon, *The 5.18 Express*, London,
Collins, 1929, chapter 1.
5 Iain Sinclair, *Downriver*, London, Paladin, 1991, p. 159.
6 Osbert Sitwell, *Penny Foolish: a Book of Tirades and Panegyrics*, London, Macmillan,
1935, p. 232. Compare David Cannadine's description (*Class In Britain*, New
Haven, Yale University Press, 1998, p. 89) of railways as the 'quintessential mid-
Victorian artefact'.
7 John Wain, *The Smaller Sky*, London, Macmillan, 1967, p. 11.
8 (A note for pedants.) OK, apart from the narrow-gauge Vale of Rheidol, in deepest
west Wales. In British Rail's first line privatisation, this railway was sold off in 1988.
9 Stanley Hyland, *Top Bloody Secret* [1969], Harmondsworth, Penguin, 1973,
p. 118. Not just steam locomotives outlived their time: anachronism attacked the
whole machine ensemble. For railwaymen staffing a diesel-powered cross-Canada
special train, the notion that a scheduled passenger train could run ahead of

schedule was laughable. 'They all thought it a great joke. Trains never ran early the world over. Late was routine': Dick Francis, *The Edge*, London, Pan, p. 106. New times defeat timetables, modern railways' holy writ.

10 Reg Gadney, *The Champagne Marxist*, Frogmore, Granada, 1979, p. 55.

11 Paul Theroux, *Riding the Red Rooster: By Train Through China*, New York, Putnams, 1988, p. 75.

12 Jan Morris, *Last Letters from Hav*, Harmondsworth, Penguin, 1986, p. 14.

13 Raymond Williams, *Border Country*, London, Chatto & Windus, 1960, pp. 25–31.

14 Peter Widdowson, *Literature*, London, Routledge, 1999, pp. 181–4.

15 Williams, *Border Country*, p. 85.

16 Raymond Williams, 'My Cambridge', in Ronald Hayman (ed.), *My Cambridge*, London, Robson, 1977, pp. 55–70; 'Wales and England' [1983], in Williams, *What I Came to Say*, London, Hutchinson Radius, 1989, pp. 64–74. The Border trilogy's second novel, *Second Generation* (London, Chatto & Windus, 1964), probes class boundaries by exploring two places which bear the name 'Oxford', yet which scarcely recognise each other's existence. One of these social worlds is built around old colleges, the other around new car factories. Williams' third novel, *The Fight for Manod* (London, Chatto & Windus, 1979), tramps ethnic boundaries. Here localism meets cosmopolitanism as a European-financed proposal to construct a vast new city in mid-Wales generates fine-grained local tensions and corruptions.

17 Paul Jennings, 'Dieselization', in Jennings, *The Jenguin Pennings*, Harmondsworth, Penguin, 1963, p. 80.

18 Modern materials and oil firing can raise this efficiency moderately, but economic calculations only make sense on short-haul tourist lines charging a premium for steam passenger haulage: Jeremy Webb, 'Back on track', *New Scientist*, 17 July 1999, pp. 42–5.

19 James Kenward, *The Manewood Line*, London, Paul, 1937, p. 7.

20 Gerald Kersh, *The Nine Lives of Bill Nelson*, London, World's Work, 1942, p. 7. Original emphasis.

21 Roger Lloyd, *Farewell to Steam*, London, Allen & Unwin, 1956, pp. 112–28.

22 John Wain, 'The quickest way out of Manchester', in Wain, *Nuncle and Other Stories*, London, Macmillan, 1960, p. 110. Other fictions supported this comfortable belief that little would change with Modernisation: see Ernest Corbyn, *All Along the Line*, London, Barrie, 1958.

23 John Trench, *Dishonoured Bones* [1954], Harmondsworth, Penguin, 1960, p. 85.

24 Paul Jennings, 'Bala likely', in Jennings, *Iddly Oddly*, London, Parrish, 1959, p. 95.

25 Not everybody mourned as accountants slashed and burned. A decade after the Beeching Report was published, J. B. Snell (*Railways: Mechanical Engineering*, London, Arrow, 1973, 160) castigated a large part of the British railway network as Speenhamland's child. Beyond profitable main lines, 'much of the rest of the network remains', he insisted,

> not because it is important or even much used by the community any more, but out of inertia. It is subsidised to keep it alive, and to keep the men in work. It has

become a form of out-relief; those employed can have little pride in their tasks and even less hope for their future. There is, true, a considerable public interest in these lines, but it is fundamentally a nostalgic one, and sometimes not healthy nostalgia but a morbid and inward-looking variety. Anyone who has true respect for railway hsitory and achiement, and a proper understanding of what railways can still do for the community, can only hope devoutly that all the remaining lines of this kind are exterminated as soon as possible.

26 Agatha Christie, *By the Pricking of My Thumbs*, London, Collins, 1968, p. 63.

27 Macdonald Hastings, *Cork and the Serpent* [1955], Harmondsworth, Penguin, 1959, p. 172.

28 Sinclair, *Downriver*, p. 6.

29 Christie, *By the Pricking of My Thumbs*, p. 67. Stepping from a Paddington–Gloucester train at a signal check, Aileen Macklin finds herself in such a place. 'The platform at her feet was still more or less intact, with the odd plant pushing up between the slabs, but the nameboards had been removed and the station building looked as though it had been hit by a shell' (Michael Dibdin, *The Tryst*, London, Faber, 1989, p. 161). When the signal lifts, her train moves off. Not until she walks down the weedy station approach, appreciating 'this quiet, these scents and sounds, the wonderful sunlight and this breeze that ruffled the little golden hairs on her arms' do we notice where our cunning author has landed Aileen: in Edward Thomas' dispeopled *Adlestrop*, now thoroughly disgraced.

30 John Marshall, *The Guinness Railway Book*, Enfield, Guinness, 1989, p. 194.

31 Not everyone would have mourned the old Euston: for Robert Lynd ('Railway stations I have loved', in Lynd, *In Defence of Pink*, London, Dent, 1937, p. 72) this terminus, 'by its very appearance, seemed to be part of the jail'. But for Paul Jennings, ('Very Great Eastern', in Jennings, *Iddly Oddly*, p. 92) prelapsarian Euston

> is the Vatican of British Railways, of all railways. It is the Basilica of St George Stephenson, complete with porticoed square and statues. It would not be in the least surprising if a procession of small boys in white issued forth on to that balcony in the main hall at Euston and filled its echoing spaces with soaring polyphony. At Euston they keep the mysteries, they serve a God of Motion, Aristotle's Prime Mover.

When the wrecker's ball flattened this basilica Jennings, in common with almost everybody else who had not been forced to work in the old Euston, castigated its replacement – this new 'black elephant': Paul Jennings, *Just a Few Lines*, London, Guiness, 1969, unpaginated.

32 The controversy is summarised in Jack Simmons, *St Pancras Station*, London, Allen & Unwin, 1968, pp. 103–8.

33 Beryl Bainbridge, *English Journey: or the Road to Milton Keynes*, London, Flamingo, 1984, p. 120; Sinclair, *Downriver*, p. 17.

34 For cogent reasons see Gordon Biddle and O. S. Nock (eds), *The Railway Heritage of Britain: 150 Years of Railway Architecture and Engineering*, London, Joseph, 1983.

35 I know of no British novel which comments on this. In Patricia D. Cornwell's *All That Remains*, London, Warner, 1993, pp. 185–6, Dr Kay Scarpetta is called to

meet her boss, Richmond's Commissioner of Health and Human Services. His department lives in Main Street Station, purchased by the State of Virginia after failing as a shopping mall. 'The commissioner resided in a suite of offices on the second level', Scarpetta reports, 'accessible by a marble stairway worn smooth by travellers scuffing up and down stairs in an era long past'.

36   For a historian's paean to this transformation, see John M. Mackenzie, 'Buildings befitting their stations: part 2, present and future', in John Whitelegg, Staffan Hultén and Torbjörn Flink (eds), *High Speed Trains: Fast Tracks to the Future*, Hawes, Leading Edge, 1993, pp. 193–202. When Liverpool Street was gentrified, at least the Great Eastern Railway's vast First World War memorial was not slighted, as Paul Jennings feared. In the late 1960s, he still often saw faded bunches of flowers propped against this memorial, with a card saying *From Alice of Ipswich* or *With Deepest Sympathy. C. W. Imbert, From his ever-loving Mother*. See Jennings, *Just a Few Lines*, unpaginated. It's an old country.

37   This crime's fame was not limited to Britain. *Hands Up, Tap Your Feet, It's a Stick-Up* was a Rio samba school's Carnival entry. Here 'a fullscale model of a locomotive parades through the *sambodromo*; in front of it a skulking figure with a bag of money represents the train-robber Ronnie Biggs, Brazil's most notorious expatriate resident': John Ryle, 'Brazil diary', *The Guardian Weekly*, 8 March 1998.

38   Michael Crichton, *The Great Train Robbery*, London, Cape, 1975, pp. 29, 114–15, 130, 179–80, 191–5. To underline comparisons with events at Linslade in 1963 (events which also inspired the train robbery in Agatha Christie's *At Bertram's Hotel*, London, Collins, 1965, 81–4), this novel's movie version bore a different title: *The First Great Train Robbery* [1978]. Director/scriptwiter Michael Crichton had ambitious plans for his movie. 'My dream was the historical world was going to be lovingly recreated', he recalled, 'and then I was going to shoot *The French Connection* inside it' (quoted in John Huntley, *Railways on the Screen*, Shepperton, Ian Allan, 1993, p. 47). Alas for good intentions; one monumental howler destroyed his mid-Victorian railway *Gestalt*. A safe's key must be stolen from the supervisor's office at London Bridge station. As the villains case the joint one day, a recently arrived train dresses the set, with its locomotive pressed hard against buffers on a terminal track. When the villains return at dead of night, this locomotive still snuggles against its buffers, with carriages still snoozing behind. Familiar with how he put his car to bed each night, Crichton evidently believed that one simply turned a key to shut down a steam locomotive, then started it up again next morning by turning the key in the opposite direction. Over the years, many shedmasters must have wished that it were that simple, with no nonsense about dropping the fire and raking ashes from boiler tubes, then lighting up from cold several hours before the locomotive was required for duty.

39   Basil Copper, *Necropolis: a Novel of Gothic Mystery*, Sauk City, Wisconsin, Arkham House, 1980, pp. 242–60; Jack Simmons, *The Railways of Britain*, second edition, London, Macmillan, 1968, p. 147. Despite its excessively up-to-date through corridor (though even this fades against an American historical whodunnit writer's chase through, and above, a full corridor express heading for Dover in 1852: see William J. Palmer, *The Hoydens and Mr Dickens*, New York, St Martins, 1997,

pp. 208–9), one passenger must clamber from Copper's train's leading carriage over the locomotive's tender in order to warn the driver to stop between stations (p. 293). Parliamentary Commissions in 1853 and 1858 recommended that a continuous rope linking carriages in a passenger train be suspended outside compartment windows, then attached to a warning bell on the locomotive's footplate. An 1869 Act made this system mandatory. It was better than nothing, but fully successful communication had to await continuous vacuum or air braking on passenger trains. Although Parliament compelled that system's introduction in 1889, this injunction did no more than ginger up laggard companies. By then 90 per cent of British locomotives and passenger coaches already were equipped for continuous braking systems. Thus it is inconceivable that passengers in main line stock worked from a major London terminus in 1880 would have enjoyed no means of alerting the train's driver or guard in an emergency. See Jack Simmons, *The Railway In England and Wales, 1830–1914: the System and its Working*, Leicester, Leicester Univerity Press, 1978, pp. 223–31. Copper's train also comes equipped with a buffet car. Unfortunately for his research, these were not introduced until 1899 (on the Great Central's new main line to Marylebone), and they did not become common until the 1930s. As his double track secondary main line railway runs through a large outer suburban village, it intersects a major road at an ungated crossing (p. 326). The Board of Trade's Railway Department would not have been impressed by that. Nor does Copper know quite enough about mechanical engineering. As his engine moves a train from rest, 'The wheels slipped once or twice, the pistons revolving swiftly' (p. 276). When a locomotive's pistons revolve, onlookers should hurl themselves behind the nearest solid wall.

40 Matthew Vaughan, *The Discretion of Dominick Ayres*, London, Secker & Warburg, 1976, p. 5; George Carpenter, 'George Jackson Churchward', in Simmons and Biddle (eds), *Oxford Companion*, p. 81.

41 Peter Lovesey, *The False Inspector Dew* [1982], London, Mysterious Press, 1988, p. 91.

42 Hugh Rae, *Privileged Strangers*, London, Hodder & Stoughton, 1982, p. 14.

43 Both George Stephenson and I. K. Brunel recommended a more circuitous and lightly graded route to avoid this precipitous ascent. Captain Moorson, the Birmingham and Gloucester's engineer, recommended attacking the bank directly, and won the board's decision: Frederick S. Williams, *The Midland Railway, its Rise and Progress: a Narrative of Modern Enterprise* [1876], Newton Abbot, David and Charles, 1968, pp. 59–60. Devoted 'small engine' line though it was, the Lickey bank's challenge eventually forced the Midland Railway into constructing one famous (and fascinating) monster. Nicknamed 'Big Bertha' after the German Army's rail-mounted siege gun on the Western Front, with her inclined cylinders and unprecedented tractive effort the 0–10–0 Lickey banker chugged up and down the couple of miles separating Brosgrove from Blackwell many times each day from 1919 to 1956: R. J. Essery and David Jenkinson, *An Illustrated Review of Midland Locomotives. Volume 4: Goods Tender Classes*, Didcot, Wild Swan, 1989, pp. 191–6.

44 Nicholas Meyer, *The Seven-Per-Cent Solution* [1975], Leicester, Ulverscroft, 1977, pp. 300–36. Evidently Meyer knew nothing about Freud's neurotic fear of train travel: see chapter 5, footnote 31.

45 Cinema audiences happily swallowed this absurdity at an even later date, watching heroic Allied prisoners escape from nasty Nazis in Mark Robson's *Von Ryan's Express* (1965) – a movie based on David Westheimer's novel of the same name (London, Pan, 1965). Also set in the Second World War, John Frankenheimer's *The Train* (1964) recognised that signal boxes controlled traffic on French railways – but using nothing so boring as bell codes. The regional traffic manager, Burt Lancaster, sits at a signalbox window with binoculars clapped to his eyes, telling the bobby which route to set up. What did he do at night?

46 Barry Perowne, 'The Raffles Special', in Ellery Queen (ed.), *Ellery Queen's Crime Wave*, London, Routledge, 1976, p. 180; Clarence Winchester, *Railway Wonders of the World*, London, Amalgamated Press, 1935, pp. 868–9.

47 Sebastian Faulks, *Birdsong*, London, Vintage, 1994, p. 343; emphasis added.

48 Derek Lambert, *The Yermakov Transfer*, London, Arlington, 1974, p. 56. Many Irish and Australian (Victorian State) trains run on 5'3" gauge tracks; 5'6" gauge is standard on Indian main lines.

49 Theroux, *Riding the Red Rooster*, p. 420.

50 Kerry Greenwood, *Murder on the Ballarat Train*, New York, Fawcett, 1993.

51 Anonymous, *Primary Colors: a Novel of Politics*, New York, Random House, 1996, p. 6.

52 C. Hamilton Ellis, *Railway Art*, Boston, New York Graphic Society, 1977, p. 113. This panegyric has a sour pendant. Benton's murals celebrated the Left *Gestalt* sustaining the 1930s' New School, as European intellectuals rescued from fascist tyranny taught evening classes to adult students in the School's spanking International Style building on 22nd Street. Times change, and intellectual fashions with them. The New School for Social Research now is New School University. As it pushed strongly into management education, School managers sold off those *embarrassingly out-of-date* Benton murals.

53 Commemorated most vividly, and only just in time (in the late 1950s), by O. Winston Link's astounding night-time pictorial confections – vast, doomed steam locomotives on the Norfolk and Western, the nation's last all-steam pike. See Tim Hensley, *Steam, Steel and Stars: America's Last Steam Railroad* [1987], New York, Abrams, 1998.

54 Ludovic Kennedy (ed.), *A Book of Railway Journeys*, London, Collins, 1980, pp. 115–16. For folk song see Norm Cohn, *Long Steel Rail: the Railroad in American Folksong*, Urbana, University of Illinois Press, 1981.

55 Roger Green, 'Introduction', to Green (ed.), *The Train*, Oxford, Oxford University Press, 1982.

56 The supplementary chapter to W. M. Acworth, *The Railways of England*, fifth edition, London, Murray, 1900, pp. 445–71 provides the model for these perorations. For other examples, pulled from my shelves almost at random, see Geoffrey Freeman Allen, *Railways: Past, Present and Future*, London, Macdonald, 1982, pp. 270–95, and Allen, *The Illustrated History of Railways in Britain*, London, Marshall

Cavendish, 1979, pp. 256–68; Nicholas Faith, *Locomotion: the Railway Revolution*, London, BBC, 1993, pp. 203–36; Massimo Ferrari and Emanuale Lazzati, *The History of Trains*, New York, Crescent, 1990, pp. 164–89; Roger Lloyd, *The Fascination of Railways*, London, Allen & Unwin, 1951, pp. 150–60; Bryan Morgan, *Railways: Civil Engineering*, London, Arrow, 1973, pp. 151–9; Michael Robbins, *The Railway Age*, London, Routledge & Kegan Paul, 1962, pp. 189–98; Ian Waller, 'Today and tomorrow', in Jack Simmons (ed.), *Rail 150: the Stockton and Darlington Railway and what Followed*, London, Eyre Methuen, 1975, pp. 165–92; John Westwood, *The Pictorial History of Railways*, London, Bison, 1988, pp. 150–205.

57   Lynne Kirby, *Parallel Tracks: the Railroad and Silent Cinema*, Durham, NC, Duke University Press, 1997. Some H. G. Wells fictions exploit railway journeys like this, offering readers extraordinary scenes that unroll before passengers' eyes: the first manned flight ('The argonauts of the air' [1897], in Wells, *The Complete Short Stories of H.G. Wells*, London, Benn, 1927, pp. 355–6); suburban Surrey devastated by a failed Martian invasion (Wells, *The War of the Worlds* [1898], edited by David Y. Hughes and Harry M. Geduld, Bloomington, Indiana University Press, 1993, p. 189); Kentish landscapes swamped by gigantic vegetation (Wells, *The Food of the Gods* [1904], London, Sphere, 1976, pp. 147–52).

58   See Alastair MacNeill, *Alastair MacLean's Death Train*, London, Collins, 1989 for the novelisation. It took so long to make a movie from MacLean's treatment that by the time David S. Jackson's *Death Train* (1993) hit the screens this Cold War plot made no sense. Cobbling together a feeble threat by dissident army officers to vaporise Iraq in order to spark a Russian military coup turned a limp movie into a camp joke.

59   Michael Dibdin, *Cabal*, London, Faber, 1992, pp. 200–12; Ian Mackersey, *Long Night's Journey*, London, Hale, 1974; Joseph Rance and Arei Kato, *Bullet Train*, London, Pan, 1981. Rance and Kato's device was copied in the movie *Speed* (1994), but with the train replaced by a boring bus.

60   James Adams, *Taking the Tunnel*, London, Signet, 1993. For a political thriller about building and opening the Channel Tunnel see Stanley Johnson, *Tunnel*, London, Heinemann, 1984.

61   John Buchan, *Greenmantle* [1916], London, Nelson, 1922, p. 167.

62   Wolfgang Schivelbusch, *Tastes of Paradise: a Social History of Spices, Stimulants and Intoxicants* [1980], translated by David Jacobson, New York, Vintage, 1993, pp. 62–3. Original emphases.

63   Perry Anderson, *The Origins of Postmodernity*, London, Verso, 1998.

64   Christopher Jencks, *The Language of Post-Modern Architecture*, New York, Rizzoli, 1977; Jean-François Lyotard, *The Postmodern Condition* [1979], Manchester, Manchester University Press, 1984; Anderson, *Origins of Postmodernity*, pp. 24–5.

65   Disdaining to follow Lyotard into postmodernity's stinking swamps, Anthony Giddens offers How We Live Now in Cool Britannia as 'high modernity' specified through ugly new descriptors – intensified detraditionalization, reflexive post-traditionalism. See Giddens, 'The social revolutions of our time', in Giddens, *Beyond Left and Right: the Future of Radical Politics*, Cambridge, Polity Press, 1994, pp. 83–7. See

also Kenneth H. Tucker Jr, *Anthony Giddens and Modern Social Theory*, London, Sage, 1998, pp. 93–5 and Timothy W. Luke, 'Detraditionalization in postmodern space-time compression', in Paul Heelas, Scott Lash and Paul Morris (eds), *Detraditionalization*, Oxford, Blackwell, 1996, pp. 109–33. Ted Benton ('Radical politics – neither left nor right?' in Martin O'Brien, Sue Penna and Colin Hay (eds), *Theorising Modernity: Reflexivity, Environment and Identity in Giddens' Social Theory*, London, Longmans, 1999, pp. 39–64) pours welcome draughts of cool sense on this gush. Like so many lapsed Leftists, Giddens still takes nuclear annihilation to be a worryingly likely fate for humankind. This *echt*-modern death infuses its own railway literature. Arthur Quiller-Couch's 'The destruction of Didcot', (in Anon (ed.), *Echoes from the Oxford Magazine* [1900], London, Frowde, 1908, pp. 127–9) anathematised the graceless station where passengers passed so many dispiriting hours waiting for Oxford trains. Q's portentous whimsy shows this junction station disappearing in a cataclysmic explosion, to general undergraduate rejoicing. One century later, a thriller laid out what would happen if Didcot really did disappear when a terrorist gang's wire-guided missile triggered a rail-borne consignment of high-grade nuclear waste on the Great Western Railway's main line somewhere west of Reading. Cremated death lies deep and crisp and even from Oxford to Winchester, with fallout killing lifeforms more agonisingly from Bristol to London: Roger Williams, *A-Train*, London, Star, 1985.

66 Thomas Osborne, *Aspects of Enlightenment: Social Theory and the Ethics of Truth*, London, UCL Press, 1998, pp. 177–94.

67 John Frow, 'When was post-modernism?,' in Ian Adam and Helen Tiffin (eds), *Past the Last Post: Theorizing Post-Colonialism and Post-Modernism*, Calgary, University of Calgary Press, 1990, p. 139.

68 'Where social scientists have appropriated [postmodernism] to provide post-Marxist and post- structuralist critiques of modernity, the debate becomes quite blurred and the issues often polemic': Roger Friedland and Deidre Boden, 'NowHere: an introduction', in Friedland and Boden (eds), *NowHere: Space, Time and Modernity*, Berkeley, University of California Press, 1994, p. 3, note 3. For an example of this blurring in action, see Scott McCracken, 'Postmodernism, a *Chance* to reread?,' in Sally Ledger and Scott McCracken (eds), *Cultural Politics at the Fin de Siecle*, Cambridge, Cambridge University Press, 1995, pp. 267–89.

69 Richard Davenport-Hines, *Gothic: Four Hundred Years of Excess, Horror, Evil and Ruin*, London, Fourth Estate, 1998. For Emett's image see p. 279.

70 Graham Coster, *Train, Train*, London, Bloomsbury, 1989; Jennifer Johnston, *The Railway Station Man*, London, Hamish Hamilton, 1984.

71 Denys Watkins-Pitchford ('BB'), *The Forest of Boland Light Railway* and *The Wizard of Boland*, Leicester, Knight Books, 1969 and 1970; Ray Pope, *Telford and the Festiniog Railway*, (1973) and other books in his 'Model Railway Men' series; Oliver Postgate, *Ivor the Engine*, London, Abelard-Schuman, 1962. For Awdry and Allcroft, see Brian Sibley, *The Thomas the Tank Engine Man*, London, Heinemann, 1995.

72 Though Wallace, Gromit and the Penguin actually scream around the carpet-riding tinplate steam outline toy trains powered by electric motors, of course. Like

so much successful children's fiction, *The Wrong Trousers* is double coded: artfully constructed to be enjoyed by pre- schoolers in one way, by adults in another.

73 Schivelbusch, *Tastes of Paradise*, pp. 85–96.

74 No great loss, perhaps, if they copied gruesome facetiousness from that doomed attempt to emulate *1066 And All That*, C. Hamilton Ellis' *Rapidly Round the Bend: a Short Review of Railway History*, London, Parrish, 1959.

75 Roland Barthes, *S/Z* [1970], translated by Richard Miller, New York, Hill and Wang, 1974.

76 Argo 443 382–2.

77 Ian Carter, 'Train music', *The Music Review*, 1993, 54, pp. 279–90.

78 Electra Nonesuch 7559–79176–2.

79 Only for some people, of course. This image is divided not only between top (empty possibility) and bottom (achieved civilisation), but also between left (European culture) and right (American nature). Part of nature, those emblematic native Americans in the right foreground have no future; a fate signalled by the locomotive's smoke obscuring their forward view. See Susan Danly, 'Introduction', to Susan Danly and Leo Marx (eds), *The Railroad in American Art: Representations of Technological Change*, Cambridge, Mass., MIT Press, 1988, p. 17.

80 See, in particular, Harlan Kennedy, 'Go deeper', *Film Comments*, 27/4, 1991, pp. 68–71 and Philip Strick, 'Europa', *Sight and Sound*, new series, 2/1, 1992, pp. 47–8. John Huntley seems to have been flummoxed by it: his otherwise comprehensive *Railways on the Screen* contains no entry for either *Europa* or *Zentropa*.

81 Geoff Ryman, *253*, London, Flamingo, 1998.

82 This system has its particular literature. For crime stories see above, pp. 176, 183, 207, 220–1, 224. John Healy, *Streets Above Us*, London, Macmillan, 1990 and Barbara Vine, *King Solomon's Carpet*, London, Viking, 1991. For undemanding romances see Maeve Binchy, *Central Line*, Sevenoaks, Coronet, 1978 and *Victoria Line*, London, Quartet, 1980; Julian Barnes' *Metroland*, London, Cape, 1980 is more ambitious and more interesting. Dorothy Meade and Tatiana Woolf (eds), *Lines on the Underground: an Anthology for London Travellers*, London, Collins, 1994 organises other writers' words by lines, branches and stations. George Benson, Judith Chernaik and Cicely Herbert (eds), *Poems on the Underground*, eigth edition, London, Cassell, 1998 reprints those pregnant little pieces which sweal tension on tedious Tube journeys.

83 This is clearly modelled on London's worst Underground smash, when a Northern Line train smashed at high speed into a terminal wall at Moorgate on 28 February 1975, killing 43 people and injuring more than one hundred. In this crash, too, the driver disabled his train's dead man's handle: but London Transport then installed new mechanisms (rapidly dubbed 'the Moorgate control') to stop a train automatically if its driver did not follow standard and regular safety procedures. Geoff Ryman does not explain why the Moorgate control failed to halt his train.

84 Ryman, *253*, p. 351.

Index

'What an excellent and informative book Debbie Garvey has produced. It will be a constant source of reference and inspiration for both those new to management and those with a little more experience in the role.'

– *Helen Connelly, Area Manager and Montessori Teacher,*
Yorkshire Montessori Nursery

'Fascinating…well supported by research…very readable… I heartily recommend this book to all setting leaders.'

– *Jonathan Wainwright, Principal Lecturer, Department of Education*
Childhood and Inclusion, Sheffield Hallam University